T0405620

Dissonant Waves

Sonics Series

Atau Tanaka, editor

Sonic Agency: Sound and Emergent Forms of Resistance, Brandon LaBelle

Meta Gesture Music: Embodied Interaction, New Instruments and Sonic Experience, Various Artists (CD and online)

Inflamed Invisible: Collected Writings on Art and Sound, 1976–2018, David Toop

Teklife / Ghettoville / Eski: The Sonic Ecologies of Black Music in the Early 21st Century, Dhanveer Singh Brar

Goldsmiths Press's Sonics series considers sound as media and as material – as physical phenomenon, social vector, or source of musical affect. The series maps the diversity of thinking across the sonic landscape, from sound studies to musical performance, from sound art to the sociology of music, from historical soundscapes to digital musicology. Its publications encompass books and extensions to traditional formats that might include audio, digital, online and interactive formats. We seek to publish leading figures as well as emerging voices, by commission or by proposal.

Dissonant Waves

Ernst Schoen and Experimental Sound in the Twentieth Century

Sam Dolbear and Esther Leslie

Goldsmiths
Press

Copyright © 2023 Goldsmiths Press
First published in 2023 by Goldsmiths Press

Text copyright © 2023 Esther Leslie and Sam Dolbear
Goldsmiths, University of London, New Cross
London SE14 6NW

Printed and bound by Short Run Press, UK
Distribution by the MIT Press
Cambridge, Massachusetts, USA and London, England

A CIP record for this book is available from the British Library

ISBN 978-1-913380-56-4 (pbk)
ISBN 978-1-913380-55-7 (ebk)

www.gold.ac.uk/goldsmiths-press

Goldsmiths
UNIVERSITY OF LONDON

Typeset by Newgen Publishing UK

For Sasha and Leda

Contents

List of figures

Introduction

Short History of the Project

In early 2018, Esther received a note from an administrator at Birkbeck stating that Professor Alexander Schoen had phoned a number of times, trying to get in touch with her. After some back and forth, contact was made – Alexander Schoen, known to family and friends as Sasha (born 29 March 1929), had seen Esther's work on Walter Benjamin and wanted to interest her in the life of his father, Ernst, childhood friend of Walter. Esther knew of Ernst Schoen – as anyone studying Benjamin would: his close friend, confidante, hustler of radio work, rival in love. But she did not know how much there was to discover – nor, indeed, how fascinating and accommodating Sasha Schoen and his wife Leda Drucaroff would be. After a couple of emails, there were visits to their East Finchley home to find out more of the personal side of the story. Sam, Esther's former PhD student, who had worked on Walter Benjamin and questions of generation and friendship, was brought in to extend and enjoy the long conversations.

Over a number of afternoons, we heard stories of Sasha and Leda's life together as they travelled the world as a result of Sasha's work on veterinary science and animal management. We heard of strange times in Berlin in the 1970s and political bias at the Free University; descriptions of various living rooms and work spaces in Dahlem and beyond. We heard about Leda's childhood in Argentina and her Communist father, her life as a dancer in Buenos Aires and elsewhere, and then, her work for the BBC Latin American and Spanish sections at Bush House and dubbing for the BBC at White City. We heard, too, about how she met Edith Piaf and we also listened to stories about her work in the antiques trade in the UK, where she was known for her acquisition of glass pieces such as those by Gallé, Lalique, Loetz and Daum, and jewellery made by Coppola e Toppo, Miriam Haskell and Schiapparelli, for example. We heard of Ernst's escape from prison in fascist Germany, his life in London, of objects and friends lost and found.

These conversations and encounters induced an imperative: to disseminate these stories – stories of innovations in cultural form, of struggle and commitment, of lives lived against or in spite of fascism in its various forms; to resurrect a life from relative obscurity, one imposed by political oppression and violence, and to rescue the contributions of an anti-fascist to thinking through the exigencies of modernity and to battling against oppression today.

We applied for some funding from the Lipman-Miliband Trust, which was kindly granted. This triggered a series of events and encounters. In early May 2019 we went on a trip to the Bundesarchiv in Koblenz, where we ate luminous food in the canteen and worked through the boxes of Schoen's archive. Here we came across address books, concert programmes, leaflets, letters, contracts, photo albums, sound recordings, scraps of poetry, dream diaries, letters, costume designs and so much more.

Two documents in particular drew our attention: a flyer from 1924, when Schoen's music was used as accompaniment for a dance by Henri Châtin-Hofmann wearing a dazzling jumpsuit (we discovered he was Anita Berber's husband between 1924 and 1928); and a score of Schoen's 1932 modernist song cycle for a dead friend, *Sechs Gedichte von Fritz Heinle* (Six Poems by Fritz Heinle). Soon after arriving back in London, we found a singer and an accompanist (Lotte Betts-Dean and Joseph Havlat) to perform the songs and organised their private rehearsal at Craxton Studios in Hampstead. We also took a trip to Kingfisher Court, an Art Deco housing estate near Hampton Court Palace, where the Schoens lived from 1941 into the following decade.

In December 2019, we staged a live broadcast of an imagined radio programme from 1932 at the Bishopsgate Institute in London. This production highlighted Schoen's anti-fascism and experimental output. Flossie Draper read part of the script, Florence Warner played the flute and the postie and we included a radio play entitled *A Pay Raise?! Whatever Gave You That Idea!* written by Walter Benjamin and Wolf Zucker and performed by The New Factory of the Eccentric Actor, alongside games, acetate projections, time travel and sonic interventions.

For March 2020 we had another event planned: a performance by Lotte Betts-Dean and Joseph Havlat of the *Sechs Gedichte von Fritz Heinle* followed by an imagined re-staging of the Henri dance, which came to be called *Tanz 23/24*, with music arranged and played by Samuel Draper, danced by Alka

Nauman and Lucie Palazot in costumes constructed by Alicia Gladston. The first lockdown resulting from the COVID-19 pandemic, however, led to the cancellation of this performance. At this point, we worked on what we thought would be a pamphlet on the life and work of Schoen. We wrote it up frantically from our places of quarantine: Esther in Somers Town, Sam in Stamford Hill. Everyone involved in the project had scattered to communicate remotely, having been released from their places of work or study.

In the meantime, Sam moved to Berlin to pursue a project on the palm reader, sexologist and friend of Schoen's Charlotte Wolff and *Tanz 23/24* took place in Warsaw on 3 October 2020 at a time when the pandemic was sufficiently floored to permit travel and events, with the incredible initiative and energies of Joanna Klass and others at Curie City, a social and art space in Warsaw. There, we imagined the struggles for queer lives in the context of contemporary Polish politics, animated by Henri's gestures and movements. That performance was reviewed by Phoebe Blatton for *Art Monthly*.[1] The concert of Schoen's music within its art and cabaret context then took place at the Bishopsgate, broadcast online on 9 October 2020.

Just before Christmas 2020 we received news that this book, drawing together the broader significance of Schoen's life, would go ahead. Since then, we have been largely writing at a distance, in various libraries, archives and museums, cobbling together our work from shared documents. We are grateful to all the people we have encountered along the way. The result of much of that collaboration is what we present to you here. We hope with this book we have gone some way to fulfilling the promise we made to Sasha and Leda, that we would bring due recognition to his father Ernst in the language he adopted in his years of exile.

Method and Structure

The forms and styles of this work retain an imprint of its previous incarnations: in lectures, radio programmes and performances, music and dance. The narrative, like the life under examination, is interrupted by the breaking in of different rhythms and tones.

Theodor W. Adorno, an acquaintance of Schoen's and a figure that appears throughout this work, spent a considerable amount of time, once in exile, exploring radio, especially in the American context. Attuned to what he saw as bad reception, he observed something he called the

Hörstreife (hear-stripe), the sound of the persistent electronic static from radio transmission.[2] This crackle undoes the false 'reality' of music and foregrounds the mechanism. He writes:

Perhaps we may say that music, normally aloof from the noise of the real world, and because of this aloofness, appearing to be 'real', loses this 'reality' when at each moment it is confronted by the 'hear-stripe', hinting so definitely at the empirical world.[3]

Imagine driving down a country lane listening to the radio. As the car moves, the transmission breaks from time to time: the volume jumps, the broadcasts cut out, white noise cuts in, other sounds and music break through. Such interference is heard especially when the radio is first switched on. Or when other electronic devices interfere.[4]

This book adopts something of this interference, drifting between publicity and private sources, real and unreal, waking world and dream worlds, the document and the spoken, the fact, the rumoured and the secret, official and unofficial forms. Where the truth of a life resides is not easily discernible. An interfering hear-stripe is a reminder of the multiplicity of experience in the world. Rather than banish this interference, we listen to it, transcribe it, de-tune further from and into it. Interruptions and interference in the flow are here emulated in the breakages in the narrative, for lack of access to parts of a life that have not been held by the archive, or are not available as matters of public or private record. One motif in Schoen's life is the loss of personal things, especially from the period before the Second World War, and yet, to counterbalance that, we found a plethora of published materials from Weimar media culture.

This work is also a historical re-tuning, when the past blares into our present, our moment. We take seriously the formal conceits of this generation's work, of Schoen's own work and carry some of their energy and impulses into our own methods.

What follows is 'about' Ernst Schoen; about his world and the world and people that surrounded him. To us he is real – a father of a friend, a kind of distant friend to us – but he is also an object of study, an individual whose traces can be found in books, in encyclopaedias and online. He left traces, intentionally or not. He innovated German radio until the Nazis came to power. He left the country of his birth for a place of greater, if still limited, hospitality. He was a composer, a translator, a dream diarist and an occasional poet; a musical arranger, recorder and producer; a theorist and polemicist. But he also represents something of a historical reference point, an antenna through which certain energies of the twentieth century passed. The peaks and troughs of this life aligned with some sort of hope and possibility in the world. Schoen's fate was personal – that of a hard beginning, of success, expulsion, innervation, arrest, exile, alienation, efforts to begin again, mostly thwarted – but it is also political and historical. He is floated and floored by waves not particular to him, but general: the militant dreams of youth, in socialism and communism, Nazism and Stalinism, to the fate of work and his own displacements. As Benjamin wrote in a review of Alfred Döblin's *Berlin Alexanderplatz* (1929): 'From the point of view of epic, existence is an ocean.'[5] Schoen's life was epic, oceanic – and subject, like Franz Biberkopf's, to the vast and inexorable waves of historical motion.

Chapter Breakdown: Form and Content

What follows is organised roughly chronologically and in two parts. The first and second part respectively convey Ernst Schoen's life and his milieu before and after exile. The final part, a coda, is dedicated to posthumous reception.

The first chapter draws on the coming of age of both Schoen and radio in the years of the war that started in 1914. It introduces a circle of friends and a circuit of exchange between them, a network that held out lifelines to each other – and railed against the world as it existed.

The second chapter tracks Schoen's work as it finds new forms in the early 1920s to 1933, his most intense period of involvement in the new infrastructures of radio and various orbiting avant-garde cultures, when he develops atonal composition, thinks and writes about jazz and co-invents the model of the *Hörspiel*, the radio listening play. This section takes the form of a series of cabaret-like fragments and short magazine-like titbits that resonate and clash with each other. As vignettes, the fragments provide instances of Schoen's work and the work of those around him. For this section, our sources are largely the print culture of the radio stations from the time – the year-book and the radio magazines of the Weimar Republic, especially the *Südwestdeutsche Rundfunkzeitung* (*SWZ*), the regional magazine for Frankfurt Radio, the station where Schoen worked, which was also known as Südwestdeutsche Rundfunkdienst AG (SÜWRAG). The transmission of this section is interrupted by a section on childhood, which takes the form of three informal lectures, based on radio talks commissioned for the station's *Youth Hour*.

The third chapter is a polyvocal account of a single year: 1933. It assembles the various accounts – from bureaucratic documents, rumours passed down in family stories, letters and pocket diaries, some contemporaneous with events, some produced much later – of Schoen's escape from incarceration in the newly established Nazi state. It is followed by a roll call, which summons up the figures from the narrative so far and recounts their whereabouts, as Schoen's network scatters.

The fourth chapter reconstructs Schoen's years in exile, after 1933. This section draws largely on personal correspondence and pocket diaries, as well as manuscripts, stories, book drafts and book reports, some of which rarely saw any light of day. As Schoen's public life is reduced to precarious work and relative isolation, this chapter returns to the biographical mode, one of tracking a life whose predominant practice consists in private experimentation: through anti-fascist songs, dream diaries and personally- and politically-charged poetry. This section is punctuated by a return to Germany, to write a report of the state of things cultural for the BBC, in 1947.

The fifth chapter follows Schoen's re-emigration to Germany in the early 1950s, where it becomes impossible to reconstitute the circles of before, not least in the context of a city divided into various sectors. Letters and dream diaries provide access to some of the successful and failed encounters and the efforts to live a life worth living. As infrastructure is remade, we explore what new institutions – including those connected to old acquaintances – come into being and what place is on offer for those whose existence was interrupted.

We conclude with a chapter on posthumous legacies and afterlives, or after-echoes.

A Preliminary Note on Names

Schoen's archive gives perplexing access to a repository of names. It logs government names, pet names and pseudonyms, as they shift over the decades. The bearers of these names are our cast of characters.

* * *

The central subject of this study was born 'Ernst Fritz Erich Schoen' on 14 April 1894.[6] He was also sometimes known as 'Ati' by those close to him, perhaps as a version of Vati, 'daddy', by some accounts invented by his step-daughter Ursula.[7]

Schoen also used pseudonyms at various points – including Hans Werdmann and Jakob Richter, also Erhard Schultze, Eliot Swift and Eric Swift.[8] We shall return to these names at various points throughout the book.

The name Ernst Schoen sometimes rings out in its adjective form: *Ernst* as serious, *Schoen* as pretty. His surname, unlike the adjective (*schön*), is mostly spelt without an umlaut, though sometimes that diacritic was used.[9]

Ernst Schoen was married to Johanna who was born with the surname Liman, but via a previous marriage had also used the name Prätorius. She is sometimes known as 'Hansi' and sometimes as 'Puma' or versions thereof. Later she used her title Gräfin Rogendorf von Mollenburg, or Countess Johanna von Roggendorf, spelt sometimes with two f's or two g's and sometimes one of each. She is also referred to as Mutti, 'mummy'.

Ernst and Johanna named their oldest child, born 14 February 1927, Nina, but she was also known at various points as 'Ninchen', 'Nini' and 'Ninibus'. Nina's sibling, born 28 March 1929, is Alexander and throughout the archives we have found references to his name as 'Sasha', 'Sascha', 'Sacha' and 'Sas'.

At points, *other* Ernst Schoens raised their heads, became mixed up in the historical recounting. There is Hans Ludwig Ernst von Schoen (1877–1954), a banker connected with the assassination attempt on Hitler on July 20 1944. And another: Ernst Ludwig Schoen (1877–1953), listed as the translator of Stravinsky's *Die Hochzeit* (The Wedding) on the Austrian Library Network. *This* Schoen is also listed as the author of a work we will also return to later in the book, 'Musik und Rundfunk' (Music and Radio) in *Das neue Frankfurt*, as listed on the Gemeinsamer Verbundkatalog, a collated library tool. When we found these Schoens, we looked at each other and wondered if we had conflated three people into one all this time. After some investigation, we concluded it was a mistake online. The author was not Ernst Ludwig Schoen, but our Schoen and we could carry on.

***

Throughout this book we slip between these names, depending on the tone or on their source. It was not always easy to decide on what attribution to use at certain points, as we moved between historical documents and records, family recollections and personal ephemera not intended for public scrutiny. We hope this page is a useful reference throughout.

Archives and Sources

A large part of this project comes out of work with and on Ernst Schoen's archive accessed at the Bundesarchiv in Koblenz. Though Schoen's archive is made up of writings in English and German, we present the German writing in translated form – all translations are our own, unless otherwise stated in the footnote or bibliography. For materials in Schoen's archive, the box number, where the document in its original German can be found, is also provided in the footnote.

The *SWZ* was accessed on microfilm at the Staatsbibliothek zu Berlin, kindly sent by Institut für Zeitungsforschung Dortmund. The dates of publication are indicated in the footnotes.

The National Archives at Kew, UK, hold a secret service file that was useful: KV 5/80. There was also a substantial amount of useful material on enemy broadcasters in Germany and Britain in the Second World War in various files.

In addition, we also accessed the following archives and cite the materials accordingly throughout the text:

Adorno-Archiv, Akademie der Künste Berlin
Walter-Benjamin-Archiv, Akademie der Künste Berlin
National Archives in Kew
Landesarchiv Berlin
Deutsche Literaturarchiv Marbach
Universitätsarchiv Frankfurt
Stasi Records Archive Berlin
Landesamt für Bürger- und Ordnungsangelegenheiten Berlin
BBC Written Archives Centre, Caversham
Museum der Dinge, Berlin

Part 1
1894–1933

Locations: Berlin, Heidelberg, Frankfurt,
Hamburg, Helgoland, London

1

Assembling and Composing:
Youth

Circles, Poems

Objects that remain, memories that persist: In the early 1930s, Walter Benjamin recalled a set of rings that bound together a circle of friends. He conjured into memory those from his past through a symbol from the world of things:

Against the background of the city, the people who had surrounded me drew close together to form a figure. It was many years earlier, I believe at the beginning of the war, that in Berlin, against the background of the people then closest to me, the world of things contracted to a symbol similarly profound. It was an emblem of four rings.[1]

The reminiscence involved a visit in summer 1914 to the shop of a prominent antique dealer on Kupfergraben, discovered by Alfred Cohn, one of the circle. Cohn had attended the Kaiser Friedrich School between 1901 and 1909 in Charlottenburg in the west of Berlin, at which a group of boys had formed affiliations and allegiances.[2]

At the antique dealers, the party were shown prehistoric brooches and clasps, Lombard earrings, Late Roman neck chains, sheet-gold breastplates, garnet-studded bracelets and medieval coins.[3] Even if the participants in this scene fall in and out of touch over the years to come, the rings they purchased there remained in the world and served as conduits for remembering a moment when the bonds were configured and confirmed:

There were, if I am not mistaken, three of us: my friend, his fiancée at that time or Frau Dorothea J, and me. C asked to see rings – Greek and Renaissance cameos, rings from the imperial period, work usually carved in semi-precious stone. Each of the four that he finally purchased is imprinted unforgettably on my mind.

Except for one that I have lost sight of, they are still today with those for whom they were intended that morning. One, a bright-yellow smoky topaz, was chosen by Dorothea J. The workmanship was Grecian and depicted in a tiny space Leda receiving the swan between her parted thighs. It was most graceful.[4]

Names were abbreviated, perhaps for shorthand, perhaps to conceal identity. The ring that was lost to Benjamin's knowledge went to his girlfriend, Grete Radt, from whom he separated shortly afterwards and who would later marry Alfred Cohn. This engagement ring fascinated him, as did the pages of Alois Riegl's *Late Roman Art Industry* (1901), which is mentioned in the reminiscence:

Cut in a dark, solid garnet, it portrayed Medusa's head. It was a work from the Roman imperial period. The proustite mounting was not the original. Worn on the finger, the ring seemed merely the most perfect of signet rings. You entered its secret only by taking it off and contemplating the head against the light. As the different strata of the garnet were unequally translucent, and the thinnest so transparent that it glowed with rose hues, the somber bodies of the snakes seemed to rise above the two deep, glowing eyes, which looked out from a face that, in the purple-black portions of the cheeks, receded once more into the night. Later I tried more than once to stamp a seal with this stone, but it proved easy to crack and in need of the utmost care. Shortly after giving it away, I broke off my relationship with its new owner.[5]

Another of these rings was destined for Ernst Schoen. Schoen had lived with Cohn for a period from 1910 after moving to a school in Lankwitz in Berlin.[6] Schoen, in this period, was interested in pursuing music, both performance and composition. Later he recalled:

In 1910, at the age of sixteen, I decided to become a composer of music. At that time I used to visit Busoni's house a lot, since his eldest son, Benvenuto, was a school friend of mine.[7]

Ferruccio Busoni was a prominent composer, performer and unconventional pedagogue, whose students included many of Schoen's contemporaries, including Kurt Weill, Wladimir Vogel and Walther Geiser.[8] Busoni passed on his pupil Schoen to a younger composer, Edgard Varèse, who lived and worked in Berlin from 1908 until 1914.[9] Schoen noted that he was 'Varèse's first and worst pupil'.[10] The young Varèse agreed to teach him 'for either ten marks a lesson or nothing'. Schoen added:

Since the first alternative was out of the question he taught me on the basis of the second [i.e. for nothing]. He took me through the harmony course devised by Luis-Thuille (followed later by Schoenberg).[11]

Schoen left Cohn's home to pursue his studies. Interest in music was supplemented with philosophy, art history and history, at various universities in Berlin, Marburg and Bern.[12]

Benjamin's story of the rings is preceded in *Berlin Chronicle* (1932) by an account of numerous attempts to construct a chart of a now scattered generation that included the four ring-holders. The chart constellated in groupings forty-eight names connected by lines. Benjamin named those on the diagram as his *Urbekanntschaften* ('primal acquaintances'), the important people of his early years. It included school comrades, familial relations, travel companions, among others.[13]

On this map, Ernst Schoen is placed next to Alfred Cohn, their names separated, or connected, by a thick black bar. This coupling was mirrored on the other side of the chart by a blotch between Franz Sachs and Herbert Blumenthal. These four names, a grouping from school, constituted the most primal acquaintances. Diagonally across was Fritz Heinle, another pole of attraction, from whom emanated members of his family as well as his comrade and girlfriend Rika Seligson and her siblings. At the centre of another cluster below was Dora Kellner, who married Benjamin in 1917 and was Schoen's lover in the early 1920s, positioned as a point of entrance to various avant-garde circles, from Emmy Hennings to László Moholy-Nagy.

This chart is shot through with war. Benjamin imagined, against a grey background of the city, a system of colourful signs that mark out the houses of friends and girlfriends, the assembly halls of the Youth Movement and Communist youth, hotels and benches, the routes to different schools, cafés whose names have disappeared from memory and the graves that he saw filled.[14]

Two such graves were filled when, at the outbreak of war, on 8 August 1914, Fritz Heinle, a poet and member of the Youth Movement, resident in Berlin for the winter semester of 1913–1914 and his comrade lover Rika Seligson gassed themselves in the kitchen of the Student Movement on Klopstockstraße, in the Tiergarten district of Berlin. Heinle was twenty years old. Seligson was twenty-three. The gas that had poisoned Heinle and Seligson was a foretaste of the toxic gas soon to be used on an industrial scale on the military front. This joint suicide was enacted in protest against the war. As the expressionist Erwin Loewenson elliptically, even telegraphically, recorded at the time:

Fritz Heinle and Erika Seligson fatally poisoned [...]. According to the newspaper: because of love troubles. According to Wolf Heinle: because of the war.[15]

This horror spurred waves of memorialisation of Heinle amongst his acquaintances in subsequent years. Benjamin composed fifty sonnets to him and guarded the literary bequest of his friend closely, making various efforts to get Heinle's poems published. Schoen wrote music and poetry for him.[16] Heinle's poetry, later motivated by sonic experiment as much as the written word, was sounded in his absence.[17] Those close to him also mimicked his gestures, his expressions.[18] There is little left in the archives about Seligson. A modest stone, at Weißensee Cemetery in Berlin, bears the long-form version of her name, Frederika, and the grave number, but no dates. Rika's younger sister Gertrude (often shortened to Traute) also killed herself in November 1915, along with Wilhelm Caro, a fellow member of the circle.[19]

One of Schoen's only surviving possessions from this period is a notebook. It opens with a dedication, written as if a single word in calligraphic handwriting: 'Von alfred am 18 august 1914'[20], only ten days after the death of Heinle and Seligson.

Alfred here was presumably Alfred Cohn and the handwriting was in a style developed by the poet Stefan George. George had founded a circle of poetic initiates. The friends around Schoen emulated such an assembly of writers and readers. They read plays that were not part of their school's curriculum: Ibsen, Strindberg, Wedekind.[21] Much later, in 1955, Schoen named this group as a 'dramatic reading circle'.[22] They harnessed culture against state, family, school. The notebook dedicated to Cohn contains a translation of a Baudelaire poem, 'Une Charogne' ('A Carcass'), that George had not included in his collection.[23] In the next decade, a number of those in the wider network – Walter Benjamin, Franz Hessel, Charlotte Wolff – went on to publish their translations of the poetry they had passed around and read aloud to each other over these years.[24]

Left in the archive are a number of photographs of Schoen and Cohn sitting together, in a field or meadow, perhaps by the sea, smoking and laughing in each other's company.[25]

In 1916, Schoen was called up for a physical examination to assess his state for war. He joined the Landsturm-Infantry Reserve Battalion III

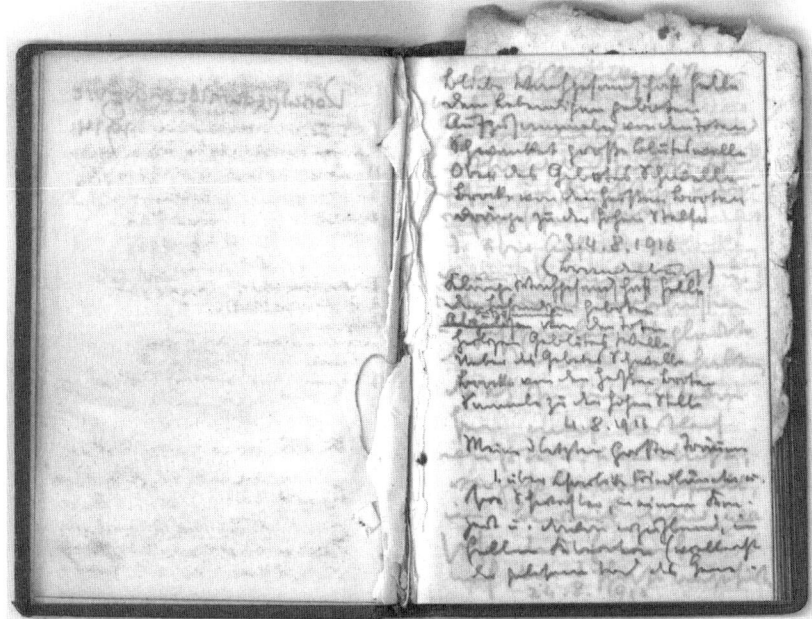

Figure 1.1 Detail from Ernst Schoen's early notebook: *Tagebuch*, BArch N 1403/1. The dedication from Alfred Cohn can be see bleeding through the page on the top left.

Photographed at the Bundesarchiv Koblenz. Copyright: Sabine Schiller-Lerg.

24, stationed in the garrison town of Brandenburg, not far from Berlin. In Brandenburg, he worked as a translator in Russian, a go-between for the different imprisoned nationalities.[26] He wrote to Jula Cohn on 23 December 1916, his location named as the Brandenburg mining wasteland 'Grube Präsident'. She copied out the letter, by hand, in Stefan George's script. Schoen lamented that he might not have any leave over the Christmas period and would not see her. He wrote of a shattering of the self in disappointment and of recuperation and how gorging on poems by Stefan George did him 'sadly good'. He told her he would go on to read some Heinle and quoted a few lines from 'Der Dichter auf dem Gipfel' ('The Poet on the Peak'), a poem originally dedicated to Rika Seligson, which he found beautiful[27]:

> Essence creature and number
> Dream and life above the ground
> Poets will paint hours
> Across the beloved mouth.[28]

The poem spoke of a soul rising above the misery of the valleys, all torment swallowed in dreams.[29] Love elevates. Songs bring peace.

Alfred Cohn had selected an amethyst ring for Schoen, one with a fifteenth or sixteenth-century profile, most likely of politician and military leader Pompey. To receive a ring from a school friend was to hold onto bonds forged prior to the dispersions of adulthood. Benjamin, in his account, was not enamoured of this ring, but it stayed with Schoen. In a photograph from around 1921, taken in Heidelberg, it could well be the ring that appears on the ring finger of his left hand. His head downturned, wearing a silk bow tie, he consults his watch and holds a cigar between his index and middle finger. A shadow of a head, likely Jula Cohn's, is cast over his double-breasted suit in the photograph, which is likely a reference for a bust of Schoen she went on to produce. Somehow this photograph made it into Benjamin's possession and later to his archive. On the back is written: 'Ernst Schoen / Heidelberg'.[30] Schoen had been sent to work at a prisoner of war camp in Heidelberg.

During these years, Schoen poured musical ideas into the notebook given to him by Alfred Cohn, ideas for compositions, motifs perhaps heard from others.[31] A number of notations from March and April 1917, all in E minor, appear under the descriptor 'Russian', though the handwriting is hard to discern. Some of the lines can be played and repeated, as if in a round, like a drinking song. Another is marked simply with 'Lamentoso', a direction for plaintive, mournful playing.[32]

Music, Towers

In spring 1918, Dora Sophie Kellner wrote to Ernst Schoen, keen to learn more about Schoen's former piano teacher, Ferruccio Busoni, who had been living in Switzerland since 1915. She reported that years ago she had heard Busoni and knew then that he was the only one from whom she would like to learn piano. She wanted to know if he was taking pupils. She wondered if Schoen might provide her with an introduction – though she recognised that she might need to practise for a while, in order to be good enough for him to take her on, as she had 'only unlearnt and forgotten since she was fourteen'.[33] Dora, with husband Walter and Gershom Scholem attended a concert by Busoni in Berlin in May 1918,[34] likely to

Figure 1.2 Ernst Schoen in Heidelberg, c.1921.

be one reviewed in the July–September issue of the pacifist journal *Die weißen Blätter* (The White Pages):

Busoni's playing: good wood! beautiful wood! transformed violin! All movements rounded, even the most angular run up gets rounded, becomes an eclipse, however sharp it is. Busoni is full of joy when he plays: he really *plays*. He can still play! It splashes about like a sonorous spinning top and suddenly the spinning top stands quite straight and becomes a rotary fountain full of colours, which whip the day into foam.[35]

In October, Kellner wrote again, in response to Schoen's letter. She had not acted on her desire to study with Busoni, but she was also saddened by news that Schoen had conveyed. Schoen's assessment of Busoni – his mediocrity as a person – did not tally with the image she carried of him and it made her loathe to contact him, despite still being gripped by his art, and even more so, by his 'renunciation'.[36] She was uncertain where to turn now in her quest to develop her playing and understanding of music. Moreover, she had acquired a piece of writing by him, in the issue of *Die weißen Blätter*, from July–September 1918,[37] which reproduced Busoni's short play titled *Das Wandbild* (*The Mural*), an opera-pantomime. He worked on this with Philipp Jarnach, based on Martin Buber's *Chinesische Geister- und Liebesgeschichten* (Chinese Ghost and Love Stories) (1911).[38]

The play was set in an antique shop in Paris in 1830. The Romantic poet Novalis was present as a student. In the centre of the stage was a life-sized painting of a Chinese girl. The shop was crammed with odd stuff, including an automaton that danced when the clock strikes eight. The shopkeeper seemed to be a charlatan. He showed his customers an ancient golden helmet from China, but Novalis wished to know who the girl in the painting was. The shopkeeper claimed not to know, but Novalis had become obsessed and had fallen in love. He rushed at the picture and entered it. The next scene took place within the painting. The two figures embraced – her hair was ruffled. A man in golden armour arrived to enchain the girl, while the young man, who wished to ravish her, hid behind a curtain. The setting returned to the shop. Novalis was now missing and the shopkeeper assumed he must be in a side room, but he stepped forward from the painting and insisted on hearing its full story. Another man in the shop realised something odd about the painting. The hairstyle that the girl had worn when he first entered the shop was now altered. He reckoned it to be a trick of the viewing angle, but was unable to find the first viewpoint again. The clock struck nine. The 'magic hour' was done.

Kellner was unimpressed by the piece and its central conceit of entering a painting, though her husband Walter Benjamin would make use of the image fifteen years later in his essay on the 'Work of Art in the Age of its Technological Reproducibility', in relaying a legend about the Chinese painter, Wu Daozi.[39] She described it to Schoen as a piece in which 'he flattened out and stylised in a terrible way an old Chinese fairy-tale motif'. And she noted that even as the background to a piece of ballet music it would still be bad. If Busoni was not a reliable guide, could Schoen himself direct her in a music course that would develop her understanding and skill? She rhapsodised about Bach and the desire to know all that came before – and Beethoven. Was time too short to learn it all?

On 4 December 1918, Kellner wrote a letter responding to Schoen's thoughts on opera that he had conveyed to her in a previous letter. The discussion became more technical and aesthetic as she reflected on music as heard and as imagined. Benjamin and Kellner had been discussing music with a musician from Wickersdorf, the Free School Community that had been Walter's milieu until the outbreak of the war. The discussions pushed them into questions of music as expression and the question of the 'expressionless'. Those who had come to inspire youthful impulses had come to disappoint just as youth itself was waning.

At some point, she insisted, they would have to develop further aesthetic strategies to break with the old. The letter closed with a request. From where she was in Switzerland, Kellner was unable to find Jula Cohn a specific book she longed to give her for Christmas: Paul Scheerbart's *Lesabéndio* from 1913, a utopian novel set on an asteroid. It had been Scholem's wedding gift to Kellner and Benjamin. She asked Schoen, in Heidelberg, to acquire it and if it were at all possible, to remove from it the fourteen poorly executed drawings by Alfred Kubin. Scheerbart disliked Kubin's images, feeling they were too anthropomorphic.[40]

This book was important to the circle of friends; like a ring, gifted for marriages and across friendships and relationships.[41] Kubin's final image in *Lesabéndio* conveys something from the future to come. It depicted the giant tower that is at the core of the narrative, a tower from which Lesabéndio will finally jump into the cloud and remain present only as a disembodied voice. While its character emanated a certain religiosity, the

tower was redolent of something of this world: the metalwork of radio towers that had sprouted up in various cities. The scratchy pencil lines appear
like metal bars riveted together. The novella's tower, built to pierce the
clouds, raged in Kubin's image like a divisive tower, a Babel raised against
God, which would fracture communication and understanding. It is suffused with the light of the head-star, glowing like a sun above it, divine in
origin or an emanation of the excessive energies of nature. However, now,
in the world around Schoen and his friends, other towers were appearing
in the fields and in the cities and they would draw Schoen and the new
wave around them.

Benjamin would eventually give Jula the engagement ring that he had
received back after splitting up with Grete Radt. But Jula went on to marry
Fritz Radt in December 1925. The circles broke apart and recombined, but
did not dissolve. Jula, for one, made a bust of Benjamin, photographed by
Sasha Stone around 1926. In recounting the fate of the four rings purchased
by Alfred Cohn (and distributed to his fiancée, to Schoen, to Benjamin's
fiancée Grete Radt and to Alfred Cohn's sister Jula), Benjamin observed
that Jula was the 'true centre of the circle's fate':[42]

And in fact she was the centre never of people but, in the strictest sense, of fates, as
if her plant-like passivity and inertia had arranged the latter – which, of all human
things, seem the most subject to vegetal laws – concentrically about her. Many
years were needed before what at that time was in part beginning to unfold in its
seed, and in part still dormant, emerged in its ramifications to the light of day: the
fate by virtue of which she, who had a relationship with her brother that by its tenderness filled to the very edge the capacities of sisterly love, was to form a liaison
with her brother's two closest friends – with the recipient of the ring depicting the
head of Pompeii and with me – and ultimately find her husband in the brother of
the woman who married her own brother as her second husband. She it was, on
the day I am speaking of, who received from me the ring with the Medusa's head.
It cannot have been many days later that I sent – after the lapis lazuli with the lute
wreathed in foliage engraved in it, after the fourth ring and to its wearer – this sonnet: 'To your finger constantly encircled [text breaks off][43]

The telling of the story breaks off at the point when it seems too complex to
recount or follow. What initially seemed quite simple, a story of four rings
and four people, becomes harder and harder to track, as rings and relationships tangled together. With more and more figures, bonds are broken
and reformed – amid the coming of new technologies and new possibilities for cultural form, such rearrangements were exacerbated.

2

Radio and Experiment: Weimar

War developed technologies and modes of communication. Radio played its part in war as telegraphy, a mechanism of communication between those directing the powerless towards death. This use was not a form of broadcasting – sending signals far and wide to anyone with a tuner – rather it went only to those who were privy to the communications of commanders. Radio in war was not initially used for sending out propaganda.[1] Instead, it operated through a five-year long continuous tapping of Morse signs: truncated, brevity codes that eventually translated back into speech. Radio communicated with the moving parts of war, with tanks as they entered into action and aeroplanes in close range. Radio allowed the earth to become a catastrophe of moving parts. It conveyed messages, but it carried a booty that could be intercepted and seized. This meant that there was also a war of the airwaves, through listening in and interception.

Radio had originated in more peaceful times, notably in the small town of Karlsruhe, where Heinrich Hertz carried out experiments to send waves across space. After the political settlements of 1848, the seizure of of colonies, the victorious war of 1871 and some class accords, there was in Germany a period of quasi-peaceful evolution, as a middle-class generated, as Ernst Schoen put it, 'larger and larger waves in the sphere of its influence', until a point when it came into conflict with British interests.[2] In the late 1880s, Heinrich Hertz deflected radio waves from a solid object at sea. In 1895, Alexander Popov made a device to detect distant lightning strikes. These experiments came together in efforts to produce devices for communication between ships. While experimenting with this in the Baltic Sea, Popov noticed an interference beat that emerged as a result of another passing vessel. He had a glimmer of an idea that the phenomenon might allow for object detection under conditions of non-visibility. In 1904, Christian Hülsmeyer was able to detect a ship in dense fog. However, he could not tell at what distance it was. He patented his device.

The first forms of radio began to emerge around 1900 in Germany as the transmission of Morse Code wirelessly, or wireless telegraphy. Much equipment had to be developed for Hertz's waves to become waves of communication: rectifiers and amplifiers, microphones and telegraphic signals, antennae and loudspeakers. This apparatus which had been conceived in peace, in a Prussian town, took on actualised form in war, under the brand name Telefunken. It meshed in time with the private interests of business and the public interests of the state. In 1906, Telefunken began transmitting long-range from Nauen in Brandenburg and soon there were outpost stations in the USA, in German-occupied Kamina in Togo and Windhoek on the African continent. News events could be communicated swiftly from and to afar. A wireless communications network was set up in the Pacific South Sea, which enabled communications to continue to flow between the army command and overseas armies and naval fleets when the submarine cables were cut by the enemies during the war. Ships adrift in the sea could mobilise their own waves and relay back and forth between land and ocean. It seemed nothing short of miraculous. Ships became small radio stations, each mast a transmitter, a floating island of transmission.

On One Fate

With war over, Schoen was soon back in Berlin, taking up jobs in the nascent communications industry. He escaped the bleak surroundings of the prisoner of war camp and left behind casual work: there was a time when he wore in or 'tamed' new shoes for other men or loosened up their suits, as requested by couturiers.[3] He got a position with *Plutus*, a critical newspaper for economy and finance published between 1904 and 1925 and edited by Georg Bernhard. After this, he became an editor with a press agency, the Wolff Telegraphenbüro from 1919 to 1921.[4] Once this agency had been in contact with all the world but when, in the years of the war, its undersea cables were cut by the Allies, its messages could not travel across the waves. Its influence was limited. The German state was now putting its resources towards a new wireless agency: Transocean News Agency. There was a short period when Schoen was assistant director of the modern art Galerie Möller in Berlin, from 1921 to 1922.[5] He went on to be press officer for the Imperial Coal Commission from 1922 until 1924.[6] Schoen, released from war, entered the world of work, as someone involved in telegraphy and press releases – communications for a modern age. War's communicative armoury was being adapted for its aftermath, to build new towers and cultures. Art extended and contorted its fruits. The manifestos of the Futurist Marinetti called for a 'wireless imagination' in new forms of poetry – 'Marconigrammes'; and for 'words-in-freedom!'[7] With the arrival of sound broadcasting, Marinetti and others imagined a new radiophonic art.[8] Schoen was to pursue something similar.

Towers, Montage, Form

Enthusiasts of modern technology deemed the radio tower emblematic of new metropolitan tempos and perspectives. On one page of László Moholy-Nagy's *typophoto* – a montaged combination of type and photography – for a film manuscript, *Dynamic of the Metropolis* (1925), a photograph of a radio mast appears.[9] Shot from below, it pierces the sky with its stark black armature, as wires radiate from it making connections beyond the photo frame. The pages of Moholy-Nagy's film script are divided dramatically by black bars that evoke the steel girders of modern towers. Sibyl Moholy-Nagy, in her biography *Moholy-Nagy: Experiment in Totality* (1950), recalls standing with her husband atop the Berlin Radio Tower, a structure that had sprung up in the German capital around the time of the film sketch's publication. From the heights of the tower, they looked down at the cars and enjoyed the play of light, gripped by the ecstasy of height, from where new transmissions, new maps, new vantage points could be found.[10] The iron radio tower was an emblem of the future, a structure pointing beyond its time, made to diffuse newness.

In 1928, architectural historian and critic Sigfried Giedion, an enthusiast of metal construction, celebrated the experience to be had:

In the windswept stairways of the Eiffel Tower, or, better still, in the steel supports of a *Pont Transbordeur*, one meets with the fundamental aesthetic experience of present-day architecture: through the thin net of iron that hangs suspended in the air, things stream – ships, ocean, houses, masts, landscape, harbor. They lose their distinctive shape, swirl into one another as we climb downward, merge simultaneously.[11]

Up there, from the aerial perspective offered through the iron bars and girders of a montaged construction, the self was battered by wind and assailed by the dizziness experienced at unfamiliar heights. Miniaturised things in the wide expanse of the sea blurred into each other, just as scenes in a film might transition in a wipe, or as dreams parade their fuzzy edges and indeterminate environs, or as attention blurs in and out of a radio show that has become background hum. Against this blur stood out the sharp outlines of the infrastructure. The new buildings of metal were open, filigree lattice, through which the wind blew, each a skeleton, hanging over the city like an X-ray of the modern torso. For Walter Benjamin, they delivered something new and strange that was relevant not just for architecture, but also for thinking:

[T]he historian today has only to erect a slender but sturdy scaffolding – a philosophic structure – in order to draw the most vital aspects of the past into his net. But just as the magnificent vistas of the city provided by the new construction in iron for a long time were reserved exclusively for the workers and engineers, so too the philosopher who wishes here to garner fresh perspectives must be someone immune to vertigo – an independent and, if need be, solitary worker.[12]

A philosophically-inclined historian captures aspects of the past via new masts, perceiving aspects in tense relation, solid in the estimation of what events are necessary and so on. This analyst has entered into a realm once reserved for those who are practical, engaged in labour. The analyst assumes the perspective of the worker, which affords new views. And a new situation: from these heights one might call for help, but also declare a new world. The radio tower was a lightning rod of experimentation and modernity. Benjamin set the Eiffel Tower as productive of new modern forms: 'Teleology of Paris: Eiffel Tower and motorways'.[13] Guillaume Apollinaire's first visual poem, 'Lettre-Océan' from 1914, captured new technical forms *as* poetry. Its title refers to the messages that passengers at sea could send to those on shore by telegraph transmission from ship to ship in a binary code of dots and dashes. 'I was on the banks of the Rhine when you left for Mexico/Your voice reaches me in spite of the huge distance', it begins. The lines of the poem spike out around a height marker – 300 metres – on the Eiffel Tower, in imitation of the aerial spokes at the top of the Paris construct. It appears to represent it in the process of radiating a telegraphic message. The poem-image is broken up by parallel bars of wavy lines that might be radio waves, sea waves or telegraph cables under the sea.

The radio tower was an experimental form, its construction mode, its materials quite new. It was a liberation from stone, made possible by precision engineering. Its many components were ground to a specific size by machines. The machines were operated by humans, but their capabilities outstripped those of humans. The tower had been imagined, designed, conceptualised in advance by skilled planners, whose designs were conveyed to workmen well trained in the construction of a complex giant out of many tiny parts over many months. Benjamin observed that the Eiffel Tower was the earliest manifestation of the montage technique. In its construction, millions of component parts came together to form a larger unity.[14] In a radio lecture, broadcast on Frankfurt Radio in 1932, Benjamin discussed 'The Railway Disaster at the Firth of Tay'.[15] Its early use of iron in construction, at a point when it was ill-understood and so had fatal consequences, contrasted with the use of montaged metals in Paris:

Eiffel and his engineers built the tower in seventeen months. Every rivet hole was prepared in workshops with tenth-of-a-millimeter precision. Each of the 12,000 metal parts was specified in advance, down to the millimetre, along with every one of the two and a half million rivets. Not a chisel could be heard in the workshops. Even at the site, as in the draftsman's studio, thought prevailed over physical strength, which was transmitted to sturdy scaffolds and cranes.[16]

Here, Benjamin is closely paraphrasing Alfred Gotthold Meyer, who noted in his seminal *Iron Construction: History and Aesthetics* (1907) how

the plastic shaping power [of iron] recedes before a colossal span of spiritual energy. [...] Each of the twelve thousand metal fittings, each of the two and a half million rivets, is machined to the millimeter [...] On this work site, one hears no chisel-blow liberating form from stone; here thought reigns over muscle power, which it transmits via cranes and secure scaffolding.[17]

A few hundred workers assembled the tower, rather than building it, from elements prepared in a factory located on the outskirts of Paris. The tower's production process undermined the division of manual and mental labour, shifting execution towards the conceptual, or the work of the general intellect, as Marx termed it in the *Grundrisse*, dating from

1857–1858.[18] Robustness that was once a property of human brawn trans-ferred to the object that was worked on, whose skillful and exact construc-tion would guarantee strength, while the workers, from draughtsmen to engineers to builders, honed their thinking skills in assembling.

For Benjamin, the Eiffel Tower was a predictive form, oriented to the future. Built as a landmark structure to commemorate the centenary of the French Revolution, it came *too soon*.[19] Its true purpose arrived after a delay, when it began to play a role in radio transmission. Its form was able to pre-figure a purpose yet to come, or still to be found. If the Sacré-Cœur was the dinosaurian ichthyosaur of Paris, the Eiffel Tower was, by contrast, another form: a giraffe, its long neck a sign of the looming hyper-technological torso of the city.[20] The tower appeared as a sign of what is to come, always on the horizon, a neck stretched ahead of a body yet to arrive. The 'completeness' of the shape could not yet be properly dis-cerned. Iron construction, like radio broadcasting, was in its infancy, its parts constructing an incomplete whole.

If it became useful for the age of aural transmissions, it was also a prod-uct amenable to a new age of visual fascination. Germaine Krull photo-graphed it for *Métal* (1928), a portfolio of sixty-four loose plates printed in collotype. She emphasised the lacework of metal bars, angular confections caught from multiple perspectives. She produced dizzying photographs of lift tracks and stairways from inside, outside, above and below the struc-ture. The tower was almost forty years old by then and Krull had found it a 'lifeless, black monstrosity', until she discovered a small stairway at its core, a little used mode of moving inside the monster. She observed: 'Everything came to life and had nothing to do with the Eiffel Tower as we had known it: iron lives!'[21] The tower gained a new life in being found again, found as something still with secrets to reveal, not that thing that was all too well known, all too much seen and represented.

Krull needed another way to see the tower again, or to make it be seen. Some of Krull's photographs of the Eiffel Tower appeared in the illustrated magazine *Vu*, in May 1928, in a collage of different perspectives. One was an extremely low-angle view of the tower, its metal struts shooting criss-cross into the cloudy sky. On the bottom left was a smaller close up of the metal bars from inside the structure. On the bottom right was an even smaller image of the entirety of the tower, but this time only as a shadow casting its gloom over the surrounding district. The photograph was shot from the tower itself and was a proof in image form of the dominating presence of the structure. Florent Fels wrote captions to accompany the three images. The one for the shadow image stated: 'From above, it appears that one disengages a little from terrestrial contingencies. One glides in thought along the length of her tower right up to the point of her sister, the shadow, which lies like the stylus of a sundial.' This tower, he notes, is the 'supreme symbol of the new era.' Showing its shadow-side implies, though, that it was also distinctly strange.[22]

Radio towers arrived in other cities as miniaturised Eiffel Towers, rapidly littering the urban landscape. Towering structures, made of many fragmented parts, might be seen to be mirrored in the form of the media they transmitted: architectural construction in metal was made of spliced parts, just as radio's programming spliced plays to lectures, concerts to conversations, children's shows to music. Modern media culture served up a choppy, distracted, syncopated, swiftly moving, clashing montage of moments, spaces and times brought together, cut across.

Entangled Lives

In this decade, engagements and marriages among the circles from Berlin fell apart and re-formed. During the winter of 1920–1921, Ernst Schoen and Dora Benjamin had an affair, meeting in hotel rooms.[23] Dora was smitten and imagined leaving Walter for Ernst. Benjamin attempted to take up a relationship with Jula Cohn, sister of Alfred and member of the friendship circle, who had come to stay in the Benjamin's home in March 1921 for several weeks.[24] Schoen had been in love with Jula Cohn from 1914 into the war years, but she reserved her affections, preferring, as she wrote in a letter to Schoen, to 'prowl around the fields', rather than be in a relationship.[25] Benjamin fell in love with her and Dora worried about him, as Jula did not reciprocate. In April 1921, Dora, in despair, wrote to Scholem about her own prowling through the streets of Berlin, singing loudly and thinking of suicide.[26] She fell ill in May and went to convalesce in a sanatorium owned by her aunt Henriette Weiß in Breitenstein am Semmering.[27] Dora insisted that Schoen go with her.[28] Benjamin visited her in the sanatorium, but was also preoccupied in trying to woo Jula Cohn in Heidelberg. While away, Dora became pregnant by Schoen, leading to an abortion in Berlin sometime before the beginning of September 1921.[29] Charlotte Wolff, then a medical student, met the Benjamins and came to know Schoen. According to one of Wolff's memoirs, she and Schoen visited lesbian bars in Berlin's Schöneberg, particularly Verona Diele on Kleiststraße and Top Keller on Nollendorfplatz. Schoen chaperoned her to the bars, only to disappear at some point in the evening, as a ruse against police surveillance.[30] At Verona Diele, the lesbian magazine *Die Freundin* (The Girlfriend) was always on prominent display. It was one of the magazines published by the *Bund für Menschenrechte* (League for Human Rights) and was devoted to education, politics, stories, advertisements for nightclubs, lonely hearts and more. This transformation in sexual and romantic life was Schoen's milieu in the early years of the Weimar Republic.[31] Walter Benjamin was apparently unperturbed by the affair between Ernst and Dora, though he was depressed by Jula's lack of reciprocity.[32] Wolff observed that the relationship between Dora and Schoen did not compromise the friendship between the two men, for Walter Benjamin, at least, was able to 'dispense with the capitalism of possessive love':[32]

The intimacy between his wife and his friend did not disturb his peace of mind: on the contrary, it brought the two men closer together.[32]

The relationship broke up in January 1922 and Dora returned to Walter and their son Stefan.[33]

Living Ears

On 31 May 1921, Edgard Varèse, with the support of Carlos Salzedo, set up the International Composers' Guild (ICG) at a meeting in Manhattan, New York.[34] The ICG advocated for premiere performances of new works under the direction, or with the participation, of composers. It explicitly sought to support the work of the living, rather than that of the dead.[35] As Varèse stated, 'Too many musical organisations are Bourbons who learn nothing and forget nothing. They are mausoleums – mortuaries for musical reminiscence.'[36] It served up, in Varèse's words, 'new ears for new music and new music for new ears.'[37] In July 1921, the ICG published a manifesto, a mishmash of ideological commitments:

In every other field, the creator comes into some form of direct contact with his public. The poet and novelist enjoy the medium of the printed page; the painter and sculptor, the open doors of a gallery; the dramatist, the free scope of a stage. The composer must depend upon an intermediary, the interpreter.

Dying is the privilege of the weary. The present day composers refuse to die. They have realised the necessity of banding together and fighting for the right of each individual to secure a fair and free presentation of his work. It is out of such a collective will that the International Composers' Guild was born.

The aim of the International Composers' Guild is to centralise the works of the day, to group them in programs intelligently and organically constructed, and, with the disinterested help of singers and instrumentalists to present these works in such a way as to reveal their fundamental spirit.

The International Composers' Guild refuses to admit any limitation, either of volition or of action.

The International Composers' Guild disapproves of all 'isms'; denies the existence of schools; recognizes only the individual.[38]

The ICG's first concert took place on 19 February 1922 in New York's Greenwich Village. Performed at various points were Schoenberg's *Pierrot Lunaire* (1912) and Stravinsky's *Les Noces* (The Wedding) (started in 1917), which Schoen went on to adapt into German for performance in 1923.[39] In 1922, Varèse returned to Berlin to launch a local branch of the ICG: Internationale Komponisten Gilde (IKG).[40] Ferruccio Busoni was its president, Ernst Schoen its secretary.[41] The committee included Alfredo Casella, Paul Hindemith and Ernst Krenek. The first concert was held on 1 November 1922, with work by Busoni, Bernard van Dieren, Hindemith, Arthur Lourié and Varèse.[42] The grouping did not last long, however; it 'crumbled away' by 1927, its promotional purposes partly fulfilled, its management too arduous for Varèse.[43]

Its leading figure caused some scandal. In March 1923, Varèse's *Hyperprism* (1921/23) premiered in New York. The audience reacted with giggles, guffaws and catcalls.[44] A *New York Sun* critic described an audience split in two: those who hissed the music and those who hissed the hissers.[45] A *New York Herald* critic reported that, at one point, Carlos Salzedo jumped to his feet and commanded the audience to be quiet. He shouted 'This is serious!'[46] Reports state that Carl Ruggles shouted from the stage that 'people who don't like this should stay away.'[47] On some days, the living had to battle not just with the dead but also the living.

Radio Infancy

After the First World War, a news service had been set up at Königs Wusterhausen, south of Berlin, to communicate daily news to post offices across the country.[48] News was to be supplemented by entertainment, with programmes based around both speech and music. Hans Bredow, from the Post Ministry, demonstrated the possibilities in front of Berlin's scientific society Urania and he was given permission by the authorities to explore further. In 1921, an attempt was made to broadcast *Madame Butterfly* from the Berlin State Opera. This led to further technical agreements concerning wavelengths and equipment and the establishment of links between a central transmitter and listening rooms. Awareness that in England in 1922 radio had been formally introduced was a spur to development. Experimental broadcasts went out from Königs Wusterhausen. From 1923, interest in radio grew among the populace. On 6 April the first radio club was founded in Berlin and almost immediately afterwards, the Verband der Rundfunkindustrie (Association of the Radio Industry) was formed following publication of the first German broadcasting journal, *Radio*. Radio was first broadcast in Germany from the attic of Berlin's Vox-Haus at the end of October 1923. By the end of 1923 there were 1,580 radio listeners.[49] A few months later, a second transmitter, Sender Leipzig, started broadcasting on 1 March 1924. At the end of that month, on 30 March, the Südwestdeutsche Rundfunkdienst AG (SÜWRAG) started broadcasting from Frankfurt. More regional radio stations followed.[50] This developing network of transmitters was accompanied by state regulation – disallowing unauthorised listening and broadcasting, insisting new listeners apply at the telephone exchange for permission to listen. Radios were limited to the reception of certain frequencies and the commercially available ones were difficult to break into and modify.[51]

Henri, Ernst, Anita

On 29 March 1924, a final concert occurred in a series that had run from autumn 1923. Its six events occurred under the title 'Tanzabend der modernen Musik' (Dance Evening of Modern Music). A handbill for the last event in the series, at the Blüthnersaal in Berlin, listed Schoen as a contributing composer, alongside Lord Berners, Alfredo Casella, Julian Freemann,

Serge Prokofieff, Emerson Withrone, Maurice Ravel, Karol Szymanowski, Eric Satie, George Auric, Paul Hindemith, Manuel de Falla, Béla Bartók, Darius Milhaud, Cyril Scott, Arthur Honegger, G. Francesco Malipiero, Zez Confrey, Igor Stravinsky, Alexander Scriabin, Modest Mussorgsky and Claude Debussy.

On the handbill, a dancer, 'Henri', posed in a jumpsuit decorated with geometric forms and with wooden planks attached to his arms. His face, heavily made up, was turned to the right. Henri Châtin-Hofmann was the third husband of the dancer and cabaret artist Anita Berber. He improvised his dances; his gestures queer, expressionistic, abrupt. The press response was mixed. F. Böhme, in the *Deutsche Allgemeine Zeitung*, on 13 October 1923, under the heading 'New York at the Blüthnersaal' used racist and racialised language to conjure up an image of Henri's 'alacrity and his glid-ing quality', which failed to 'master the impulse of the core body'. Only the costumes impressed the reviewer, but the 'local audience here applauded with delight'. The *Berliner Börsen-Zeitung*, from 16 October 1923, focused on how Henri's dance revolved around his hands. Again, the costumes drew the eye: 'Equally original as the dances were the American's cos-tumes: flashy, bizarre, curious, "worked out", moreover coquettish, like his whole demeanour'. Again, in the *Berliner Börsen-Zeitung*, this time from 28 October 1923, these were remarks on the womanly appearance of the dancer, who spoke an 'eloquent language of the hands'. A demarcation of what is proper to Germany creeps into the review:

The particularly prominent feature of this dancer, which manifests coquetry, all manner of make-up and other grooming arts and which make up an essential part of these dance performances, is admittedly uncongenial to the German sensibility.[52]

And again, in the same newspaper, from 1 April 1924, the final evening was reviewed. New dances had been promised, but in the end, there was only repetition of old ones. The reviewer was disappointed. But the audience was 'able to admire his art of communicating expressively through his hands'. He sang, as it were, with his arms and hands. His agility with these body parts was exceptionally free and subtle. The fact that Henri bore a strong feminine trait in his artistry, stronger than any other dancer tended to possess, appeared psychologically characteristic of the particular gift of this dancer, according to the reviews. The fine oscillations of the hand imparted to his whole physicality something soft, delicate, feminine and effeminate.[53]

Klaus Mann wrote up his memories of the decadent couple, Anita Berber and her husband Henri, for the theatre journal *Die Bühne* (The Stage).[54] Mann recalled cocaine use in her rooms, with Henri in the shadows, as Berber told wild stories of hypnotising animals and murderers whose killer grip she had evaded. Mann, just eighteen years of age at the time, watched a weakened and drugged Henri pine for food, once all the money had gone. The teenager bought him a Wiener schnitzel and amused himself as Henri fell on it in hunger. At the dances in the Blüthnersaal, Henri was seen as something of a clown. He came to interrupt the stale ballet, to shock. Schoen's music appeared suitable to accompany this interference, this interruption.

Radio Roles

In 1924, radio for purposes of entertainment and information began in earnest: the first play, the first opera and concert transmissions, news, weather reports, stock exchange updates, an outside broadcast to greet an airship on its maiden flight over Stuttgart. On 10 April 1924, an Arbeiter Rundfunk Klub (ARK, workers' radio club) was founded, to be followed by many others. The club focused on teaching workers to build their own radios. In time, though, such clubs began taking critical stances towards programming and there was a burgeoning demand for worker-controlled radio stations.

In 1924, Ernst Schoen was called to Frankfurt, to the newly founded Südwestdeutsche Rundfunkdienst AG (SÜWRAG). The station was led by Hans Flesch, who was keen to introduce some experimental approaches. As Flesch declared, 'In the beginning there was experimentation' and Flesch was there from the beginning.[55] He continued his previous engagements with X-ray technology and the science of electromagnetic waves, first explored when he was a medical student.

Schoen was recommended for the job by a relative of Flesch: 'Are you looking for an intelligent, literary, musically trained man. I have him here in Berlin. Shall I send him?'[56] On 1 June 1924, Schoen began work

Figure 2.1 Front and back of a flyer from Schoen's Archive in Koblenz: *Kompositionen ('Ati's Compositions')*, BArch N 1403/55.

Photographed at the Bundesarchiv Koblenz. Copyright: Sabine Schiller-Lerg.

as a programme assistant, but quickly advanced to become Programme Executive, then Leader of the Programming Department and, soon, Flesch's deputy.[57] He opened the doors of the studio. An array of commentators on politics, arts, science, technology all passed through the doors of the SÜWRAG over the subsequent decade.

On 15 May 1924, Flesch was witness to the marriage of Paul Hindemith and Gertrude Rottenberg and he was married to Gertrude's elder sister Gabriele. The Hindemiths went on to occupy the top two storeys of a fourteenth-century tower on the south side of the river Main.[58] Circuits of filiation and collaboration became live. On 1 April 1926, to mark the station's second birthday, Schoen's portrait and name (styled as Schön) appeared in a constellation of portraits and names, surrounded by statistics about the Frankfurt station's expansion. These had swelled from 43 listeners on 1 February 1924 to 80,089 on the same day two years later.[59] Upon hearing that Schoen had the post at SÜWRAG, Walter Benjamin expressed interest and even considered applying for the position of editor of the radio magazine.[60]

New Love

A few years after all the tangled affairs in the Berlin circles, Schoen met Johanna (Hansi) Liman.[61] Hansi met both Schoen and Sasha Stone through their dramatic entrances at Walter and Dora Benjamin's New Year's Eve party: Stone arrived with a white greyhound and moments later Schoen arrived and bowed, saying *Schoen, Schoen, Schoen*.[62] In 1925, Hansi was living with her seven-year-old daughter, Ursula, in Berlin, following a divorce. Schoen married her within a few months, on 3 March 1926.[63]

There is a photograph of Schoen, stamped with the address and details of the photographer Sasha Stone, the source of his future son's name. Stone's photograph depicts Schoen at the 1927 Frankfurt World Exhibition of Music, standing in the Mechanical Department, with Hansi. His hand is on his hips and he wears a hat, a bow tie and an elegant suit. On plinths are musical instruments and on the wall is a constructivist mural.[64] This Frankfurt was modern and modernist. The work at the radio station would remake music and reach the world.

G

Schoen orbited another circle: the G group and its journal *G*, a magazine inaugurated in 1923 with the subtitle *Zeitschrift für elementare Gestaltung* (Journal for Elementary Composition). The publication drew together a number of artists and writers, at the intersection of Dada and Constructivism. Raoul Hausmann was present at the early meetings – as a writer, photomontagist and painter and optophonetist (a person who works with the visualisation of speech). Werner Graeff was part of the circle too, an engineer concerned also with automotive design. Also present was the architect Ludwig Hilberseimer, director Charles Métain, writer Tristan Tzara, artist George Grosz, photomontagist John Heartfield. Walter Benjamin and Ernst Schoen were also there,[65] and Schoen and Dora Benjamin are credited as contributing editors.[66]

The third issue from June 1924 contained Benjamin's translation of Tzara's essay 'Photography from the Verso'. Raoul Hausmann also wrote on fashion. Mies van der Rohe and Ludwig Hildesheimer contributed work on industrial forms. Graeff considered car design and the need for new technology. George Grosz wrote about himself and Kurt Schwitters wrote on poetry. There were thoughts on the Luna Park and contributions from Hans Arp and Hans Prinzhorn. Ernst Schoen (as Schön) wrote an article under the title 'The Theatre Muse'. It was illustrated with a photograph of the 'King of the Rodeo', Tex Austin. A tumble of invective mocked Berlin's theatre scene and Germans in general for their cultural failings. Schoen wrote:

The teutonic religious-pacifist epidemic began to manifest itself back in the day through a flood of brotherly dramas (that was our revolution), which at that time excited unheard-of outrage. Nowadays no one can even remember a title, let alone an author's name. Today's continuation of that epidemic are groups of young dilettantes, of both sexes, who, with confused presentations, badly translate boring old mystery plays into doggerel verse, dash through Germany and environs (Haaß-Berkow-Plays, Plays of the Lübeck Dance of Death). These are unimportant from a cultural point of view, but unfortunately shockingly important from the point of view of the nation's health, for the spreading of this epidemic amongst our confused youth must end in a new flagellantism.[67]

Mock-medievalism plagued the scene. Theatre in Europe and the US was only for 'Spießer', a contemptuous word for the cultureless petty bourgeoisie. The real leaders in Berlin theatre – those who had an ounce of cosmopolitanism – were stock brokers who threw their money from time to time into short-lived venues for operettas or revues. They manufactured a sentimental swinishness that piqued Schoen's interest.

Radio Magic

Radio-specific forms were invented. The first *Hörspiel* was broadcast in Germany on 24 October 1924 and was called 'Zauberei auf dem Sender' ('Broadcasting Radio Magic') with the subtitle 'Attempt at a radio grotesque'. The *Hörspiel* was a type of radio play that presented radio not merely as a technology, but as technology mediated by social relations, a realm of conflict, negotiation and work.[68] The first one was written by Hans Flesch,[69] and it involved his creative assistant, named in the script as Ernst Schön, as well as other figures at the station. Schön composed electronic music. The play began with the familiar announcement:

> ANNOUNCER: 'Frankfurt am Main on wavelength 467—Frankfurt am Main on wavelength—'.

Whispering can be heard in the background. Radio stages its own malfunction, its fear of silence. The FAIRYTALE AUNT, a teller of traditional children's tales, enters and requests two minutes speaking time. The station switches its electric connections on and off, in a chaos of confusion about what should be broadcast. In the play, listeners phone in to complain that they have paid their licence fee and yet there is no broadcast. The FAIRYTALE AUNT makes a case that the radio should provide more stuff for children. Sound effects – the screaming of sirens and a kettledrum – herald the intervention of a booming voice announcing that the station has lost its mind. A battle ensues between the words of the FAIRYTALE AUNT, who argues that the public is no longer satisfied by what radio provides for them and an ANNOUNCER who is reading out US trading information. In time, these voices are drowned out by various musical motifs. After a scratching sound, Flesch returns:

> ARTISTIC DIRECTOR *(disturbed)*: Well — what — what was that — for God's sake — what — give me a glass of water — please — Mr. Schön,

did you ... *(gurgling sound of water being poured)* ... Thank you *(drinks)*, Schön, did you hear that on the monitor?

Schoen replies:

CREATIVE ASSISTANT: Yes, Herr Doktor, everything.

Things get more chaotic. The DIRECTOR hears music, while the others do not:

ARTISTIC DIRECTOR: [...] While all of you were standing around, there was... but why are you looking at me like that? What is it now? Mr. Schön, please, answer me!
CREATIVE ASSISTANT: Well, Herr Doktor — we have — I mean — but there wasn't any music just now — there was nothing to be heard...

Can music be heard, if no one is playing it, the artistic director asks? His team suggests hallucinations or the intervention of another radio station. The network director insists there cannot have been any music, for had there been, an honorarium payment would without doubt have been immediately demanded. The FAIRYTALE AUNT has vanished, but her place is taken by a 'typewriter lady', whose clattering could be heard – though the men observe there are normally no typists in the broadcasting station, only in the offices. The station director begins to dictate events, but is drowned out by an uncanny music. A magician intervenes. He was a visitor to the station some days before and had been prevented from performing his tricks:

MAGICIAN: I have avenged myself. I taught a lesson, but not an Esperanto lesson. A magic lesson. You didn't want to believe in me. I forced you to believe in me. Why didn't you let me perform my magic tricks in the radio for people; harmless, cheerful enchantments that would have pleased people, I begged you urgently enough to believe me that radio listeners could become radio watchers by the force of my power. You laughed at me! People could have seen all these amusing things in their electron tubes, seen them in their detectors, seen, yes, Herr Doktor, *seen*, just as you see me standing before you. Yes, more than that, just as these same radio listeners can see me now. *(Speaking to the apparatus.)* Ladies and gentlemen, look very closely, very closely into your radio, in the temper colours of your amplifier tubes, into the crystal of your detectors — I will count to three — on three you'll all see me, attention, one — two...[70]

The assembled party calls for him to be delivered to the madhouse – but he in turn, states that they were prepared to do the same to the ARTISTIC DIRECTOR some moments before. An attempt is made to get the station broadcasting as normal. The ANNOUNCER interjects: 'Frankfurt a. M, on wavelength 467 – we will now play "The Blue Danube" by Johann Strauss.'[71] The musicians begin but it comes out distorted. It reverts to the correct tempo, but is stuck on the first bars, which repeat endlessly – like a scratched record, as one of the station workers observes. The *Hörspiel* ends with a homily from the artistic director. The station wants order not chaos and if insufficient attention is paid, chaos may reign. The station managers need to be strong and keep on their toes to hold it all together – if it falls apart, they may as well shoot themselves. 'The Blue Danube' resumes as it should.

Radio, it would seem, is magical, a way of conjuring meaning from the chaos of the world, ordering it and placing it before a listening public. The magic referred to here is the new technological magic of radio, a capacity Flesch explored further as tape technologies came into being. That Flesch turned to magic in the context of the most advanced technology is not a singular association when it comes to radio. Such insights can be found reflected elsewhere. In 1927, Richard Oswald's silent film *Funkzauber* (Radio Magic) was released. A review in the *Berliner Zeitung am Mittag* (Berlin Midday Newspaper), by Billy Wilder, described the plot as about a man who attempts to listen to radio without a licence, for free, in the woods, in a police station where he is held as a vagrant and in his hovel of a home. The Berlin broadcasting studios appeared, as did popular presenter Alfred Braun, and so the viewers saw – though did not hear – how listeners are afforded 'hours of the liveliest entertainment from a magical distance.'[72]

Radio was magic, yet it drew on cool technical rationality. As a result, it was a precarious activity, ready at any moment to collapse into nonsense. And yet this nonsense had its charms and showed the extent to which an art of sound effects and a playing with presence and absence, of voicework and reflexivity about a medium, of ear-splitting cacophony and soothing sounds, could produce intelligent humour. And the magician hinted too at what was already coming into view: television, another magic.

Magical Ether

Radio hosted a confrontation between the technical and the supernatural. A novel from 1924 mirrored this. Written by Paul Rosenayn and titled *Der Ruf aus dem Äther* (The Call from the Ether), it concerns a man who receives radio messages from outer space. Alien messages invade the home on radio waves. Radio was a medium of the other world. A film from 1925, titled *Radiofimmel* (Radio Craze) presented images of radio as a blazing light in the blackness, a luminescence existing in outer space. Radio was the sun. Radio was a ball of streaming light. Radio was light waves.

In its first decades, a relation between radio and telepathy emerged, even if, despite repeated experiments on the fringes of science, no positive connection could be established. In 1924, Robert H. Gault attempted to transmit data by thought alone, but the experiment concluded only that thought waves were not carried in airwaves. In February 1927, V. J. Woolley, member of the Society for Psychical Research, worked on an experiment in telepathy with the BBC, with agents thinking of selected objects and audiences attempting to divine what they were. Again, no positive evidence was gathered.

Radio was a modern means of communication, but, as explained in a prehistory of broadcasting authored by Schoen across the second half of his life, it was the outcome of experimentation with waves that went back to the use of magnets in China in ancient times.[73] Schoen's prehistory encompassed legends about electricity in medieval times and superstitions about electricity gleaned from art of the eighteenth century. He began with a legend about a shepherd named Magnes, tending his goats on Mount Ida in Crete. Following his herd, he played his shawm and traced his way with his long staff. Suddenly he found himself rooted to the spot. He could not move his iron-nailed shoes, nor his ferruled staff.

Schoen provided a mythic origin to the discovery of magnetism, or the lodestone, and one that could be explained only by stories of atoms floating in currents from one material to another. This property in nature was mobilised by emperors in China, a thousand years before compasses were invented. The ancient Romans, Schoen reported, used the power of magnetism to manipulate objects using forces of attraction and repulsion. A Roman priest, for example, constructed an oracle of letters made of iron and placed it on a stool. He suspended a ring on a thread above the letters, which caused them to rearrange themselves in a certain order to further the priest's goals. Schoen comments:

Then in those times, just as today, a governing class exploited the monopoly of knowledge to procure their political objects.[74]

Such manipulation was used more recently, noted Schoen, for in the First World War: 'a German general would not move his troops without consulting an anthroposophist'.[75] Superstition pervaded the battlefield. Distorted and pressured by the demands of unequal class societies, science was far from neutral – indeed, like any other system of power, it was subject to myth and superstition. And sometimes a quasi-explanation just filled the vacuum – quite literally in the case of ether.

Call the two devices, from one to the other of which Hertz sent his wave, electric circuits, oscillator and resonator, sender and receiver, or however you like, true it remains that the force exercised by one of them on the other cannot activate through the space between them immediately, without taking time, but that the electrification of the first of the circuits causes first of all a transversal wave, similar in velocity to the light wave, a wave, which again, after having been transferred to the second circuit, causes the electric current in it. Electricity – the oscillation of waves, progressing through all space, pervading every matter, undulation of a medium which for a time was called ether for lack of a better name, but whose substance and entire being had to be left alone again as one of the great interrogation marks for future theory and research.[76]

As much as radio was modern and technical, it also tapped into some sort of other side, a wave realm that is indistinct and magical, for want of a better expression.

Ether Magic

In Germany in the 1920s, radio was a technology whose possibilities were extensively debated intellectually and its capacities were pushed in experimental directions. The language of ether featured prominently. Ether was an emblem of radiophonic communications' capacity to span the world and to smash through time and, thereby, to become the most dominant form of the future.[77] Radio's 'bridging of the spatial and temporal distance' meant that it 'suddenly empowered people from one location to speak to any number of people at any number of locations in the world'.[78] This was a kind of magic and it was a force, or power, in all the senses of those words. An advertisement in the 1930 German radio year-book depicted a dynamic collection of Arcophon loudspeakers from Telefunken, with 'Sound True to Life'. Its tubes hover above three sheeny sets, in three subtly modulated patternings that seem like ether emanations.[79]

There is another ether, the compound used to anaesthetise wounded soldiers on the battlefield, as elsewhere, in an effort to undo the war's effects on their bodies, the agony of death and dying. Anaesthetics: sometimes the surgery involved repairs to a face that had been blasted away and by the art of the surgeon, needed to be made whole enough again. And if not whole, then functional. Ether, anaesthetising, suffused a body with feelings of euphoria or stupor, so that surgery might occur. It took away sensation, abstracted it, pushed in the opposite direction to the *aesthetic*, an enlivening of feelings, an intensification of sensations perceived through the body. Ether aids the process of healing, but it does so by stealing consciousness. What dangers lie in that?

Only a medium could retrieve missing words, from the other side of life, or from the markings on the palm, somehow divined from the future. Or a medium could come into being, whose whole purpose was to transmit voices, to convey them as part of a new language in the modern world, developing a vocabulary that broke with the past and its wars and brutal iniquities. Ether could not numb the pain of war enough. The devastation of the earth, the ripped open mud shafts for trenches and the battered cities quivering under the fear of gas warfare, prompted so many things to be rethought, as well as undone, in the wake of a devastating embroilment of pain and technology, in which language turns mute or insufficient. Language needed a new outlet and new articulation.

Gas vs Gas

In a 1925 newspaper article attributed to Walter Benjamin, but written at least in part by his wife Dora, titled 'Die Waffen von morgen' ('The Weapons of Tomorrow'), it is predicted that the strange names of chemical compounds developed for the next war would soon tumble easily from the tongue, just as the new words 'Trench', 'U-Boot', 'Dicke Bertha' and 'Tank' did in the First World War. War introduced new technologies or found uses for burgeoning interventions. It also created new atmospheres and sensations. The author imagined a future of chemical warfare to come:

In the streets of Berlin, a smell like that of violets disperses in beautiful, bright spring weather. This endures for a few minutes. Then the air becomes suffocating. Those who do not manage to escape its reach will after a few minutes no longer be able to make anything out, will be momentarily blinded. And if they still don't manage to escape, then they must suffocate. All this can happen one day without any aircraft being visible in the air, without the whirring of any propellers being audible. When the sky is clear and the sun is dazzling. Yet, unable to be seen or heard, 5000 metres in the air, sits an aviation wing that drops *chloroacetophenone* – tear gas – the 'most humane' of the new agents, which, as is known, already played a role in the gas attacks of the last war.[80]

Toxic gas was destined to enter the field of battle, as much as the streets and homes of the city, to make them lethal zones, or in Benjamin/Kellner's words, to literally take the breath away. Kellner's novel *Gas gegen Gas* was later serialised in *SWZ*, the regional magazine for Frankfurt Radio.

New Frankfurt, New Studio

In 1926, the *SWZ* ran an announcement on a new set-up for the Frankfurt station. In an axonometric cutaway, the station was laid bare, mapped out without a roof. Features included a conductor with an orchestra, a recording of a play and a number of places to work and relax and eat. Everything appeared idyllic, well-positioned, busy, functional; a doll's house of technological modernism.[81] In another article from the same year, this time about new rooms at the Frankfurt Broadcasting Station, there was mention of a room for staying at the studio overnight and it came complete with a *chaise longue* and access to an indoor swimming pool.[82] Reports in the world's radio press focused on the gleaming white of the building, its ultra-modern nature, projectors to avoid crackling papers and the latest recording and broadcasting technologies.

Camilla von Zöllnitz, die Heldin unseres neuen Romans: „Gas gegen Gas"

Figure 2.2 Front cover of *Südwestdeutsche Rundfunk Zeitung*, Frankfurt am Main/Kassel, 19 October 1930 (Volume 6, Number 42).

Photographer unknown.

Headphones and Haircuts

Radios affected bodies. In the sculpture *Mechanical Head: Spirit of Our Age* (1919–1920), Dadaist Raoul Hausmann bolted together a hairdresser's dummy head, a T-square, a pocket watch mechanism, a spectacles case, a nail and a screw, a travel cup, a tape measure, a yardstick poking from the head like an antenna. Though no radio is present, it anticipated the formation of a subject: wired-up, mechanical, anonymous; subject to measurement and augmentation.

Given weak signals and insufficient power for loudspeakers in early radio technologies,[83] early sets were used with headphones – *Kopfhörer* in German, literally 'head-listeners'. Radio was largely a solitary activity, as only one headphone set could be connected to each device. Paintings depicted this aloneness, such as Kurt Günther's *Radionist* (1927); its central figure with a cigar, his eyes slightly glazed over. This radionist reads while listening along to what is on the radio, a common practice in the early days facilitated by the radio programme magazines. Kurt Weinhold's *Mann mit Radio (Homo Sapiens)* from 1929 shows a man naked but for his headphones that attach him to the radio device. He sits alone with this mechanical apparatus. In the 27 December 1925 edition of the *SWZ*, an advert for Dr Nesper's 'original' headphones appeared. It made claims about their lightness and elegance, amplification and the purity of their sound. The company's worldly reach is emphasised through a number of racialised silhouettes in profile, each wearing headphones.[84] On another page we see two large portraits of radio listeners; above, a figure reclining on a chair; below, one on a sofa. Both are listening in.[85] Radio was to be delivered to the individual, directly into the ears, as the listener relaxed in modern and well-appointed rooms.

On the front cover of this issue is emblazoned the title: 'Which hairstyle fits best with headphones?',[86] alongside a portrait of Lisa Rado from the Frankfurt Opera. She gazed into the camera, headphones curved around her face: a small aerial protrudes from the right-hand side. The question on the front cover is repeated throughout the issue and answered largely pictorially. Lucie Mannheim from the Berlin State Theatre, actor Jutta Jol, singer Irene Ambrus, star of a revue Anita Franz and Berlin opera singer Ella Hoffmann each sport a slightly different hairstyle. Again, the question: 'Which hairstyle fits best with headphones?' An array of women, all posing, smiling, haircuts on display, are involved in this scientific quest. Finally, the answer is given in cartoon form: 'Headphones and the ladies' hairstyle – as imagined by a funny reader'. To avoid knots and tangles, the solution is the *Bubikopf* (literally 'lad-head'), an 'ideal', radio haircut. This was a haircut for the modern woman, the *neue Frau* who listened to the new media form.[87]

The invention of loudspeakers eradicated headphones, but it let in magic and myth. Two adverts from the *SWZ* of 26 August 1928, both for Delta loudspeakers, presented two figures at a table. Invoking what would now be considered an Orientalist scene, the origins of the voice appeared to come from the sky, from the ether, from one person playing a flute and another reading from a book. Out of the loudspeaker horn emanate lines representing sound waves. Loudspeakers haunted the room, bringing into presence those absent.[88]

Movement

With the advent of the loudspeaker, people were freed up to dance while listening. *Tanz-Programme* or dance programmes litter the schedules. With the advent of the loudspeaker, people were freed up to dance while listening. *Tanz-Programme* or dance programmes littered the schedules. On 6 December 1925 the front cover of *SWZ* was emblazoned with the title 'Dance on the high seas'.[89] Experimental dance was also represented in 1925, through the names Anita Berber, Mary Wigman and others.[90] Listeners might also dance along at home.

Solve the Puzzle

The *SWZ* provided its readers with a number of puzzles in each issue in the *Rätsel-Ecke* (puzzle corner) or *Bunte-Ecke* (colourful corner). Find the ten words whose first and last letters can be read backwards to make a humorous proverb.[91] Complete the crossword puzzle in the shape of a four-leaf clover (see Figure 2.3) or a star, bell, ship, rabbit, tree or house in other issues.[92] Decipher the cryptogram. In another puzzle, readers are asked to cut the newspaper into strips and rearrange them to form an image, making a new whole from the parts.

Figure 2.3 'Die bunte Ecke' ('The Colourful Corner'), *Südwestdeutsche Rundfunk Zeitung*, Frankfurt am Main/Kassel, 28 December 1930 (Volume 6, Number 52), p.14.

Publications, Adverts

In 1929, those in charge of national German radio decided to publish a yearly handbook (*Jahrbuch*) reporting on developments within the sector. Hans Bredow, radio commissar, wrote in the introduction to the first one:

The public demands good radio stations. It would also like to know what points of view contribute to programming and according to what conceptions and fundamental principles the men, to whom so valuable a good as radio has been entrusted, reach their decisions.[93]

The year-book reported on radio activities across the year in all the various stations in Germany. It also aired the problems associated with the form, in order to facilitate public discussion of key issues within the industry. Bredow referenced the 'will to culture' (*Kulturwillen*) of radio and expressed a hope that the year-book, with its report on the year's achievements, demonstrated that deeds follow the will.

The first pages of the *Jahrbuch* were given over to advertising. Siegfried Kracauer had, in the same year, divulged the 'main concerns' of the new white-collar salaried masses through the 'surface level manifestations' of adverts and articles in popular magazines. He listed, as if flicking through the pages, the array of products and problems: 'pens, Kohinoor pencils, haemorrhoids, hair loss, beds, crepe soles, white teeth, rejuvenation elixirs, selling coffee to friends, dictaphones, writer's cramp, trembling – especially in the presence of others, quality pianos on weekly instalments, and so on.'[94] Such advertisements were strewn throughout the outputs of flourishing print culture, including in the pages of the *SWZ* and the year-books.

A circuit between listening and reading, for example, was represented on the inside cover of the 1929 *Jahrbuch*: 'Those who love radio read *Die Sendung* (The Broadcast); Those who read *Die Sendung* love radio.'[95] Radio was a listening activity, but it was immediately accompanied by a reading culture. The listener should read in order to listen and listen in order to read. *Die Sendung* was just one of many radio magazines, journals, pamphlets and books conveying the new medium into its present and towards its future. An advertisement a few pages further in for *Funkstunde* (Radio Hour), the official magazine of the Berlin Radio Society, indicates that it was crammed not only with schedules from across the networks, but also with photographs and images of 'World Radio', extra information on radio lectures, literary content and 'much of interest for everyone'.[96] Radio was for everyone and everyone would find something in, on or through it.

The second advertisement in the year-book had stark, modernist, asymmetric black bars counterbalancing a blockish sans-serif font and it demanded: 'Become a Participant in Radio! Register at any postal organisation. Monthly fee only 2RM [*Reichsmark*].' Each person was commanded to sign up – and in so doing became not a passive recipient, but an active participant (*Teilnehmer*) in this new world of culture. Then followed advertisements for equipment. One of these, for a Grawor-Sektorphon loudspeaker, depicted a group of older men and younger women together in a room, heads slightly bowed, in acts of collective listening. Their gazes did not coincide and each one looked into a middle distance with unfocused eyes. Above their heads hovered an image of the decorative front of the loudspeaker and above that floated a fuzzy image of the head of Beethoven, whose sounds flutter through the ether. The image suggests a séance. There was a mystery and magic in the technology still.

A few pages after advertisements for network devices and dry cell batteries, a very different image of the coming radio listener appeared in an advertisement for TEFAG (Telephone Factory) equipment. A cartoon depicted a happy-looking man slumped on a small armchair, eyes closed, indulging himself in the sounds emanating from two large pieces of technology and all atop a map of the world, with the tips of Africa and India visible. Behind the man and the radio equipment is the TEFAG logo. It was a fist, like the fist of a revolutionary worker, balled around three wires, bending them into wider coverage.

A few pages on was an advertisement for *Ikarus*, a magazine about motorised and aeronautical travel and culture. It was officially linked to the first German flight carrier Lufthansa and was also directed at those who drove and were passionate about cars. Radio listeners were cosmopolitan, an inhabitant of the world. They connected with the wider world through their sense of hearing, as well as moving through it by air or on wheels, as free as waves.

The editorial content of the year-book ranged from essays on the pre-history of German radio, its organisation, problems to do with the type of culture to be communicated on the airwaves, what instruments and voices broadcast well, what workers wanted from radio, how it carried and preserved traditional local culture. There were discussions about how to approach literature on radio or what a lecture was for, what the technology did or did not do. Some issues dealt with what was broadcast, whether it was legitimate to play only extracts from operas, what new forms of drama might be developed, who was listening and how – and what children might do with radio. There was a section on technology, on oscillation research and the state of broadcast and reception technologies. A miscellaneous section reflected on the flight of a Zeppelin airship as an event suitable for radio broadcast. Other contributions considered news on radio, the uses of radio in school, women as radio listeners, a day in the life of a radio-listening farmer, interference and ways of overcoming it, the rights and duties of a radio listener. There was also a long list of birthdays, death days and anniversaries, embedding the medium of radio in the process of memorialisation.

Jazz!

Jazz was in the orbit of Frankfurt Radio and Schoen regarded this musical genre with interest. From 1925, SÜWRAG had its own jazz band, led by Paul Hindemith's brother, Rudolf. At its peak in 1927, the band played weekly.[97] The style was New Orleans and Dixieland jazz, performed by ensembles such as the Berlin-based Weintraub Syncopators and American bands such as Sam Wooding's Society Syncopators who toured Europe from 1925 to 1927.[98]

In 1925, a young composer, Mátyás Seiber, arrived in Frankfurt from Hungary, attracted by its musical avant-garde, though he soon took off to join the musical ensemble on an ocean liner as a cellist playing popular music on transatlantic journeys. In 1927, he suggested to Bernhard Sekles, director of the Hoch Conservatory in Frankfurt, that he teach a jazz class there. The appointment was controversial – deliberately so, in order to cause a stir in the music scene. There was fervent discussion of the need for blood transfusions into German music and the importation of existence-threatening anti-Germanness through atonality, international-ity, Americanism and pacifism.[99] Just before the class was about to take place in 1928, it was attacked in racist terms by Bruno Danicke, a member of the Prussian parliament from the Deutschvölkische Freiheitspartei (The German Popular Freedom Party). Seiber was eventually dismissed as a sordidly un-German teacher. Even the *New York Times* reported on the controversy and included a line from Carl Nielsen, stating that jazz 'is nasty and deathlike music, always the same, because its creators steal from one another'.[100]

In 1927, as this controversy unfurled and as the SÜWRAG jazz band played in an anodyne way, far from the unpredictable improvisations and syncopations of hot jazz, Ernst Schoen published an article titled 'Jazz und Kunstmusik' ('Jazz and Art Music') in the journal *Melos*.[101] It began with a summary of a number of articles that appeared in a special edition of the Viennese modern music journal *Anbruch* in 1925, the first time jazz had been written about in German music journals. Schoen's interest was in the musical value of jazz and how it was being positioned as the 'realisation of the well-known American desire for a national art in the realm of music'.

Only Americans – despite examples such as Stravinsky's *Ragtime* and Weill's *Mahagonny* – could, by 'blood, education and heart', hold the spirit of jazz. Germans (presumably understood here as ethnically white Germans) should not. But jazz had, he claimed, revitalised European music, offering new techniques, including 'vibrato, glissando, overtones, expansion of the available tonal scale, syncopation, and it has drawn new instruments', for example, the saxophone and the banjo, into art music. Opera was absorbing jazz. Schoen cited Ernst Krenek's *Jonny spielt auf* (Jonny strikes up) (1927) and compared jazz with certain aspects of Wagner's use of the leitmotif.

Schoen addressed the controversy about the jazz school, as Seiber publishing a teaching book on jazz drumming had brought that back into focus once again. He mentioned the 'little press storm, which was understandable in eminently politically agitated times such as today's'. In the intervening months, stylistic elements of jazz had entered into 'art music' and were 'peaking in what Wiesengrund-Adorno characterised as the Surrealism of Weill's *Threepenny Opera* music'. Schoen was pragmatic about teaching jazz at the conservatory, given most music that was being performed was drawing on it. Seiber's jazz teachings were affirmed by Schoen – he had studied in the USA and he had a knowledge of music beyond jazz, 'even adopting a critical stance towards jazz'. Schoen concluded with a number of questions:

Should it not by now be superfluous to discuss the influence of Jazz on art? Should Weill's work not rather give us cause to, for once, draw into consideration the possibility of a curative influence of art on Jazz? Should it not, as is the same for all genuine art, have shown us repeatedly the consolatory value of a world ordered by spirit and flooded by soul.[102]

Sonic Portraits

In May 1926, Ernst and Johanna Schoen visited Walter Benjamin in Paris, together with the photographer Sasha Stone.[103] Stone supplied Benjamin with photographs of cluttered-up nineteenth-century interiors for his social analysis of the past and he also made a montage for the book jacket *One Way Street* (1928). Stone photographed Schoen on a number of occasions around this time. A picture from the mid-1920s depicts Schoen as smartly dressed in a white shirt and black tie, his hair swept over, a professionally commissioned image, perhaps.[104] This portrait was cut and pasted onto the cover of a large oblong book, his head reaching the top line of the stave, his eyes in the middle, between two crotchets or quavers. To the left is a large alto clef. On the spine is written *Quartette* (Quartets) and on the back, in English, as if a poem: 'The lines, circle on the back cover are red. / The rest is black. / Sasha Stone'.

Another portrait of Schoen by Stone featured in the *SWZ* in May 1929 and Schoen pasted a cut out of it into a scrapbook. In the picture, Schoen is smiling, holding his eldest child, Nina on his shoulder.[105] In another portrait, he was perhaps a little older, his fringe more curled and, once more, wearing a white shirt and tie.[106] Schoen put Stone in touch with Varèse and he produced portraits and press photographs for him too.[107] Stone supplied other pictures for the Frankfurt magazine *SWZ* of people playing sport, actors including Max Pallenberg on New Year's Day 1929, clowns, circus performers – all themes addressed in his wider work, which included photographs taken at Erwin Piscator's theatre, images of Ernst Busch, Chaplin, Tilla Durieux, as well as nudes.[108] On 27 July 1929, Stone presented a lecture on the radio on photography as the new 'Weltsprache', or language of the world. In this instance, Stone's face peers out of the *SWZ* – a photograph of himself by himself.

Radio technology mobilised waves that could not be seen to convey sound from one place to another. Photographic technology captured in chemicals a moment in time that would otherwise disappear into history. One held onto something that was fleeting; the other amplified passing sound so that it might disperse widely. In being held onto and amplified, the moment and the event were made available for broader reception and analysis.

On 11 September 1927, the *SWZ* ran a promotion for a lecture by Dr Carl Adolf Schleussner, an industrialist and founding investor in the radio station. His talk considered four images, two of which appeared in the paper: a chest X-ray and a fingerprint from a forensic record.[109] Just as the finger print, to a hand reader, might reveal a horde of observations about a person's fate and character, so too might handwriting reveal something to the graphologist, something that Benjamin later wrote about in the pages of the *SWZ*.[110] What if music or sound might do the same, revealing aspects of character or fate, or, simply, a fuller picture of the individual? In one issue of *G* was an advert:

> Musical Portraits
> better likenesses. more fashionable
> and a tenth of the price of painted ones

> Musical Advertisements
> in business life and on the street indi-
> vidually and universally designed by Ernst Schoen.[111]

Was this a joke? Did Schoen ever complete one? How would they have sounded?

In a journal, *Gebrauchsgrafik* (Utility-graphics) from 1930, an advert jumps out from the page: SASHA STONE SEES YET MORE.[112] Sasha Stone Atelier advertised its services and referred any potential clients to satisfied customers at the German Railway, the Belgian Parliament, the German Linoleum Works and more. New eyes that saw more in visual portraits, new ears that heard more in sonic portraits. The question of musical illustration came to the fore again with the development of film. With leitmotifs, music could signal people or moods.[113] Music could not photograph life, it could not document life, but it could say something more, perhaps – could it provide better likenesses at a tenth of the price?

Circus Towers

In a photograph, a line of people appear huddled in the body of a biplane: they have poked their heads through a slit, in a contraption that shows the city of Paris from above in the background, with the Eiffel Tower in the centre and a panel of an aeroplane in the foreground.[114] The Eiffel Tower, or rather its painted copy, almost touches the base of the plane: a painted prop propelled out of a painted landscape. On the reverse side of the photograph are scribbled the names of the plane's passengers in pencil: on the far left, the Chilean composer Acario Cotapos Baeza, next to him 'Puma' (another nickname for 'Hansi'), Edgard Varèse and next to him, the Italian painter Joseph Stella, both of whom were involved in the ICG.[115] At the far end is Ernst Schoen, slumped over the fuselage of the plane, his coat draped like a cloak, his hat positioned at an angle. At this point Schoen was right above Paris, one of modernity's nodal points, with a group of contemporary experimenters.

Such fairground attractions got the attention of Surrealists – there is, for example, a 1923 photograph of André Breton, Robert Desnos, Joseph Delteil, Simone Breton, Paul Éluard, Gala Éluard, Max Morise and Max Ernst in a similarly constructed scene. In the same year, Paul Morand commented in poems about a Florida fairground: 'For 60 centimes, MODERN PHOTO will photograph you, as an aviator, as Jesus, with the crown of thorns, AT NO EXTRA COST.'[116] The image, made on the cheapest photographic paper, was developed onsite and could be used as a postcard, as it came ready stamped. In 1929, Jean-Gérard Fleury described the possibilities of fairground photography at the Foire du Trône:

In an aeroplane, an ocean liner, on the Croisette in Cannes or the Promenade des Anglais in Nice, on the Esplanade des Invalides, atop the Eiffel Tower, let yourselves be photographed, sirs, let yourselves be photographed [...] with your ladies [...]. Nice, Paris, Cannes [...] You will never have travelled so much: it is the photography booth that, for 6 francs, will fly you over the Eiffel Tower, like Lindbergh the day after his transatlantic flight, or over the Côte d'Azur, like a wealthy islander.[117]

Figure 2.4 Ernst Schoen (on the right) with, left to right, Acario Cotapos Baeza, Johanna Schoen, Edgard Varèse and Joseph Stella in a fairground photography booth above a painted Paris. Dated c.1928.

Photographer unknown. From Schoen's Archive in Koblenz: BArch N 1403 Bild-110-036. Copyright: Sabine Schiller-Lerg.

Capturing the Street

On 20 November 1927, Schoen's colleague at the radio, Dr Paul Laven, published an article in the *SWZ* on the 'wandering microphone'.[118] The capacity to do outside broadcasts was improving. 'Sound portraits' (*Hörbilder*) had been part of radio practice since Hans Flesch and Hans Bodenstedt experimented with them in 1924.[119] Recordings could be made anywhere between the land and the sky. In the street, the boxing ring. On motorbikes, in airships. When the airship *Italia* crashed over the North Pole in 1928, Friedrich Wolf produced *SOS Rao-Rao-Foyn/Krassin rettet Italia*, a live broadcast of a rescue attempt by the crew of the Krassin.[120] The 1930 *Rundfunk Jahrbuch* was dotted with photographs that point to reportage of real-world events. One image depicted the juggler Enrico Rastelli seated on a large ball representing his dance partner. Another figure stood next to him with a microphone, in 'A Dialogue with Rastelli'. Beneath this was a photograph of a fireworks display at Berlin's Luna Park: 'The large fireworks display in Berlin's Lunapark was portrayed on radio.' Fireworks made their own symphony, each crackle and boom conveyed to all parts of the city via the airwaves.[121]

The process of radio, the workings of the crystal that caught radio waves and relayed them through the earphones, transformed the possibility of what could be heard and where that sound could be captured, produced and transmitted. The street became a place not just of reception, of hearing anew, but of potential production and realisation. Varèse's oscillating refrain 'New ears for new music and new music for new ears' posed a question for music. Orchestras that previously only sought to represent the sounds of nature – of cuckoos, nightingales, storms – turned to the sound of other, second and emergent natures: of trains, factory sirens, parades, the moods and movements of the city. In turn, these sounds could be heard again, received via radio apparatuses in automobiles, on carts, listened to in a state of semi-distraction, blended again with sound and images that cannot be fully blocked out.

The score for Paul Hindemith's 1922 *Suite for Piano* was published with a striking cover (which Schoen writes about in his essay 'Jazz und Kunstmusik'). The lower half featured a street scene scribbled in pencil. Trams next to bicycles, coaches next to omnibuses. There were lamp-lights and telegraphs, shop windows and billboard stands, all swirling in a single scene. People walked in all directions, as in a George Grosz drawing. The chords thundered and jumped around interrupting the flow of the music. It was march-like and cabaret-like. Another example of musical urban cacophony was Varèse's *Hyperprism*, first performed at an ICG concert during its second series at the Klaw Theatre on 4 March 1923.[122] Varèse centred the percussion instruments. One critic remarked that it resembled 'shrieks from a zoo, the din of passing trains, the hammering of a drunken woodpecker, a thunderbolt striking a tinplate factory.'[123] Varèse's *Ionisation* (1931) also featured a variety of instruments, including triangle, anvil, parade drum, snares, claves, bells, sirens and chimes.[124] Another work, also performed at ICG,[125] Arthur Honegger's *Pacific 231* (1923), introduced the sound of a train to the concert hall. With radio, the train entered the home.

* * *

Interruption: Childhood and Radio

Preface

In the second half of the 1920s, two children joined the Schoen household: Nina on 14 February 1927 and Alexander, nicknamed Sasha after Stone, on 28 March 1929. These two children occasioned new waves and techniques.[126] They were born into a technological and social world in flux. Radio proposed innovations in the home and the family: the creation of new pedagogies and new techniques of entertainment. It played music with and for the young. It woke children up and sent them to sleep. Parallel technologies recorded their voices and played them back. Through and with radio, the child faced and intervened in the forces of modernism and modernity.

Many of the tensions and complexities of radio in its relation to children and childhood can be grasped through a short history of the radio programme, *Jugendstunde* (*Youth Hour*), which was transmitted every day on Frankfurt Radio and overseen for some years by school headteacher Karl Wehrhan. Programmes were usually thirty minutes long. Each listing in the *SWZ* stated the specific target age for the programme. There were talks on foreign lands or lectures about domestic and exotic nature, which offered 'colourful images'. There were insights into the world of technology and science, such as 'The Secret of Radium' on 5 October 1928. There were daring first-hand reports of climbing the North Cape in the Arctic. A short talk on 16 November 1927 explored how youth might support the German War Graves Commission. There were many occasions when songs from the German playbook were performed. And there were fairy tales, read by women called *Märchentanten,* Fairy Tale Aunts. There were other aunties at the station: a *Kasperltante,* named Liesel Simon, well known on the Frankfurt scene for her puppet theatre. There was also an *Elternstunde* (Parent Hour) under the direction of Karl Wehrhan and Hans Flesch and later, Schoen. On 12 June 1927, Dr Alfred Bloch advised on the problem of 'Youthful Showing Off' and on 27 November 1927, school choices were the theme. In 1929, Schoen oversaw an episode on 'The child who is quick to learn'.

The *Jugendstunde* oversaw children's transition to adulthood and the world of work. Periodically, the programmes gave careers advice. They presented new paths available in a modernising Germany of white-collar workers and consumers and they were addressed to boys and girls. On 13 November 1925, there was a show on the 'Joys and Cares of a Nursery Worker'. On 29 November, the theme was 'The Young Girl in the Office'. And on 13 January 1928 'Hairdresser and Milliner'. The following month, boys were introduced to apprenticeships in banking and insurance.

On 29 December 1930, Walter Benjamin picked up the theme of careers. The programme was listed in the relevant issue of the *SWZ*, a magazine that now looked fully modern, rationalised, its fonts less fiddly. The title of his radio talk, 'Carousel of Jobs',[127] begins with an evocation of how career choices appear to a fourteen-year-old about to enter the world of work. The possible career paths spin past like a carousel onto which a leap must be taken, without being able to see properly what is speeding by. The right job was not a properly thought out choice, but rather what is momentarily possible, given unemployment and precariousness, or the effort just to hold on. Even the skilled worker, in very many cases, 'can no longer count on keeping his job'. Benjamin warns his audience that he will not touch on the widely used 'performance tests' that measure aptitude, nor the careers counselling that he knew to be widely available for young people. Benjamin was interested rather in the ways in which the demands of work, the habits instilled, combined and reformed the nature of an individual; how behaviourism merged with psychology and how 'gesture, affinity and ability' made an individual suited to certain types of work, even to jobs that did not yet exist, but would in the future. This new science of work, Benjamin noted, had been well advanced in Soviet Russia, under Aleksei Gastev's influence, the then director of Moscow's Ministry of Labour.[128] Soon, the Sixth International Conference on Psychotechnics, he observes, was to take place in Moscow. But Benjamin put his own twist on this psycho-materialism. Work was our fate and it was through our bodily contortions and the mental attitudes required in work that we came to understand the connections between inner and outer, self and world:

You all know of graphologists, palmists, phrenologists, and the like who claim to glean deep insights into people from particulars of physique, posture, etc. Regardless of how one mistrusts them, there remains much that is interesting and true in their observations. They assume that there is an indissoluble correlation between the inner and the outer. In their opinion, size, physique, and genetic material determine fate, just as fate, in their opinion, effects changes to the lines of the hand, the gaze, the facial features, etc. But what fate would more consistently call forth such effects, both inner and outer, than the job? And where would such determinations be easier to make than at the job, where thousands of people are subjected to the same fate day in and day out?[129]

Benjamin used the broadcast to ask listeners to participate in research. He requested that listeners send to the station personal descriptions of the influence of jobs on mood, views, on relationships to colleagues, on how the self who began in the job relates to the self of today. 'The material you provide will be reviewed in a second report and presented along with the conclusions that can be drawn', Benjamin remarked.[130] Mysticism was close to professionalism, critique close to self-help, hope close to despair. The technology of the radio, as much as its interaction with the child and the adolescent, encapsulated all of these complexities, tendencies and contradictions.

Programme I: 25 Minutes

Radio was often given a lifespan. The first article to appear in the 1930 *Rundfunk Jahrbuch* was by the historian of technology and science Franz Maria Feldhaus and detailed '2000 Years of News Technology'. It opened with a depiction of the Ancient Greek technique that placed those enslaved within shouting distance of each other in order to transmit news along a line. It finished with the contemporary radio installations at Königs-Wusterhausen that serviced Berlin.[131] The next article described the state of the capital's studio in 1923. Back then, *crêpe paper* cascaded down the walls to reduce reverberations. The past seven years seemed like an eternity. Photographs of recently outmoded radio instruments were contrasted with later models as if they were the relics of another age.

Radio might have grown up, but it was also still a child, not yet an adolescent. Bertolt Brecht, in 1932, drew an analogy between the ageing of a person and the ageing of radio:

I am not sure if it is finished yet, but if so then this youngster [*Jüngling*] who needed no certificate of competence to be born will have to start looking retrospectively for an object in life. Just as a man will begin asking at a certain age, when his first innocence has been lost, what he is supposed to be doing in the world.[132]

Radio asked itself what it was doing. Could it write its memoir, its history, and account for its place in the world as a person might? Its development could have gone in many directions but radio was and remained subject, like everything, to the forces of history: war, militarism, the dumb violence of capital shaped by technological forms. If the history of radio could be understood as a technology still in its infancy, it was an infancy with its own history and prehistory. Schoen framed his studies of radio in similar terms. In his unpublished work, *Broadcasting: How It Came About*, he titled the tenth chapter 'In the Nursery of Broadcasting' and, in a summary version, sketched its contents:

History of experiments in wireless telegraphy since 1795. Joseph Henry and the Smithsonian Institution. Mahlon Loomis and the typical inventors of early industrialism. Bowman Lindsay, another example of the tragic fate of the 'self-made man'. The wireless experiments of Professor D. E. Hughes. Dolbear's wireless experiments. Edison and wireless telegraphy. Development of electrical science and industry in Germany. The Rathenaus. Descriptions of the process of wireless telephony. Sir Oliver Lodge's on the tuning of wireless transmissions. History of the coherer. Sir Joseph A. Fleming and his oscillation valve. His career and beliefs. History of the generators of radio. Lee DeForest and his audion. His career.[133]

The nursery was a place of transformation. A place of screams and cries but also sleep and silence; and the coming into language, into voice.

The growth, development and numerous potentials of radio were marked by anniversaries. As it grew older, the *SWZ* diligently marked the birthdays of the station with elaborate front page spreads that might be displayed in the home like birthday cards. In 1926, after two years of Frankfurt Radio, the front cover celebrated the increase in listeners (from 43 listeners on 1 February 1924 to 80,089 on 1 February 1926) and scattered on the page the photos and names of the regulars: Headmaster Wehrhans, Thomas Mann, the Fairy Tale Aunt and many more, including Schoen.[134] It was a family of radio people. On 23 March 1927, the *SWZ* marked the third birthday of Frankfurt Radio with a front page: a drawing of the city, with a sky that radiated with the waves of transmission.[135] The article that followed declared 'We are celebrating a birthday!' 1927 marks the fourth birthday of the Südwestdeutsche Rundfunk Gesellschaft.[136] The year after, an article marked five years with images of erected masts and various bits of modern radio equipment.[137]

Other calendar events figured: The front cover of 1 January 1928 exhorted *Prosit-1928-Neujahr* ('Cheers–1928–New Year'). 'Everyone listens to radio' was written below and an octagonal shape contained eight types of 'everyone': Chaplin with a dog, two people shaking hands, a worker, a clown, as well as a number of bourgeois types.[138] Radio set the times – in hours but also years with calendars printed in the newspaper. The arrival of the year 1930 featured a collection of cartoons to mark three decades of the new century. 1900 was encapsulated in an aristocratic ball and a serene scene in a living room. 1910 evoked wild parties and an austere family scene. 1920 was marked with demonstrators, strikers, those injured in war and slick modernity in home life. A large question mark hovered over 1930.[139] Still in its childhood, only seven years old, German radio had yet to fully be defined or fully define its future. It was learning to speak, to find forms and interests and dispositions.

Of Schoen's own childhood not a great amount is recorded, apart from some bare facts. He was born on 14 April 1894, child of architect Otto Schön from the Eifel district of Germany and Joanna, born Grodnick-Grodinsky, whose family had come from Russia. His mother, who was Jewish, had her son baptised as Protestant.[140] The father left the family when Ernst was six months old – he went to the USA, where he died in 1918. Schoen grew up with his mother and grandparents and, around the age of sixteen, he left home to spend a period at the house of his friend Alfred Cohn.[141] In a picture of Schoen as a child, from the turn of the century, he is outside in a forest, in contrast to the more traditional photographic studio. He is dressed in a sailor suit.[142] Schoen's wife Johanna gazes out of a picture from a similar time, but from another social sphere.[143] Johanna was the daughter of a writer, Paul Liman. The foggy memory of childhood is carried through into the fogginess of these photos, for they are products of a technology also still in its infancy. Sound, too, is carried through time from early recordings, conveying a fog, the audible presence of an atmosphere marked on phonograph or wax cylinders.

The etymology of the word 'infant' points to one who is not able to speak (from *in-* 'not, opposite of' and *fans*, the present participle of *fari* 'to speak'). The retrieval of infancy confronts inarticulacy and so comes into the world through memory, projected and constructed. To retrieve childhood is thus necessarily an adult projection. Childhood is not only lost to the archives but is a lost archive. One channel for the remembrance of childhood might be in dreams, which Schoen archived frequently in subsequent years.[144]

His dreams evoked scenes from his childhood, or its projection. On a night shift at work at the BBC, on 10 June 1946, Schoen dreamt of relatives. The scene was a family gathering. There were not enough chairs for guests. Schoen greeted his eldest great-aunt (perhaps his Aunt Linda) and her husband. He wore a tailcoat with a white buttonhole, white gloves and had a stick with a silver knob under his arm. She wore a black evening dress with a black lace overhang. They made their way to their apartment where one of his cousins, dressed darkly, leaned against a wall. Another asked for a glass of water. Hansi replied that they would make coffee for

Figure 2.5 Ernst Schoen in 1896. Studio: Mdm. Lili, Berlin.

From Schoen's Archive in Koblenz: BArch N 1403 Bild-109-022. Copyright: Sabine Schiller-Lerg.

Figure 2.6 Johanna Schoen in 1903. Studio: Alfred Leonhardt, Berlin-Schöneberg.

From Schoen's Archive in Koblenz: BArch N 1403 Bild-110-002. Copyright: Sabine Schiller-Lerg.

everyone. At the entrance a relation asked Ernst if he had any chlorine. In another dream that year, from 4 July, he dreamt that he encountered Nina, his daughter, who he named 'Ninchen', as a little girl. She looked poor, he noted, like in a bad photo from the time. She played with a group of other children, tyrannising them. He noticed a friendly and pretty-looking girl with a round face, straight hair and a blue skirt. The dream ended there. Another spoke to the embroilment of various contemporary and histori-cal events. On 29 May 1948, Schoen dreamt that he was in a Jewish chil-dren's home in Tel Aviv, which would shortly be attacked and stormed by Arabs with artillery. It was only a couple of weeks after the destruction of Palestine. He cautiously crept up a narrow staircase and then swung him-self over a bannister, carefully, because a child was hidden under each step. He asked if people were hiding to trick the Arabs. He recalled a feeling of total hopelessness and wondered if it was still worth living in the face of these children sentenced to death and other atrocities. The children here represented innocence and vulnerability. Upon waking, he wondered why 'the children did not leave the house and disperse themselves as guerillas' and he thought of 'their child skulls, with close shaven hair, and their large sad eyes.'[145]

Dreams may contain trauma, anxiety, but they also offer a new way to speak, perhaps new proposals for living. Radio, too, might be reparative and offer another future. In the 1930 *Jahrbuch*, one article speculated on radio in 1950, by when it might have matured and entered its middle-age. It mused on everlasting tubes and optical transmitters using infrared light and wireless connections receiving programmes from across the world effortlessly in a reduced-size device that was radio, television, telephone, facsimile transmitter, all in one. Everything could happen at a distance. The writer dreamt up remote-controlled aeroplanes and an automatic cooking pot that prepared and cooked food for all the city's inhabitants. A cartoon showed a well-paid city Head Chef remotely tasting the food through a device. There was also a cartoon titled 'Insurance Salesman's Dream'. Its caption described a remote-controlled fire engine of the future that was able to conjure rain out of the clouds in any required quantity. Another depicted a young woman with her infrared pocket truth detector exposing the ill-intent of an already married suitor.[146] Radio's future could be one of total social and technological transformation.

This transformation started with speech and with those who were granted speech through new technologies. Though radio plugged listeners into an apparatus, restricted movements, it also demonstrated a tendency, even a dream or a desire, to animate. At various points the *SWZ* encouraged children to engage in model engineering. In 1932, instructions for making a model plane drew children into the world of modern construction and a possible career future for them, or a possible means of escape when the time came to flee.[147] Instruction extended into art making. The *SWZ* published, for example, the results of a competition for the best picture painted by a child. They reproduced images of boats, animals and flowers.[148] Radio also encouraged those in its vicinity to emerge out of muteness, to find expression.

Many children's books from the time showed animals interacting with radio sets. Valentin Kataev's *Radio-zhiraf* (Radio-Giraffe) from 1926, for example, depicted a number of animals listening and broadcasting into microphones: a giraffe, an ape, an ostrich.[149] And so, just as animals might learn not only to listen and broadcast over the airwaves, so too might humans, both child and adult, learn to harness the energies of radio: to speak back or speak for the first time, in new voices and languages.

Much of Schoen's radio work relating to children came about through discussions with his childhood friend Walter Benjamin. It often involved an interplay between the heard and the written. At 20:15 on Sunday 3 January 1932 a programme was advertised in the *SWZ* for 'Poets with Keywords' ('Dichter nach Stichworten').[150] Benjamin presented it. Adapted from a Baroque parlour game, the programme supplied listeners with a series of seemingly unrelated words with which they were to construct sentences. Benjamin declared them into the microphone: KIEFER, BALL, STRAUSS, KAMM, BAUER, ATLAS. The German speaking listener might have discerned some punning: KIEFER means both pine and jaw; BALL could be a toy ball but also the dance; STRAUSS means bouquet, ostrich and struggle; KAMM a comb, ridge and neck; BAUER is farmer but also a cage; and ATLAS is the map but also satin. The audience then sent in their playful linguistic constructions. To translate any of those entries is to fix meanings, but here is an attempt:

Under the pine tree
with trembling jaw
in pink satin
Gretchen leafs through the atlas
and then hurries to the ball
the ball is made of snow

Oh woe, my bouquet
there is a struggle!
She threatens with the comb
her neck bristles
If you were only in a cage
you good-for-nothing farmer![151]

This 'coming to voice' also took place in the private sphere. When the radio played, the child might sing along, reply, disobey the requisite passivity of the form. Schoen too, as a professional with access to equipment, brought recording to his home in the early 1930s, producing shellac records by deploying state of the art technology in a domestic setting. In the Schoen archive, these domestic recordings of song and voice are listed on a record index, alongside commercially available vinyl: Edgard Varèse, Hanns Eisler and Jacques Offenbach, among others.

On them, we hear voices and singing. Nina wants a silk scarf. Then there is talk of a trip to Africa. There they will ride on a Jumbo, an elephant. Nina says she wants to take off all her clothes and get darker skin. Then the family talks of going to Berlin, where Papi is. In Berlin, they will visit a toy shop. Nina wants a song about Red Riding Hood. Hansi suggests 'Hansel and Gretel get lost in the woods' and Nina sings it.[152]

Later, in another recording session, Ernst and Sasha appear. 'Jetzt Geht's Los, Jetzt wird Ernst!' ('Let's make a start. Now it gets serious'). Nina and Mama talk about Switzerland and the railway trip there. Ernst asks Nina if she would like to sing a Swiss song, which she does. Sasha then sings. Then they discuss a trip to Switzerland and how they missed Papi at the train station, because he came to greet the wrong train. To make up for it, he brought two bouquets.[153]

In this recording, still accessible today, voices are not only preserved, but conserved in a certain state. Recording allowed for the performance of a dialogue, the accentuation of a social interaction, between parent and child and child and child. The recording became another ear, a new ear. Tell me how you are feeling, the medium asks. Do something else, it commands. At times the parents might leave the scene and the child might operate the device, talking to it, talking to themselves, talking to their future self. At this point the child becomes an operator, engineer, producer. This recording practice was never only a private or domestic one, it was one that came to and returned to the public sphere.

The place of children on the radio was revisited numerous times in the early years of the *SWZ*. On 17 January 1926, a front cover declared 'Rundfunk im Kindermund' ('Broadcasting Babytalk'). A child sat below the words, smoking a pipe, playing the adult.[154] On the inside pages too, an adult's face was placed on the body of a child.[155] On 7 March 1926, the front cover repeated the same title and included a picture of a child with a rabbit.[156] On the inside page: the title and theme continued with numerous photographs – including a baby wearing headphones.

In 1926, other adverts for equipment started to appear in *SWZ*. In one for a microphone, a child wears headphones, its smile beaming out from the page like a sunflower.[157] As much as flowers are drawn to the sun, this microphone is a sun that draws the eye and ear of the consumer or the play-ing child. The sun's rays mingle with the waves of sound and promise sunny futures in a world where energy comes at us from our new appliances.

Programme II: 25 Minutes

Picking up where we left off: issue 49 of the *SWZ* from 1926 presented a series of images of a child interacting with a sound horn. In the first pic-ture the child sat beside the sound horn. Then the child ventured to look inside. The child then took the sound horn from the apparatus and placed it on their head like a hat.[158] Throughout issues of the magazine, children are shown as users of headphones. The 1 May 1927 edition of the *SWZ* included a drawing of a child pressing the earpads, listening intently.[159] Radio might teach speech but it also endeavoured to teach listening. This is a process that could go awry: it could be subverted, whether intentionally or not. Listening – and its mediation – was explored in work for the young listeners of the young medium too. The 1932 adaptation by Benjamin and Schoen of an 1827 fairy tale by Wilhelm Hauff, *The Cold Heart*, uses fairy tale characters stepping into 'Voice Land', a non-visual space commu-nicated by radio, in order to dispense lessons on morality and economics and what might be heard and how.

DUTCH MICHAEL (rudely): Well then, Mr. Announcer, let us in already.

ANNOUNCER: Not so fast, Dutch Michael, you brute! It's not that easy! You can come into Voice Land and speak to thousands of children, but I patrol the borders of this country and there's a condition you must first fulfill.

LISBETH: A condition?

ANNOUNCER: Yes, indeed, Miss Lisbeth, and one that will be especially difficult for you to fulfill.

LITTLE GLASS MAN: Well then, name your condition. I am certainly used to conditions, I often set them myself.

ANNOUNCER: Alright, listen closely, Little Glass Man, and you others too: whoever wishes to enter Voice Land must be very modest. He must surrender all finery and relinquish all external beauty, so that nothing is left but his voice. However, his voice will then be heard by thousands of children simultaneously.[160]

During this time, listening practices entered other settings beyond the home. The 1931 *Jahrbuch* focused on the use of radio in schools. In one photograph young boys in a Berlin school leaned out of a window to build an aerial. Others constructed a loudspeaker. Examples from school radio programmes are given: Hans Christian Andersen fairy tales for children of ten years of age and above; a journey into fairy tale land, with records, for seven year olds; a game with *Rumpelstiltskin*, for eight and over; a geographical introduction to Germany; a musical trip around Europe; a celebration of Johannes Kepler, for twelve years and above; recordings with indigenous groups in Mexico; some Mozart, Bach and Beethoven; dispatches from a submarine cable, for thirteen years and over; Berliners as soldiers in the Thirty Years War, for 10 years and over; a trip to the planetarium, with a Berlin school, for over-twelves. There are language lessons too, in English and French. Such was the educational offering for a German child in these years.[161] The classroom was not only a place for listening but also for recording. A year prior, the *SWZ* ran an article entitled 'With a microphone in school' for a music lesson.[162] The 1932 *BBC Year-Book* observed that every third school in Germany listened in to school broadcasts.[163]

In the Soviet context, technology was employed to transform school children into 'workers, technicians, and engineers of tomorrow'. For example, at around the same time, the Soviet state 'initiated a special movement organised around Stations of Young Technicians', 'schoolchildren were encouraged to test and develop their technological creativity by building working models of radio receivers, power plants, cars, and even flying vehicles'. They were sometimes called 'Young Techies', communists not just of the future, but of today.[164] This was a different context to the German one, but both involved the invention or construction of new customs, in the production or construction of new humans, born again in a new, if fragile, post-war political context.

Schoen commissioned Benjamin to deliver regular lectures on diverse topics for children in their home setting. He made programmes on Berlin dialects, the petrification of Pompeii, counterfeit stamps, slum housing, manufacture, the history of the Bastille prison, witch trials and the history of toys. Some dealt with their home city of Berlin, with unusual aspects of the changing city space, such as its puppet theatre, its guttersnipes, factories and brass works. Some programmes looked at charismatic and marginalised historical characters, such as Kaspar Hauser or Roma people. The tension between modernity and magic echoed in radio programmes on eccentric and supernatural figures or phenomena: witches, demonic Berlin, Dr Faust, Cagliostro. Some programmes addressed swindles and crimes: bootleggers, postage stamp swindlers, robber bands. Some dealt with historical events, especially catastrophes such as earthquakes or structural collapse, fires and floods. One might suspect Benjamin was encouraging the young to run amok, to learn of the violence of the world so that they might start to counter it or use it for other ends.

Benjamin's radiophonic work extended to plays. *Radau Um Kasperl* (Much Ado about Little Kasper), written by Benjamin, was broadcast on 10 March 1932.[165] Schoen wrote the music and worked on the sound effects. It was an hour-long play and the story was as follows: One foggy day Kasperl is sent to the market to buy some fish. On the way someone from the radio station asks him to come in and do a broadcast. Kasperl goes to the studio, but has no concept of what radio is and is nervous. Having established that an acquaintance in Putzingen would be able to hear the show, he directs a torrent of abuse at him. Chaos ensues and Kasperl has to go on the run. He gets into various tangles at the railway station, the fairground and the zoo, where he is finally cornered. He returns home and goes to bed. Unbeknownst to him, a microphone had been concealed in the bed. His tirades after waking up are cut together and broadcast and the radio station has won – it has got its Kasperl material. Kasperl receives 1000RM for his unwitting trouble.[166]

The themes of the play were various and complex. It educated the listeners as to the types of permissible radio discourse. It demonstrated the mobility of radio broadcasting, its omnipresence in the city. It dealt with radio's intrusion into the most intimate space, the bedroom. It reflected on the alienation and commodification of cultural work – and, significantly, did this by using a folk-theatre figure Kasperl, now displaced into a new media environment. The play was written as an experiment in the proper place and tone of radio discourse. It asked who the subject of radio might be. It incorporated dialects and sonic play. It reflected on the place of radio in the home, its breaking through the separations between public and private zones. It also considered the alienation and commodification of cultural labour. In doing all this, it made radio itself an object of discussion. It laid bare the mechanisms of radio, its means of reproduction. It also used the specific capabilities of radio. It was sonic and opened in the fog, as if to suggest the demotion of vision and promotion of hearing. The dialogue used word games and dialect. It deployed a myriad of sound effects and noises. Through this specific aspect, Benjamin worked on an interactive radio culture, where the children were asked to contact the radio station to guess what sounds were heard during the show. The listing notes add: 'As the title implies, Kasper's experiences in this play are also connected with Radau (*racket, row, hubbub, din*). Children are asked to suggest what the noises mean and to share their opinions with the radio station.'[167] Did Benjamin and/or Schoen ever open these post bags?

If children were able to listen at home and at school, they might have also listened in the concert hall. On 14 December 1927, a number of compositional experiments for children were included in a programme of a

Figure 2.7 Postcard advertising a concert of children's music from 1927.

From Schoen's Archive in Koblenz: *Kompositionen ('Ati's Compositions')*, BArch N 1403/55. Photographed at the Bundesarchiv Koblenz. Copyright: Sabine Schiller-Lerg.

concert at the Meistersaal in Berlin. Along with pieces by Satie, Poulenc, Debussy, Stravinsky and Bartók, Schoen's compositions, *Sechs Lieder für Kinder* (Six Songs for Children) were included.[168] Written also in 1927, these were premiered by Alice Schäffer-Kuznitzky (voice) and Alice Jacob-Loewenson (piano).

Circles collapse and new circles form. The singer Alice Schäffer-Kuznitzky was perhaps a regular at the Meistersaal (where Henri had danced),[169] and, at an evening recital on 10 January 1930 by the November Group, also part of Schoen's wider circles, she sang a work by E. W. Sternberg, which set to music poems by Else Lasker-Schüler, Stefan George and Ricarda Huch.[170] In 1922, the pianist Alice Jacob-Loewenson married Erwin Loewenson, who was around the youth circles in Berlin at the outbreak of the 1914–1918 war.[171] She studied piano, composition, comparative musicology,[172] and was influenced by Busoni's pedagogical piano recitals, as were Schoen and Kellner and others in the circle. She also gave piano lessons, became prominent in a number of Jewish educational institutions[173] and published in the *Jüdische Rundschau* (Jewish Review) before eventually fleeing to Palestine after 1933 where she continued to teach, write and work for the radio.[174]

Schoen's archives provide us with not six, but eight songs for children – two were either not performed or else not yet written at the time of the performance. The songs are short and playful; they avoid a prescription of childlike innocence, rather addressing their audience with volatility, humour and dissonance – modernist, jerky and atonal. But what was the context of the performance? Would children be present? How would they have sat – would they have been able to move around? Would they have had to sit upright in chairs?

The performance was reviewed in the Berlin press in subsequent days. On Monday 19 December, the journalist Otto Steinhagen wrote in the *Berliner Börsen-Zeitung*:

The applause was much less the following evening in the Meistersaal, even though there were new (i.e. atonal) children's pieces and children's songs to be heard. It was not because of the singer, Alice Schäffer-Kuznitzky, who was greatly appreciated, nor because of the pianist, Alice Jacob-Loewenson, but rather because this music rarely hit the right note as children's music, and in many cases it is not even new, but simply atonally distorted.[175]

Steinhagen stood by his opposition to atonality in the nursery. In 1933, the leading English-language journal for musical discussion, *The Musical Times*, published a summary of current debates, including 'a whole-hearted denunciation, by Hans Bassermann, of Erich and Elma Doflein's *Geigenschulwerk* (Violin Schoolwork), in which violin pieces were intended to familiarise young players with atonality'. In the article, Steinhagen wrote:

Unless atonality is strictly excluded from the children's curriculum, the next generation will be utterly incapable of appreciating the classical and romantic masterpieces. How can we explain to a child the world of significance that lies in a Schumann harmony, if its ears are rendered insensitive by the action of cruel discords?[176]

The article goes on to cite Steinhagen from November's edition of *Musik* where he attacks Ernst Toch in a similar vein:

Every player of new music knows how awful is the consciousness of giving listeners music for which they have not yet an ear. And this is why Toch, addressing an American audience, adjured them to 'train their ears for the new music of to-day, as they had trained them for that of Bach, Beethoven, and Wagner'.[177]

Criticising atonality in 1933 was a political act, just as it already was in 1927. To train the ear out of a certain tradition, a certain version of tradition, into a new sonic world. What, then, should children's music be like, if not atonal? It might be functional: it might rock a child to sleep, or calm a child down. It might also express an ideal, an atmosphere. For children's music to be atonal is to cross a line. Rather than allow the child to be brought up out of itself, it apparently imposed fashion and history onto innocence.

The songs that Schoen wrote for performance granted the child a sense of humour. Some were short and abrupt. They expressed or reflected certain realities of life: boredom, routine, the death of a soldier, anxiety, upset. As such they held to a pedagogical method, or counter method. In his alphabet song, Schoen took a traditional model from a children's primer and played around with it. The lyrics:

Say 'a' with the finger
Say 'b' with the toe
Say, what the little thumb
caught with the little finger
a, b, c, d, e;
c, d, e, f, g.[178]

In 1943, this song's original pianist, Alice Jacob-Loewenson,[181] published a book that brought together her piano method as *Boker, Boker: A Palestine ABC for Piano* (בקר בקר: אלף-בית ארץ-ישראלי לפסנתר).[180] The *SWZ* also published alphabetical primers throughout this period.[181]

In 'To the Planetarium', from *One Way Street* (1928), Benjamin evoked a 'cane wielder' who 'proclaimed the mastery of children by adults to be the purpose of education'. Who would trust this person, he asked. 'Is not education, above all, the indispensable ordering of the relationship between generations and therefore mastery (if we are to use this term) of that relationship and not of children?'[182] To point, or to use the cane, was to proclaim the mastery of children by adults. It ordered the generations. Radio and new music offered a different accord between what had been and what was incipient between the generations.

As much as the domestic sphere was a place of recording the voice, of coming to speech, both privately and in interaction with the public sphere, it was also a place of musical experimentation. Nina spoke on the domestic recordings but Nina also sang. And Schoen wrote small pieces of domestic music, all left in the archive: a 'Kanon für Hansi', a song 'There is a Little House' and other domestic work. This represented a childhood that stretched into the decades to come, times of displacement.

The title of 'There is a Little House' is hard to decipher, as with much of Schoen's handwriting. It could say 'there is a little noise' but also house and horse, or even Hitler. The first section reads:

Oh, isn't Nina a very special child?
But Sascha is also a very special child?
How I am so grateful.
That my children are such special children.[183]

Then there is a change of tone:

There is a little house above the sea,
A little garden and a cherry-tree.
I guess, the cherry tree is blooming now,
And blossoms float around like springtime snow.

After all our longing,
After all our strain,
After all our struggling
And all our pain,

Figure 2.8 Facsimile from Schoen's 'Kinderlieder', from his Archive in Koblenz: *Kompositionen ('Ati's Compositions')*, BArch N 1403/55.

Photographed at the Bundesarchiv Koblenz. Copyright: Sabine Schiller-Lerg.

After all our grieving
Our hope shall be:
Let's keep the little house above the sea.

And in the garden there's a little place,
Bless'd more than all the world with charm and grace.
And charm and grace are ever there anew,
For, sitting there, my only love, are you.
After all my longing,

After all my strain,
After all my struggling
And all my pain,
After all my grieving
Our thing is this:
It is the house, the garden and it's you![184]

The lyrics are poignant, tragic, almost naive. There is a dedication on the bottom of the first page. 'Puma von Ati, 7 May 34. And that should be a word! L[on]d[o]n.'

A piece called 'Childish Blues', dated 16 June 1942, was written for Sasha and Nina to sing at their home in East Molesey, London, when the Schoens' lived at Kingfisher Court. Sasha was thirteen years old at the time, Nina fifteen. There is something or someone listed as 'B' on the stave, perhaps a *Blockflöte* (a recorder), or another person. The lyrics go: 'Boys are naughty' and 'girls are...' then 'Yes, love and harmony!' This version of the blues, or jazz was sanitised, kitchified. As music written for the domestic sphere – either to teach, or just to pass the time, perhaps as a gift – there are a number of parallels: Anna Magdalena's *Notebook* (1722–1725) or Leopold Mozart's pieces for his daughter Nannerl (written between 1759–1764).[185] The radio newspapers had previously printed scores, to perform at home.[186] Schoen contributed to this tradition.

Programme III: 18 Minutes

In 1926, the *SWZ* ran an advert for its *Rundfunk-Märchenbuch*, a book of radio fairy tales prompted by the station's *Märchenstunde* (Fairy Tale Hour): a large cloud with inflated cheeks blew out puffs of vapour, while children in babygrows tumbled in the sky.[187] How might the modern city accommodate children in new ways? Walter Benjamin's review of Alois

Jalkotzy's *Märchen und Gegenwart: Das deutsche Volksmärchen und unsere Zeit* (Fairy Tales and the Present: German Folk Tales and Our Time) (1930) focused on its cover:

It is a photomontage: winding towers, skyscrapers, factory chimneys in the background, a powerful locomotive in the middle distance and, at the front of this landscape of concrete, asphalt and steel, a dozen children gathered around their nursery teacher, who is telling a fairy tale.[188]

Children were exposed to the forces of modernity, to the factories and mineworks that would employ them, the skyscrapers that would house them, the trains that would transport them. This was their environment, far removed from the aristocratic and peasant worlds of traditional fairy tales. They gathered at the base of these looming presences. They listened in, attentive to the story being told, whether in person or over the radio. The infancy of the technology was the hope of childhood: listen, speak and gather again. There was danger in this, but also the expectation of a future with new energies.

Paul Hindemith's *Wir bauen eine Stadt: Spiel für Kinder* (We are building a city: a play for children), from 1930, included a cast of children in a project of urban construction. Hindemith composed the music, Robert Seitz and (later) S. B. Lewertoff the words. The *SWZ* ran an article on 1 February 1931. An image showed students from a local school, the Lessing-Gymnasium in Frankfurt, perhaps performing, perhaps in rehearsal. The children declared:

> We are building a new city,
> It's going to be the most beautiful one,
> It's going to be the most beautiful,
> We'll go with buckets and shovels,
> And wagons and horses,
> And dolls and cars,
> And everything we have,
> We'll go together,
> We'll build a new city,
> And it'll be the most beautiful one ever built.
>
> If you give me stones, I'll give you sand.
> If you fetch me water, I'll stir in the lime.
> We'll build the houses. We'll put roofs on them.
> We'll build roads. We'll build trams.
> If we all help each other, our city will soon stand.[189]

How would the children arrange the streets, the houses, the rooms? Would they erect radio towers and broadcast from them?

In Schoen's archives are a number of photographs of 20 Fuchshohl in Frankfurt. Schoen was registered as living at 21 Taunusanlage, next to Frankfurt's *Alte Oper*, at the time of his marriage to Johanna. Married life continued in nearby Kronberg in the Taunus and, in 1931, the family moved to a newly built modern settlement in Frankfurt's Ginnheim.[190] The photographs of the new home are hard to read as personal images – the interiors are empty, modern, plain. Why would they put two chairs on the end of the bed? The house is devoid of people, things. Might the photographer, Hanna Mandello, female pioneer of the Leica camera, have used the occasion of the family's moving in to explore rather cool scenes of everyday life, or was the family especially neat and tidy?[191]

20 Fuchshohl is part of the *Siedlung Höhenblick*, the 'High View Settlement', built in 1926–1927. The apartments were originally rented, designed by Ernst May, a planner and developer of modernist estates. This was the New Frankfurt, for new eyes, ears and lives. In 1928 the *SWZ* ran an article on Ernst May.[192] Radio and building went together, Ernst May lived in the development, as did the architects Carl-Hermann Rudloff and Max Cetto, the graphic artist Hans Leistikow and the painter Willi Baumeister.[193]

This new architecture housed a new family and its domestic life: one photo depicts the nursery, simply decorated.[194] Plain curtains covered the window and there was a white unornamented wardrobe and two cots. Unlike the other rooms in this series of photographs of the house, the nursery appeared occupied: There was a rocking horse slightly aslant, some bedding in the crib, a photographic portrait on the wall.

But the children were absent and so was a caregiver. In 'Thought Figures' from 1933, published in *Die literarische Welt* (The Literary World), Benjamin tied storytelling to a process of healing. He imagined a sick child in a crib who is told a story by his mother. He asked how this scenario might be considered restorative. The answer could be found through the hand gestures of the storyteller, the mother who leans over the bed of the ailing child. Benjamin drew a lesson from the Merseburg Spells (*Merseburger Zaubersprüche*) – a collection of pagan spells from the ninth century, discovered by Georg Waitz in 1841. These consisted of a magical imperative

Figure 2.9 Nursery at Fuchshohl 20 in Frankfurt. Dated 1929–1933.

Photographed by Hanna Mandello, Frankfurt am Main. From Schoen's Archive in Koblenz: BArch N 1403 Bild-110-006. Copyright: Sabine Schiller-Lerg.

formula, preceded by a narrative in which a similar past occurrence is described. The spell referred to in Benjamin's essay was conjured to bring about the healing of a lame horse. Benjamin suggests, enigmatically: 'If we reflect that pain is a dam that offers resistance to a current of narrative, it is evident that the dam will be pierced when the gradient is steep enough for everything that crosses its path to be swept into an ocean of blissful oblivion. Stroking marks out a bed for this torrent.'[195] Pain collects in the dam and is pierced through speech. An advert from the *SWZ* from the time profanes this image for the domestic sphere. It recommended 'bright, jolly colours for the children's room'. A child slept soundly, the figure, perhaps the mother, hovered anxiously above.[196]

In 'A Family Drama in the Epic Theatre' (1932), a commentary written in the wake of the premiere of Brecht's play *Die Mutter*, Benjamin provided a more radical account. (On 1 May 1932, the *SWZ* ran a cover portrait of 'Die Mutter' for Mother's Day).[197] Benjamin's article began with a simple maxim borrowed from Brecht: Communism is not radical, rather, it is capitalism that is radical.[198] In relation to the family, Benjamin noted, capitalism 'insists upon the family at any price, even where any intensification of family life can only aggravate the suffering already caused by conditions utterly unworthy of human beings.' Communism did not seek, according to Benjamin, simply to 'abolish family relations. It merely tests them to determine their capacity for change.' The mother's 'social function' was not to simply 'produce the next generation', but to provide the labour that reproduces the living labour of those around her: in this case, her son. Pelagea Vlassova, the protagonist of *Die Mutter*, is forced to feed the worker, to reproduce his strength and to do it also while impoverished. She found food and cooked dinner, she held her child and clothed him and then her songs lulled the child to sleep.

The question raised by Brecht's play, according to Benjamin, was whether 'this social function [of the mother] become[s] a revolutionary one, and how?'[199] Following on is the radical claim: 'If the mothers are revolutionised, there is nothing left to revolutionise.'[200] Benjamin surmised:

What are the objections to Communism? She sings: Learn, woman of sixty. She sings: 'In Praise of the Third Cause'. And she sings these songs as a mother. For they are lullabies. Lullabies for Communism, which is small and weak but irresistibly growing. This Communism she has taken unto herself as a mother.[201]

Healing, as much as care and the singing of lullabies, should be understood as a social process, enacted not just through the mother's care of the child but mutually, for the abolition of the very categories. Schoen was, at this point in Frankfurt, paid a great deal, lived a comfortable life and no one in the family could be compared with Pelagea Vlassova. If the mother was a worker, so was the domestic servant who kept the family home clean and tidy.

The photo of the crib evoked care and childhood through sleep. Schoen wrote music for children, both to energise but also put to sleep: one song was close to a lullaby, the fifth song of his music for children, entitled 'Tenderness'. It captured something of the sympathy doled out to the child who is perhaps unable to sleep:

Little hushbabies
Hushabye

Make little eggs
Makes eggaleg

Little hushbabies
Hushaban
Begin the song from the start again!

Little hushbabies
Hushabye.[202]

Alice Jacob-Loewenson wrote lullabies, publishing *Variationen über ein jüdisches Wiegenlied* (Variations on a Jewish Lullaby) for piano with the publishing house Mizmor.[203] This lullaby was about a cradle and so it truly was a cradle song or *Wiegenlied* – not all songs for children are about the place of sleep and some are about waking. *Frère Jacques*, for example, might be sung to soothe a lively child to sleep or to rouse to wakefulness. Its titular subject, Brother Jack, is to awaken and ring the morning bells to wake up the other monks for *matines*, the morning prayers. These songs are soothing. Their rhythms are repetitive and gentle, often in 6/8 time, with a swinging motion, to rock the listener to sleep with words. Like all old things that have existed since we were small and since our species were young, mist covers the origins of the word lullaby. Some say that the word derives from 'Lilith-Abi', Hebrew for 'Lilith, begone'. Get ye hence Lilith, the demon who steals children's souls in the night. Others say that the word comes from the word 'to lull' – which may mean a pause or a rest, or to sing, even if badly, perhaps just a sound made with the mouth to soothe the child – *lul lul lul* – spliced together with the word 'bye', from goodbye, god be with you, goodnight, let the day lull, let us pause until morning.

Lullabies have been sung by caregivers seeking to send their dependents to sleep for many, many years – in ordinary environments, sung out of tune or sweetly, but always as an intimate, domestic act. But composers of the classical world of music have donated their share of lullabies too: the *Berceuses* of Chopin and Busoni, Stravinsky and Tchaikovsky and the *Wiegenlied* of Schubert and Brahms, for example, the latter the stuff of music boxes. Brahms, it is said, suffered from sleep apnoea, startling himself awake with an untuneful snort repeatedly through the night.[204] A cradle song should summon up sleep again, counter the disturbance. The final words of the first verse of his *Wiegenlied* are not reassuring or calming, but terrifying, an insistence on God's whims.

Guten Abend, gut' Nacht,
mit Rosen bedacht,
mit Näglein besteckt,
schlupf unter die Deck':
Morgen früh, wenn Gott will,
wirst du wieder geweckt.

Good evening, good night,
covered with roses,
adorned with carnations,
Slip under the covers.
Early tomorrow, if God wills it,
you will be woken up once again.

* * *

Alien Furniture

Advertisements adorned the pages of the 1930 *Jahrbuch*. There were adverts for other magazines that spread radio culture. And there were many adverts for radio equipment. One advertisement politely inquired as to whether the reader had already attempted to see if their device using alternating current would not work better with Rechtron's demodulated tubes. An array of cabinet-style loudspeakers from Nora followed, before some publicity for a newsletter from Dralowid and a drawing of Isophon's loudspeaker, which loomed, massive as a concert hall, above the behatted heads of men crowded around its base. Here the radio replaced the venue and brought it into the home. Audiences once amassed in the old cultural institutions of the city gathered within domestic space. Another advert was for a Helios-Dynamus radio with 'natural tones', which boasted the capacity to replicate the atmosphere of the broadcast space, lending the feeling of actually being there. Radio was not in the home. The home was in the radio studio or the concert hall. Modern citizens learnt to be comfortable elsewhere, citizens of the airwaves, from wherever these emanated. Radio challenged the divisions between the public and private. For radios – as new pieces of alien technology – to find a place in the home, they had to blend in. At times they looked like fireguards, fireplaces, cabinets, suitcases, cocktail cabinets, carriage clocks, jewellery boxes, even cigar and cigarette cases. But Brecht had already written that radio was not an 'adequate means of bringing back cosiness to the home and making family life bearable again'.[205]

Clown Time

In his conversation with Schoen, published in 1929, Benjamin claimed that radio possessed a quality that takes the impulses of cabaret further: 'Simultaneously, radio had to take advantage of its superiority over cabaret in this specific regard – namely, its ability to gather, in front of the microphone, artists who would be unlikely to come together in the space of a cabaret'.[206] He quotes Schoen at length. But radio could also bring cabaret into the world of radio. Cabarets and clowns featured in the pages of the *SWZ* throughout the twenties. On 30 July 1929, the front cover featured a photograph by Sasha Stone: a line of clowns holding their palms beside their faces as if blowing raspberries. Cabaret stars also appeared: Velaska Gert on the front page of the issue from 10 November 1929; Claire Waldoff in February 1926 in an article about *Überbrettl*; another on comedy and cabaret. On 9 November 1930, the paper also published a sociology of the circus by Dr Hans Hartmann.[207] Schoen would later return to this theme.

Melody Maker

Schoen's journalism appeared in the radio press, but he also wrote music criticism in the heavyweight journals of the day, including *Melos* journal, founded in 1920 by Hermann Scherchen. Schoen contributed several articles and there were debates across contributions. In 1928, he wrote on the sociology of the opera, on music on the radio and on musical education, considered under the heading 'Cartels or Socialisation' and reflecting on musical individualism in contrast to collectivity. In 1929, debates continued over what radio music might become, alongside reflections on Stravinsky's influence and radio compositions for the Baden-Baden Festival.

An essay by Schoen in *Melos* in 1929 considered the question of a composer's influence.[208] Of what does this influence consist? Is it in working methods or in the idea of a stylistic epoch – and under what conditions does it endure? In Schoen's account of how the music of a composer's legacy seeps into or warps what follows, he mentioned 'the problematic role of [the] prophet', referring to Busoni.[209] The essay dazzled with its musical analysis and it ruminated on form – the syncopation and polytonality of 'the *Passagenwerk*' (used in a musical context, but perhaps referring to Benjamin's arcades work) of Stravinsky's Piano Concerto produced, he stated, a 'devilish equability'. And in the present 'sterility' had led to 'an artistic Fascism of musical work': plodding Rococo, academicism paraded as the great national art and Hindemith taken captive by *Gebrauchsmusik*. Applied arts were the order of the day.[210] Schoen writes:

Of course one can evade the intellectual demands of atonality on this party on the eve of the wedding. But then one overlooks how it represents one of the cleanest consequences by way of which musical creativity today might integrate its word in the chorus of singular artistic works across time.[211]

German Jazz

On Friday 13 June 1930, a jazz concert was scheduled, broadcast from Karlsruhe, for the hundred minutes before midnight. It was mixed in style. There was an overture by Theodor Munz for trumpet, saxophone, bass, piano and drums, followed by a piece called 'Potpourri' by Kurt Weill from the *Threepenny Opera* (1928), featuring the Mack the Knife theme. There were a couple of fox trots and some numbers by Karl Haas, the band's leader.[212]

Colleague Critique

On 10 April 1930, Schoen wrote a letter to Benjamin, responding to questions that Benjamin had asked of him, presumably for an article. He provides a thorough profile of the politics and personnel of German radio and the culture officials. He outlines their previous experience: Hans Bredow came from a career in telegraphy administration and in the war, he was involved in the organisation of the German wireless field stations and received, with the founding of German radio, his own state secretariat. Schoen stressed who was 'particularly stupid' and who reactionary. Magnus, he notes, is 'relatively skilled and engaging'. He had undertaken a study visit to see United States radio in situ, which he admired. Schoen commented that US radio was 'famously exclusively an advertising means for private entrepreneurs'. He discussed political uses of radio – relating how the May Festival had been banned from broadcasting on the airwaves, despite it not being in any way political. Things had started to shift. The most prominent case of political uses of radio to date, he observed, are the ministerial speeches in favour of the Young Plan for reparation and against Alfred Hugenberg's petition for a referendum on the matter, which caused such a stir in the right-wing press. 'All other political uses revolve around liberation celebrations, flag waving and such like. Typical for the political ideology of radio are the so-called political dialogues of the German airwaves, at which parliamentarians from the German National Party to Social Democracy exchange pleasantries.' He elaborated the vested interests in radio in a section titled 'Press Demagoguery' – it included the tyranny of the Frankfurt City Health Office over medical talks; the influence of the great shipping firms on the programme in Nordische Rundfunk AG (NORAG, Northern Radio AG), the Hamburg broadcaster; the presence of various ministries of trade and industry, agriculture and craft. He included a section in his report on the censorship of poetic works.[213]

Precarities, Positions

In the late 1920s, there were nine workers at Frankfurt Radio. They oversaw around ten hours of radio a day. The station relied on drawing in freelance writers and presenters.[214] There was also a heavy reliance on Frankfurt institutions to provide programming.

In the letter to Benjamin in April 1930 detailing the situation at the radio station, Schoen mentioned various institutions, religious entities and choirs and societies, such as the Housewives Union, all of which offered programmes. A Frankfurt newspaper and the trade unions each had a half hour programme slot per week. The public health office was his particular bugbear, with its medical lectures. All this material was not the reason the station had a strong reputation amongst artists and scholars. Despite having a reactionary industrialist, Carl Schleussner, as an investor, the station had fostered experimental work and employed leftists. Freelance engagement by the radio station in Frankfurt was a coveted position. There was the promise of a large listenership, the benefits of a liberal atmosphere at the station and generous honoraria, especially compared to what was usual in print media.[215]

The elections of 1928 resulted in a coalition in Germany led by the Social Democrats, who were now able to significantly reduce censorship. In the first half of 1929, Schoen took over as artistic director, after Flesch moved to Berlin. But unlike Flesch, he did not get a seat on the governing board. And this despite the fact that Schoen had been energetic at the station. He had made some cost savings too, by combining two stations through a complex technological process.[216]

Radio Robots

A contribution in the 1929 *Jahrbuch* of German radio by Ernst Hardt considered the relationship of workers to the radio. It cited a poem that had been submitted to Cologne Radio in 1928 by a factory carpenter, Karl August Düppengiesser, from Stollberg. For Hardt, it expressed the strength of desire on the part of workers to 'become human through radio':

> Radio Wave
> My arm is already an aerial, feels the weave
> Of miracle waves, feels the desire of that world
> Of the never seen, which lights up hope in me
> To believe in a human reborn life.
>
> Peoples, millions of lives conscious of power
> Whose belief in truth has been soured,
> To you, waves, hungry, in your path
> lift listening ears big with hope.
>
> Wave, be aware of your multiple forces,
> And weave, which entangles us all,
> At the world's wheel – entrusted to you by a higher hand –
>
> To the spirit of the new, broad human breast.
> Then your deepest desire has worked out too;
> The human, the world, that I glimpsed far from time.[217]

The human has become a radio, its circuits prostheses. The *Jahrbuch* closed with a number of lists of radio societies and networks across Europe and equipment suppliers and countless magazines to spread the appendages of this new human, these new bodies.

Hot Love for the Thing

The opening ten pages of the 1930 *Jahrbuch* were advertisements. Radio culture, or radio technology, remained in development, subject to improvements. There were technological wonders, which the wealthier could purchase or the radio hams dreamt of emulating. There was advertising for the hobbyists who picked up their Dralowid parts, a firm praised in the 'winged words of amateurs'.[218] There was a burgeoning literature: monographs about coils and condensers and mains supply receivers; radio listings magazines printed in *gravure*; and for the others, a 'Workers Radio' periodical, supported by more than 400 clubs. And there was an advertisement for *Rundfunk-Rundschau*, self-promoting as independent and placed opposite an advertisement for the Imperial Radio Society's monthly annotated directory of new radio publications. Mingled among adverts for regional radio magazines and specialists were adverts directed at schools and children. The 1931 *Jahrbuch* began its content proper with a call out to listeners. The year-book, it stated, was to be a work of reference, one that taught and entertained, as well as preserved wireless culture for posterity. To cultivate this function, it requested photographs and drawings from listeners, especially those related to the early days of wireless news transmission and radio.[219]

But everything was still up in the air. The opening article concerned 'Contemporary Questions of German Radio', and reprinted a speech delivered by radio chief Hans Bredow in September 1930. Bredow reflected on the increasing decentralisation of German radio, as regional centres began to produce their own content, but he noted that the costs were unsustainable. He argued for more integration – facilitated by cabled connections between the twenty-seven German stations – to cut costs, without reducing quality. The push was towards unification: programmes were broadcast on all stations. He pointed to the local interests and mentalities that persisted in radio – comparing it to the days of the postal carriages: 'Each person believes that he must stay, as much as possible, in his own locality, and fails to understand that technology has obliterated the tight limits.'[220] Technology might also facilitate localism, with ultra-shortwave radio making it possible for local organisations to develop a parallel communication network. He also praised radio internationalism – his example was a Mozart serenade, broadcast from Salzburg to over fifty-three European stations. Politics had become bound up in radio, because radio existed at a time when 'the German people stand under the sign of political ferment', and so radio had to remain 'supra-party-political'.[221] Bredow ended his speech with the evocation of what radio needed to see in its advocates: 'Hot love for the thing, hot love of the people and humanity in all its parts and layers'.[222] Radio was a passion, a universalising and binding one. Hopes remained high.

Studio Updates

This was a time of investment and growth. At the start of 1928, the studio presented a new musical organ. It is featured on the front cover of the *SWZ*.[223] Paul Hindemith wrote a piece for its inauguration: *Konzert für Orgel und Kammerorchester*. The music began with the trumpets, an announcement, fugue-like. When the organ struck up, it washed over the ears, as if one had dived into a body of water.

Infrastructure continued to accumulate in the studio over the years to come. The 1931 *Jahrbuch* included photographs of new instruments well suited for radio use: an electric organ invented by Jörg Mager, pioneer of electronic music and a Trautonium, which produced sounds through a resistor wire pressed in different ways and at different points to alter pitch and produce vibrato. Hindemith wrote some trios for Trautonium and gave a public performance with pupil Oskar Sala at the Berliner Musikhochschule Hall under the title 'Neue Musik Berlin 1930'. The use of recording on records was also discussed in the *Jahrbuch*.[224]

One article in the 1932 *Rundfunk Jahrbuch* provided a tour of the newest radio stations in Germany, each different according to specific local needs and inflections. Rapid development in terms of broadcasting technology and acoustic and artistic relations altered the requirements of space for performance and rehearsals, technical equipment and administrative staff. What had begun as rented offices became in time purpose-built radio stations. One of the recently rebuilt stations was in Frankfurt, designed by Willi Cahn with ample studios in the Eschenheimerstraße. Its large broadcasting room had a trapezoidal shape. The features included recording rooms, moveable walls and a stalactite ceiling (*Stalaktitendecke*) to subdue background noises.

Animal Radio

In the 1929 *Jahrbuch* an illustration entitled 'The *Deutsche Welle* brings stimulation to everyone' depicted a large bubble, with the word 'Everyman' in it. It was abutted by smaller bubbles labelled 'Parents, Teachers, Educators', 'Art Lovers', 'Children and Pupils', and other small bubbles with 'Housewifes and Mothers', 'Doctors', 'Lawyers', 'Civil Servants', 'Farmers', 'Traders', 'Workers' – and these were further specified as manual and office workers, 'artisans' and 'technicians'.[225] All these groups had been brought into proximity, but they also possessed worlds for themselves and radio needed to address them all. There was another group bound into radio transmission from the start: animals. A collage of images depicted animals, from elephants to seals to birds, conveying their 'voices' on radio.[226] To whom did they communicate? What did they say? Perhaps theirs was the sound of a modernity yet to be deciphered. A cartoon a few pages on showed a man holding a bird up to a microphone. Musical notes rose from its beak. Somewhere else on the network a cat listened and curiously poked its nose into the receiver. There were photographs of lions in front of microphones. The capture of animal noises surfaced from time to time. On 15 May 1932 the *SWZ* printed a picture: a pair of shoes could be seen, a body bent over, holding sound equipment close to a number of chickens in a coop.

Radio Models

'Here, we will first have to develop a series of models and counter-models of techniques of negotiation', said Schoen in his conversation with Benjamin.[227] He went on to provide three examples. The first was an interaction with the boss,[228] which could be a prediction of a *Hörmodell* first broadcast on Radio Berlin, on 8 February 1931, under the title 'How Do I Deal with My Boss?' ('Wie nehme ich meinen Chef?') and later on Frankfurt Radio on 26 March 1931, as 'A Pay Raise?! Whatever Gave You

That Idea!' ('Gehaltserhöhung?! Wo denken Sie hin!').[229] 'A Pay Raise?!' was written by Benjamin and Wolf Zucker. The Frankfurt broadcast was directed by Schoen and it aired during the evening, between 20:30 and 22:00. It was followed by a discussion between a workers' representative and its co-author Dr Benjamin. The second and third examples of models and counter-models were on crime and divorce.[230]

Slogans

In his 'Conversation with Ernst Schoen', Benjamin quoted his interlocutor as saying 'Give every listener what he wants, and even a bit more (namely, of that which *we* want)'.[231] Was there a match between what audiences want and what the programmers want? Could one lure the other, pull them towards an idea of what was worth listening to, develop them culturally, educationally, politically? And who was this *we*: the crypto-Communists and radicals of the radio station, who were at odds with the radio authorities? Radio was a medium, as Hans Flesch thought, with political and social functions.[232] But to what ends? Did the audience know what it wanted or get what it was given? The German Communist Party in 1932 asserted what they wanted when they graffitied a slogan on a fence, encouraging listeners to tune in to Radio Moscow: 'Clear the tracks for red radio'.[233]

Archive Towers

When we first met Alexander Schoen, he reported that his father was one of the first people to broadcast internationally from the Eiffel Tower. Perhaps a vinyl record still existed of the event.

One day at the archive of the Akademie der Künste in June 2021, looking through the 1930 *Rundfunk Jahrbuch*, we discovered a photograph of a group of people huddled on the side of the Eiffel Tower. It is captioned: 'Roaming Microphone 1: Report from the Eiffel Tower in Paris to the Frankfurt Station'. One of the figures in a white shirt, hair slicked back, looked like Schoen. Then a second image, perhaps a celebration before or after the transmission. The caption: 'Roaming Microphone 2: In the Antoine beauty salon in Paris'. Schoen now has a jacket on, surrounded by

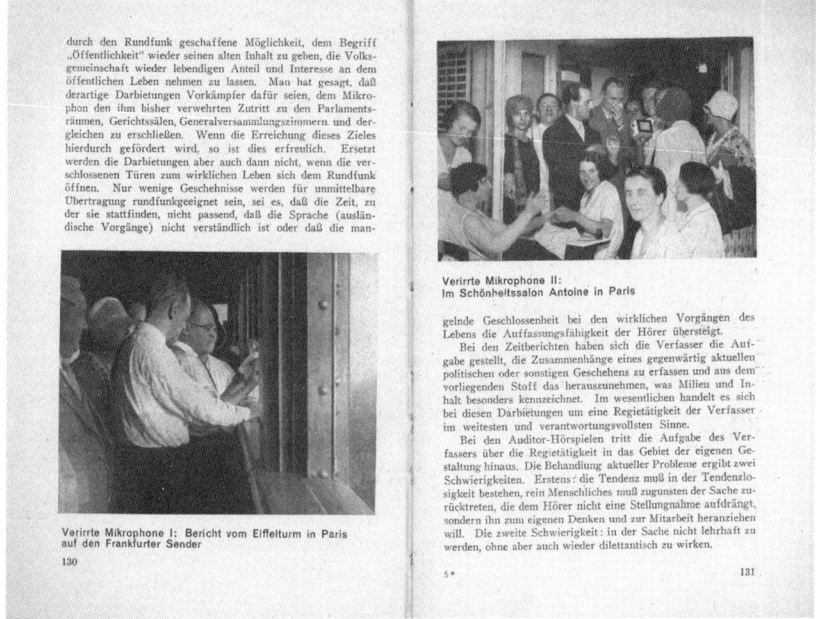

durch den Rundfunk geschaffene Möglichkeit, dem Begriff „Öffentlichkeit" wieder seinen alten Inhalt zu geben, die Volksgemeinschaft wieder lebendigen Anteil und Interesse an dem öffentlichen Leben nehmen zu lassen. Man hat gesagt, daß derartige Darbietungen Vorkämpfer dafür seien, dem Mikrophon den ihm bisher verwehrten Zutritt zu den Parlamentsräumen, Gerichtssälen, Generalversammlungszimmern und dergleichen zu erschließen. Wenn die Erreichung dieses Zieles hierdurch gefördert wird, so ist dies erfreulich. Ersetzt werden die Darbietungen aber auch dann nicht, wenn die verschlossenen Türen zum wirklichen Leben sich dem Rundfunk öffnen. Nur wenige Geschehnisse werden für unmittelbare Übertragung rundfunkgeeignet sein, sei es, daß die Zeit, zu der sie stattfinden, nicht passend, daß die Sprache (ausländische Vorgänge) nicht verständlich ist oder daß die man-

Verirrte Mikrophone II:
Im Schönheitssalon Antoine in Paris

Verirrte Mikrophone I: Bericht vom Eiffelturm in Paris auf den Frankfurter Sender

130

gelnde Geschlossenheit bei den wirklichen Vorgängen des Lebens die Auffassungsfähigkeit der Hörer übersteigt.

Bei den Zeitberichten haben sich die Verfasser die Aufgabe gestellt, die Zusammenhänge eines gegenwärtig aktuellen politischen oder sonstigen Geschehens zu erfassen und aus dem vorliegenden Stoff das herauszunehmen, was Milieu und Inhalt besonders kennzeichnet. Im wesentlichen handelt es sich bei diesen Darbietungen um eine Regietätigkeit der Verfasser im weitesten und verantwortungsvollsten Sinne.

Bei den Auditor-Hörspielen tritt die Aufgabe des Verfassers über die Regietätigkeit in das Gebiet der eigenen Gestaltung hinaus. Die Behandlung aktueller Probleme ergibt zwei Schwierigkeiten. Erstens: die Tendenz muß in der Tendenzlosigkeit bestehen, rein Menschliches muß zugunsten der Sache zurücktreten, die dem Hörer nicht eine Stellungnahme aufdrängt, sondern ihn zum eigenen Denken und zur Mitarbeit heranziehen will. Die zweite Schwierigkeit: in der Sache nicht lehrhaft zu werden, ohne aber auch wieder dilettantisch zu wirken.

5*

131

Figure 2.10 Double spread from *Rundfunk Jahrbuch*, published by the Reichs-Rundfunk-Gesellschaft in Berlin, 1930.

No photographer listed.

fashionable types, possibly among them Helen Hessel, fashion journalist and acquaintance from Berlin who was also involved in the broadcast.[234] On the following page is the start of an article entitled 'Music and Hörspiel', by Ernst Schoen.

The sight of the photograph hit us: this moment, from 3 September 1929, we thought had been lost, left unseen. Schoen's name is nowhere near his image on the page, it could only be found by flicking through and recognising the scenario and his frame and clothes. It felt like seeing an old friend. A couple of months later the image also appeared in the *SWZ*.[235] This caption confirms it is Schoen and that he is standing with Dr Paul Laven. The caption notes that it is a 'microphone that has gone astray'. The modern experimenter could clamber to the top of a mast and send signals across borders. And then descend into echoing underworlds of the metropolis.

Broadcasting Trotsky

At 18:05 on Wednesday 8 January 1930, Frankfurt Radio broadcast a reading from Leon Trotsky's autobiography *Mein Leben* (My Life). Ernst Schoen is listed as *Referent*, as contributor.[236] It was preceded by a light concert of Mozart and Dvořák.

Citizen Radionists

The final articles in the 1930 *Jahrbuch* considered listenership, the concentration of radio shops, the ways in which people could help the development of radio, whether through reporting on interference or becoming young radio hams. The author admonished those who show insufficient community spirit in radio clubs, using them as places to complain about technology or programming. The journal closed with 'Ten Rules', which included checking antennae, not complaining, not fiddling with the receiver, not playing the radio too loudly, connecting with groups and clubs and spreading the word of the joys of radio to friends.[237]

Blind Films

A reprint of a 1928 lecture by Hans Flesch, eventually published in the 1931 *Jahrbuch*, raised the question of the relation of the film and recording to the *Hörspiel*, or rather what was specific to each and how a purely acoustic medium could come into proper existence. How could a play be written and performed specifically for radio with its unique technical capabilities, rather than relaying a traditional performance of a play in front of the microphone? How could the form be developed for radio with the same precision that film provided? The solution, for Flesch, was to use sound film as a recording and editing mechanism, to cut out any accidental sounds and to allow the incorporation of montage, overlays and other devices. Indeed, two years after Flesch's speech, in 1930, Walter Ruttmann used the sound strip on film to make his radio play – or 'blind film' – called *Weekend*. The following article, indeed, logged the broadcast of *Weekend* on Berlin Radio on 13 June 1930, along with F. W. Biscoff's *Hallo, Welle Erdball!!* (Hello, Wavelength Earth Speaking!!), which was subtitled 'sound symphony'.[238]

Radio With Pictures

Hans Flesch and Ernst Schoen co-authored an essay on 'Music in Radio' in a reflective section of the 1929 *Jahrbuch* on the state of affairs five years after the start of German radio. Music, as their opening statement put it, was the easiest thing to think of in relation to radio. It appeared to be transmittable without limit. A wealth of musical treasures lay at the radio's disposal. Any problems concerning a true-to-reality reproduction of the musical artwork appeared to be small and simple to overcome. Technological development allowed constant progress towards being able to broadcast impeccable musical reproduction. Despite all of this, they noted, music on the radio and reflection on music on the radio was the most difficult thing of all. Sound reproduction was good and the radio could broadcast lectures and concerts. But absent from all of this, they claimed, was something that more and more radio offerings were addressing: 'the domain of existence of artistic sensation'. At issue was the transmission of contemporary music, 'sound art' that required support from its equally new medium. It was not just musical history that deserved to be aired. Radio music needed to be able to deal with modern music. The highlights of the year in music were outlined, including Schoenberg's own conducting of an early work. It was the Frankfurt station, where both writers were based, that was the most committed to music and in particular contemporary music, 'cultivation of which for a whole gamut of reasons belongs to the main areas of its activity'.[239] Paul Hindemith, Béla Bartók, Philipp Jarnach, the Baden-Baden Music Festival, Ernst Toch and Kurt Weill and Franz Schreker and others were supported by commissions from radio. Radio became a patron of the arts.

Flesch also wrote a second piece on radio music for the year-book. It began with the observation that radio occurred inside the home of the listener. Because of this, it was easier to affect the listener spiritually – but this meant there were more obligations. Flesch observed how music played by non-professionals used to involve a sometimes laughable and ambitious amateur dilettante attempting the classics, plagued by the lack of opportunities to hear talented musicians perform the works and squeezed by a lack of time to practice. He noted more modest efforts on the part of amateur players to play extracts from 'the greats' in order to improve their appreciation and understanding of the music. They had only rare opportunities to hear it in concert. The arrival of the gramophone and the broadcasting of concerts made these attempts somewhat redundant, as audiences could listen to excellent reproductions of works by professional players. Flesch worried that the technical mediation of the works was preferred to the experience of it inside an overcrowded concert hall. The 'divine spark' could not be conveyed in this way.[240] Radio, he insisted, had to develop the capacity to understand the difference between different modes of listening and not be complicit in the 'mechanisation of the masses'. Radio was mediator and preparer and thus remained a servant of the work, aiding listeners to attain artistic enjoyment by taking up into themselves what Flesch called 'the score for everyone'.[241] It was not a question of learning the formal aspects of music, but of hearing compositions again and again and absorbing the music. Flesch's attention turned to new music, music that was made for radio from the very beginning. He imagined a music not yet in existence, made of the peculiarities of electrical oscillations and he dreamt of continuing advances in microphone technology. And he returned to the location of where these efforts were received: in the home, the most intimate setting, to which we are most 'connected'.[242] The grand symphonies of Beethoven and Strauss were hardly emotionally bearable in concert halls, let alone the home. More subdued works were better suited here.

What forces might radio have unleashed on us, the domestic listener connected to a greater world? Flesch concluded with a quotation from Thomas Mann's *The Magic Mountain* (1924): 'Music, as a final incitement to the spirit, is invaluable — as a force which draws onward and upward the spirit she finds prepared for her ministrations.'[243] The article was followed by reflections on the psychology of the radio music listener and what type of effect was developed in relation to technical mediation. There followed perspectives from four contributors. One, Jaeger, considered the aural torture endured by city dwellers subjected to urban noise, including that of workers in the factories. This prevented them from developing a sense for music and so a particular music needed to be developed specifically for them. Flesch's contribution noted that film music existed in order to cut off the sense of listening and to allow focus on the visual elements. How was it different in the home, he wondered. There was nothing special to grab our attention at home and so our listening sense prevailed, he insisted confidently. The radio listener had open eyes, but did not see, because thought processes had been stimulated: The radio listener 'is especially receptive to the effects of radio', stated Flesch in a round-up of radio opinions.[244] Listener *was* receiver.

Dummy Heads (Still Life)

From the start, radio was a technical pursuit, as understood by radio hams and hobbyists. Many radios were constructed from kits and they could be mended, exchanged, adapted, improved. Neologisms emerged: *Funktechnik* and *Funkwissen*,[245] radio-technique or -technology and radio-knowledge. *Rundfunk*, the word for radio, was a new coinage by Hans Bredow in 1923, specifying radio waves that transmitted in a circle. To help out and inform the enthusiast, the supplement *Radio-Umschau* (Radio Survey) began to appear as an insert into the *SWZ*. It was edited by Leipzig-based electrical engineer Dr Peter Lertes, who also wrote an early book on electronic music, one on wireless telegraphy and various works on radio clubs, as well as co-inventing the Hellertion and the Heliophon. The pages of *Radio-Umschau* were scattered with frequency tables and diagrams of circuits, including valves, wires, switches, resistors and potentiometers.

In his 'Conversation with Ernst Schoen' (1929), Benjamin quoted Schoen on the infrastructure of the radio: 'the scraggly figure of the loudspeaker, or of headphones bulging on ears like tumours with the hanging entrails of the cord', and argued that it was suited to the 'poetry of Aragon or Cocteau, or to a painting by Beckmann or, better, de Chirico'.[246] This paraphernalia of radio – headphones, cables, microphones, projectors – was the stuff with which the new poetry and new art must engage. But also, they became parts of bodies, next to bodies, wired up to them. The loudspeaker was a figure, the headphones growths, the cords entrails. Radio and its technical means become the subjects of literature and painting, but more than that, they might be the most necessary subjects for modern artworks.

This artistic-technological tendency was rendered in a painting by Willi Baumeister, a neighbour of the Schoens in Frankfurt – Baumeister at number 26 Fuchshohl, the Schoens at number 20. Painted in 1930, *Still*

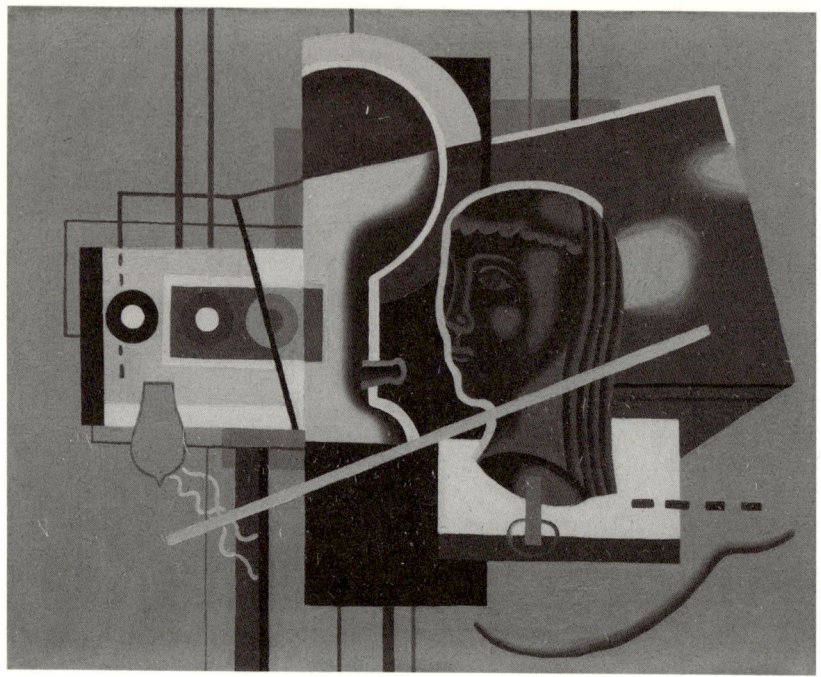

Figure 2.11 Willi Baumeister, *Still Life*, 1930; oil on canvas; 26 x 32 1/4 inches; Saint Louis Art Museum, Bequest of Morton D. May.

Copyright: 2022 Artists Rights Society (ARS), New York/VG Bild-Kunst, Bonn.

Life with Head (Stillleben mit Kopf) was a gift for the Schoens. The head of a woman, modelled on Schoen's wife, Johanna, was in profile, an outline, tending towards a Bauhaus-style abstraction or a diagrammatic image by Fernand Léger. The head, chopped at the neck and placed on a rod, was as smooth as the newly deployed dummy heads inseparable from sonic recording. These arrived in the 1920s – sleek, almost featureless heads, the size of a human one, with little holes for microphones for binaural recording in concert halls or for radio drama. The ideal but artificial listener received sound vibrations on behalf of a listener to come.

In Baumeister's painting, arranged around the dummy head were the dials, amplification and antenna of radio, an imitation of the diagrams in *Radio-Umschau* and other publications. Painting was still and silent. This painting, with its name *Stillleben mit Kopf*, punningly included the German word for silence – *still*. Baumeister had been a Dadaist. His subsequent work, slick and cool, seemed far from the chaotic, anti-war clatter of Dada, but there was an echo in the dummy heads of the Marc Janco masks, danced in by Emmy Hennings at the Cabaret Voltaire in 1916 – those that evoked Hennings' own dolls and puppets, shaken angrily against a brutal world, her voice loudly declaiming poetry in an attempt to mobilise rhythm in order to remake all the values of the world. *Still Life with Head* came to hang in the house in Fuchshohl, shrill, of the moment, but soon to be lost in the years to come – silent to its origin, speaking perhaps elsewhere, displaced out of its context.

Flaubert

Benjamin's letters to Schoen just after the First World War were littered with references to Gustave Flaubert. On 27 February 1917 he wrote that he was 'busy reading' Flaubert's *Bouvard et Pécuchet* (1881), his 'most difficult work'.[247] Later, the next year, he wrote that he had now read all of Flaubert's novels except *Salammbô*, a novel he names as *Camet d'un fou* (though he expresses doubt) and *Novembre*.[248] On 26 May 1930, Frankfurt Radio broadcast *Flaubert Before the Public Prosecutor* by Ernst Schoen and Ludwig Marcuse. It appeared listed as a foreign programme worth hearing in BBC regional newspapers on 14 July.[249]

Hands

For the 1930 *Jahrbuch,* Hans Flesch contributed an essay on the artistic challenges of radio. Flesch emphasised the way that radio did not respect borders and so insisted on international programming. But crucial, he noted, were the efforts taken to persuade contemporary artists and authors to produce work that conveyed itself adequately on the radio. Frankfurt Radio led the way and Paul Hindemith was mentioned as one who rose to the challenge and laid the path for others. The Frankfurt station delivered a series of radio-specific compositions with work from Paul Graener, Ernst Toch, Hermann Reutter, Kurt Weill and many others, all examples of what he called 'musically-productive forces'.[250] The contribution was illustrated by a two-page collage of 'Hands in Radio', a photographic study by an artist named Sentke of hands cut from bodies plucking, bowing, fingering and striking musical instruments.

Constricting Circles

At the radio station, Schoen provided work for his old friends and contacts – those, for example, who had been around the journal *G*.[251] Critical thinkers were invited in: Benjamin, Adorno and Leo Löwenthal, among others. Alfred Auerbach, a left-winger who was a specialist in dialects and radio plays, appeared more than a hundred times, as did Dr Alfons Pacquet, a travel writer and a Quaker.[252] But it was not all that easy to openly support leftist politics at the station and it rapidly became ever more difficult. For example, in 1928, Hans Flesch had brought author Ernst Glaeser in to run the literature section. Glaeser was forced to leave SÜWRAG in 1930 because he had publicly stated his support of the Communist Party in an election appeal on the part of a proletarian-revolutionary writers' organisation. Politics and culture became squeezed.

Dada Delay

In 1930, Schoen engaged in a lengthy correspondence with Raoul Hausmann. It began, in June, with Hausmann's comment that his friend Kurt Schwitters had mentioned some possibility of lecturing opportunities at the radio station. Schwitters indeed was soon to present a 25 minute lecture on 'Form in Art and Typography' at 18:05 on 9 September 1930.[253] In the *SWZ* for that week, there appeared an accompanying article that brought abstract shapes into the popular magazine.[254] The raggle-taggle contents of this *SWZ* were enclosed by an amusing and rather Dadaistic cover with a working man leaning onto a traffic bollard in Munich – it gave way and the two of them, rubberlike, bent down towards the pavement.[255] The caption: 'The Rubber Traffic Bollard or The Wiser Head Gives In'.

Schwitters' article included a graphic by Constructivist Carl Buchheister, who collaborated with Schwitters in the late 1920s. In this 'single form variation', some sickles circled around an empty centre. Some of the sickle forms were flipped over. Schwitters commented: 'One recognises that an image that emphasises the centre simultaneously streams over its edges'. It was an image of dialectical form – perhaps with a slight gesture at a political interpretation with sickles and dynamic movement, containment and excess. A second reproduced image was an abstract composition by Wassily Kandinsky. His caption described how it, too, posited an organising centre and also lines that emanated or broadcast (*ausstrahlen*) outwards. The language could almost be mistaken for a conceptualisation of the radio station. A third reproduced image was one within Schwitters' style of *Merzbilder*, his name for his version of the Dadaist assemblage. A series of rectangles were laid at an angle, thereby breaking through the resistance of the lines of the frame and thereby emanating or broadcasting (*ausstrahlen*). Displaced circles produced tension.

The fourth art image was a composition by Mondrian from 1918. It had, Schwitters noted, no centre and no negative parts. For this reason, it did not spill or emanate beyond its borders. The other images were drawn from the realm of graphic arts. There was a receipt by Robert Michel for the Frankfurt seed shop Kahl, with its innovative and dynamic use of the arrow to communicate without words. A second advertisement was by Max Burcharzt for spiral springs, which divided its elements into groups for comprehensibility and used colour communicatively. A third example was a flyer for a Dutch cable factory by Piet Zwart – simple, dynamic, in tension and communicating graphically rather than with words. The final example was by Schwitters, a page from a catalogue for centrifugal pumps by Weisse Söhne in Halle. It was a table, a spreadsheet.

Schwitters remarked of his own work that the thickness of lines related to their function in dividing categories. It was not an overtly modernist piece. It was a very orderly and ordering piece – and not what one might associate with Dada or Merz. It was a functional work that conveyed information through numbers and codes and layout, just as the listings on the next and subsequent pages presented, more or less clearly, information for radio listeners so they might tune in at the right time to the desired programme.

Another former Dadaist was to be invited in to show a broader public what he could do in order to make sense of this modern age. Hausmann noted in his response to Schoen that he was about to travel for three months, but suggested some themes for the autumn: the new type of novel by Joyce, Lawrence, Dos Passos, Ehrenburg, Döblin, Jahnn and 'the virtually unknown Aage von Kohl'.[256] Another suggestion was the end of New

Objectivity and Surrealism in the visual arts. Hausmann suggested also reading fragments from a novel he was writing – perhaps *Hyle*, which he had started in 1927. He finished the letter by reminding Schoen that they were old acquaintances from Berlin and the circle around *G* and hoped that this would lead to employment. They agreed on the visual arts lecture, focusing on the end of New Objectivity – a twenty-five-minute lecture with a payment of 75RM and travel expenses of 75RM. This was to be recorded on 15 September at the Frankfurt station and Schoen noted in his invitation letter of 5 September that he would be glad to resume the acquaintanceship.

The correspondence continued. A letter on 19 September 1930 asked if the lecture had caused any consternation in the press. Hausmann offered to speak on simpler themes such as men's clothing, a long-held concern of the *SWZ*. In January 1931 he offered a lecture on film and noted that he was personally acquainted with Eisenstein, Dovzhenko and Ermeler and was a member of the League for Independent Film. On 22 September 1931, he mentioned his upcoming radio lecture on men's clothing. He had sent photographs to accompany it as an article in March 1931: an American moccasin shoe, a polo shirt with half-length sleeves and a beret plus sleeveless pullover and white trousers. He hoped that he might also still be able to deliver a talk on 'film and its development', which had been delayed because of a lack of time available in the programme for film discussions. Hausmann requested that it be broadcast in the near future or if not, that he received a fee despite the programme being pulled. In May 1932, Hausmann attempted to interest Schoen in some work he had done on the new photographic vision. On 2 June 1932, Schoen wrote in response to Hausmann's proposal of a conversation with Werner Graeff on 'what the photographer sees' with a curt refusal: 'It is too difficult conceptually for our listeners.'

Peace Plays

A contribution in the 1930 *Jahrbuch* by Hans Flesch reported from the Berlin Funkstunde studio and opened with a description of an experimental *Hörspiel* broadcast on 18 August 1929. The announcer preceded it with the following words: 'For radio, this wonderful synthesis of technology and art, en route to transmission, the line is true: In the beginning was the experiment.'[257] The essay was a plea for radio as an experimental form and noted that what seemed inconceivable – sport reportage or dance lessons – because of the missing visual aspect, became commonplace in time. The magazines helped to bring visuality to radio: dance lessons were published from time to time in the *SWZ*. Included in the *Jahrbuch* as an example of experimental practice was the script of the *Hörspiel* broadcast on 18 August 1929. It was by composer Werner Egk and writer Robert Seitz and titled *Ein Cello Singt in Daventry* ('A Cello Sings in Daventry'), an English town that became known for its mast, listed in Germany throughout radio directories and papers of the period. The programme featured a cantata for tenor, double choir and orchestra. The libretto – written in German and English, in the hope it might be picked up internationally – concerned a man assailed by the turbulence of the city, after having worked for ten hours in an office: train lights, sky signs, traffic lights, scurrying crowds, fortune tellers, match sellers, paper sellers. The 'sky-signs', or advertisements on the clouds, were persistent and followed the man into his home in a quieter side street. Consuming cigarettes and books did not enable him to shake off the bustle of the city. He turned on the radio and heard a cello broadcast from Daventry. Divided by sea and language, the man felt as if the foreigner was in his own home and playing for him: 'A faraway land calls out a greeting to me.'[258] An early radio play broadcast in Germany was about radio itself and its magical ability to bring peace – and that was peace between two nations who little more than a decade ago had been at war.

Stimme/Stutter

A recording of Schoen's voice is preserved from 10 October 1930. Entitled a 'Talk-Runde', it was a conversation between Schoen, Friedrich Karl Roedemeyer and Richard Plaut.[259] Schoen's recorded voice sounds rapid, clipped – the speed and the well-rehearsed and structured sentences apparently helped him to speak without faltering.[260]

Early on in our meetings, Sasha reported that his father spoke with a stutter apart from when he was on the radio. If talking is a thing and requires bodily things, so too the body might need extensions: technological objects, such a microphones and headphones. The voice is worked by the radio. On the radio, use of the voice *is* work.[261] It has to obey its demands.

The discipline that examined and diagnosed stuttering or stammering developed in the 1920s in the wake of the traumas of the First World War. Could Schoen's stammer have developed in childhood but remained with him in adolescence, because of the war? Was his very expression shot through by the events of that war (as, indeed, his friend Walter Benjamin thought)? In Schoen's post-war compensation file, he argues that events – of the Nazis – 'severely aggravated a nervous speech disorder.'[262] In this sense, the recording we have of Schoen's voice from 10 October 1930 is the recording of a voice at once fragile and suspended between two catastrophes.

Requiem for Berlin

> But your brother
> Is dead and dead
> Is the stone over him.[263]

The past lived on: from the war that started in 1914, from the aftermath of the war that ended in 1918, to the November Revolution and the quashed uprisings of 1918–1919. Kurt Weill's *Berlin Requiem* (1928) set words written by Brecht. It was a cantata for three male voices and wind orchestra commissioned by the Reichs-Rundfunk-Gesellschaft (State Radio Company) and initially called – as stated in the *Berliner Morgenpost* – 'Memorial tablets, epitaphs and death songs.'[264] Weill had started to write in a style suited to radio transmission: the acoustic restrictions of the broadcasting studio; the instrumental and orchestral possibilities favoured by the microphone; the spread of vocal registers and the harmonic limitations which radio imposes. Through the music, the city-dweller was confronted with death – a death not just of a person, but of possibilities of living – after a failed uprising and in the midst of world depression and uncertain futures.

The *Requiem* was intended to be broadcast on all stations, but Brecht had failed to show the poems to the Reichs-Rundfunk-Gesellschaft for prior approval. When the completed work was submitted in the spring of 1929, all but two stations – Frankfurt and Cologne – balked at airing it,[265] given the extent to which the cantata dwelt on morbid themes and brought into focus the bodies of those slaughtered during the uprising. It eventually premiered on Frankfurt Radio on 22 May 1929 with Hans Grahl, Johannes Willy and Jean Stern as soloists, accompanied by the Orchestra of the station, conducted by Ludwig Rottenberg. It was never to be performed in Berlin. The work of mourning was left unheard.

The Leipzig premiere of Weill's *Mahagonny* (1930) was interrupted by demonstrations in the stalls. One audience member was said to cite Goethe: 'An age is ending here and now, and you can say you were present.'[266] This age was ending, perhaps, but another was beginning. By 1933, after the total capture of the *SWZ*, along with everything else, by the Nazis, articles included titles such as 'The National Revolution Has Won.'[267]

Airship

In the 1931 *Jahrbuch*, a report detailed events around an accident that befell an English airship on 5 October 1930 – it was notable because the text had been written at the scene of the accident on the day it occurred. It was offered as proof of radio's 'mediating role that transcends time and space.'[268] The inside frame of an airship looked like a radio tower. It was a floating tower. Radio floated in and made waves that conveyed the news across the realm.

Promise

Like the surrounding culture of the time, radio was voluble and experimentation was its watchword. At the Frankfurt music festivals, experimental composition met new media and new technologies of musical and sonic expression, such as Jörg Mager's electronic microtone generator, the spherophon. Kurt Tucholsky noted cynically in 1930: 'Due to bad weather the German Revolution took place in music.'[269] It was a critical statement, a dig at the inability of the German revolutionary leadership to carry out a successful revolution – but perhaps it had a positive truth to it too. The new media and genres of radio, of recording, of music for avant-garde film, theatre and expressive dance, demanded experimentation and there were those who stepped up to that challenge.

Radio, as ceaseless chatter, as private whisperings or public pronouncements, as unconventional or educational, did not develop in overly experimental directions. It did, however, open a small window of experimentation. Schoen was able to explore radio's specific capacities and pushed the medium in various directions. Schoen attempted over many years to develop and theorise the possibilities of radio, writing weekly ideas and theses on radio for the specialist press. He published more than sixty articles in a German radio journal in the course of a few years. His motive was to counteract 'bourgeois laws of inertia'.[270] Radio was of social and political significance. It would overturn bourgeois sclerosis. It would teach about the modern world and its arrangements. It would democratise Germany.

Hans Flesch criticised the way in which cinema had simply tried to adapt theatre into its medium. The point of the new art was to find appropriate forms of expression, both cinematic and radiophonic. Indeed, there were those who argued that theatre was an outmoded medium and radio should work in coordination with sound film, as both were engaged in the technical reproduction of sound and with mass reception. In the late 1920s, imageless radio and soundless film seemed to exist at a perfect meeting point. In 1930, Alfred Braun, Berlin radio producer and announcer, stated: 'Radio is analogous to sound film alone – not to the theatre'.[271] In July 1932, a journal called *Blätter des Hessischen Landestheaters*, which Schoen wrote in on occasion, put out a special issue dealing with the state of theatre and radio.

Benjamin's contribution 'Theatre and Radio' was published alongside extracts from Brecht's essay, 'The Radio as an Apparatus of Communication'.[272] Extracts from a conversation between Ernst Schoen and Kurt Hirschfeld, a theatre director and dramaturg in Zurich, were also included.[273] Benjamin pointed to the potential of radio and theatre to meet in new forms, such as listening models and plays dealing with problems of everyday life, such as marriage difficulties and schooling. He noted that radio had at its disposal technological and technical resources and it was its role to generate cultural forms, formats, genres, styles that could take best advantage of these resources, while engaging large audiences. Citing Brecht's epic theatre as his model, he recommended radio approach drama from the perspective of the human in crisis – this is someone who was 'a reduced, debarred person subjected to various trials and judged'.[274]

Culture, he noted, was to be replaced with training, distraction with group formation, as sets of listeners form alliances, united by common interests and inclinations.

Schoen, in similar fashion to Benjamin, emphasised the pedagogical impact that radio might have, including through its remediation of classical theatre. A discussion of opera on the radio, for the BBC house yearbook in 1934, explored how ludicrous early attempts to broadcast opera in Germany had been, as the listener, like a latecomer to the auditorium, was forced to confusedly attempt to follow the action, but hampered, because the listener misses out on all sorts of cues and was exposed to the rumble of scene changes. At best, the performance acts as a record. Schoen writes:

That is why I agree with the relay of opera performances, as long as they are not regarded as artistic productions but as *reported* art – comparable to the reproduction of pictures in a book – and so long also as they are restricted to the proportion corresponding to the number of opera-adepts amongst listeners, and strictly limited to the best of their kind in matter and performance.[275]

The actual task of opera broadcasting, like other dramatic forms, consisted in this: 'the future lies with those broadcast producers who, like, for instance, the conductors Scherchen and Rosbaud in Germany – both bitter enemies of relayed opera – strive constantly for a form of radio-opera that is essentially original and its own.'[276] Schoen began his article with an anecdote from German radio some eighteen months earlier. There was to be an audio pageant of one of the former German Grand Duchies and so historians were consulted. One old scholar remarked on how one episode in the seventeenth century would lend itself especially to broadcasting, because of its wonderful costumes. The old failed to grasp not only the possibilities of the medium – they did not even understand its constitution. Schoen remarks that 'any child could have told the poor old man that it is not its purpose to make an exhibition of stage dresses and decorations in its transmissions, and that, in fact, its performances are largely done in shirt-sleeves.'[277] The participants are workers, not so different from the imagined audiences. The listeners are as intelligent as children, that is to say, they are radio's equal. Schoen advanced experimental modes in the context of technology, mass audiences, progressive politics.

Radio music would be 'music that is played nowhere'. Only 'works on the basis of electricity, tube technology and electromagnetic waves' are the appropriate form of radio music. And so, electronic composition was born.[278] For Schoen, radio could discover the laws of its medium through reporting, including talks and interviews, 'artistic programming which, due to the works and performers, is satisfactory to the most demanding of listeners', and the 'communication [...] of major events and important personalities', both scholastic and artistic.[279] He developed what has now become a customary form. The music that was presented on the radio station was introduced by a short lecture. In this way, he attempted to draw in new audiences to sounds and forms that would otherwise strike them as unfamiliar.[280] Radio was not a medium directed at elites. By law, the radio station had to develop in accord with cheap radios and aerials, so as to ensure that it be heard widely amongst 'broad circles of the middle class and the working class, who are not able to obtain expensive apparatuses'.[281]

New Routes

In 1929, Brecht experimented with theatrical and radio form with the work *Der Lindberghflug*. Integral to the work was the engagement of listeners with radio, characterised by Brecht in the essay from 1932 for *Blätter des Hessischen Landestheaters* on the possibilities of radio as 'a kind of resistance by the listener and for his mobilization and redrafting as a producer'.[282] The radio play was in cantata form, with music by Kurt Weill and Paul Hindemith and it was performed for broadcast by the Frankfurt Radio Orchestra. Weill was a proponent of 'absolute radio art', along the model of abstract 'absolute film', and in reference to his former teacher Busoni, whose 1907 manifesto had called for 'absolute music' through conscientious and long experimentation.[283] The sounds should be technical in a genuine sense.[284] On its first performance, at the Baden-Baden Chamber Music Festival, the composition was transmitted into a number of surrounding rooms from an area that had been temporarily set up as a broadcasting studio. The next day's concert performance had a stage divided in two, with one side occupied by the ensemble, chorus and speakers. This represented the radio. On the other side, behind a screen, sat one performer in shirt-sleeves, representing the listener. This figure sang the part of Charles

Lindbergh, the transatlantic aviator. Brecht had hoped that the radio version would have put the listeners in their homes in the role of Lindbergh, singing the part to complete it. Brecht developed the interactive aspects of his play subsequently, arguing that school classes should produce versions where they filled in the aviator's part. The practice was taken up in a certain way in a regular broadcast from autumn 1931 titled 'Music Making with Invisible Partners' (*Musizieren mit unsichtbaren Partnern*): chamber music was played on the radio with vocal or instrumental parts missing and the listener at home was invited to fill in.[285]

Composing Still

Schoen had found new ways to work with radio and musical theatre, composing two radio cantatas, *Die kleine Tages-Serenade* (1930) and *Der Tag des Herrn Karl*, which premiered on 30 May 1932 with Hanns Eisler's *Tempo der Zeit*.[286] The flyer for a performance at Darmstadt remains, alongside a listing of the performers: Heinrich Allmeroth, Regina Harre, Martha Liebel and Heinrich Kuhn. The serenade was also played in a live concert programme in February 1930 in Berlin, along with some compositions by Walter Gronostay and the public playing of two Deutsche Grammophon records, 'Lustige Hirtenweise' (Merry Pastorale) by Walter Gronostay and 'Modernes Schlachtgeräusch' (Modern Noise of Battle), probably by Edmund Meisel.[287] Preserved on vinyl is a record of Hansi singing 'Der Neugierige' from Schubert's *Die schöne Müllerin* (1823), accompanied probably by Ernst.[288] The lyrics:

> I ask no flower,
> I ask no star;
> none of them can tell me
> what I would so dearly like to hear.

> For I am no gardener,
> and the stars are too high;
> I will ask the little brook
> if my heart has lied to me.[289]

Schoen worked within the art song tradition, programmed them and wrote them.

Technical Furniture

Radio connected the big corporations to domestic space and advertising developed a complex language to communicate, in one image, new technological developments for consumers. The 1931 *Jahrbuch* opened with a full-page advertisement from Siemens: 'In the Signal of the Giant Dial', it read. A large radio dial arced the page, like a rainbow whose colours have been substituted with numbers and calibrations – an anti-rainbow, then. Siemens' radios had enlarged over ten years, and as the graphic showed, the bowed form in the number 2, representing the year 1921, is widened into a 3, to represent the year 31. In this way, graphic design tracked the expansion of the numbers of radio listeners across a decade. In 1921, the radio apparatus had at best two valves. By 1931 they had three. These valves allowed the broadcasting of high-quality speech and music and the receivers increased in sensitivity. Progress was assured. Overleaf was a full-page advertisement for Grawor-Sektorfar magnetic loudspeakers available at Grass & Worff: '100% Dynamic'. The word 'dynamic' blared from the sound membrane in the sketch of a radio speaker, widening upon exit, like soundwaves spreading across a room. The design was reminiscent of Soviet modernism and was perhaps an example of Greenberg's kitsch, whereby avant-garde visual innovation became commercial hooks. In any case, this table-top speaker with its four-pole double power system had a luxury casing in walnut.[290]

1931 Listings (Snapshot)

One article in the *Jahrbuch* introduced the work of the Berlin 'Funk-Stunde' in transmitting current day affairs and events. There is the 'Interview of the Week', and examples given included Dr Curt L. Heymann and Rabindranath Tagore on contemporary India, the actor Max Pallenberg and the Minister for the Occupied Territories, G. R. Treviranus. A panoply of voices was brought in to comment on politics and art and other things in the news. Of special note was a talk from Minister of Justice Prof. Dr J. V. Bredt on Article 48 of the constitution, which two years later would come to play a devastating role in German history.[291] Amidst all the sport reportage and medicinal chat and literary reviews were also more controversial themes, such as Alfred Mühr and Ernst Toller debating 'the Cultural Bankruptcy of the Bourgeoisie', Dr Paul Friedländer and Josef Joos on 'Political Education of the Youth', alongside discussion of rationalisation and unemployment, as well as reflection on the technical and artistic potentials of radio – an ever-present theme. Of the numerous names listed in one article – those of composers, playwrights, politicians, directors, technicians, critics and so on – all were male, apart from one of the authors of the 'Story of the Week': Alice Berend.

Speaking Back

In 1932, Brecht wrote that radio 'is purely an apparatus for distribution, for mere sharing out'.[292] The listener had been pacified, insulated, made to sit back to receive only handouts. Their reactions were privatised. From this position, Brecht made a proposal to:

change this apparatus over from distribution to communication. The radio would be the finest possible communication apparatus in public life, a vast network of pipes. That is to say, it would be if it knew how to receive as well as to transmit, how to let the listener speak as well as hear, how to bring him into a relationship instead of isolating him. On this principle, the radio should step out of the supply business and organise its listeners as suppliers. Any attempt by the radio to give a truly public character to public occasions is a step in the right direction.[293]

There had already been attempts to deal with this problem of passivity. The 1930 *Jahrbuch* reports from Frankfurt on the *Hörspiel*, specifically the 'Auditor' series, whereby listeners were included in the process by giving them the roles of judge and jury, as in a courtroom. Another *Hörspiel* on current affairs asked listeners to comment, in the hope they would think for themselves rather than deliver ready-made standpoints. To listen to the radio was to both audit the events of the work and be provided with the opportunity to comment in response.

New Frankfurt, New Houses

To be modern is to be always modern, ever renewed. Fritz Wichert spoke of the necessary 'vitalization of radio', even something so young needed constant refreshing. And his envisaged mode of 'vitalization' was to set about programming by using the energy of 'a fight'. Wichert devised a lecture format to achieve this in which 'polar, antithetical or contrary' lectures were delivered in a series titled 'Thoughts on the Time'. In 1927, Le Corbusier, who had designed a modern housing estate in Stuttgart, battled against Paul Schultze-Naumburg, who was working on his book *Art and Race,* eventually published in 1928, a tract that would become a key ideological text for the National Socialists in the coming years.[294] Radio – as much as architecture – was a battleground.

The pages of the *SWZ* tracked the building of a new city more widely. In 1926, an article documented new industrial constructions: market halls, gas works, cranes, chimneys.[295] Construction sites also became part of a vision. In 1930, the front cover of the newspaper showed a worker hovering above a pit, his face reflected in its surface. Wooden pollards jutted out. It appeared as a photomontage, but it was a photograph of construction itself. In the new age, buildings curved.[296] The city took on a new face.[297] On 5 January 1931, there was a programme scheduled on today's glass architecture by Dr Curt Gravenkamp.[298] The newspaper ran an article to compliment it. Mies van der Rohe's glass house in Berlin was featured, alongside Edwin Gutkind's children's house in Berlin-Lichtenberg, as was a house with a large window that looked out onto a forest. The Bauhaus was featured a year later, for a broadcast on 14 February 1931.[299] A love letter to modernism. In 1932, the paper ran an image of a cross section of a house. In it everyone and everything had its place.

Slime Radio

One article, by Martin Rockenbach, from the 1931 *Jahrbuch*, considered poetry in relation to radio, through a negative assessment of radio by Hermann Hesse in *Steppenwolf* (1927). It quoted a point in the novel where the protagonist Harry has been shown a wireless set belonging to his landlady's nephew. Harry considered the nephew 'a victim to the charms of wireless', a worshipper before the 'god of applied science', dedicated to an instrument that can only prove, and imperfectly at that, a long-held wisdom about facts and forces held by thinkers for thousands of years. Hesse wrote:

I told her that the omnipresence of all forces and facts was well known to the ancient Jews, and that science had merely brought a small fraction of this fact into general use by devising for it, that is, for sound waves, a receiver and transmitter which were still in their first stages and miserably defective. [...] The discovery would be made – and perhaps very soon – that there were floating round us not only the pictures and events of the transient present in the same way that music from Paris or Berlin was now heard in Frankfurt or Zürich, but that all that had ever happened in the past could be registered and brought back likewise. We might well look for the day when, with wires or without, with or without the interference of other sounds, we should hear King Solomon speaking, or Walter von der Vogelweide. And all this, I said, just as today was the case with the beginnings of wireless, would be of no more service to humans than as an escape from themselves and their aims, and a means of surrounding themselves with an ever denser mesh of distractions and useless activities.[300]

Rockenbach wanted to counter the idea of a flattening out of culture through radio, placing his hope in the fervent desires of youth to develop their innerness. He also picked apart the vague and speculative nature of Hesse's claims about the unreality of time and space. Rockenbach challenged a scene later in the novel, where Harry described the experience of a half-dream, a magical theatre of fantasy, in which Mozart switched on the radio and Handel's *Concerto Grosso* in F Major played. He heard 'the devilish tin trumpet spit out, without more ado, a mixture of bronchial slime and chewed rubber, which the owners of gramophones and subscribers of radio have agreed to call music.'[301] This was distortion. Mozart was wielding the last weapon of art's extermination. Mozart was teaching a lesson – the glory of the music remained somewhere in the air, but the radio demonstrated only its own clueless mechanism, 'its spiritless business-doing.'[302] Radio was a site of struggle: between idea and appearance, eternity and time, divine and human. It turned a glorious tone into slime, spoilt it, scratched it. It was all we had, because this was our life, our world, our modern world. Radio was an analogy for a world that was vaguely miraculous and largely foul. But all this criticism, all this existential hatred of the mechanical, would be resolved, stated Rockenbach, if Hesse could be sent the latest, most technically accomplished receiver.

In opposition to Hesse's scepticism, Rockenbach proposed the writer Hans Heinrich Ehrler, who had embraced radio. Ehrler championed the act of speaking to his compatriots through a little can, reaching thousands of ears, his lips forming syllables, with tone and colour, not the voice of a metal membrane or a tinny hum. It was a hidden mouth with magical sounds that swooped across the land. Perhaps to mitigate the fact that Ehrler was a reactionary (who would indeed be drawn in a few years to the *Nationalsozialistische Deutsche Arbeiterpartei* [NSDAP]), the author also evoked a working class that was hungry for experience and education and sought its soul in radio by listening to the worker-poet Johannes Becher and his 'Ballad of a Radio-listening Farmhand.'[303] In Becher's ballad, reprinted in the volume, a young man thought about how his father once held a shell to his ear and told him to listen to the sea. The father died and the shell was lost and the boy was taken on as a vassal and worked hard. One day on the farm, an aerial was erected and a radio installed. The waves flooded in – the boy, everyone there, could hear the world. The radio replaced the shell – it opened out beyond the small parameters of life. It brought the ocean back to the boy, but his hard work did not stop and he wondered if the roar he heard was the roar of the cities and their streets. Something was offered but could not be taken. Not yet. Something threatened. In the pubs, the skat players asked each other 'Do you hear the sea?':

> And they snoop –
> And we: the sea
> Flow through the streets and crackle.[304]

Sea, radio, revolution all collapsed into one great wave.

State and Feelings

An address by Hans Bredow, published in the 1931 *Jahrbuch*, was followed by an essay from the minister Hans Goslar, on the relation between the state and radio. The contemporary state, he argued, must remain in close and direct contact with its people and it must consider those people as a social whole. Radio made it possible to address everyone, not just specific classes or groups, or party adherents. It allowed multiple perspectives, experiences, lives to come to voice, to be aired, in order to spread knowledge and culture and generate empathy and understanding. When Goslar used the term for the radio receiver, *Empfangsgerät*, it was as if the listener became a receiver, but the German word *empfang* resonated with the word for feeling, *empfinden*. The simple line drawings that accompanied the essay illustrated a worker and a peasant and an intellectual and a businessman shaking hands and looking each other in the eye. The types were clearly demarcated, but they had to be brought together under a common umbrella of interests. To develop a relationship between state and people, the author recommended improvised talks from ministers about the day-to-day life of the state.[305] Goslar recalled a summer's day in a small central German spa town with a loudspeaker conveying the morning ceremony of parliament and the evening ceremony of the Berlin authorities as they honoured the Constitution from the *Sportpalast* (Sports Palace). There he was, in the countryside, far from the capital and yet he and the nation participated 'in the same rhythm and pulsebeat,'[306] in a 'feeling' that rolls like a wave across the whole land. There was no longer one central place separated from a locality, but rather the breathing of the same air and a common *Reich* of experience.[307]

BBC Afar

German radio tracked the work of the BBC. In an article from December 1932, Sir John Reith's face stared out, like a death or Halloween mask. Photos of the new Broadcasting House adorned the page. The bright façade on Regent Street loomed (in a photo that is almost identical to one published in the *BBC Year-Book* from the same year – even the shadows fall across the building in the same way[308]). The chapel, with zodiac symbols atop, was also in the year-book, captioned: STUDIO FOR RELIGIOUS SERVICE. Beside was a picture of Eric Gill's statue of Prospero and Ariel ready to be hoisted into place on the front of the building. And there was the corner of a studio room (*Geräuschraum*) with the modern materials all listed – wood, metal, rubber, felt and granite.[309] The *SWZ* named the room: 6D. On the corner are some water taps. An article from the 1932 *BBC Year-Book* clarifies the function. 6D is an effects room

equipped with machines for the production of every conceivable noise, and an important feature is a central elevating and rotating table, the top of which is fitted for the convenient manipulation of various small machines. The equipment also includes a large tank for water noises; an elaborate electrical effects group; a wind machine; a railway noises group; various types of floor materials for floor effects; a compressed air group, including hooters and foghorns; a small piano; a barrel organ; special doors for opening, shutting, slamming, etc.; suspended sheets for thunder; and drums of various sizes. The Gramophone Studio contains six turntables to be used for 'mixing' a variety of noises such as Bank Holiday noises, applause, etc.[310]

The *SWZ* article detailed the history of the BBC, costs of the new facilities and Reith's role. If Germany looked to Great Britain, Great Britain looked back. The BBC year-book for the same year kept a close eye on the technological and social situation of radio in Germany. A large aerial image of the newly constructed Berlin *Funkhaus* (broadcasting house) was included.[311] There were comments on Dr Bredow's visit to England in May 1931.[312] The BBC year-book discussed the differences between the organisations: decentralisation, for one, in Germany.[313] There was a long discussion of 'congestion in the ether', after the installation of a high-powered transmitter at Mühlacker, near Stuttgart. It interfered in the broadcasts across Great Britain, making a more or less continuous whistle or the sound of a German programme softly playing in the background.[314]

Time Running Out

On 29 July 1932, *Die Sendung* published an article. The question 'Wer macht die Rundfunkprogramme?' (Who makes the radio programmes?) was blazoned across a page with four images. Schoen was in the centre. To his left was Hans Rosbaud. To his right, Franz Wallner and Wilhelm Schüller. If the question were to be asked a year later, after the Nazi ascension to power, these names would have changed; so, too, did everything – the programming, the ethos – to ensure that those who remained were not targets of the new regime.

The organisation of German broadcasting as a network of nine financially independent regional companies, supported by private investment, was undergoing transformation. Up until this point, fifty-one percent of Reichs-Rundfunk-Gesellschaft shares were held by the Reichspost, which owned all the fixed assets and collected licence fees as well as providing the means of transmission and delivering the Marine Service and the Wireless Service, which conveyed news items on behalf of the government to the regional stations, from which they were able to choose what they wished to air. There had been many debates over the political uses of radio – with a declared tendency towards 'neutrality' or non-partisan programming or the scheduling of predominantly 'apolitical' content. This system was overseen by a series of centrist parties in coalition in government, led by the Social Democratic Party of Germany.

From 1929, more and more pro-government content had begun to appear on radio, with lectures and speeches by government officials and party representatives – this did not include Communists in the main.[315] From 1930, when the coalition collapsed and the government began to rule through presidential decree, the voices on radio reflected the interests of the incumbent government and its sense of what constituted permissible political debate. The Nazi vote was beginning to climb, until there was a stand-off between General Paul von Hindenburg and Adolf Hitler in 1932. President Hindenburg appointed Franz von Papen to government as Chancellor on 1 June 1932. In the campaign for the July 1932 parliamentary election, Nazis were allowed onto radio, along with other opposition parties, but the Communists were barred. These Nazi radio appearances – Georg Straßer on 14 June and 29 June 1932 and Joseph Goebbels on 18 June 1932 – were evidence of von Papen's desire to build links to the Nazi Party. His efforts to distance himself again later that year meant that the Nazis were given less airtime during the November 1932 election campaign.

Von Papen's presence as Chancellor triggered a large-scale reordering of broadcasting. In the second half of 1932, state control was firmly exerted and the regional broadcasting companies were centralised. The Ministry of the Interior took control. Von Papen's Interior Minister Wilhelm von Gayl decreed that each regional station devote an hour a day to a Berlin programme called *Stunde der Reichsregierung*, Government Hour. Ministers would be given the platform to hold formally 'unpolitical' speeches in favour of government policies.[316]

Such overt attempts to instil government-friendly propaganda into the listening masses were not very successful – and von Papen failed to attain a majority in the Reichstag in the November elections and resigned. He returned, appointed again by Hindenburg, as Vice Chancellor to Hitler's Chancellor on 1 February 1933. From then on, until the Parliamentary elections on 5 March, the Nazis began a radio campaign, with Hitler speaking on the radio sixteen times over five weeks. Other Nazi officials clogged the airwaves too and they blocked the appearance of most of the opposition parties. Goebbels, for one, was a commentator on the torch-lit procession for the Führer on the evening of 30 January 1933.

The pressure was being felt broadly. Dr Franz Wallner, who replaced Glaeser in the literature section at Frankfurt Radio, introduced some programmes on 'Neglected Poets' and also interviews with contemporary literary figures. In June 1932, he was denounced in a nationalist newspaper, *Deutsche Zeitung* and accused of favouring 'leftist' and 'non-German' artists,[317] and his programme was characterised as 'centrist-Marxist'. Schoen was effectively demoted, made answerable to the administrative manager Dr Wilhelm Schüller.

On 3 September 1932 Benjamin wrote to Adorno from Poveromo, Italy. Life was getting more precarious, work more unstable, friendship more fractured:

At the moment, however – and this touches upon my chances of getting to Frankfurt – I am even less than ever master of my own decisions. I know neither when I shall be able to return to Berlin nor how things will work out there. I shall almost certainly be here for the next few weeks. After that I shall probably have to return to Berlin, partly to deal with the problem of accommodation, partly because Rowohlt seems to be insisting on publishing my essays after all. In itself, however, the temptation to remain in Germany for any length of time is certainly not very great. There will be difficulties everywhere and those arising in the field of broadcasting will probably ensure that my appearances in Frankfurt are even rarer. If you happen to know how things are going for Schoen, please let me know. I have heard nothing from him. That is all for today.[318]

Schoen was unable to give Benjamin any more work at the station.[319]

Past Songs, Coming War

As progressive hopes faded, thoughts turned back to the doomy days before the war of 1914–1918. The friend who had ended his life in protest against war resurfaced as the proposer of a new language, one of complaint in song. In 1932, Schoen composed music for *Sechs Gedichte von Fritz Heinle* (Six Poems by Fritz Heinle).[320] If, as Benjamin pointed out in 1916 in 'The Role of Language in Trauerspiel and Tragedy', music was the language of pure feeling, then these songs represented a fractured expression of love, stretched out over a number of decades, between the dead and living:

Denying all mercy
Flying far towards the East
To which I delay admitting
Of any hidden illusion

It lies on cooling pillows
Stored over time
With fluctuating conscience
Ready for torment or for action.

When I awake each morning
As in a lighted mirror
My hands reach up
To feel my face.
When I awake at night
The shadows don't betray my hands
The mirror cracks.

Over the hill with sharpest views
Cries suppressed in glowing illusion
Beneath feathers, nodding spitefully
Fortunately sprayed into the sunshine.
While little frogs in valleys
Croak in fear with tripping steps
Decorated with wandering daisies
In procession crying coarsely.

Believe that you remain
With awakening illusion
The night – the night – slumbers deeply
Into sleep.
Only your dreams know
You are tearfully alone in your pillow
Quite small.

Sweet pain, silent pain
Love is never still
Divides the flowers and flees away.
Swings upwards, swings upwards in deep waves
Up towards the proud dream circle
To where one must return.
Sweet fortune, smallest thing
Can only be granted by love, brought by love
That no one can completely win.

Jubilation was served
Your sinking voice still just ready
Meets the clatter of the rider
Reflecting in bed
On the empty joy
That every honest cadet
On horseback will proclaim.[321]

Memories of Heinle returned, like a refrain or chorus. Schoen was not the first to evoke his friend in the form of song or lyric. Benjamin had written a series of sonnets, which directly mourned his friend's death: a conjuration of poetic telepathy to communicate with a dead friend who had entered a transcendent realm.[322] It had been Benjamin who met Heinle in Freiburg-im-Breisgau, where both were enrolled in the university and involved in the youth movement. Happy in each other's company, they hiked in the surrounding countryside and made merry in taverns by night. Benjamin wrote excitedly to his school friends in Berlin of his new acquaintance. He had introduced him to the circle. Here is one of Benjamin's Sonnets for Heinle.

> Sonnet 34
> I sat one night to ponder on myself
> And round me thy sweet life did stir
> The mirror of my mind glanced back
> As hadst thou just looked out from in its depths
> Then came the thought: Thou sucklest me
> Into thy breath I shall my self surrender
> For like grapes hanging are thy lips
> Which have mute witness borne to inmost things
>
> O friend thy presence has been wrested from me
> Like one asleep whose hand looks for the wreath
> In his own hair so in dark hours I for thee
>
> Though once thy cloak did round me go
> As were there dancing and from within the midnight throng
> Thy look did snatch the breath out of my mouth.[323]

Benjamin read his seventy-three sonnets out loud to others in his circle, like an act of communion, broken telephony. So precious were these sonnets to him that he passed them to the librarian Georges Bataille in Paris in 1940, at the point when he knew he had to flee and must be parted from his archive. In her memoir, Charlotte Wolff wrote that the way Benjamin 'spoke of his friend, the poet Heinle, could leave one in no doubt about his love for him.'[324] Heinle's descent into muteness foreshadowed what Benjamin analysed as the poverty of communication in the post-war period. To bring voice, and song, to radio, was an effort to counter the silence.

Lichtenberg

As reaction took a firmer hold in Germany, Walter Benjamin worked on his final radio work, which had been commissioned by Berlin Radio.[325] It was a fantastical play about the physicist and astronomer Georg Christopher Lichtenberg, merged together with some ideas from Paul Scheerbart's astral novel *Lesabéndio* (1913). In the final months of the Weimar Republic, Benjamin burrowed into two authors that he and his friends had revered and discussed since their school days. The play was set on the moon, in a crater that had been named after Lichtenberg. The Moon Committee for Earth Research, all named after characters in *Lesabéndio*, were investigating humankind, who were represented by Lichtenberg. The committee was exploring human happiness or its lack. Benjamin adopted Scheerbart's inventive technologies from *Lesabéndio*, which perhaps seemed slightly less fantastical in a radio age. There was the Spectrophone, through which everything happening on earth was heard or seen. There was the Parlamonium, with the help of which human speech – which grated on the ears of the lunar inhabitants as they were used to the beautiful music of the spheres – was translated into music. And there was an Oneiroscope, which allowed the dreams of earthlings to be observed. The play opened as a broadcast to the audience of the meeting of the Moon Committee. On the back of his copy of the play that was never to be broadcast, Benjamin noted the results of the elections in Germany, perhaps as he heard them announced on the radio. One radio message – an electoral result – would be the means of eclipsing the other – the experimental radio play. Beneath his jotting down of percentages gained by the parties, with forty-four percent going to the Nazis, Benjamin drew a bird. He called it the *Wahlvogel*, the election bird, its wings seemingly broken. He who had to take flight drew an image of the flightless.[326] He who took flight was one of many who had to find a route out.

Voices, Circles

For the circle around Schoen and Benjamin, the practice of reading aloud went back to the *Lesekreis*, the communal readings of poems, the debates on student politics. It took on technological forms: reading aloud on the radio. On 4 March 1934 Adorno wrote to Benjamin, remembering an evening in November 1932, when Benjamin stopped off in Frankfurt on the way back from Poveromo: 'Incidentally, you were familiar not only with the general plan, but also with the two scenes (the cemetery and the haunted house) which I read out at Schoen's place, on the very same evening when you read us the first instalments of the Ar... (I nearly wrote: the Arcades! What a telling lapse!), no, of *Berlin Childhood*.'[327] Benjamin's voice was soon to leave the radio waves. Voices, at this point, were intimate, both transmitted publicly and uttered privately, soon to be dispersed along various lines of flight.

After the elections of March 1933, once the Nazis were affirmed in power, thorough reforms of broadcasting took place immediately, as part of a broader assault on the freedom of the press. At this point, all radio station employees deemed politically unreliable lost their posts. Evidence for dismissing Schoen was plain to see. Quite apart from who he had engaged to speak at the station and the experimental work he had advanced, his detractors might point to statements such as this, in an interview with the radio magazine *Die Sendung*, from 1932:

From the very beginning, I was of the opinion that radio has to be, in the broadest sense of the term, a political instrument. Politics I understand in general to be: applied morality.[328]

New Heads

As the Nazis seized power, the *SWZ* ran a headline: 'New Heads and New Voices on South West Radio'. The station and its newspaper had a new focus now – front covers celebrated the Nazi assemblies, such as the victory procession of the SA through the Brandenburg Gate by torchlight in January 1933, a Nazi Party Rally in Nuremberg and Potsdam Day in March 1933. Broadcast in full on the radio, Potsdam Day marked the reopening of the Reichstag, following the fire that had been reason enough for mass arrests of any opposition. In an article from the following year, military leaders towered large over a mass of bodies in a crowd making the *Sieg Heil* gesture. 'Work is the highest virtue,' declared one feature. The 'event against un-German books' was depicted. Youth wore uniforms. A musical concert under the title 'Strength Through Joy' was presented.[329] The German *Volksempfänger* radio was featured in the pages within months. The circumscribed nature of its reception – restricted to the local broadcaster and the German sender – was openly paraded. 'The national revolution is victorious.'[330]

During the tenth German radio exhibition, Goebbels gave a speech on 18 August 1933:[331] 'What the press was to the nineteenth century, radio will be to the twentieth.'[332] Radio was captured – and by 25 October 1933, it was possible to imprison Hans Bredow, whose stepping down had been reported as voluntary in the *SWZ*[333] On 15 April, Walter Beumelburg was to be made director of Südwest-Deutscher-Rundfunk, displacing Wilhelm Schüller. But Schüller was able to use employment protection law to stay in place until 30 September, when he left 'voluntarily', so to speak.[334] In one copy of *SWZ*, among a row of new heads was the new director of Frankfurt Radio, Beumelburg. A caption read: 'We come from war. Our purpose is to complete the revolution which began in August 1914.'[335]

One issue of the Nazi programme press, *Der Deutsche Sender*, devoted a full page to those who had been displaced and put on trial. A photograph, with the sneering caption 'Men of Merit', showed the arrival at Oranienburg, the concentration camp for political prisoners outside Berlin, of Kurt Magnus, Hans Flesch, Heinrich Giesecke, Alfred Braun, Friedrich Ebert (son of the first President of the Weimar Republic) and politician Ernst Heilmann. They stood before an SS officer, as for a roll call, in loose and crumpled suits. Beneath the photograph a number of men were shown in small head portraits, such as would have been used to affirm worth and status a year or so before. The roll call was not quite the same as on the photograph. Kurt Magnus was there, as was Giesecke. These two were managing directors of the Reichs-Rundfunk-Gesellschaft (RRG, Reich Broadcasting Corporation). Alfred Braun, of the Berlin drama programme, too. Hans Flesch appeared. There was also Secretary of State Hans Bredow, Dr Hans Roeseler of Silesian radio, director of the Mitteldeutsche Rundfunk AG (MIRAG, Mid-German Broadcasting Corporation) Fritz Kohl and radio pioneer Professor Friedrich Georg Knöpfke. At the bottom of the page a caption, in ironic tones, notes that this was a draft of a Roll of Honour for the 'Systemrundfunk', the Nazis' derogatory term for Weimar Radio.[336] Weimar democracy produced systems. Nazi autocracy was to cultivate something else.

Radio's capture was visible even on the outside of the radio house in Frankfurt. For example, on 11 November 1933, on the eve of Germany's plebiscite about leaving the League of Nations, the radio house was

Figure 2.12 The puzzle page from the *Südwestdeutsche Rundfunk Zeitung*, Frankfurt am Main/Kassel, 3 September 1933 (Volume 9, Number 36), p.7.

doused in light and, above the by now present eagle and the swastika, were words that read 'Whoever does not go to vote on 12 November is a traitor to the *Volk*'.[337] Several of the leaders of the 'System Radio' were put on trial. On 5 November 1934, proceedings began against nine figures accused of 'breach of trust in relation to commercial law', fraud, document falsification, favouritism and betrayal of a client. The accused were in the dock for eighty-nine days.[338] There were microphones in the courtroom and parts of the trial were recorded onto discs so that they might be played on the radio. One form of radio eclipsed its predecessor and felt fully justified in broadcasting the violence it sought to enact. The accusations could not be substantiated and in June 1935, Flesch, Magnus and Bredow alone were charged simply with financial mismanagement.

Radio was now on a war footing – the old guard had to be replaced. War was a reference point in this age of Nazi cultural war. On the front cover of the Westdeutscher Rundfunk AG (WERAG, West German Broadcasting Corporation) radio magazine for 24 September 1933, despite the fact gas masks impeded speech, the situation still required the soldier to broadcast in one. In the same way, newspapers continued to run images evoking the 1914–1918 war. Nazi radio suffused the atmosphere with its ideas and put the nation on total martial footing.

Solve The Iron Cross

The new fascist regime captured all aspects of life and culture. Even the puzzles – present in the *SWZ* from the start as squares and diamonds, but also animals and other forms, including ships and houses – were now composed of militarist iconography. On 3 September 1933, an iron cross – the symbol of German and Prussian militarism – appeared at the centre of a crossword. Solve the puzzle. In order to play you must already be at ease with the symbols of the state.[339]

On the radio, in April 1931, Walter Benjamin had described someone swept up in the Mississippi Flood as 'a shipwrecked person adrift on the wreck, having climbed to the top of the mast which is already torn apart. But he has the chance from there to give a signal for his rescue.'[340] The cry of protest, or for help, at a moment of crisis – shouts of *m'aidez! mayday!* – could be best made from this height, where a panoramic view is possible. At this point, the flood had engulfed the mast of the radio station, as much as the city.

3

Wires Cut and Crossed: 1933

There is a small, pocket-sized diary in Schoen's archive, printed for use in 1931, but overwritten with the events of 1933.[1] Time goes awry in this period of crisis. In a letter to Hansi, from London, on 29 November 1933, Schoen noted that it was around 6pm, but he could not be sure as, yet again, all the clocks had gone askew.[2] When Schoen was forced to flee a newly authoritarian state in 1933, he entered uncertain times. This 1931/33 diary is indicative of the problem of taking stock of this year and its sequence: a life had become untimely, its habits displaced, its traces muddled, confused, overwritten.

As Edward Said later argued, the exile is, quoting Wallace Stevens, held in a 'mind of winter', in which a

life of exile moves according to a different calendar, and is less seasonal and settled than life at home. Exile is life led outside habitual order. It is nomadic, decentered, contrapuntal; but no sooner does one get accustomed to it than its unsettling force erupts anew.[3]

Perhaps nothing encapsulates Schoen's life more than this statement.

The 1931/33 diary notes that Schoen was arrested on 3 or 4 March 1933.[4] This is corroborated in the files that document his case for compensation for damages accrued during the years 1933 to 1945. It stated, in official scrawl, that Schoen was held from 3 March to 7 March 1933, in the police prison in Frankfurt.[5] Some accounts claim that 'On 3 March 1933 [Schoen was] arrested for several days for political reasons'.[6] The arrest was recorded in the *Frankfurter Allgemeine* on 10 March 1933. The report, glued into a scrapbook kept by Schoen, reads:

Released from custody.

As communicated by the Tel. Union of the Direction of the Southwest German Radio A.G. the co-worker of the programme department Schön, was taken by the police into custody temporarily. In the meanwhile Schön has been set free once more. The reasons for the arrest could not be established.[7]

A testimonial letter was later provided for Schoen as part of a compensation case, on 5 August 1954, by his former colleague, the lawyer Kurt Magnus, who was the managing director of the Reichs-Rundfunk-Gesellschaft (State Radio Company) until March 1933.[8] Magnus swore under oath that Schoen was arrested for a few days around the beginning of March 1933. He noted, too, that he was arrested a second time in the middle of April 1933, after he had also been dismissed from the radio 'for political reasons'. Magnus was unable to attest to the length of the second arrest. The 1931/33 diary logs some precise dates. On 15 April, Schoen was taken into custody again. He was back home on 21 April.[9] A total of seven days. The file in the compensation case notes, in contrast, that he was in Hamburg's penal institution Fuhlsbüttel from 14–29 April 1933. The record is muddled.

Reasons given for the arrest are sometimes more specific. According to Sabine Schiller-Lerg and August Soppe's 1994 biographical sketch of Schoen's life, Schoen was rumoured to have tried to cut off the main radio transmission cable during an election hustings speech by Hitler.[10] Schoen wrote to Benjamin about this accusation, on 28 June 1933:

As a result of the elections of 4 March I was taken into custody, for the first time, for 48 hours. Reason given, as revealed by my very right wing lawyer, was an anonymous letter, in which it was established that – as was true – on the day of Hitler's election speech, I had a *Hörspiel* rehearsal at the Broadcasting Station. From that the charming conclusion was drawn that I might have wanted to sabotage the speech technically. A particular nicety is that I was driven in a private Nazi car with streaming pennant to cast my vote.[11]

Reference to the accusation was repeated in a letter sent from Schoen to his lawyer, Dr Fraustädter, in 1958.[12] An acknowledgement of Schoen's legitimate case for compensation, on 24 April 1954, gave the following reasons: he was a 'Mischling' of the first degree – his mother was Jewish. In addition, the acknowledgement stated that the reactionary press had attacked him from 1931 onwards.[13]

The events are related in the compensation file in the following way: After an anonymous claim that he had cut the transmission cable during a speech by Hitler, Schoen was arrested and brought to the police prison in Frankfurt. Simultaneously, he was dismissed with immediate effect from his position at the radio station. After four days in custody he moved with his family to Hamburg, where he was once more arrested. The reason given this time was for favouring Socialists and Jews at the radio station. Fraustädter's account notes that he then fled to England in May, as a result of his wife's interventions and attested that he was racially and politically persecuted.[14]

Dr Fraustädter's name crops up in Momme Brodersen's *Klassenbild mit Walter Benjamin: Eine Spurensuche* (Class Portrait with Walter Benjamin: In Search of Traces) (2012), a book that tracks the fates of those who appeared alongside Benjamin in a school class photograph from 1912. Brodersen describes Werner Fraustädter as 'a committed lawyer who, as a social worker, legal advisor and publicist, stood up for the rights of stateless people who had been displaced by the turmoil of war in the then German Reich'. Fraustädter was likely also a member of the Social Democratic Party of Germany.[15]

Schoen's compensation file provides numerous claims and reasons for his persecution. Exiles who seek redress were compelled to recount the circumstances of their oppression again and again, as if the experience of it were not enough to last a lifetime. According to a testimony related on 22 October 1952:

In March and then again in April 1933, I was arrested after anonymous accusations by a National Socialist. Had the efforts of my wife to release me from the second detention not succeeded, I would probably not have got away with my life.[16]

In another official statement, as part of the case for compensation, on 21 December 1953, the lawyer Willhelm Schüller, who had worked at the radio station with Schoen, stated that Schoen was persecuted on racial grounds, as he was a half-Jew, and also on political grounds.[17] Schüller adds that he was arrested because of baseless denunciations by a radio colleague who was desirous of his position. Kurt Magnus in his testimony, in February 1954, described him as a half-Aryan.[18] A friend, Else Mertens, for her part, in December 1933, stressed that he was 'politically persecuted'.[19] On 15 March 1954, Schoen submitted proof of his racial heritage through a photocopy of the release certificate of his mother from Theresienstadt Concentration Camp.[20] He also noted in this statement that the anonymous accuser had said he favoured Socialist and Jewish people in his programme making.

Another source of evidence about events in March and April 1933 is an account by Alexander (known to us as Sasha) Schoen: 'Mutti's Story', which he wrote in 2016. The story of his father's escape was passed down as family history over the decades, but elements of it were only disclosed after many years. Of the first arrest, Sasha wrote:

I was only three years old when the police arrested Ati [his name for his father] the first time and the High Court in Frankfurt sentenced him to eight years for actions against the State on a trumped up charge of having cut the wires linking the Frankfurt transmission of Hitler's speech on his ascension to the presidency in 1933, to the wider radio-listening public. What a farce! Nobody actually believed that a wireless transmission could be interrupted simply by cutting an imaginary wire. In fact, one of Ati's secretaries presented the 'very same scissors' that he had used to do the deed! In court, Ati gave a long speech accusing Hitler and his Nazi goons of a long series of crimes. It was 1933 and still possible to oblige the courts to listen to a defendant's statement.[21]

Alexander Schoen narrates how in jail, after the first arrest in Frankfurt, his father 'became a vocal and popular agitator' and that 'he managed somehow to escape from gaol after just eight months, slipping past the guards during a transfer from one section of the gaol to another and to return home as fast as he could in order to destroy as much documentary evidence linking his radio work to his many friends in the music, theatre and literary worlds as he could' before the Gestapo could track him down.[22]

These months should be days – the rest is part of a narrative passed down as part of the family story. Although 'he managed to destroy a large number of letters as well as published or still not published written documents', according to Sasha, 'his feverish work was not missed by our cook', who

phoned the police and informed them that my Dad was at home destroying documents. My sister and I stood still, held tightly by my mother, Mutti, while about five police in their stupid helmets and two grim-faced, plainclothes officers, the Gestapo, grabbed my father and bundled him off in their large black-curtained van. This time, without the need for any court proceedings, he was taken by train to Hamburg, where a judge swiftly sentenced him to life in the State Penitentiary at Fulsbüttel.[23]

The 1931/33 diary suggests a slightly different timeline, that Schoen went underground in Hamburg prior to his second arrest. The entry for 14/15 March recorded 'to Hamburg' and on the line below: 'Ernst, Nina, Hansi'.[24]

But why Hamburg? Perhaps it was known to Schoen as a place of escape, where certain networks of solace and shelter could be found? According to some accounts, Schoen was sheltered there by the judge Otto Friedburg, or possibly with friends of Friedburg.[25] We know from others that Friedburg provided shelter for those at risk from the authorities. The violinist Betty Francken, for example, who was eventually murdered at Sobibor on 16 July 1943, moved in with 'the family of Dr Otto Friedburg, a judge with whose family she was acquainted' after her previous landlady emigrated to Brazil in May 1937.[26] Also: Olga Löwengard, born 1864, who was sent to Theresienstadt and murdered there on 12 November 1942. Another: Wolf Kruszynski, born 1874, who took his life on 19 November 1939.

According to the Hamburg telephone books, Friedburg moved homes several times after 1933. In 1934 he was listed as living at 115 Isestraße, next door to an address given by Schoen. While staying on Isestraße in Hamburg, Schoen wrote a film script, entitled *Der wunderbare Punkt* (The Marvellous Point).[27] In 1935, Friedburg moved south to 19 Immenhof. Between 1938 and 1940 he lived slightly to the west on 31 Hagedornstraße. By 1941, he was no longer listed in the Hamburg telephone book, as he was, like Schoen, in London.[28]

It seems that Schoen was taken from his safe house in Hamburg to the prison at Fuhlsbüttel.[29] And, according to Sasha, while his father was again incarcerated, Hansi and Nina spent time with Friedburg working out what to do:

Mutti stayed at home for three days after Ati's re-capture. However, my sister [Nina] remembers that Mutti spent a great deal of this time away from us with my Dad's lawyer, Otto Friedburg. I believe he was the only person who knew what she was intending to do. I was very agitated, while my sister, who was two years older, appeared to be inexplicably calm.[30]

Official records of Schoen's time at Fuhlsbüttel are lacking, given they were destroyed during or after the war. Schoen's experience is detailed in a poem, dated 23 March 1943, a decade after his incarceration. The long form poem was eventually published in 1950, in German, under the pseudonym Hans Werdmann in the collection *Londoner Elegien* (London Elegies). In it, he remembers the conditions, the Communists he met there and he reflects on his own lack of self-sacrifice and political bravery. It is another form of evidence of what happened:

In the courtyard of the police prison the green Minna receives us
The door slammed shut. The engine started.
Comfortably it shook me on my bench. Opposite
Pathetic haggard and cheerful, a garrulous old man,
In front of us a wall, behind which voices rang out,
Because back then quite rightly they still separated
Us politicos from the criminals.
Behind us, the barred window. From a long clean street
Spring looked in with its first bitter buds.
Heavy was my heart.

State Prison Fuhlsbüttel. Not one of those old
prison citadels, no, sober modern hygienic.
After the admittance examination, through the quiet echoey
Monster building rattling up the stairs. The SA man
Unlocks the doors. And I am finally back
Among people.
                    For you should know: Once you have been
Caught in the net that is stretched out
Over the shore of the offices, to which the crowd is constantly
constantly washed up, once the machine of destruction,
Has sucked up resistance and once
The iron door is slammed behind you,
Then you are in the realm of the shadows. Unlikely
Is the return. From cell to cell only knocks
The hopeful death worm of the Morse Alphabet,
And disunified remain the nightly
Cries of dreams.
                    But you must also recognise,
Who remains lively, who still thinks of you and of me,
He stands at the farthest, highest edge of the barricade,
That separates us from eternity. You may not know of him
But he knows all about you. And still the dying
Say it wordlessly: We live! We are the avengers!
And the other slogan: Never again senseless suffering!

Nineteen scrutinising faces looked at me. And barely
Were the doors closed, all three surrounded me, took
Crockery and blankets from me and the little suitcase
And began to make a bed for me. And when I
said: I am not in the party, then one replied:
Here we are all one party.

                              In the evening, when we twenty had stretched out,
half undressed next to and on top of each other on our
plank beds the stench was strongest
Of sour bread and urine. Jokes flew, until finally
The last call for silence had faded and the long
terrible lonely night came.

                              I don't want to talk about it,
How we waited for one day after the other, each one for that and yet also
Each for all. Will you be called or you or I
For interrogation or for deportation? Or else, as it then became sure
For some of you comrades: Will they leave us here to rot
And only with the whip and the boot heel, only with a dark cell
And rope to help along the trial of the shadow life of those who fought
and the others who had not even fought properly.
I will not speak of the bungled together
        Chess game made by ourselves nor
Of the stupid old issues of the *Illustrated London*
        News, which were our reading
Nor of being led to the showers, when we saw the grey
Bald shaven faceless phantoms of the prison trusties
In their striped clothes scurrying round the corners with lordly superiority
Of those who were at home, just as we until our last breath
Would never be at home here, speak not
Of the walk, when we went one behind the other wordlessly
Rattling down the echoing stairs, then lining up at the exit
Next to the cancerous flowerbeds of the prison-officials
To finally on command creep round in circles.
When I was shown the Deputies, the Mayors, the Trade Union Leaders,
When behind the barred window here and there the faces of corpses pressed
        themselves again the panes
To catch a glimpse of a friend, a comrade-in-arms from afar
Or when we were allowed to walk together in groups,
Sone sent a ball over the rubble field next to the prison and I
stood alone at the furthest end, next to the wall, from where one could
maybe catch the smell of the outside and the advancing Spring.

But I'll bear witness to you, Sailor Karl of the best Frisian batch!
You dictated to me your memories of the cruise of the "Falke",
Where a couple of blokes, types like the Feme murderers
Thought they could have you
Shipped you off to Bolivia as cannon fodder.
And you Lothar, farmer, Hitler Youth, Strasser, CP and Fuhlsbüttel
That was your short meteoric career. Every day at six
You held, according to the good old traditions, political lessons
None of us knew at the time how long this would be our lives.
Then suddenly, after only a period, Lothar, our paths parted again
And when I think of you today, the ten years since then
Seem short to me because I could do so little in them
And long again, because you the youth of then
Are now a man, should you still be alive.
My way, comrades, was the safer one, but yours the more important.
Whenever the mire of life, dictated to us by our worst enemies,
Wishes to assail me I think of you;
Always when I see good comrades bogged down in small unnecessary things,
I think of you and always
When I feel like despairing over my own defeats
I think of you. But only if I should ever forget you,
Then shall I be truly cursed, comrades.[31]

23.3.43.

Sasha detailed the final nights of his father's incarceration, and how the story came to be known:

In the relative calm of our small flat in the outskirts of London, Ati told us that the prison Governor came alone to his cell at around 2 to 3am, in the darkest part of the night and quietly whispered that he was to get dressed and follow him. Ati was too surprised to say anything, and followed the Governor along sound-less, unlit corridors and countless barred and bolted gates until they reached the main double doors that were normally guarded by several warders. The Governor unlocked both doors and pushed Ati into the outer yard where Otto [Friedburg] was standing at one of Ati's official cars. Before climbing into his car, he heard the prison doors clang shut behind him.

'You have two hours to get out of Germany, after which the Gestapo will re-arrest you and return you to Fuhlsbüttel... if you're lucky!', Otto said, ominously.

'Why did they let me out?', Ati asked. 'I've no idea', Otto answered. 'I only got a message from the local police yesterday. I was told to collect you from Fuhlsbüttel today and not to ask any questions.'

Otto drove Ati at high speed to the port of Hamburg.[32]

Sasha also recorded later the identity of the prison governor:

Ati learnt many years later that the Governor of Fuhlsbüttel's name was Solomann and that, although he was not Jewish, he had been arrested shortly after Ati's escape, and died in Buchenwald concentration camp.[33]

Even the prison guards were not safe from the enemy when the enemy was victorious.

The way in which Schoen left prison has a series of secretive details at its core, unknown even to him at the time. This has been summarised in some of the academic accounts as relating to the personal intervention of his wife with the responsible authorities in Berlin.[34] Sasha recalled that the nature of this involvement was unknown to his father:

It was not until after my father died in 1960 that Mutti told my wife how it was that Ati had been allowed to 'escape' from the state penitentiary and to flee from Germany. In early 1964, during one of our frequent visits to Mutti in her apartment in Hampstead, and when I had left to do some shopping for her, she told my wife to sit next to her on the sofa. She asked my wife to fetch the bottle of Benedictine and proceeded to polish off three tumblers of the liqueur in quick succession.

She then told her the following story with the injunction not to reveal it to anyone.

'Back in Frankfurt, when Ati had been re-arrested by the Gestapo,' she said, 'I made plans with our lawyer, Otto Friedburg, to save my husband from a fate that seemed inevitable. I travelled to Berlin and stayed overnight with a close friend, Karla Hoecker.'[35]

The name Hoecker, a musicologist, was recorded in one of the address books – her address 37 Andreezeile, Berlin. In his account, Alexander Schoen adopts his mother's voice, relaying the secrets afforded to his wife, Leda:

'Early the following morning, I took a cab to the newly established Gestapo head-quarters and, marching past the guards, I demanded to see the Commanding General on a "personal matter". I gave my name as Countess Rogendorf and was led to an office near the front door by the ranking duty officer who demanded to know the reason for my request. I said it was none of his business to ask that. The officer made the mistake of nodding his head in an upwards direction, seeming to point to the General's office.

"The general does not see casual visitors. You must write for a formal visit and wait for an appointment," he said. "Please leave at once".

'Without answering the officer or even looking at him I pushed past him, ignored the pistol he snatched from its holster and as rapidly as I knew how started to climb the broad staircase in the direction of the office that had been nodded at by the officer.

'I climbed up and without taking any further notice of the soldier who had been ordered to escort me to the exit, I continued to climb up the imposing stairway to the first floor. Two armed guards attempted to stop me, but with a brief gesture and an imperious "Hände weg!", I pushed past them and approached the only door outside of which two further armed guards were standing. Again I pushed them aside with the same curt command and opened the first and second of two doors that led into an extravagantly large office. Behind his desk that stood in the centre of the room was the bulky frame of the man I knew must have been the Commanding General. The two guards who again grabbed me by the shoulders but were again sharply pushed away, attempted to explain who I was and that I had a personal message for the General.

'My thoughts were a mixture of revulsion at the sight of the General, which presented a gross image of a pig dressed in a black, much decorated Gestapo uniform that was intended to terrify his subordinates, and dark thoughts that were addressed to this satanic apparition.

"My name is Countess Rogendorff and I demand that you release my husband Ernst Schoen immediately from gaol in Hamburg. He has been imprisoned illegally, but has committed no crime."

'Instead of removing his own weapon, he coughed loudly and burst out laughing.

"Madame, please sit down and explain what this is all about", he spluttered.

'He ordered the guards to leave, rang a bell on his desk and ordered coffee. Too surprised to say anything further but retaining as severe a face as I could, I sat down opposite the desk. I again told him my husband's name and demanded that the general should order his release at once.

"I know who he is and have to say that we consider him to be a dangerous criminal and a threat to the Third Reich. But I'll examine the circumstances of the case."

'When the orderly arrived with a tray, he poured out two cups of coffee and added cream, still with a grotesque smile on his podgy face.

'I pulled myself together and stretched out a hand to his shoulder, just touching his podgy neck. "I know that you will be able to release him when you realise that my husband is completely innocent."

'I was thirty-five years old at this time and considered to be an exceptionally beautiful and fashionably dressed young woman. I must explain that now, over thirty years later, the following three days and three nights alone with Satan were a nightmare. I had been installed in a small, fully furnished apartment on the same floor as the general's office and, although I had forced myself to accept the drama of a brutal and sadistic seduction that had been prepared in my mind days before, I remained openly self-composed until my final release and escort by two guards to the Hauptbahnhof in Central Berlin.'

This dramatic and brutal scenario was the payment made by Mutti in exchange for two hours of freedom from the Fussbüttel penitentiary, from which Ati was rescued by Otto Friedburg with the connivance of the prison Governor. Until his death in 1960, he always assumed that somehow the Governor had been involved in the planning of his escape and that he would finally pay the price for that with his own life; as indeed he did!

Mutti always considered her actions during her visit to the Gestapo head-quarters to have been so shameful that she would never tell anyone about it. My wife was outraged at this assumption and told Mutti that the whole saga was an extreme example to all women of the outstanding courage of a young woman in the face of a terrifying ordeal. How could she think anything different?[36]

The account tallies possibly with documentary evidence, though the companion in Hamburg, according to the diary, was philologist Bruno Snell, not Friedburg. In the period when Schoen is in prison, there is a note in the 1931/33 diary, on Monday 17 April: 'With Bruno Snell to Berlin'[37]. Two days later, on Wednesday 19 April, there was a note – 'Afternoon back in Frankfurt'. Perhaps that covers the 'three days and three nights alone with Satan'. Schoen was released the following Friday. Elsewhere in the extant documentation, the name of Waffen-SS officer Gustav Krukenberg is mentioned. Krukenberg was the Reichs Radio Commissar and manager of the Reichs Radio Company and leader of the radio department of the Reich ministry for Popular Enlightenment and Propaganda.[38] Hansi's intervention with him in Berlin apparently led to the window of opportunity to escape for Schoen.[39]

The family's escape from Nazi Germany became part of a family mythology – a story of survival and resilience. When we first met Sasha and Leda, they told us this story. Hard to tell, hard not to tell.

April is often given as the month when Schoen escapes to London.[40] Some add more details: 'Schoen fled to London at the end of April; his family followed shortly afterwards, leaving behind all their belongings'.[41] Others specify the means: that he fled on a ship to Harwich, England.[42] But evidence suggests that he did not leave immediately – or, at least, if he did leave, then he returned to Germany soon after. In any case, he sorted out living arrangements in his new home, London, a city he had visited before and knew.

Hansi wrote a letter on 18 May 1933 to the Police Captain Abraham in Hamburg. She complained that they were in limbo since discussions between Friedburg and the police seemed to have stalled and this was disastrous as no money was coming in to feed the family.[43] Schoen had been prevented from working and unable to seek other 'possibilities of existence', as he was not allowed to leave Hamburg. She noted that a friend in London had offered him a temporary creative role. She implored the police captain to find out if the restrictions could be lifted and if a passport could be acquired or even a visa, so that London could indeed figure in future plans. She finished the letter with the argument that in the weeks that had passed no valid reasons for the restrictions had been presented: 'no positive material has been found, whereby the suspicion could be proved that this was a case of baseless rumours'.[44] Abraham had just been made the leader of the Hamburg police, where he would stay until October 1933 before beginning an illustrious career through Nazi institutions, including SS-Brigadeführer and Major General of the Police.

The radio press, now run by new men, quickly let its opinion be known. In the *Volksfunk*, on 15 August 1933, a comment appeared:

Ernst Schoen's sympathies for Soviet ideas, only actually expressed in his private life, and his musical tendencies must have led the men in authority to decide to effect his dismissal.[45]

After Schoen's removal from the airwaves, another programme aide, a composer and musical enthusiast, Carl Stueber, took over Schoen's role, until he moved in the summer to the radio station in Leipzig. His rapid rise could be attributed to the fact that he was the leader of the NSDAP work cell from 1926 onwards and had published articles on music in the Nazi newspaper, the *Völkischer Beobachter*.[46] He had joined the NSDAP on 1 February 1932.[47]

In Schoen's pocket diary, an entry on 23 May 1933 recorded 'Ernst to London' and there are notes about Frankfurt in the days after. On 31 May a note in the diary states 'Sasha to Hamburg'.[48] Later, on 10 June: 'Bentheim–London' then 'evening to London'.[49] On 9 July 1933, Schoen signed off a manuscript, written in English, called 'Death and the Clowns'. Dedicated to his Hamburg friends, it was written in London. It was a call for work to be 'the legitimate continuation of play, instead of an economical punishment' and it insisted that 'every creative imagination be allowed to grow on its place in the common' and hoped that 'the right of existence' be no more 'the duty of penal servitude'.[50]

Certainly, there was no definitive break with the homeland at first. Otto Friedburg appears again in the diary and in a photograph in Schoen's possession of a boat full of passengers. On the reverse is written 'Spring 33, Heligoland with Otto Friedburg'.[51]

In the photograph, Sasha and Leda helped us identify `Mutti' as the figure in the lighter coat smiling directly at the camera, next to the figure clad in a black coat and hat, at the highest point of the image. Below and to her immediate left is Ernst, who is sitting on the side of the boat, wearing a lightly coloured cap. Perhaps next to him is Otto Friedburg in the dark hat. Helgoland crops up in the 1931/33 diary but not as early as spring. On 22 July someone recorded, with its alternative spelling, 'back from Heligoland'. Could this entry refer to the trip on which this photograph was taken?

A feature on Helgoland (spelt Heligoland) appeared in the *SWZ* only a month before, on 18 June 1933, placing it within its political swirl. The

Figure 3.1 Helgoland with Otto Friedburg, from Spring 1933.

Photographer unknown. From Schoen's Archive in Koblenz: BArch N 1403 Bild-110-077. Copyright: Sabine Schiller-Lerg.

radio magazine described it as an 'Edda in stone', a place of myth and mystical light and the former site of Ernst Haeckel's biological research. Its political fate is evoked: exchanged between Germany and England along with Zanzibar in 1890; Schoen, like the island, caught between states.

At some point over these months, Schoen made it to London. Alexander Schoen recounts a dramatic and sudden departure from Fuhlsbüttel:

He knew that the first boat leaving Hamburg was a Russian vessel the 'Felix Dzerjinsky' bound for St. Petersburg via London. He had already arranged passage and personal documentation, so Ati was stowed in a small cabin without any further formalities.

The SS Felix Dzerjinsky was a Soviet merchant passenger ship, in operation from 1926 to 1955. There is a reference to it in the diary with a slightly different spelling: 'Felix Dzerdjinski has set off', but this appears on 17 October. The vessel was a so-called London refrigerator ship, built by the Soviet North shipyard and used on the Leningrad–London route in the 1930s to transport perishable goods such as butter and eggs in refrigerator holds. The passengers were mainly English and the cabins were comfortable with furniture of fine woods and good quality carpets – all designed by well-known painters and decorators from France. Hanging on the wall were newspapers for everyone to read – a Soviet technique for spreading information and the political line – alongside pictures of Lenin. The crew were Soviet and called the passengers 'comrades'.[52] The boat is also mentioned by name in the diary on 9 and 11 November. Alexander Schoen's story continues with the boat's arrival in Harwich where:

the English police were waiting for him, having been alerted by Interpol to arrest him and return him to the German authorities without delay.

None of this happened, however. 'What it is to have friends in high places!' he thought.

According to Alexander Schoen, two old friends of Ernst, Lord Reith and Anthony Asquith, were waiting at the police station where Ati had been installed in a holding cell.

Both men were extremely angry that Ati had been arrested in England.

'How dare you arrest this man?' Lord Reith demanded of the station commander. 'He is a good friend of ours, a friend of England and a great and innocent man who deserves to be treated as a hero.'

We know from notes retained in the archive that Schoen knew the son of a former British Prime Minister, actor Anthony Asquith and it is likely he knew Asquith's sister Violet, by then part of the Bonham Carter family, for she helped those persecuted by Nazis to find their way in London, likely including Schoen.[53] Reith would, in some sense, have been an unlikely figure to come to Schoen's aid. In his diaries, in December 1922, Reith had noted a motivation and a context for radio quite different to that which animated Schoen: To complete the task of developing the nation through broadcasting, Reith had to 'take Christ with me from the very beginning and all through this difficult work. I cannot succeed otherwise [...]. I can do all things through Christ.'[54] His earthly political sympathies were reactionary. He opposed the unionisation of staff at the BBC. According to his daughter, in 1935, over lunch at the Carlton Club, he revealed to Guglielmo Marconi his admiration for the dictator Mussolini, who he thought spread democracy by non-democratic means.[55] His friend, Theodor Wanner, head of South Germany's broadcasting service, conveyed to him his fears as to what was on the horizon in early March 1933, a point at which Schoen was imprisoned. Reith revealed his disbelief in his diary:

9 March 1933: Dr. Wanner to see me in much depression. He said he would like to leave his country and never return. I am pretty certain, however, that the Nazis will clean things up and put Germany on the way to being a real power in Europe again. They are being ruthless and most determined. It is mostly the fault of France that there should be such manifestations of national spirit.[56]

Wanner was dismissed from his post, and on 13 March 1933, he was attacked in his apartment and suffered a brain concussion.[57] The perpetrators were never pursued. His further comments to Reith about being terrified to speak out about what was happening in Germany on pain of being shot were dismissed and Reith continued to argue in support of the new regime. Reith admired Hitler's actions in the Night of the Long Knives in 1934, when many supposedly disloyal stormtroopers were murdered: 'I really admire the way Hitler has cleaned up what looked like an incipient revolt. I really admire the drastic actions taken, which were obviously badly needed.'[58] In 1936, he wrote in his diary: 'I have a great admiration for the German way of doing things.'[59] He praised Hitler as efficient in his annexation of Austria, even when he was required officially to oppose the regime. Indeed, he even came to admire what Schoen's successors did with and to German radio, noting in his diaries that: 'Germany has banned hot jazz and I'm sorry that we should be behind in dealing with this filthy product of modernity.'[60] His office, according to employee Richard Lambert, contained 'a hard solitary chair for nobodies, or offenders; an upholstered armchair for senior subordinates or persons of standing; and a sofa, reserved for high dignitaries, or for individuals whom the interviewer wished to impress by close personal proximity'.[61]

Schoen's 1933 pocket diary notes, on 23 May: 'Ernst to London'. In Alexander Schoen's account, after arriving in Harwich:

Ati's passport was taken from him and not returned until several years later when he was granted political asylum. He was also not given a work permit until war broke out in 1939. Without a passport he was unable to accept an invitation to join the NBC, New York, as head of their new foreign service, nor a similar invitation from Moscow Radio.[62]

What of the other members of the family? There is movement, a shifting around, perhaps to sort out things, find a space to be. According to the 1933 diary, on 25 May there are notes about trips involving Frankfurt, Hannover and Oeynhausen. On 31 May, Sasha was on route to Hamburg. 30 June, Puma sets off from somewhere, perhaps London, in the evening and arrives in Hamburg the following day. There is also a note about Rotterdam on the same day.[63] On 5 June, someone arrived in Hamburg. On 11 June, another trip to London was logged. On 15 July, a note in the pocket diary alludes to the trip to Helgoland, returning on 22 July.[64] 7 August saw a trip to England. Again, an entry on 7 September: 'In evening to Hamburg'.[65] And then, on 9 October: 'Off to London'.[66] Gradually the traces settle into London links and London lives to be lived.

1933: Roll Call

What happened to everyone else, to the friends and acquaintances and employers and employees, those close and those distant, in 1933 and shortly after? And what happened to their possessions, as the Nazis secured their grip on power? How could they be contacted?

What was the new status of these people as they scattered across the world, broadcast, narrowcast, radiating out from Germany, slipping underground, emerging into light or staying, heads down, getting by? Refugees? Cosmopolitans? Migrants? Exiles? Émigrés?

Anita Berber was already gone, having collapsed in Damascus and died shortly after returning to Berlin in November 1928.[67]

Hugo Ball had also died of cancer in 1927.[68]

Walter Benjamin was travelling across Europe, trying to find places to live on very little money. He had considered taking his life a year prior to Schoen's escape, drafting letters to Schoen, among four others. 'Dear Ernst', he wrote, 'I know you will think back on me in a friendly spirit and not altogether infrequently. For that I thank you. Yours, Walter.'[69] He never sent these letters, but he preserved them along with the will, in which Schoen was to be left Paul Klee's painting Die *Vorführung des Wunders* (The Presentation of the Miracle) (1916), a painting that eventually made it to the Museum of Modern Art (MoMA) in New York.

Willi Baumeister lost his Frankfurt art school professorship and had to work commercially. His painting, presented to Schoen in 1930, with Hansi's face and knobs and dials, would, in any case, at some point make its way to the Saint Louis Art Museum.[70]

Ernst Bloch eventually made it to the US with the architect Karola Piotrowska.[71]

Bertolt Brecht and Helene Weigel went to Scandinavia, where Benjamin joined them. Brecht worked on his manuscript of *Round Heads and Pointed Heads* (premiered in 1936). Hanns Eisler visited to play through the music for the play.[72]

Alfredo Casella continued to compose music. His fascist sympathies were compromised by the passing of anti-Jewish laws in Italy, in 1938, which affected his Jewish wife.[73]

Henri Châtin-Hofmann eventually moved back to Baltimore and spent a number of years in an asylum where he died in 1961.[74]

Alfred Cohn was learning, according to his sister Jula Radt-Cohn, to be a beekeeper in case he had to leave Germany and needed a skill.[75] He soon fled to Barcelona, where he tried to support his family by selling fashion jewellery.[76]

Hans Flesch, Schoen's predecessor at the radio station, was arrested, sent to prison and recruited into the army. In August 1933 he appeared in Oranienburg Concentration Camp and later in the *Rundfunkprozess*, an eighty-six-day show trial that sought to prosecute former radio employees for alleged corruption during their period broadcasting in Weimar, which took place in the Regional Court of Berlin in 1934.[77]

Otto Friedburg went to London in March 1938[78] and was naturalised as a British citizen a decade later.[79]

Valeska Gert left for London, where she started work on a short film written by Humphrey Jennings, *Pett and Pott: A Fairy Story of the Suburbs*.[80]

John Heartfield fled first to Prague and then to London, producing fierce anti-fascist work throughout.[81]

Raoul Hausmann took refuge in Ibiza.[82]

Paul Hindemith was condemned as an 'atonal noisemaker' by Goebbels, but was allowed to remain in Germany on condition that he wrote tonally. His brother Rudolf also stayed and led the symphony orchestra of the General Government of Krakow in occupied Poland.[83]

Schoen's pianist and friend Alice Jacob-Loewenson was on her way to Jerusalem.[84]

Ernst Krenek emigrated to the US in 1938.[85]

Gretel Karplus was in England, after her husband Theodor W. Adorno had left Germany to be at Merton College, Oxford.[86]

Germaine Krull was taking pictures for detective fiction books.[87]

Dora Sophie Kellner, then separated from Walter Benjamin, was in exile, running a boarding house in North West Italy.[88]

Paul Laven would go on to broadcast from the 1936 Olympic Games.[89]

With his sister Erika, Klaus Mann participated in a political cabaret *Pepper Mill*, before they were both forced into exile.[90]

Hanna Mandello left Germany for Paris in 1934. She worked there as a fashion photographer under a new name, Jeanne Mandello, doing commissions for magazines such as *Fémina*, *Harper's Bazaar* and *Vogue* and fashion houses including Balenciaga, Guerlain, Maggy Rouff and Creed.[91]

László and Sibyl Moholy-Nagy moved first to the Netherlands, then to London, then to Chicago.[92]

Ludwig Marcuse took refuge first in Sanary-sur-Mer and then, from 1940, in Los Angeles.[93]

Jörg Mager would die impoverished in 1939 of heart failure in Aschaffenburg.[94]

Lisa Rado had already died, in 1928, of a heart attack, a day after appearing on stage.[95]

Friedrichkarl Roedemeyer became one of the leading scholars of radio in the Third Reich.[96]

Liesel Simon, the Frankfurt puppeteer, eventually fled to Ecuador to join her son. She died there in 1958.[97]

Gershom Scholem was in Jerusalem, collecting and cataloguing hundreds of kabbalistic manuscripts at the Hebrew University.[98]

Sasha and Cami Stone were living in Brussels, where they worked on publishing a collection of nudes titled *Femmes* in the French magazine *Arts et Metiers Graphique*.[99]

Mátyás Seiber was dismissed from the Hoch Conservatory in April 1933 and returned to Budapest later in the year.[100]

Kurt Schwitters had just finished his *Merzbau* and would leave for Norway in the coming years, only to be interned on the Isle of Man in 1940.[101]

Leon Trotsky was offered asylum in France, but forbidden from entering Paris. Simone Weil arranged for him to hold a secret meeting at the house of her parents.[102]

Kurt Weill fled to Paris. There he worked with Brecht on the ballet *The Seven Deadly Sins*, premiered on 7 June 1933 at the Théâtre des Champs-Elysées in Paris.[103]

Edgard Varèse had begun new experiments in electronic composition, including one, *Ecuatorial*, for two theremins, premiered in New York in 1934.[104]

Mary Wigman remained in Germany and ran the Mary Wigman-Schule until 1942.[105]

Charlotte Wolff was in exile in Paris, about to start work as a hand reader. She was hosted there by fashion journalist Helen Grund, wife of Franz Hessel.[106]

Part 2
1933–1960

Locations: London, Frankfurt, Düsseldorf, Hamburg,
Paris, Berlin, Yugoslavia

4

Exile Life

Everyday Existence

On 19 November 1933, amid reports on disturbances in Palestine, Budapest students in anti-Jewish riots, German-American boycotts and the fiancée of a Rothschild family scion converting to Judaism, a short article appeared in the *Jewish Telegraphic Agency* with the headline: 'Ernst Schoen, Reich Playwright, Joins British Broadcasting Corporation':

The British Broadcasting Corporation has acquired the services of Ernst Schoen, former director of programs of the Frankfort-on-Main radio station, who has emigrated from Germany on account of the Hitler persecutions.

Herr Schoen left the Frankfort station where he had been employed for nine years, following an anonymous letter received by the station authorities that he had been giving preference to Jewish performers.[1]

The name 'Jacob L.' is recorded in Schoen's diary from around that time, listed at the *Jewish Telegraphic Agency* at 109 Fleet Street.[2] Contact had been made.

The first pages in Schoen's pocket diary, its 1931 dates scratched out and overwritten to serve for 1933, are a record of numerous names and addresses in Hampstead and surrounding areas: the Montessori School on Willoughby Road; someone called Feldberg in Parliament Hill, perhaps the refugee scientist William Feldberg; Westfield College on Kidderpore Avenue. The diary contains details of daily lives and encounters – he sees 'The Black Shirt' on the number 8 bus. There were people to contact or things to remember, some ticked off, some left unmarked. He jotted down new landmarks and locations: Liverpool

Street Station and 50 Porchester Terrace, addresses in Croydon and Tottenham Court Road. London postcodes were written out in German format. Sometimes the city became absorbed into former patterns, such as when a stretch of Finchley Road, dense with refugees became known, even by London taxi drivers, as Finchleystraße. There were new calculations in new currencies. Mention was made of Bertha Bracey at Friends House on the Euston Road. The address Lea Steps, on the Vale of Health, appeared – an address that Schoen gave to Walter Benjamin and others as his place of correspondence in the early weeks.[3] Regular reminders to pay storage charges appeared.[4]

The diary registered places and people. The names Reed and Schoenmann appeared as well as a meeting at 200 Gray's Inn Road with photographer and roller-skater Percy Brown. This address was home to newspapers that might provide work: *The News of the World* and *The Sunday Empire*. On 14 June, a note recorded the move of someone, perhaps Schoen himself, into a twin bedroom. On 10 August, 'The Well of Loneliness' and 'Radclyffe Hall' were scribbled down, perhaps a recommendation.[5] In mid-August 1933, the National Liberal Club address appears: a place where Lady Violet Bonham Carter was a frequent presence, as was Sir Thiruvalayangudi Vijayaraghavacharya, a high-ranking Indian civil servant who met Hansi on the train from Harwich to London[6] when she arrived in England.[7] If old circuits were broken, others might be revived. Albrecht Theodor Andreas Graf von Bernstorff, relative of Hansi's, was also in London, a Rhodes scholar who had worked since 1923 as a diplomat in the German Embassy. He fell out of favour with the incoming Nazi regime and was relieved of his post in London in 1933.[8]

The names pile up, as a migrant made efforts to establish himself as a public presence: Kadi and Schönemann, Jaeger, Hans Seligmann, *Sunday Graphic*, H. Zander, Paul Wegener, Kurt Singer, Jack Goldschmidt, Elias Avery Lowe.[9] There were tips to be swapped; old bonds to be relinked. The musical offer in London entered the mix: an outing to the Kolisch Quartet and New Bond Street to hear Schoenberg's music; a concert at the Aeolian Hall.

On 24 November, Schoen attended a BBC concert and he reviewed it for the BBC listing magazine the *Radio Times*, in an article titled 'Notable Music of the Week: Music from Austria'. In the back of the diary are jottings on the Hamburg-Grimsby line and the London North Eastern Railway

Boats, which travel Wednesday to Sunday, on a thirty-hour passage costing 35RM.

In early January 1934, an entry noted the name of Brian Mickie at the BBC – Schoen meant Bryan Michie, who was then in charge of the Sound Effects studio, described in a contemporary profile as 'a two-storey apartment that looks like a power house in one of Fritz Lang's fantastic films of the future'[10] Schoen reminded himself to wear a tie. Work opportunities cropped up. One note reads: *Evening News*, Sales Manager, Advertising Department. There were high society encounters: the occasional meeting with film director Anthony Asquith and the prominent family of the Bonham Carters. A letter from 19 July 1934, on Gainsborough Pictures notepaper, invited him, for example, to lunch at Lady Bonham Carter's house on Radnor Place, W2.[11]

The back page of the diary also recorded the address of Lucy Backhouse, 50 Higher Drive, Purley. She was a Quaker serving on many charitable committees, including the Friends Committee for Refugees and Aliens. For Schoen, all the necessities of life required reproduction in a new context. And all the while the regularity of family life continued. Special days to be remembered: Nina's name on 14 February, her birthday. Ernst and Hansi's wedding anniversary on 3 March. These festival days were traces of continuity in a life otherwise interrupted.

In the Land of the BBC

Some crumbs of work were offered by the BBC. Schoen joined an organisation that professed to have broad ambitions for radio and how it might improve the quality of life. In Britain, radio was under the control of the state and rival stations were forbidden. John Reith, the first Director General of the BBC, had extolled the capacity of radio. Radio promised, he noted, 'the expression of a new and better relationship between man and man'.[12] It would form the basis of a utopia, an idyll brought about by his own energies, which were those of a 'practical idealist'.[13] Reith perceived the unequal distribution of actual things in the world as a 'natural law' of unfairness that might be counteracted by wireless' inherently democratic ability to be shared. Radio presented no barriers to the enjoyment of the 'best in every department of human knowledge, endeavour and achievement'. Through this offer, the children of today would become good, sensible citizens of tomorrow.[14]

Schoen provided the organisation with some 'services', as the *Jewish Telegraphic Agency* report put it. One of Schoen's contacts at the BBC was Edward Clark, an employee in the music department mentioned in the 1934 *BBC Year-Book* as one of the figures who had conducted music for the programme *Children's Hour*.[15] Clark was also responsible for producing a number of important world and British premieres (some of which he also conducted) and was associated with avant-garde composers in Schoen's extended circles, including Arnold Schoenberg, Anton Webern, Alban Berg, Ferruccio Busoni, Igor Stravinsky, Béla Bartók and Paul Hindemith.

Rather than steady work, Schoen lived off chance commissions and support here and there. On 1 November 1933, the *London Evening Standard* reported that Schoen was writing plays for the BBC: 'Former German Radio Chief Writing Plays for the BBC'. In a copy of the report, clipped out and taped into a scrapbook in Schoen's possession, someone, perhaps Schoen himself, had written down: 'mistake' and below that 'no, not for the BBC'. His quoted words to the journalist were: 'I have written several radio plays, and have also done some producing work for the BBC'.[16] Things were garbled in a language newly adopted.

Schoen adapted to writing in English; even if he retained a German syntax in his prose. As one of his services, he was invited to contribute an article to the 1934 *BBC Year-Book*, which covered programming from 1 November 1932 to 31 October 1933. His contribution 'Broadcast Opera in Germany' begins with an anecdote, a 'once upon a time' story that occurred only a year before. It concerned a professor who thought that a broadcast of a pageant set in the seventeenth century was well suited to radio because of the wonderful costumes it would display. The professor, ignorant of the fact that radio is not a visual medium, failed to understand, according to Schoen, the reality of performances that are 'largely done in shirt-sleeves'. Any child, he noted, could have put the poor old man right. Most also know about the division of labour within the studio.[17]

In his contribution on opera and broadcasting, Schoen conveyed radio as a technical medium that had, within its short history, developed an extraordinary capacity to reach lots of people. He wrote:

Every listener, and still more every broadcaster, will remember, I suppose, with a tender emotion the times when the fact that a sound uttered before a microphone

could be heard a couple of miles away, without a wire between, was enough to sat-
isfy the highest wants of all concerned. In these times of Paradise and innocence,
broadcasting people were eager to put every sound and every noise within their
reach before the microphone. The producers, in their search for programmes of
any sort, went to the opera directors amongst others, asking them the permission
of putting the microphone in front of the stage and of transmitting the operas to
broadcast listeners.[18]

In the early days, the 'magic' of radio was enough to make it an object of
fascination. But, in time, it needed good broadcasting material. Emergent
technologies are conceived in the light of what preceded them. Opera was
first broadcast by placing a microphone in front of the performance.

In so doing, by the way, they merely followed a tradition, already existing in the
legendary days of the first telephone, when first (I think) the King of Bavaria and
then other sovereigns and wealthy people listened to opera performances through
their special telephone lines. The difference, of course, was that what was then a
privilege of the happy few was now to become accessible to the masses.[19]

If this democratic potential is realised, argued Schoen, the battle begins to
find an aesthetic proper to it in relation to the new technical reality: artistic performance on the part of the 'speaker' is separate from the acous-
tics of the listening environment and so the very performance of drama
on radio is a fragmented and re-montaged process that bears little relation to the 'physical completeness' of theatre. He considered the problems
inherent in broadcasting drama, how it relies on a single physical sense –
hearing – without reciprocity and how it addresses detached individuals.
Radio, therefore, deals more easily with statements, such as sports reports
or poetry recitals, without the need for discussion and light music, or well-
known 'serious music', to provide 'emotional sensation'.

Dramatic production married awkwardly with radio and it needed
still to find a genuinely popular form that matched its discursivity. Schoen
mocked the tendency in Germany to broadcast from the opera house.
It provided the listener with a fuzzy experience, akin to pressing an ear
against the wall of the concert hall, only to pick up muffled sounds, con-
textless laughter. The silence on stage was inexplicable, as the mimed
scene unfolded and the endless rumble of scenery changes were simply
confusing to a listener. Such transmissions might continue to exist, but
not as artistic performances in themselves, rather as 'reported' art', akin

to the reproduction of pictures in a book. The last part of Schoen's article proposed the modern way forward: not relayed opera, but radio opera as composed by Hans Rosbaud or Hermann Scherchen. Schoen sought to intervene in the aesthetic debates even in this new context. He brought with him experience of an advanced and experimental practice. But his ideas found little resonance.

A few pages after Schoen's contribution in the 1934 *BBC Year-Book*, there is an article by John Gloag, titled 'Learning to Broadcast'. It gave advice on how to speak on the radio. Do not use words of more than two syllables, unless absolutely necessary. Speak slowly. Picture your listeners in armchairs and try to be conversational. Do not rustle your typescript. Throw each page on the floor as you finish with it. Do not drink on air. Be humble. It has an illustration, a photograph of Miss Megan Lloyd George and Sir Oswald Mosley discussing 'Fascism' in the radio studio.[20]

Hostilities

On 24 November 1933, the BBC's programme magazine, the *Radio Times*, published a short piece by Schoen on 'Music from Austria'. In the regular 'Notable Music' section, he endeavoured to understand the chamber music of Haydn, Mozart, Beethoven, Schubert, Brahms and Reger historically. That the sonata had rigid rules, he claimed, was an invention comparable to electricity, the innovations of French painting and the political science that shaped diplomacy in nineteenth-century Europe. But even as composers developed the form, they

poured in the acid of its dissolution, and, by encouraging a tendency to dissonance, by experimenting in new harmonics and modulations, and by finding new pleasures in new discoveries and in the retreat from an ordered consonance, a new form in music was presently evolved, a form almost without form – the 'fantasy'.[21]

Introducing Schoenberg into the discussion, Schoen revealed that a 'great daily paper used the vulgar unoriginal expression "composer of cacophony"'. At performances of Schoenberg's and Webern's work by the Kolisch Quartet, he had witnessed both applause and invective from the audience. The quartet was to play on the coming Friday at the BBC Public Chamber Music Concert. Schoen wrote of Webern:

It would be idle to pretend that the normal average listener can like or even understand his work. There is an undeniable and natural antagonism between the conservative music-lover, whose preferences and innate sympathies are for the past, and the artist, whose nature it is to create the new: and it is not possible to judge fairly between these conflicting opinions.[22]

Schoen recommended that the adventurous listener 'plunge head first' into 'dangerous and unfamiliar waters' to experience 'the strange sounds of nature imprisoned in a score', an experience 'naked and lonely'. Here a listener might attain 'artistic revelation'. He concluded with some thoughts on Ernst Krenek who, unlike Webern with his commitment to absolute modernity, explored whether modern composition could be original if based on traditional forms. In this small way, through this article placed in a popular listings magazine, Schoen attempted to open radio listeners' ears to the unfamiliar, setting it within the tradition of developing musical forms.

On 12 January 1934, Schoen published another short piece in the 'Notable Music' section of the *Radio Times*. The article 'Hindemith and Applied Music' opened with praise for Hindemith who had revived a once prevalent tradition of music: *Gebrauchsmusik*, a kind of utility music favoured also as a political vehicle by Hanns Eisler and Bertolt Brecht. Hindemith's technique is difficult, he argued, but pleasurable to perform. This article sought to introduce certain strains of modernist composition in Germany to an audience that needed to be reassured about difficulty and newness.[23]

On 9 February, he wrote again in the 'Notable Music' section on 'Bartok and Musical Folklore'. Here he insisted that the most exciting music is that which developed the folk music of anonymously composed dances and songs into artistic music. Johannes Brahms was named as the importer of a strand of folklore into classical sonata and rhythm. Bartók, too, transformed music of 'mere ethnological interest into that of high individual genius in the sphere of art'. Schoen criticised Bartók's compatriot Zoltán Kodály for converting the same folk music into sentimental romantic harmonies. Arguments were to be had about the course of musical development.[24]

In April 1934, Schoen faced an openly hostile encounter. The essay on 'Music from Austria', from November, was paraded in an influential music journal as an example of a defence of extremism in music. An opinion piece, 'Wireless Notes', appeared in *Musical Times*, a key publication for all things musical in Britain. It was signed by the pen name Audax and was vicious:

Some of the arguments put out by apologists for the extremists are funny. I call them arguments, but they scarcely deserve the name. There was Herr Ernst Schoen, for instance, in the *Radio Times*, not long ago, repeating the old stuff that 'There is an undeniable and natural antagonism between the conservative music lover, whose preferences and innate sympathies are for the past, and the artist whose nature it is to create the new; and it is not possible to judge fairly between these contending opinions.'[25]

Schoen was labelled an extremist and Audax was determined to undermine his analysis, in order to speak up for popular taste:

This is full of fallacies. Always we get the sting in the tail: 'Hands off: you are not able to judge.' Does this frighten anybody now? The simple truth that blows these pussyfoot arguments off the floor is revealed when we ask, 'How comes it, then, that the bulk of the music we sniffed-at lovers of the classics now know to be great was realised as such by the vast bulk of those who first heard it?' (And remember how badly played it mostly was in those days.) If extremists deny this, it is useless to argue further: their historical knowledge is simply lacking. If they don't deny it, why should they argue that things are so entirely different now? No, Herr; it sounds all very *schoen* ['nice' in German], but it won't wash. Of all the feeble cases, that of extremism seems to me the feeblest. Never, in spite of all our begging, do propagandists for it tell us constructively wherein lie its powers and beauties. Extremism is the biggest swindle ever perpetrated in honesty by the simple-minded, self-deceived.[26]

Audax, despite the name's gesture towards boldness, defended the music lovers' unadventurous instincts in knowing what is great music and he insisted that they are not unequipped to judge the new music – they simply heard it for what it was – bad. Audax sensed that lovers of the classical past were being criticised as lacking knowledge. Classical music was recognised as great from the very first chord that was played and continued to be so. New music lacked power and beauty. Those who championed it were simple-minded and delusional. They did not know their own tiny minds. On 24 April, Schoen marked his diary with a note: 'Audax, *Musical Times*, *Radio Times*, Webern.'[27] How could he get a foothold in this musical environment that was apparently so hostile to experimental approaches?

Through 1934, contacts accumulated and there is evidence of work here and there in the pocket diary. On 6 April, Schoen noted payments from the *News of the World* and the *Chicago Tribune*. Again, on 9 April, this time followed with a list of photographs and two names, Stone and Stern, likely Sasha Stone and Grete Stern. He mentioned a performance of *The Barber of Seville* at Sadler's Wells and picking up a driving licence from the Automobile Association at Coventry Street. He continued his efforts to keep in touch or make contact with other refugees. In the middle of March 1934, Bertolt Brecht wrote a letter to Schoen, whom he addresses as 'Dr.' from Svendborg, Denmark: 'I can imagine that things are not going all that rosily for you, but at least you are not concentrated', a verb in reference to the camps. He continued: 'It is interesting that certain musical and pedagogical tendencies have got on people's nerves.'[28] He gave Schoen permission to try to do things with his work in England and asked after his old friend, theatre director Jacob Geis. Everyone was looking for someone in these years. The letter was never sent. On 18 March 1933, Walter Benjamin discussed the question of emigration in a letter to Adorno. He was pleased that Adorno had secured a post in England. He reflected on London. He had spoken to someone who had been there recently – 'still the gate of the world', especially if one speaks English. He told Adorno he would see Schoen there: 'That he still has his family with him is no bad testimony to the sustainability of English soil.'[29]

In May, Schoen left Lea Steps in the Vale of Health, Hampstead, and, on 22 June, moved to an address in Belsize Park, while the two children boarded at a school in Woodford Green. He published again in the *Radio Times* edition of 15–21 July 1934 – a piece titled 'Opera Did Not Fall From Heaven', with the subtitle 'But Singers Sometimes Do'. It was a homage to mezzo-soprano Conchita Supervia and written for the occasion of a rare performance in London of Monteverdi's *The Ballad of the Ungracious Ladies* (1604). Schoen provided a potted history: Opera had its origins in Renaissance feudal Humanism and held onto a conviction that the form would continue to develop as long as humans had imagination. There were no more pieces in the BBC's *Radio Times* after this. Audax's shadow was long.

The diary entry for 30 July noted future travel by car to Lehrter Bahnhof in Berlin. Underneath is a list of expenses, associated with a return to Berlin on 15 August: tips for luggage carriers and on the ship.[30] Other jottings referred to The National Union of Students on Endsleigh Street and the Academic Assistance Council. Brecht's sojourn in London, at 24 Calthorpe Street, is also recorded. Later in the year, on 17 December 1934, Schoen noted down Brecht's address (and by proxy Benjamin's Scandinavian refuge).[31]

The Schoens sought out whatever help they could get. In August 1934, Johanna Schoen wrote to the Academic Assistance Council offering to sublet a furnished room with breakfast. The request was forwarded to the Committee for the Assistance of German Refugee Professional Workers.[32] Life scraped by on handouts from a church charity and a Quaker. In autumn 1935, the editor of the *New York Times*, Arthur Hays Sulzberger, sent $250, after the High Commission for German Refugees, based in Geneva, requested assistance for Schoen.[33]

On 13 October 1935, Schoen wrote to Benjamin and mentioned a meeting with Adorno and Edward Clark. The three had eaten together. Schoen was incensed by what he called Adorno's 'theory of the social significance of music in the nineteenth century that was almost schizophrenic in its snobbism'.[34] Adorno talked of the 'flight' from the 'commodity character' of 'banality', and compelled economic, aesthetic and psychological concepts under one single heading. Schoen thought this akin to the inferior thinking of what he called one-year volunteers of Marxism, like the officers who bought a shorter period of conscription. He added that Adorno's thought processes were more reminiscent of Grock, a popular blundering Swiss clown than the adept juggler Rastelli, about whom Benjamin had also written in 1935.[35] Schoen wondered if Oxford University was to blame.

On the same day, following the meal, Adorno wrote to the composer Ernst Krenek. He apologised for his delayed response, blaming it on the fact that his time in London was occupied with BBC matters.[36] Adorno was trying to get some *Lieder* he had composed performed on BBC radio, but he could not say if he had been successful. Clark, he reported, had given the impression that the *Lieder* might be performed, along with Krenek's, but nothing definite was said. In his opinion, this did not stem from malevolence on the part of the BBC, but rather disorganisation. The BBC had requested he write two essays, one a detailed analysis of Berg's *Lyric Suite* (1925–1926) for programme notes and the other an essay on Krenek for *The Listener*.

Schoen had his own proposals. In 'Music for Broadcasting: Should It Be Specially Arranged', written for the *BBC Annual* in 1935, he wrestled with the question of how music might determine the form of radio and vice versa. He reviewed the technical situation, the improvements in transmissions, which meant that many types of music could now be broadcast adequately, even if it was still necessary to adapt to sonic defects. But what people wanted was not talks, symphonies and plays, but rather entertainment, jazz and news. Schoen approved of intervening into works of the past, making them more radio-friendly, more comprehensible. But the most significant question for him was that of the social situation of radio music. Three images accompanied the article. One was a painting by Adolph Menzel of music at the court of Frederick the Great. Entitled *Flute Concert at Sans Souci*, the image showed musicians playing in close proximity to a noble audience in a grand ballroom, looked on by vast oil paintings under grand chandeliers. The King is playing, his back is turned to the audience, a high music stand blocks his view to other musicians. The second image was of La Scala in eighteenth-century Milan – grand in scale, the stage far from the audience, the performers dwarfed. The third was a photograph captioned 'The listener at home'. A domestic environment, three people sit close to the radio. One figure leans back and relaxes. Two others are sitting more upright. All appear rapt in concentration. They are listening together, apart.

What is the social situation of art, asked Schoen, and what 'very particular form of human society' was it made within? He imagines 'the poor solitary listener in front of his loudspeaker' who is 'overwhelmed by all the incompatible specimens of our music museums, each of them once meant for a very definite type of community, and now the poor man is not even told a word about the whys and wherefores of this musical farrago'.[37] He continued:

We are told that the famous man in the street wants 'none of your high-brow stuff' when he comes home tired from the day's work and turns on his loudspeaker. But nobody has ever seen him, this fabulous monster, nor been able to tell us what entertainment really is. I can tell you. For the man who is doing hard and tedious factory or office work day after day, it may be the latest song-hit, for another one, favoured with leisure and refinement, it may be the playing of chamber music. What a man understands by entertainment is entirely dependent on his general claims on life. This bestially low standard of entertainment of the man in the street is neither willed by him nor predestined in him but forced on him by artificially keeping down his claims on life.[38]

Culture as conveyed on the radio could exist, Schoen concludes, as 'more than an adornment, as something more than one of those sixpenny luxuries that tyrannise the life of the middle classes'. But it could do so only 'if a real social need can be thought of which broadcasting and nothing else but broadcasting will answer'.[39] To remedy the situation, Schoen proposed practical measures: 'a few examples of ways in which reconsideration and revaluations could enable music, more effectively than at present, to do its share in the general task of making the man in the street a man fit for the world'. To achieve this, he recommended:

- Introduction of an experimental music department.
- Selection of the best works and parts of works (a very difficult task, but not at all a matter of 'taste').
- Performance of these in documentary form (i.e. in associative connexion with their social and political surroundings, or in connexion with other works of similar or opposite form and style).
- Sociological comparison of musical and other types of work.
- Performance of 'light' music of to-day and demonstration of its derivation from classical forms.
- Demonstration of how far 'light' music is light and how far only bad.
- Awakening of interest in the combinatory laws of elementary musical technique. Little musical problems, musical competitions, musical puzzles.
- Not only performances of music for music's sake, but introduction of music wherever it serves a useful purpose, and demonstration of this use (for instance, in the news and running commentaries).
- Adaptation of all musical material for the very peculiar social situation of the solitary listener.
- And most important of all: Resuscitation of the communicative forces of music (formation of listeners' groups for music and continuous collaboration of listeners and listeners' groups on the microphone side).[40]

Amid the practical and programmatic recommendations, Schoen was motivated by a larger question. What music is worth broadcasting to all? To illustrate the naïveté of radio programming, he mobilises a prejudiced and colonialist image. The microphone, he argues, picks up everybody and everything that can be made audible. This indiscriminateness he compared to what he calls 'the bush-negro who adorns his naked beauty with the ornaments of top-hat, collar, and shirt-sleeves'. The implication is that what is available is drawn on, because it is there and can be – and in the process some sort of natural beauty is compromised. He uses a second analogy, 'that of the baby who wants to eat everything within his reach, solely because this is the only way yet known to him of assimilating his surroundings'.[41] Radio, in this view, grabbed what it could because it had not reflected on what was desirable or apt. Radio wanted to be assimilated by and assimilate to the world that already existed and could barely imagine a different one. Schoen evoked long-held and stereotyping tropes of modernism – that non-Europeans and children are somehow more authentic and immediate, even mimetic. Radio, by contrast, so the argument goes, needed artifice and mediation. It would also be later used to fight against the European militaristic-colonialist project that had determined its invention.[42]

What might Schoen think he could smuggle into BBC radio? And what other forces had a critical interest in what was broadcast? Communists in Britain at the time appeared not to theorise radio as a form, nor try to use it – they pointed out the spread of cheap sets in the Soviet Union, which could effectively educate and propagandise and, sometimes, they denounced what they perceived as lies on the BBC. The British Communist Party's *Daily Worker* carried some BBC schedules, but they appeared less prominently than the Moscow listings, for which, from 1934, a technician was available to tutor listeners on how to tune in to faint signals.[43] As there was a shift on the part of democratic societies towards fascist regimes as the main enemy, a certain rapprochement took place between national Communist Parties and democratic governments and, under a policy of the Popular Front, intellectuals joined the Communist Party and broadened its base by annexing with progressive cultural forces. From autumn 1935, a *Daily Worker* column reviewed programmes on BBC radio.[44]

* * *

Towards the back of the 1934 *BBC Year-Book*, a picture of Hitler at the Berlin Wireless Exhibition shows him looking indifferently – his eyes not meeting anyone else's – at a set of valves and radio paraphernalia thrust before him by the hands of a man in a black coat whose profile is caught indistinctly. Pressed up against and around Hitler are at least three SS agents, eyes alert, taking measure of the scene.[45] This photograph accompanies an article, published anonymously, on 'The Re-Organisation of German Broadcasting', which observed how German broadcasting had transformed in less than a year from 'an aggregation of privately-owned companies loosely bound to a point above' into 'a publicly-owned system of iron-bound centralisation, taking instructions from the Minister for Propaganda himself'. Continuity existed in terms of organisation – technical control lying in the hands of the Post Office, the central organisation still known as the Reichs-Rundfunk-Gesellschaft (State Radio Society). However, where previously 'the centre existed by virtue of the regions', now the opposite was true.

The article explained how the changes began in July 1932 with the introduction of the principle that the senior officials must be acceptable to the government of the day. By November, programme officials were being asked to follow the spirit of the leading German National People's Party. The political grip tightened after the March elections with Hitler's confirmation in power. A broadcasting department was formed within the Ministry of Propaganda under Eugen Hadamovsky. Many previous officials, if they were still in post, were dismissed if Jewish and alleged to be incompetent or politically suspect. At the opening of the Berlin Wireless Exhibition in August 1933, Hadamovsky proclaimed, as the *BBC Year-Book* reported:

All that happens in and through broadcasting to-day happens in order to create so broad a basis for National Socialism among the people that one day the entire nation will be drenched through and through with our philosophy, that one day it will be a thing taken for granted and an intimate need felt by every German to confess National Socialism.[46]

The article concluded with the state's plan to provide a radio set for every home and a programme of propaganda in the form of posters and mobile vehicles with loud speakers to draw in new listeners.[47] It could have noted the recent name change at Schoen's former radio station: SÜWRAG was renamed Reichssender Frankfurt in 1934. The station was reborn.

Weak Signals from New York

Jazz was a topic of discussion for the new exiles during the 1930s. Mátyás Seiber, the Hungarian composer, known to Schoen from Frankfurt, lodged at 32 Belsize Park, NW3, in 1936. In January 1936, Adorno was in correspondence with Seiber about a draft of an article on jazz – he wanted Seiber's comments.[48] Adorno had wanted a group of paid researchers, including Seiber, from a variety of disciplines – economics, social research, musical analysis, musical history and psychology – to take on the question of jazz. Questionnaires for music publishers and composers were to be read alongside a social theory of music. These means would track how jazz succumbs (according to the thesis) to social pressures and turns into a commodity, its musical promise corrupted. Adorno was particularly keen for his research team to discover how a 'hit' is made. The collective project did not come into being. The work on jazz eventually found form as Adorno's article 'On Jazz.'[49]

On 24 January 1933, on the eve of Nazi rule, a concert was broadcast from Geneva on SÜWRAG. Programmed to follow a Mozart performance, it was announced as an international concert, which began with '1. a) English, b) Cuban Rhythms, c) American cocktail, d) Musical eccentrics.' Then there was '2. a) Three South American songs, b) Three North American songs.' After this followed jazz: '3. Black Magic: a) Negro spirituals [...], b) Black-brown fantasies, c) Tiger-Ragtime.' The concert moved on to a 'Russian Fantasy' by Bob Engel. Those performing were listed as the Jazz-Symphoniker under Jean-Marc Pasche. Soloists included Jean Wiener, Clément Doucet and M. Hugues.

Was the radio jazz from Geneva the type of jazz that Adorno heard and railed against? Jazz that did not understand or sought to overlook or erase the jazz of the black experience? What did it mean to criticise jazz, if this aligned your aesthetic predilections with those of the fascist enemy? From 1933, the Nazis had moved against jazz in all its forms. In 1935, Hugo Hartung's radio play *Jonny spült ab* (Jonny Does the Dishes), with music by the composer Bernhard Eichhorn, was a parody of Ernst Krenek's *Jonny spielt auf* (Jonny Strikes Up), which had brought jazz themes into modern art music. The fate of jazz in the fascist context meant that those who performed it were reduced to parody and menial work.

On 1 October 1936, Schoen wrote to Horkheimer, who resided in New York City, at 429 West 117th Street. Schoen lived at 32 Belsize Park, London NW3.[50] After promptings from Adorno, Schoen shared a paper: a comprehensive study of broadcasting in all countries using historical materialist methods. It was a plan for a book that he hoped to complete – but he expressed doubts that he would manage it. The letter's tone was deferential. He wondered if the manuscript might fit with the Institute's plans to publish documentary and critical materials on propaganda and promotional activities. He asked if it would be permissible for it to be published in the Soviet Union as well; and if he might be able to use a pseudonym, as he feared for his paid roles at the radio station? He asked if a more lasting collaboration might be possible, a modest but regular one, noting that he was particularly interested in the social situation of art and artists during times of imperialist crises. He had completed studies, he noted, on the social symptomatics of art movements, their styles and use of material and also the current forced regrouping of artists in music, fine arts, poetry, theatre and film. He requested individual commissions, but also offered to gather source materials or book reports in the field. He concluded:

Forgive this digression. Perhaps the chapter on Germany in my study will remind you of the times when you were an occasional witness to my camouflage attempts on Frankfurt radio, those times which, as a consequence, made me a political émigré.[51]

Schoen attempted to remind Horkheimer of past connections. And then the inevitable:

With many kind wishes and compliments to you and your lady wife, also from my wife.[52]

A postscript appeared after the signature: 'By the way, I speak and write French, English, Italian and also a little Russian.'[53]

Adorno followed up on similar matters. On 29 June 1936, he had written to Horkheimer:

Mr Schoen has been telling me about his work on the history of radio. I have the impression that under certain circumstances this investigation might be included in a study of propaganda or that we could get a journal article out of it. I have encouraged him – of course with no commitments and no promise of an honorarium – to send you an outline. Perhaps it will result in something useful. Schoen is living under desperate circumstances and belongs among the decent political intellectuals.[54]

Adorno returned to this matter later in the year, on 26 October 1936, after he had received the forty-one-page manuscript of Schoen's radio work entitled 'On the Function of Radio in the United States, England and Germany'. He had read it right away, but it was unclear to him how it sat alongside his own project and he wanted to express his opinions, in case Schoen's article gave the embarrassing impression that this bore any relation to the ideas he had in mind.[55]

It is self-evidently out of the question that we publish it in this form. For one, because of the political pronouncements, which might be all well and good in their scene (although I myself would doubt the political effectivity, if the foundations are so narrow), but for which we are certainly not the place; and not to mention the hymns to Russia, to which one shows, I think, the most loyal attitude at the moment by remaining silent. But also because of the quality of the content. There are a number of very interesting and also new materials in it, but the conclusions that are drawn from them are quite schematic and empty, i.e. the dialectical concretisation of an ideological phenomena, which appears to us as one of the most urgent tasks of theory, is quite misjudged here, with its consistently repeated – and to some extent blind assurances against the concrete moment – that radio is a class instrument etc, which we certainly do not doubt, but as a generality, however, is quite pointless to assert. Best of all would be the work appearing in an explicitly political journal such as *Left Review* or the *New Statesman* or over there in something like the *New Republic*. I've already looked around on those grounds; but it is hopeless, partly because of the length, which, even with radical cuts, is still many times longer than what is possible there; but also because this work, which is so fatally reminiscent of Dreyfuss's employee investigation and appears like a parody of a scientific study, would still appear much too academic there.[56]

Adorno invited Schoen to visit and speak with him about it. Perhaps the contribution could be reduced to the empirical parts and cut to fifteen pages. Adorno wondered if he could clarify for Schoen some of the theoretical consequences and work with him to rewrite it. But he left it in Horkheimer's gift to decide if it was usable. If not, he should let him know quickly, so that he might cancel the meeting. He encouraged Horkheimer in any case to send £5 to Schoen, because of 'Schoen's desperate poverty'.[57]

Horkheimer wrote to Schoen on 27 October 1936, describing the process by which something could be published at the Institute, various levels of processing and inspection, involving the department, himself and then Wiesengrund-Adorno. He advised that the manuscript might not be quite right. He also insisted that the manuscript could not appear in any other languages. He told Schoen that the journal was set up to publish work by close associates of the Institute. Appearing only three times a year, there was little room for essays. As it was one of very few independent German language publications, many scholars who sent unsolicited work could not be published. Horkheimer was more interested in what Schoen could deliver in a bibliographic review. He informed Schoen that the Institute was conducting studies into authority and the family and, in connection with this, they were interested in the sociological significance of radio, its function and role in social conditioning. He asked for an assessment of books published on these topics in the last two years. Horkheimer mentioned how the Institute hoped one day, when it had the financial means, to publish monographs and should that come to pass, he would be happy to discuss the proposition again.

The letter breaks off a little at the margins, but there appear to be no references to Schoen's impoverished and precarious situation or recognition of his predicament, simply the convention of wishing the wife all the best, with one extra thing in parentheses: '(Does the beautiful colourful Parisian scarf still exist?) My wife trusts your recommendation the most'. Schoen was reduced to a fashion consultant. On 30 October, Adorno wrote to Horkheimer that the meeting with Schoen was going ahead and that he would try to extract some empirical material from the work and leave out the theory. On 23 November, Adorno reported back on the meeting. He let Horkheimer know that Schoen 'behaved very nicely and unpretentiously in every way and approached everything with understanding – without falling into soapiness':[58]

He is a decent, very cultivated and informed man and has had those types of decisive experiences which I called, in a discussion with Pollock, 'lifting up the stone and seeing the worms beneath'. I believe that, in the field of his specialist knowledge, directed in the right way, he can be of use and that he deserves to be encouraged by us. On the other hand, I am fully aware that he is not to be regarded as 'theoretically gifted' and does not claim to be so himself. So in discussion with him I soon renounced my original idea to formulate his large essay in terms of theoretical interpretation, as that would have meant simply writing the essay myself and this was not the idea.[59]

Instead, Adorno pushed for removal of the 'crudely offensive *politica*'. Schoen obliged. They reserved the right to cut more.[60] And, Adorno suggested, they could print some of it in a smaller font, to take up less room. Schoen was also happy to undertake a review of radio literature, as Horkheimer had requested. Adorno pressed for payment to Schoen, noting that he did not even have money to make a trip from London to Oxford.

Horkheimer responded on 8 December, indicating that they should remain in correspondence with Schoen, but it was unlikely that the journal would publish his book discussion, as his review essay was dealing with year-books, which was not something they reviewed.[61] Horkheimer reported bad news on 22 February 1937. Schoen's discussion was unusable: 'He simply cannot do it.' He proposed that Adorno let Schoen know that the material would be used for internal discussions only and he should be paid a further £5 for his efforts.[62] On 2 March, Adorno replied that he was sorry the work was unusable, but appreciated the offer of £5 and hoped it would get to Schoen very quickly. On 23 March, Adorno reported that he had seen Schoen, who had shown him the rejected writings. Adorno agreed with their rejection and admitted that he had no heart to solicit any more work from Schoen.[63]

Opera Groupings

One flyer grabbed our attention in Schoen's Koblenz archive. The front had a modern flair – with sleek black, red and white graphics. Inside, a black and white map depicts each central London music venue, from Cecil Sharp House in North London to the BBC Maida Vale Studios in the West. In a land without music, London appeared as an oasis of tepid leisure and cultural consumption. In this landscape Schoen became a performer and producer, in an organisation called the Opera Group. The mission was set out:

THE OPERA GROUP has been founded for the performance of all kinds of opera except grand opera. There are many more small operas than great ones, and their artistic appeal is at least equal to that of the latter. Their range covers the whole period from the very beginning of opera up to the present time, and they are particularly characteristic of transitional periods such as our own. Thus, THE OPERA GROUP aims at making known to a wider public the charms of these operas, and also at stimulating the creative interest of composers in this particular form. [...] THE OPERA GROUP aims at convincing the public of the specific theatrical appeal of opera. [...] [T]he Group does not wish to scare individuals.[64]

On 31 January 1936, newspapers, from the *Portsmouth Evening News* to the *Sheffield Independent*, gave notice in their radio listings of a broadcast of performances by the Opera Group, with Ernst Schoen as director and mezzo-soprano Betty Bannermann and sopranos Nora Colton, Honor Terras and Eugenia Triguez. A few months later, on 30 April, a notice of the Opera Group's work appeared in the *Yorkshire Post* and the *Leeds Intelligencer*. The report included expression of the 'hope to repeat the London programme on tour, both in England and abroad, if public support warrants it.' It continued: 'Mr. Ernst Schoen is the producer, Mr. Georg Knepler is conductor, and among the eleven members of the company are Howard Hemming and Betty Bannermann.' It is likely this performance that Adorno remarks on favourably in a letter to Seiber on 28 May 1936:

Schoen's performance made a brilliant impression. Kneppler [sic.] is truly a quite excellent musician. Of course the soloists barely give anything of their own and the question remains whether one can bring something legitimate into being entirely without any initiative from the staged individual. But perhaps the people are capable of development. In any case, I am much more optimistic about the enterprise, sans phrases, than I was at first.[65]

He finishes:

Greet the Schoens warmly on my behalf, and be in touch soon.[66]

The Opera Group made it into national and regional newsprint. On 29 November 1936, there were listings in the *Belfast Telegraph* and the *Sunderland Daily Echo and Shipping Gazette*, among others, and a broadcast by the National Programme, transmitted from Daventry, of 'Comic Opera in Beethoven's Time'. Schoen was again listed as director and it was performed by the BBC Orchestra (Section C), led by Laurence Turner and conducted by Georg Knepler.

On 10 March 1937, there was a short review of the Group by Crescendo in the *Daily News*. This dispatch on the previous night's music at Cowdray Hall noted that 'the Opera Group, sponsored by Ernst Schoen, gave some examples of contemporary opera; Two Czech composers, Janáček and Alois Haba, opened this curious entertainment, preceded by a commentary by

Edward Clark, who spoke on opera in general and not on the six excerpts on the programme'. The review was negative:

The 'House of the Dead' and the 'New Earth' – this latter illustrating hunger and desolation – sufficed as far as I was concerned and if many of the audience had been as honest, they too would have left the hall.[67]

The *Radio Times* listed the first broadcast of Jacques Offenbach's comic opera *Bluebeard* (1866) on 7 July 1937 on the National Programme from Daventry and on 9 July regionally, performed by the BBC Revue Chorus and The BBC Theatre Orchestra. It was written and adapted for the microphone by Kathleen Nott and Ernst Schoen and, as Schoen had proposed in his 1935 *BBC Annual* article on musical adaptation for broadcasting,[68] it was condensed into a forty-five-minute production.

Schoen frequented other music scenes. He was a member of the International Society for Contemporary Music. A ticket is preserved in the archive with 'Complimentary' stamped on the top, from when the Opera Group performed a selection of English Opera from 1680 to 1768 on 19 June 1938 at the Royal College of Music.

Another brochure survives, from a performance of Dr John Blow's *Venus and Adonis* (c.1683) and Charles Dibdin's *The Ephesian Matron* (1769). Some of the costume designs for these performances remain in the archive: kitsch, flamboyant, opulent.

On 10 August 1937, the Opera Group presented scenes from Otto Nicolai's *Merry Wives of Windsor* (1848). The performances sparked a discussion of the place of opera and questions of difficulty and adaptability. Must high opera be avoided, as it would not be tolerated by the audiences, either in the halls or listening through the radio? In an article in the collection of cuttings in Schoen's archive, the journalist Garry Allighan stated 'Opera Must be Condensed to be a Radio Success'. Did the technology of the radio, as much as the technology of the audience, determine this truncation, this lightness, and so on? Under the title 'Ear, Without Eye', Allighan wrote:

Ernst Schoen, director of the Opera Group, showed last night that opera has to be adapted for the microphone if it is to be acceptable. He took Otto Nicolai's operational version of the Shakespeare play and presented those scenes which possessed nothing but aural qualities.

[...]

These [...] scenes [...] lost nothing by being presented for the ear only without the aid of vision.

The opera was reduced to microphonic proportions in scenes and running time. The result was a self-contained and concise sound-drama.

This is, I am convinced, the form for studio opera. An hour is the ideal length for this type of entertainment and with a good cast, full chorus under Leslie Woodgate and the B.B.C. orchestra conducted by Georg Knepler, the joint-founder with Ernst Schoen of the Opera Group, the perfect musical broadcast was achieved.

If the B.B.C. were to arrange for the Opera Group to broadcast similar studio-opera weekly they would please a very large number of listeners.[69]

What of the demand of the heavy, not the light, to reflect on the heavy world? Though the Opera Group often worked within the orbit of lightness, it also carried over some legacy from Schoen's Weimar years. In 1938, for example, Schoen conducted the Opera Group in excerpts of Brecht's *Threepenny Opera* (1928) for a Festival of German Music, which had been organised alongside a 'Festival of Twentieth Century German Art' at the New Burlington Galleries.[70] The festival was a riposte to the Nazi 'Degenerate Art' exhibition touring in Germany after 1937. Alongside it, a 'Degenerate Music' exhibition took place in May 1938 in Düsseldorf. Hans Severus Ziegler – hater in equal measure of what he called 'Negroidism' and atonality – produced a booklet for it.[71] On one page a collation of images – a cover of *Melos* journal, the cover of an issue of *Anbruch*, dedicated to Gustav Mahler, with an essay by Adorno and a handbill for Krenek's *Jonny Strikes Up* – was captioned 'In these pages Musical Bolshevism was souped up'.[72]

Among the Opera Group cuttings collected amongst Schoen's things is an article from the *Evening Standard* from 27 August 1938. The head-line: 'Aliens Are Flooding Our Music Market'. Neither Schoen's name nor Knepler's is used, but they might well have been. It reads: 'Alien musical conductors and orchestrators have been pouring into this country...' and continues, quoting a representative of the British Authors and Composers Association, 'The point is that what they are doing is just what a competent British musician and composer could do. There is no particular art in a good deal of it.'[73] England had provided a shelter, but it was not necessarily a safe and welcoming one.

To Be British

On 19 June 1939 the *Deutscher Reichsanzeiger und Preußischer Staatsanzeiger* published a list of those who had been stripped of their citizenship four days previously. Included among 141 names are: Ernst, Johanna and Nina Schoen.[74] The following year, in 1940, Schoen got a position as a translator in the German section of the BBC External Services department. With a more stable position came a new address. Hansi recorded it in her 1940 diary: 99 Greencroft Gardens in South Hampstead.

Established in 1938 during the Munich Crisis, the German Service of the BBC was an extensive broadcasting service attempting to change the minds of Germans.[75] News and commentary appeared alongside satirical broadcasts. It operated from Surrey Street and, after 1941, from Bush House. By 1944, it was broadcasting for four hours a day. Schoen and others worked on translation materials to underpin the broadcasts, under the leadership of Carl Brinitzer.

The BBC External Services department, the umbrella organisation under which the various polyglot language sections existed, was a Tower of Babel, as a *BBC Year-Book* from 1948 called it.[76] Antonia White described it in *BBC at War* (1942):

At the beginning of the war the BBC was broadcasting in nine languages: to-day its news bulletins go out in no less than thirty-nine. At the outbreak of war the European news service was broadcasting in French, German, Italian, Spanish and Portuguese. Almost immediately Polish and Czech were added. Since then N. F. Newsome, the editor, has had over and over again to recruit yet another language staff at short notice till now the schedule of his department includes twenty languages, and the daily transmission of 300,000 words in thirty-six hours of broadcasting. Working elbow to elbow in stuffy basement rooms by artificial light, the seventy-five editors and sub-editors deal with the incessant stream of news that pours in from typewriters, telephones and tape-machines. Each diverts part of the stream into the channels of the particular country for which he works, emphasises the points most likely to interest its inhabitants and presents them in the way that appeals to their temperament and psychology.[77]

Here, Schoen was limited to the role of an observer, a translator of others' words, listening in. Those who were allowed to broadcast had to fit a particular type: the polyvocal was reduced to the monologic, whose voices must be pinched and without accent.[78]

Radio in the Mirror

Schoen had left German radio behind, but German radio still made its way to England. There were various ways for the Nazi regime to occupy the airwaves. Transmissions saturated Germans with Nazi ideas, music, cultural approaches, but there was also diffusion outwards across the world. The existing foreign service on shortwave, a sampling of German language broadcasts from across the regional stations, was augmented and amplified. At first, it was directed at Germans living abroad, with the aim of giving notice, beyond the borders of Germany, of the desires and deeds of National Socialism.[79]

One particular poster depicted a German fortress on a hill, surrounded by low mountains, lakes and tiny settlements. 'Germans, your Heimat is speaking to you' ran the title and in smaller letters beneath: 'On the Short Wave Station'. The radio tower hovers higher than all the surroundings and from it, pulsations of circular waves emanate like a sun.[80] The chimes of the Garrison Church at Potsdam sounded the 'identification signals' – distinctive tones on shortwave to permit listeners with simple receivers to tune into the right frequency and the correct time. The broadcasting towers of Zeesen, rising high above the Brandenburg pines, carried, as promotional materials put it, the voice of Germany and German music around the world. It was not uncommon to find such a description with depictions of short waves emanating in multiple directions to conquer the broad waves of the seven seas and separate home and abroad. The music might be 'German' – but from 1941 what that meant was a prohibition of music featuring muted horns, atonal melodies, or with a 'distorted rhythm' (*verzerrte Rhythmen*).

As much as it was martial, the technology of radio was also presented as a type of magic, conveyed by mysterious tubes, antennae, masts and wires. The German shortwave station taught a new ABC comprised of the letters of the call signal of Berlin shortwave radio, 'the magic series DJA to DJR'.[81]

Brecht and Eisler wrote a song in 1942, while in Hollywood. A small apparatus has carefully been looked after, part of the home effects carried from place to place by exiles. It was both a conduit of useful information and a means of keeping the words of the oppressor close.

You little box that I carried in flight,
Carefully, such that the valves would not break,
From house to train, from ship to train,
So that my enemies could to talk to me,
Where I lay and at my pain,
Late into the night, first thing in the morning
Talking of its victories and my troubles
Promise me you won't suddenly go silent again![82]

External Services broadcast in the German language from England to Germany. The German station Reichssender Hamburg (Imperial Broadcaster Hamburg) amongst others, broadcast to the British Isles in English and Gaelic. There were various Lord Haw Haws prepared to do what were effectively presentations of Nazi propaganda, most famously William Joyce. Numerous others, many of them women, broadcast from the *Rundfunkhaus* (Broadcasting House) in Berlin, wrote manuscripts, read them, or read the words of others. The content ranged from cultural presentations to news and current affairs.[83]

Vivian Stranders announced the news in 1942. A large secret service file on him reveals he had been under surveillance from the 1920s, when he posed as a British secret service agent in Belgium.[84] The British Security Services suspected him of working for the German state. By raiding a hotel room, proof was obtained of his engagement as a spy for £2 a day and that he was drinking heavily. Evidence that he was a bigamist was also found. Eventually the French authorities arrested him on espionage charges and he was sentenced to imprisonment for two years. In the 1940s he lived on Hauptstraße in Berlin and was paid 60RM per show.

A curious case was Frances Dorothy Eckersley, a comrade of William Joyce and donor of funds to help the National Socialist League find a new headquarters in London. Through her contacts, Joyce was taken on by the radio station. At the end of 1939, Eckersley and her son James Clark joined the external service of the broadcasting station in Berlin. His father was Edward Clark, Schoen's friend and music advisor to the young BBC. Clark and Eckersley, daughter of an army officer and his estranged suffragette wife, were in a marriage from 1922 to 1929, when she left him for another BBC employee, chief radio engineer Peter Eckersley, who had a close association with Oswald Mosley.

The marriage was dissolved in December 1929, on grounds of adultery.[85] The adulterous lovers were in the Independent Labour Party, but Peter followed Mosley into the New Party. Dorothy Eckersley, who had been drawn to Stalinism, visited Nazi Germany in 1937 and was impressed. She worshipped Hitler.[86] She joined a group called The Link, which strove to strengthen Anglo-German bonds. A friend, Margaret Bothamley, was an active Nazi in a number of groupings, such as the Anglo-German Fellowship, the Nordic League, the Right Club, the National Socialist League and was the secretary of the inner London branch of The Link.

Bothamley also founded the Imperial Fascist League, which Dorothy Eckersley joined. Eckersley went to Berlin with her son and sent him to school there. Eckersley began broadcasting on 15 December 1939, announcing, acting, archiving and translating and she brought in friends such as Bothamley. From February 1942 to January 1943, she analysed English newspaper reports and BBC programme content in order to ascertain which items German radio should contradict.[87] She broadcast as Jeanette in a series of plays called *Women to Women* until May 1943. And then things began to unravel, through illness and her efforts to extricate herself from her situation in Germany. The radio station was keen to keep her son broadcasting, but she felt things were falling apart and kept him away. Eventually they were arrested by the Gestapo and interned in Austria and northern Italy, until the British released them at the end of the war. There was a trial in July 1944 of the two of them, though the son was exonerated on account of his youth and inexperience.[88] He had cooperated in the internment camp in June 1945 by giving as many names and details of English-language broadcasters on the *Kurzwelle* (shortwave) as he could muster.[89] Eckersley was found guilty in 1946 of assisting enemy propaganda through broadcasting and sentenced to twelve months imprisonment.

Margaret Bothamley broadcast from July 1940 until March 1945, writing her own features and delivering them. In her defence statement, taken by Major R. W. Spooner, Bothamley stated:

The reason I worked at the Rundfunk was that it was my only opportunity to warn English people of the danger England was incurring in being influenced by propaganda against Germany and in favour of Soviet Russia. I was troubled by the decay in morals in English education, especially in the co-educational schools and by the activities of the Sexual Reform Society, whose leader had come to London from Germany, as well as by the change of policy at Unionist Headquarters. I have proof of war being planned against Germany from 1907 and onward. I have proof from English sources of all I used to say. I was troubled at doing these broadcasts; but I felt like a mother who saw her children in danger and could only call to them from a house which was not on speaking terms with mine.[90]

There was also Jack Trevor, real name Anthony Cedric Sebastian Steane, a British actor who became a speaker for such shows as *Victory Over Microbes* and *Club of Notions*. He was convicted at the Central Criminal Court in January 1947 of assisting the enemy and sentenced to three years' imprisonment. He managed to successfully argue that he had been pressured into it all by the Gestapo and the sentence was annulled after an appeal. There were various others, English Nazis, upper class types, just like the people Schoen parodied in his unpublished 1942 play written in English, *Distinguished Company*. Sir Osbert Nosey, the Hon. Waldorf Oscar MP, Captain Ramshackle and others gather to discuss how they can court Hitler and take over the world. And they collect in a living room that Schoen sketched: a living room with a dining table, perspective askew and a picture of Hitler above the fireplace.[91] This was a social and political scene Schoen had to contend with.

But still they did their part for the British state. The presence of Hansi and Ernst at wartime night duty was recorded in one of the entries in the 1940 diary for both of them: Air Raid Precaution (ARP) volunteer work in war time. On 21 May, from midnight to 4 a.m., Hansi worked on gun post duty. From October of that year, during the Blitz, several high explosive bombs ripped through the area.[92]

To not be British

In time there was another improvement in living arrangements. Schoen and the family moved to a rented flat in a swish modern development called Kingfisher Court, in East Molesey, a suburb just down from the Thames by Hampton Court.

Nikolaus Pevsner included Kingfisher Court in his London surveys, remarking: 'KINGFISHER COURT, 1933 by Guy Morgan. Quite interesting as an early essay in the modern style, i.e. early as England goes. Two small blocks of flats, three storied, with, on the roofs, sunroofs of concrete designed like station platforms.'[93]

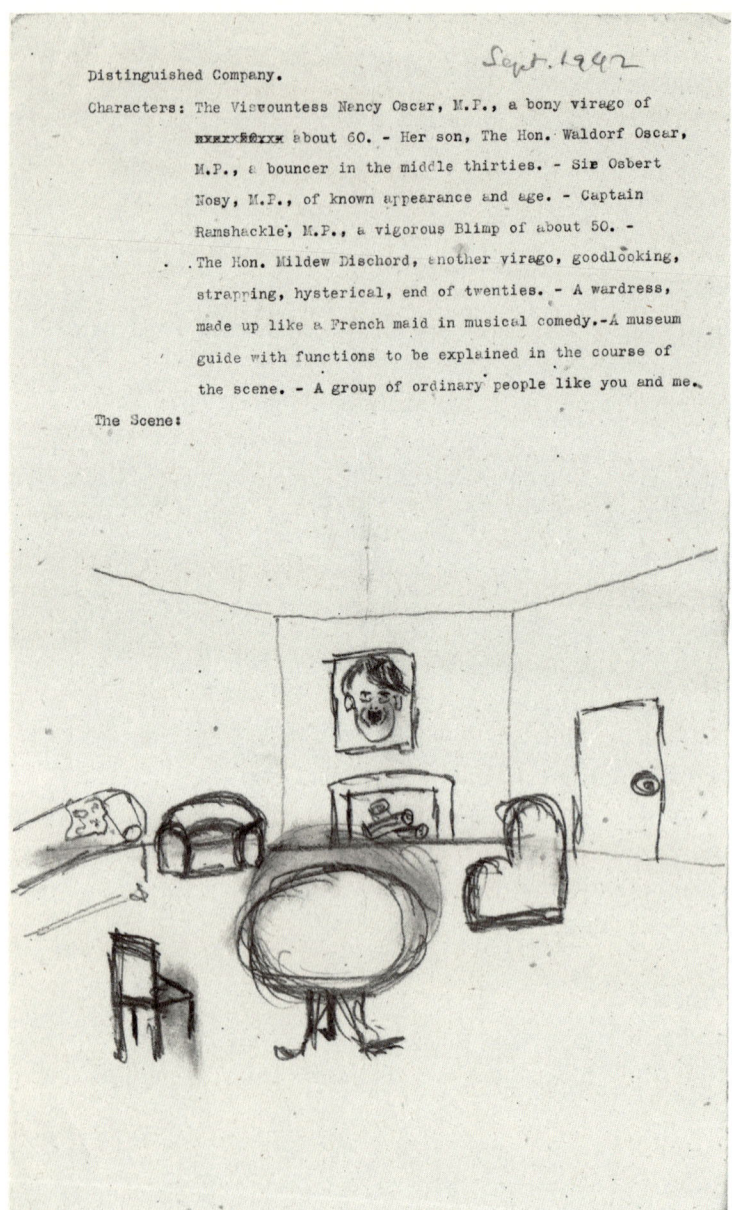

Figure 4.1 Set for Ernst Schoen's play *Distinguished Company* (1942), drawn by himself.

Photographed at the Bundesarchiv Koblenz. From Schoen's Archive in Koblenz: *Bühnenstücke, Filmmanuskripte und Rundfunksendungen*, BArch N 1403/69. Copyright: Sabine Schiller-Lerg.

This transitory architecture, of coming and going, suited the Schoens, given, until the 1970s, units were mostly still only available as rentals. Here the Schoens floated, with something more than a mast to cling to, at least for a while. The environment was modernist and glamorous. It had tennis courts and a swimming pool, a bowling green, a cocktail bar, a sunken garden, a pond and a self-named Country Club. It attracted actors and directors, given its proximity to film production studios.

They lived at flat 43, on the upper floor, overlooking the River Mole, a small tributary of the Thames. In an interview from 1984, Georg Knepler described being with Ernst Schoen and Hanns Eisler in Schoen's lounge. Knepler remembered a painting that Schoen valued: 'Something constructivist [...] something to do with radio, there were wires, and a microphone and a head'.[94] It was *Stillleben mit Kopf*, a portrait gifted in Frankfurt days, by their neighbour Willi Baumeister. Knepler added that 'Eisler poked fun at the picture and Schoen in turn found it strange that Eisler who had a sense of novelty when it came to music proved not to possess it in a neighbouring medium.'[95]

Letters in the archive chronicle disputes over the rent and the facilities. In one dated 8 July 1942, the management of the building requested an annual fee of 10/6d to maintain the upkeep of the pool, an increase as a result of the war.[96]

In the non-working hours in his day, Schoen wrote poetry into which he poured his frustrations, anger and fears. The opening poem in his collection *Londoner Elegien* (London Elegies) vented spleen against England. Composed between 27 February and 7 March 1941, 'Peace and War', begins with an image of London in peacetime, a place of

> human mildew on the rind of the earth
> And the largest abscess on a limp and pregnant body
> A fascinating old woman: England,
> London: Millions of tightly compressed
> Identical little houses built quickly out of dirt.
> Inside bridal trousseaus of garish upholstered furniture,
> Sat to pieces before it is paid off.
> In front of the cold fireplaces gas ovens for cooking and warming,
> Aspidistras in every window
> Radio howls come from all the windows
> On the corners of the streets churches, pubs and cinemas.
> Here and there the beauty of buildings, gardens and people:
> Sheen on the fungus.[97]

The vision was bleak. He wrote about men of good old Celtic stock weakened by work and thin beer and women who are either embittered lesbians or wailing, nagging birth machines. He wrote of misery, observed from an open-topped bus and of gateways leading into the belly of the earth, where a warm stinking wind hit the descender like a fist in the face. Down in the underground, trains flung people out or sucked them in, a sticky mass, from one nothingness to another. That was in peacetime. And in war-time nothing much had changed. One was still pursued by the nightmare of rows of houses, all identical. There was no arrival, just a sense of being back at the beginning for ever and ever. Sometimes, a bomb whipped away the façade and it was possible to see a mirror hanging on its hook or a bath tub looming in the air or a ruptured armchair crowned in a red white and blue flag. Only when the darkness fell was the ugliness, rubble and misery concealed. The hellish stinking underground was the shelter now. The platforms were dense with those who have taken to sleeping down there, no longer travellers but a populace. The poet detailed a life that developed in the artificial light of the tube. There was gossiping, eating, laughing, loving and fighting and sometimes an accordion played tunes for a party. Everyone huddled there together.

> Until one night a merciful bomb breaks in and releases
> everyone from their spunkiness.[98]

Schoen's desolate poem referred to an incident on the evening of 11 January 1941 at Bank tube station, where a bomb's destructive shockwaves travelled through the booking hall, down the escalator and stairs to the platform, killing more than fifty people, or in Schoen's dejected view, releasing them dramatically from their English stiff-upper-lippedness.

He had become embittered but also more fervently political. Under the rubric of *Gebrauchsmusik*, he wrote a number of political songs in 1941. The 'Heimkehrlied' (The Home Coming Song) spoke of wandering and displaced people, as they creep through and across lands in a quest for liberation and a return to somewhere called home. One hundred years ago it was the communist spectre stalking Europe. In 1941, it was more bleakly the efforts of various peoples and groupings to win back territory and political autonomy from the Nazis.

We have wandered since '33
Following the stars,
But some of our travelling companions
Left before us.

First the Hungarians wandered
Far over mountain and valley,
As the Admiral on horseback
Made himself King of the Hapsburgs.

And then, as Mussolini
Marched into Rome,
The best Italians could not remain
In their homeland any more.

We left our home,
When Adolf Hitler came,
This impudent Nazi terror
Took our body and life from us.

We are a colourful heap,
That you see coming now,
And some of those who walk with us,
Barely know where we are going.

Liberals and Socialists are
Amongst our number,
And Jews wander with Christians,
Men, women and children together.

And behind us follow more,
The Austrians are joining us,
The Czechs and the Poles are wandering
The Spanish too, man for man.

Dutch, French and Belgians,
Norwegians and Greeks too:
The army, in which we wander,
Never stops coming.

We wander over the Alps,
Carpathians and Pyrenees.
We creep through the woods at night,
We swim through rivers and seas.

No internment camp
Terrifies us, no border soldier,

No police jail,
No passport office, no barbed wire.

First we wandered to Spain,
To Czechoslovakia,
To France, to England, to Holland,
Wherever room could be found for us.

Often we had to keep on wandering,
Sometimes even over seas,
And then with heavy steps
Fascism came behind us.

From France we went on to Spain,
From there to Portugal;
The cells and barrack camps
Greeted us everywhere.

From England it was on to Australia
And to Canada too,
And then back again to England;
No stopping near or far.

Our fathers wandered in this way too
A hundred years ago,
But their wandering was not in vain,
It had meaning and purpose.

When Marx and Engels hiked
And Herwegh and Freiligrath,
That was progress for all,
The socialist state.

And so we wander in the homeland,
And we fight until it is freed.
Out battle cry: Down with Hitler.
Our weapon: unity![99]

A second composition, in a similar style, titled the 'Anti-Hitler Song', portrayed waves of opposition to Fascism across Europe.

From Murmansk down to the Black Sea
Workers, peasants and soldiers defend
Their land against Hitler's fascist army,
Against Hitler's bloody cruel deeds.
From the Don up to the Finnish lakes,
Their call rings powerfully and clearly:

We will put a stop to the Nazi armies
And a stop to Hitler, this year!

From England's factories and aircraft hangars,
From the conveyor belt, from the workbench,
From the pilots, from the commando troops,
From every ship and every tank,
Sound out the voices of the bravest, the best
In an ever growing, louder and louder choir:
We forge the weapons, we fight in the West,
And we prepare the second front.

Partisans are the Czech saboteurs,
The revenge for the dead of St Nazaire.
Norwegian teachers, and deserters
From Bulgaria and Austria, they form an army
Of avenging against the Nazis and strike
Now the last annihilating blow,
The Greeks, the Dutch, Belgians and Poles
Stand ready for the Day of Retribution.

From the Ruhr, from Mannheim,
    from Hamburg and Bremen,
From Gestapo jails and the military hospitals
Can be perceived a quietly threatening tone,
From every labour camp, from every concentration camp
And from the bloody wounds of parting
The German mothers rise to speak:
An end to the mad Nazi dogs
And an end to Hitler: Right now, immediately![100]

Its location and date were given at the end: London, 1941.

Water and War

One poem from *Londoner Elegien* was titled 'Seestück' (Sea Piece) and
opened with an image of a frozen body plunged into the sea, only to
later surface from the depths. This small moment of release – a submerg-
ing into freely willed death, or *Freitod* – is undermined by the gulp of air
snatched after life fights back. The poem continued with Schoen's recollections of various seas: the North Sea visited as a child, with its dunes
and glassy grey water pooling around rocks; the Atlantic, the Adriatic and
Olympic cloudscapes; the coast in damp England. Unforgettable, though,
is the Mediterranean. The poem described swimming out into the sea

and looking back at loved ones far away on the beach. Fear arises about not being able to make it back. But one does and those on the beach barely noticed your absence. The beaches in his imagination here were at Le Lavandou on the Favière Coast, where Brecht spent summers and Benjamin visited. He thought, too, of Homer and wine and Charon's boat across the River Styx. He recalled sailors leaping off their steel-grey destroyers and diving into a bistro. They emerged with a copy of the Communist newspaper *l'Humanité* under their arm. Were these soldiers still watching over their posts, but now as dead men, marshalled in a skeleton parade.

> Ah, have not all seas become
> Red seas of blood salt lakes seas of tears?
> Why do they not spill over the shores?
> Are they not full to overflowing with the
> Ludicrous iron tower supports of tank fleets,
> With the swimming men-cities of death, now themselves
> Dying in the green glassy deep sea landscape.[101]

If the seas had become conduits of war, should not sea monsters devour the 'cities of death'? There was a glimmer of hope. One day children would play on beaches again. Waves would again gently lap against coasts.

The end of war was approaching. Coming from the seas and from the air and through the fields in September 1944 were Allied troops. They came from the West – Aachen was the first city to fall. From the East, the Red Army advanced. As a result, the radius of Nazi German broadcasting began to shrink: and anyway electricity was cutting out. Radio station houses were bombed and destroyed. Frankfurt Radio's house had been pegged as the evacuation building for the control centre of German radio in case of severe damage in Berlin. It was hit by bombs in March and September and moved to a temporary requisitioned site in Bad Nauheim.[102]

In the *BBC Year-Book* of 1944, a note on the German Service discussed the difficulties of striking the right attitude on radio, as victory against 'the main enemy' proceeded. What is the right tone to adopt when broadcasting to a people in defeat?

Crowing and sneering will not help; one must be factual, restrained, objective, above all accurate; the opportunities for light relief are few. Happily the service can always draw on Hitler, whose past speeches, recorded by BBC engineers when they were broadcast and played back at appropriate moments, provide a lively and arresting way of reminding our German listeners of past triumphs and unrealized arrogant hopes. All the evidence shows that Hitler himself is quite outstanding as a propagandist on behalf of the German Service of the BBC.[103]

What had been a sign of power, exercised through a total saturation of the airwaves with ideology, became its own indictment, as Hitlerian pomp was undermined and rang out as evidence of failure, documents of vain-gloriousness or hubris.

Ends or Beginnings (Dream Worlds)

One practice that remained experimental, uncensored by the press or crushed by the indifference of the audience in the host country, was Schoen's habit of dream transcription. It became a work in its own right, a ritual of remembrance and transcription. He wrote out his dreams, mostly in German, in pen or pencil, then often typed them up on a typewriter. A modernist practice, perhaps surrealistic, perhaps therapeutic. It gives some sort of access to his life, his occupations and preoccupations through these years, when what occurred was far from any official channels.[104]

Schoen typed up a dream that he had on the night of 27–28 November 1939. In the dream, as in the world, the family lived in cramped conditions in Belsize Park. In the dream, they were even more squeezed, living only in the left-most part of the house:

On the wall, a poor white little bud bloomed on a thin stem. I wanted to pick it and to do that I had to pull it through a ring. As I did that, the bud on the stalk broke with a loud human cry of pain. In a later part of the dream, Hansi informed me, to my delight, that she had inherited, along with the whole house, in which we had only lived in such a small uncomfortable part, also the title of Reigning Countess. She dampened my joy though, in informing me that while the title also goes to the children, it does not go to me, since I only married into it.[105]

Something fragile tried to find an existence and failed. The dream provided a sense of joy – such elevation, socially, above this, a promise of space and status. That, too, was snatched away, from Schoen at least. Perhaps he could not bear to snatch it, even in a dream, from the rest of his family.

* * *

Interruption: Sleep and Dream

Schoen dreamed about the BBC – sometimes his dreams about the BBC took place at the BBC, in a specially designated sleep room, in Brooklyn Hall, Bush House. An article from the 1934 *Year-Book*, entitled 'How

Broadcasting House is Run', explained something of how the BBC's buildings catered to the rhythms of the working day:

More mundane matters need the attention of the broadcasting staff, and such
commonplace factors as food, and even sleep, have to be catered for within the
walls of Broadcasting House. As has been said, rehearsals of many programmes
are taking place daily, and every session must be broken at some given time for a
'breather'. In the basement at the broadcasting headquarters there is a restaurant
which must be capable of providing meals or light refreshments throughout the
twenty-four hours of each day, since a fifteen-minute interval does not afford time
to the artists to go outside for a coffee.[106]

And given the imperial reach of the BBC, the sun never set not only on its
territory but on its work. As the 1943 *Year-Book* acknowledged, the BBC
'Overseas Service' could never sleep,[107] but, as is started a decade before,
its workers must:

The Empire transmissions run into most of the early morning hours – and the
staff on night shift must be fed at the normal mealtime intervals as though it
were day. Furthermore, it is not possible for one Announcer to cover the late
evening and early morning programmes (finishing with the Canadian Zone
at 3am), and also to take the Australasian Zone transmission, which begins at
certain times of the year at 5.30am. Neither is it economically practicable to
expect these members of the staff to live either on top of the building or per-
manently in a near-by hotel. As a result, arrangements must be made whereby
one Announcer may go to bed at 3am and be able to get a reasonable period of
sleep (which means that his quarters must be sufficiently quiet to enable him
to sleep whilst the day-time staff arrive and work), whilst the man who starts
announcing at 5.30am must have facilities for sleeping up to the time he has to
prepare for his programme.[108]

These 'late night programmes' also helped out the sleepless in proximate
time zones. Some sought radio out to pique interest before sleeping.
A little quip in *Wireless World* from 9 November 1934 made a complaint:

AND SO TO BED
      It is one of numerous bees in the bonnet of the BBC that the British listener
can stomach nothing heavier than dance music after 11 p.m., and this is why
so many of us roam the European ether as the evening draws to a close. The
Germans delight in 'Serenades' – soothing concerts of classical and semi-classical
items, which are far more conducive to subsequent slumbers than many of the
hot dance numbers that hurtle from the BBC aerials.

Frankfurt, for example, is giving a Beethoven concert by the station orchestra this evening from 11 o'clock to midnight.[109]

The 1942 *BBC Handbook* stated that some people, those on different work hours – 'shift workers, fire watchers, and civil defence services' – had different 'interests [to] those trying to sleep' at regular hours.[110] Radio might wake some people up, but put others to sleep.

The BBC annuals periodically addressed questions of sleep. In 1928, there was an announcement about new headphones that leak no sound so as not to wake someone sleeping nearby.[111] There are stories of nurses whose final task of the day was to remove headphones from their patients who have fallen asleep in their hospital bed.[112] One year-book reported on a scientist, a Professor Seligman, who asked listeners questions about their dreams to assist in his 'investigation of type dreams' in relation to place, gender and ethnicity. Certain dreams were common to every people, no matter what their 'social culture'.[113] A report from 'the post bag' from 1938 told of a listener who asked whether the BBC 'was interested in photographing a dream by means of television apparatus'.[114] A decade later, a year-book reported on a night of television broadcast at Alexandra Palace:

You will not forget your night at the Palace, but home is the place. There are no loose ends on our television screens – no frantic cue-ings, no cold sweats, no trepidations, no call bells, no groping 'previews' – but only the serene, unruffled dream-worlds that are born of these controlled frenzies.

One night at the Palace, yes, but home for a thousand.[115]

Radio put people to sleep as much as it woke people up. In the 1939 *Handbook*, the recently departed Head of the Programme Correspondence Section, Mr R. W. P. Cockburn, noted a letter from a correspondent who wrote:

I much enjoy listening to your late dance music, and I know I am not the only one. But having been tuned in for about three-quarters of an hour I drop off quietly to sleep. I suggest, therefore, that an alarum clock or something of a similar rowdy nature should be unleashed at the microphone between the interval of 11.30pm and the ensuing programme of gramophone records.[116]

The BBC made dreams, lured into dreams, infiltrated dreams. It also pulled listeners back into the waking world, the world of clock time.

As an employee, Schoen slept in the sleep room and also dreamt there. On 14 July 1945, he dreamt that he was travelling through a Berlin destroyed by war with a man called Avrach.[117] In the dream, the war was drawing to a close and Schoen saw a sign pointing a way through the wreckage. The dream evoked imprisonment, a claustrophobia, a sense of going round and round in circles, getting nowhere, accompanied by the desire to get out. They entered a lion house. The cages might open at any point. Or, they might shut in the wanderers. Joseph Avrach was Polish, his birthplace was Łódź – the signpost pointed to Połód, a village in eastern Poland, close to the border with Belarus. Signs in the landscape were omens. A return to somewhere on the horizon? 'Molet' is a Polish word for a knurl or a ridge, a small protuberance, sticking out from an object to help in gripping. Eyes looked East, back to Avrach's homeland. Was there something to hold onto, a ridge to head for, a vantage point, or an advantage in this game of hide and seek? Or were there just more traps? Fate and future were bleak in this landscape.

Schoen's dream in the early morning of 23 January 1945 returned again to the destroyed city of his birth to find only an uncertain place amongst his former compatriots. English and German architecture merged. Wondering about being open or covert, a spy or a family man, he tracked past routes from days long gone:

I was secretly in Berlin for investigative purposes. Somewhere in the area around Uhlandstr, I got off the bus and decided to walk home along a long street, parallel to Kurfürstendamm (I had spoken to Sascha about my way to school the day before.)

I saw the name of a cross street, Herderstr., and thought, yes, that's right. I walked down the long street, surprised to see no devastation at all. I saw two-storey wide modern brick houses, similar to those in England. Then I noticed that these houses only looked like this because the upper floors had been taken down. On the right, in a room, open to the street, were people who knew me, including an old woman, similar to my great-aunt Jeannette. I wanted to carry on, then I recognized them and they me. They were surprised to see me. They were anti-Hitler and asked me mockingly: 'Aha, we suppose you are coming from Leipzig?' – 'No, from London,' I said proudly. They were amazed. I said I have to get home quickly. A young girl (not very young) did not believe me, thought I was a spy. She said suddenly 'give me your coat'. I gave her my green plastic mac. She put it on. I turned and went out with her and the others. A man was standing there, who looked quickly at me and then at a photo that he was holding in his hand. I pulled my hat over my forehead and we went up to him.[118]

Was he part of this group, this other Germany that might yet emerge from the ruins? Did he bear resemblance to one who might be looked for, as comrade or as enemy?

* * *

Poetic Portraits (Roll Call)

Towards the end of the war, Ernst Schoen developed a prolific private poetic practice. Figures of the Weimar spume were encapsulated in sonnet form in poetic physiognomies, sometimes bitter, often melancholic, condensations of lives and his relationship to them: Edgard Varèse, Benny Busoni, Walter and Dora Benjamin, Gershom Scholem, Bertolt Brecht, Friedrich Podszus, Sasha Stone among others.

It was a roll call, a reckoning but also a memorial practice. Upon hearing of Benjamin's suicide, Schoen composed a sonnet, on 14 March 1941:

> In truth you taught me to honour the poets
> Over lemonade and filled baguettes.
> We read the works of the great who are dead
> In which you remain for ever entangled
>
> And then you composed your own work
> And words, friends, women became messengers
> From once to now that blaze on in me
> Before they scatter forever into nothingness
>
> Finally Paris where roofs, books, walls
> Gave you once more the desire to live
> Then suddenly word was that on a frenzied
> Flight from the Nazis suicide was your end
>
> I cannot believe it, how could I ever have believed
> That our wanderings would one day come to rest.[119]

Brecht wrote a similar poem, in which he named Benjamin a refugee – a *Flüchtling*, someone who takes flight, which emphasises instead the act of *moving*, but not necessarily reaching a place of refuge. This is one who flies and cannot land. Benjamin was arrested, 'in flight', and remains forever a *Flüchtling*.[120]

On 2 November 1945, Schoen returned to another suicide: Fritz Heinle, the young poet whose death by suicide had so deeply touched the Berlin circle at the start of the First World War. He wrote a poem dedicated to his memory:

Make peace with you for the complete surprise
When in our young days you preceded us
As we argued over the meaning of life
And every argument faded out in word and rhyme

Make peace with you who sang like a prophet
From whom verses glided glowing from the lips
Like tree resin drips fragrantly from sore cuts
Like rain above the slopes of home

Make peace with you who strove after peace
And quaked before the blood vision of war
So much that hand in hand with your girlfriend you yielded
And hand and hand from life he crept

Now I think every day of you distant friend
I who survived you from war to war.[121]

Three days later, he wrote a second poem for Heinle. The language was more desperate, as it focused on suicide, 'gas death', an act which put an end to their childhood. Schoen lived on 'with blood-splattered hands'.[122]

He also composed a poem for Sasha Stone in July 1944. His photo-eye created a world, but disregarded reality, abandoned projects and riches.[123] As late as June 1960, Wladimir Vogel let Ernst und Hansi Schoen know that Stone had died many years before, of tuberculosis in 1940.[124] The poem mourned someone it did not know to be dead. The poems about others were often bitter, pointed – reflecting on a time gone, no longer to be regained.

1945–1952

Battling Legacies, Fighting Adorno

In the years following the Second World War, tensions manifested across the network which had been drawn together and flung apart. Some breakages could not be repaired. Traces of enmity are to be found in letters here and there, including those exchanged between Hannah Arendt and Gershom Scholem, as they discussed the possibilities of getting Walter Benjamin's writings into print posthumously. Schoen ended up again in the loop.

On 16 December 1945, Scholem sent Arendt two articles by Benjamin. These had not been published before and he stated that he chose to send them to her rather than to the Institute for Social Research 'because of Wiesengrund's bizarre behaviour – that for almost four years he didn't bother writing me a single line and then, a few months ago, sent me a copy of the Institute's memorial issue, and without even an accompanying letter.'[125] Scholem also noted that it was a result of the fact that the Institute was 'sitting on' Benjamin's literary estate, as if it were its possession. This drew Scholem towards Schoen, for he knew that the Institute did not have all of Benjamin's unpublished writings, as they were distributed amongst himself, Arendt, Dora Sophie Kellner, Gustav Glück, Schoen and others. Could these outsiders not band together and produce their own edition of the writings, he wondered? Scholem mentioned that he was keen for the correspondence to be published, but not in a language other than German. Benjamin was a complex writer, Scholem noted – it would be impossible to render him into English.[126]

On the same day, a year later, Arendt wrote a letter to Scholem, prompted by some correspondence from Alfred Cohn, which she included and within which Cohn had included words from Schoen. The voices intermingled, the correspondents, mediators, channelers of ideas of others' ideas. Cohn wrote:

Ernst Schoen, a common friend of Walter Benjamin's and mine, asked me what is happening with Walter's literary estate. I replied to him – which I'd also heard from Walter himself – that all of his manuscripts, as photocopies, are either with the Institute for Social Research, or they are with Gershom Scholem at the Hebrew University.

I know nothing about the precise distribution of the manuscripts. Now Ernst Schoen, who better than anyone else perhaps is familiar with, and has mastered, Walter's manner of thinking, has offered to collaborate on the publication of his literary estate. In case the question of the publication of the estate ever comes up, I'm of the opinion that one should accept this offer. It is not necessary for me to spell out for you my friend's qualifications.

Perhaps it would be simplest for you to be in direct contact with him, and then the two of you can discuss all the details. He wrote: 'Perhaps you can tell Mme. Blücher-Arendt exactly what I wrote Gershom Scholem, and I'm fully convinced of it: that neither Palestine nor the US would be the right place for such a publication, but rather first of all it should be in German, that is, it could be in Switzerland. And then perhaps there could be a French translation because still today France is the one country where one could expect his manner of thinking to be best understood. Finally, maybe at the very least there could be an edition for a very narrow circle of readers in England and the US. All of this, and precisely in this order, is what I could attempt to undertake.'

Hence, my dear Hannah, I am merely a middleman, though a middleman who out of self-interest is highly motivated to see the plan carried out, and quickly. I am convinced that Walter told you about Ernst Schoen. He's basically a musician, though is passionately engaged in all things related to culture, and for years he's been a program director for London radio. His address is:

43, Kingfisher Court
East Molesey
Surrey, England.

I have done my duty, that is to say, I've carried out what I set out to do. I very much hope that the immediate consequence of this will be a positive result. One last thing. Since his days at Frankfurt Radio, Ernst Schoen has had serious quarrels with Wiesengrund. He specifically asked that his plan not be shared with Wiesengrund. I have no idea if and how you get along with Wiesengrund-Adorno, nor do I know if he is interested in Walter's literary estate. Be that as it may, I urge you to respect my friend's wishes.

Drop a line to keep me up-to-date on what happens, and my very best to you,

Alfred Cohn.[127]

Adorno was to be excluded. The project was to be held onto more tightly by the original adolescent groupings. Was Schoen's elevation to programme director at the BBC an error or an effort to boost him, to grant 'basically a musician' more status?

On 25 December, Scholem replied to Arendt, informing her that he had already let Schoen know that he intended to publish Benjamin's writings with the New York publisher Schocken, under Arendt's guidance. He did not wish to derail the process by introducing Schoen into the proceedings. Should it all fall through, he would be prepared to return to Schoen's 'friendly offer'. Nonetheless, he requested that Arendt write to Schoen to find out what might be included in a volume of posthumous writings. He advised caution:

I advise you to write to Schoen about what Schocken's volume might include. You should treat the man well. (While he can also be abrupt, he's very good-natured.) Schoen wrote to me that Wiesengrund is angry with him because it had come to his attention that he, Schoen, called him a 'little snob'.[128]

Proposals, Suburbia

Schoen might have basically been a musician and not in any way a programme director at BBC radio, but he was still committed to the capacities of radio to renew itself and the world.

On 10 May 1946, he issued a ten-page proposal for a radio station in the British Occupied Zone of Germany. The manuscript begins with a statement about radio as an instrument of political power, a vehicle for the formation and influencing of public opinion. This is a basic fact that needed to be grasped and that others had failed to recognise before. He elaborated on how the leaders of radio in the Weimar Republic, under pressure of reaction, and in 'a catastrophic flight from responsibility', had allowed themselves to declare that radio is non-political or supra-party. On these neutral grounds, it had broadcast the words of its enemies. He explained how the Nazis had shrewdly prepared the takeover of radio, beginning in July 1930 with newspaper articles by Horst Dressler-Andress and the establishment of a 'Reichs Union of German Radio Participants'. Through this they gathered the right people in the right posts to make sure they could control who came to stand in front of a microphone. Schoen counselled on how best 'progressive and democratic forces' might establish a radio station that does not fall victim to hectoring, hysterical propaganda and mis-education. It required expert personnel and a complex division of labour: a radio engineer as technical director, an economist as financial director, a musician as musical director, a theatre professional as drama director, a political journalist as news director, a teacher as leader of the school and youth section, a worker as director of the workers' radio programming, a politically organised woman as director of the women's hour, a farmer as leader of farmers' radio and so on. His recommendations were precise. The news should not be delivered in the pseudo-objective manner of the British, but rather in the lively manner of US radio. Lectures and discussions should act as the 'tribune of democracy' and deliver content from around the world. On music, he wrote: 'It is hard to say if musical plumbing of the loudspeaker is in part guilty of bringing about mass stupefaction and mass neuroses, or if it has added to the life of the individual cheerfulness, dynamism and rhythm'. It was certain. though, that music was essential and that it should appear montaged with words. He imagined excerpted plays and educational programmes.[129]

On programming specifically for workers, Schoen recalled how the leaders of radio in Weimar debated what to call the service and decided upon the apolitical sounding 'Hour of Work'. Workers and intellectuals were largely separated, resulting in the most interesting experiments in radio being carried out by politically uncertain intellectuals, while the workers' movement more or less followed the 'line' tediously: 'If the German working class today is to co-determine again, in any leading role, intellectual as well as material rebuilding of the nation, then, as in all other matters, so too in radio, conviction does not get to decide by itself, but only in combination with the strictest self-criticism in terms of quality.'

Schoen observed how disastrous it was that the workers' movement ignored those who worked on the land as labourers and small-scale agrarians. Farmers' radio provided an opportunity to discuss land reform, to find out what is happening in the Soviet Zone, as elsewhere. This, as an area of modernisation, should become one of the key parts of radio, rather than the embarrassment it was, in opposite but equal ways, in the Weimar Republic and under the Nazis. He ends critically: '[T]he coming German radio must never again congeal into self-satisfied and reality-evading bureaucracy, rather it should, from the very start, be a meeting place for any warm-hearted attempts to lend lively expression to progressive forces amongst the German people and relate to progress across the whole world.'

In February 1946, there was a flurry of correspondence between the Schoens and Major Atkinson, Foreign Director of the BBC until 1932. Atkinson was a Germanophile and translator. He was pleased to have received a letter from the Schoens – he thought that they had vanished 'in the continental maelstrom'. He had written a previous letter, he reports, that clearly had not arrived in 1944 and then, around Victory in Europe time, he had enquired at the BBC to see if Ernst was still employed and was told that he had left.[130]

Traces left in the archive point to tensions in the suburban enclave. On 12 June 1946, the estates manager Arthur Speed wrote to 'Mrs. Schoen' complaining that 'Mr. Schoen' had been using the squash courts without subscription and that a payment of 2/6 was required, to be given to a Mrs. Packer.[131] Schoen replied on 14 June 1946 that the people using the courts were his children and it complied with the terms of the tenancy.[132] Other

letters revealed other tensions. On 2 July 1946, Arthur Speed again wrote
to 'Mrs. Schoen':

Madam, I have had a complaint from your neighbours that you are creating a nui-
sance by throwing fish bones and other offal out of your windows. This is a serious
menace to health and I must ask you to please refrain from doing this and place
your garbage in the proper receptacles which are provided for that purpose.[133]

New management took over the complex in 1950 and bemoaned the fact
that 'the general tone and appearance of the property has gradually deteri-
orated'. More fees were demanded to halt the 'downward trend'.[134]

Other signs point to a settling in, a feeling at home. *The London Gazette*
published details of British naturalisation in its issues. There is an entry,
from 20 September 1946, that reads:

Schoen, Alexander. Child of Schoen, Ernest Fritz Erich.
Schoen, Ernst Fritz Erich; Germany; Programme Assistant, British Broadcasting
Corporation; 43, Kingfisher Court, East Molesey, Surrey.[135]

The date of naturalisation was 27 July 1946.

Popular Voices, Translation Practice
War and exile had drawn on Schoen's facility to speak and read languages
other than his mother tongue. The post-war period – life in exile, a precarious life as translator, routine work on German Service radio – returned
him to a close engagement with words, language, mediation and communication across contexts. He devoted much of these years to translation,
or rather to the attempt to get translations into the world. He consulted
the programme of the progressive Unity Theatre in London, to see if the
plays staged there could be translated and played elsewhere, or to see if
the theatre directors might be interested in works he could convey to them
from Europe. He read through old and new drama and novels and poetry
in various languages. The move between languages and national contexts
were part of a political practice, one of communist internationalism.

In 1947, under the pseudonym Hans Werdmann, Schoen edited a collection of poems: *Voices of the Peoples Against Fascism*. The voices in the
collection that were to be heard – or read – were an international society
of revolutionaries and resisters. There was poetry from Yugoslav partisans,

German songs from the pro-Republican brigades in the Spanish Civil War, Russian songs of protest and lyric poetry of dissenters in the concentration camps of the Second World War. Schoen thanked two friends in his introduction, A. L. Lloyd, a former merchant seaman, poet and folklorist and the actor Herbert Lom. Both had been instrumental in securing material and Lom had completed rough translations of a few poems in Czech. In the introduction, Schoen praised the upcoming English-language poets, the symbolist David Gascoyne, the intellectual Marxist John Manifold who was an Australian poet and a poet David Martin who hailed from the industrial North of England. He also gave a sense of his London circles. Sylvia Townsend Warner, for one, had been involved in a staging of Brecht's elements from *Furcht und Elend des Dritten Reiches* (Fear and Misery in the Third Reich) in 1934 and his *Die Gewehre von Frau Carrar* (Mrs Carrar's Rifles) at the German *Kulturbund* in exile in 1942.

Schoen's pseudonym Hans Werdmann was a quasi-anagram of *der Wandersmann*, 'the travelling man'. Schoen, too, was wayward, wandering. The pseudonymous author spoke in another key, full of complaint, quite unlike Joseph von Eichendorff's 'Der frohe Wandersmann' (1823) who had no worries, no need of bread, surrounded by brooks that spring from the mountains and larks that buzz with pleasure. This new wanderer was witness to an aftermath of horror and an ongoing alienation. Exchanged names allowed for fresh starts or no traces.

Pseudonyms were prevalent amongst the exiles. Adorno, for one, used Hektor Rottweiler. The exiles also referenced the figure Peter Schlemihl, from Adelbert von Chamisso's novella. Schlemihl sold his own shadow. He was hapless, clumsy, as his name signifies in Yiddish – something like the 'Mr Bungle', who Benjamim wrote about in relation to his childhood.[136] Mr Bungle holds tight to the child's side, breaking things, making trouble. Schlemihl, shadowless but in possession of his soul, strides the world in seven-league boots, seeking nature's secrets.[137]

Schoen was bootless and confined to Europe. With Hans Werdmann he found a name to hide in, both from political judgement or oppression as much as from the traumas of memory, of the present, of previous experience, imprisoned, for example, in Fuhlsbüttel in Hamburg. Schoen also used the name Jakob Richter a decade later, for a number of publications: 'Der getretene Hund und die kostbaren Öfen' ('The Kicked Dog and the Expensive Ovens'), 'Die drei Herren im Feuerofen' ('Three Men in a Fire Oven') and 'Ein erstmaliger Fall' ('A First Case'), all from 1960.[138] When official names get you nowhere, try others.

Germany in Ruins, Return to Frankfurt

In 1947, Schoen was sent by the BBC to Germany. He was tasked with compiling a report on cultural institutions amid the ruins. His officially logged report detailed the state of book and periodical publication, radio, film, theatre and other cultural activities in a number of German cities. This occasioned, as he put it, 'a certain amount of comparison between the propaganda methods of the occupying powers.'[139]

The first stop was Düsseldorf, in the British Zone, where the radio people he spoke to were unable to ascertain how many listeners existed, as a decline in moral standards meant many were tuning in unlawfully. Numbers were likely declining, as there were few new sets to buy in the shops and a lack of valves and other spare parts, except for some available on the black market. Three-quarters of the radio sets were the Nazi *Volksempfänger* or homemade detector sets, both with very limited tuning abilities. Foreign stations – such as the BBC – could not be picked up. In winter, there were frequent interruptions to the electrical current, as the occupying powers limited the allocation. People retired early to bed. The paper allocation was small too and so newspapers were very slim. He recommended more interzone communication to help publishing and spread resources. He also pointed out problems with licensing newspapers. Publishers from the pre-Nazi days had been favoured, owing to issues connected to the process of denazification, barring newspaper editing to younger 'striving' incomers. Schoen also relayed complaints about the poor quality of the British films in the cinema, a choice dictated by the Rank Organisation and the small budget available.

Schoen complained about structures, about the contradictory information given by officers responsible for culture, propaganda and education in the Control Commission Group, the British civil servants and military personnel running local government, policing, housing and transport in the British Zone in North-West Germany. One civil servant complained that all the 'best people' had gone back to England and only 'sharks and the hyenas remained.' He closed his Düsseldorf report with a word on the opera. The opera house was unable to fill the seats reserved for the Allied Nations on two nights weekly and the doors were flung open to Germans. At a performance of Beethoven's *Fidelio* there were around thirty allies and the rest of the audience were Germans. And yet, complained the management of the Opera House, all the ticket receipts go into the British fund, as Schoen put it in his report to the BBC – likely the fund for relief and rehabilitation of displaced peoples and orphaned camp survivors.[140]

In Frankfurt, under US occupation, things were more hopeful. Listeners were increasing, more sets were being manufactured. Schoen spoke to Eberhard Beckmann, who was appointed by the US occupying troops to run Frankfurt Radio in 1946. Beckmann was satisfied with the smooth functioning of radio under the Americans, who had loosened their hold. There was, though, Beckmann observed, a distrust of those Germans who worked with the occupying Americans. The serious elements of radio programming, especially talks, had been cut right back: 'he is of the opinion that the German listening public is too tired to accept more than good entertainment, and that the confidence of listeners has to be regained, before more serious material can be offered to them.' He explained the proposals for a new independent structure for radio under the Americans, separate from the Post Office and with the director chosen by a group consisting of representatives of government, political parties, religious organisations, the trades unions and the youth movement. Unlike in Düsseldorf, the listenership was expanding. His report on publishing from Wilhelm Hollbach, prominent journalist and briefly US-appointed Lord Mayor of Frankfurt, was less positive. There were few readers and fewer reviews. The periodicals were poor quality, 'bought by the housewife as wrapping paper'. There was, according to Hollbach, too much emphasis on 'responsibility and re-education', whereas conveying 'the fundamentals of historical and political knowledge' would have been more useful.

Schoen visited Dolf Sternberger in Heidelberg, who he described as 'emphatically a non-party man'. Schoen was present at a meeting where Sternberger and 'distinguished' people of the 'Aktionsgruppe', a kind of German Fabian Society, discussed Alfred Weber's proposals for a constitution for Germany. American state attorney Jempner told them brusquely not to meddle in such matters, as they were not their concern. In the French Zone, Schoen had heard from an acquaintance that involvement in enterprises such as the Aktionsgruppe would be grounds for imprisonment. Schoen gave details of Sternberger's publication, *Die Wandlung* (The Transfiguration), noting that periodicals were on the rise, owing to a hunger for intellectual guidance and a lack of books. An anecdote revealed that one publisher in Munich had acquired the entire paper stock of Nazi newspaper *Völkischer Beobachter* and a former Nazi publisher, Franz Eher Nachfolger, was now churning out books indiscriminately.

Schoen's next stop was Hamburg where he visited the publishers Dr Claasen and Rowohlt and learnt that there was a better method for deciding what should be published in the British Zone than in the American.

The report closed with some words about the reception of BBC services in Berlin. Gustav Leithäuser, at Berlin University, Director of the Heinrich Hertz Institute for Wave Research and technical advisor for Radio Berlin, told him that long wave transmissions were only receivable in winter in dark hours and in Berlin, hardly then. The medium wave reception in Berlin was too weak and failed entirely in summer. The Russian wavelength produced interference. Shortwave transmissions were obtainable during the day, but insufficient for the reception of music and frequently disturbed by distortion. There was selective fading during the news and English lessons. Leithäuser suggested a technical solution, as well as programme recommendations: frequent and speedy repetition of the best British transmissions by the British Forces Network, particularly concerts, using the Magnetophon, a German reel-to-reel tape recorder discovered by the Allied Forces during the invasion in 1944–1945.[141] The waves had to be managed and corralled. England, that 'land without music', was to send music to be received, no longer under conditions of experiment and innovation, but as an effort to conquer airwaves and distract minds that might otherwise be intent on fomenting yet more racist disasters.

On this fact-seeking mission for the BBC, Schoen kept a diary of his private thoughts and observations. It began on 4 October 1947 with a preamble about awful people and shabby conditions en route to Liverpool Street and then on the overnight ferry. Once on a German train, conditions were 'sour, worn out and comfortless'.[142] He recorded details of travelling surrounded by Occupation personnel. Food was paid for with occupation tokens and drinks were bought at highly subsidised occupation prices. He came to realise that everyone around him was from the Control

Commission Germany. He observed the officers' wives and children, people from the NAAFIs (Navy, Army and Air Force Institutes), the officers of all types, a 'petty bourgeois' bunch with inferiority complexes and guilty consciences that turn them into 'ghosts of the multi-coloured world.' He observed that there was much material here for 'novels, comedies and bitter satires.' Eating roast beef and mustard sauce in the restaurant car, he entered Germany for the first time in more than a decade. There was little damage across the border with the Netherlands and he wondered if there had been fighting there at all. Once transferred to a military car, he was driven – the price paid in cigarettes – to Düsseldorf. The vehicle crossed the Rhine, the river appearing bleak and still. And then came the ruins. He was taken to a Control Commission hotel and chatted with the butler there, who had been a prisoner of war in Scotland. Schoen was reminded of the Germans who worked at the BBC and in the British universities and were well looked after. Good connections were cultivated in the prisoner of war camps. On his way to the opera to see *Fidelio*, he remarked that the air stank of illegal dealings and some people were dressed far too well. Others had just been clever with what little they had. On the streets he passed piles of rubble, heaped up but not removed. One modern block smelt of burning and had been giving off smoke for two years.

On the route to Frankfurt, he observed 'the hell of a beaten and occupied Germany.' Human ghosts milled in Hogarthian, Brueghel-like possession, misery and evil. He went to the Excelsior Hotel, where, for one night, he shared a room with an American on his way to a posting in Berlin. To pass time, the American read a cheap thriller printed especially for the American forces in brochure form. As he finished each page, he ripped it out and threw it away. The American longed for women, cigarettes and whiskey. The next morning, 9 October 1947, Schoen passed by ruin after ruin. Opera Square, Hotel Imperial, places he had visited with Hansi, were all gone. Part of the new natural history of destruction. The back entrance to the Opera House, 'whose walls still stand', bore a ragged notice: 'Public Monument: Out of Bounds.' Schoen was billeted with the friend of a BBC secretary, a Mrs Schmidt, and plumbed her for opinions. She was interested in the Oxford Movement, the Anglo-Catholics who wanted to revive the Church of England. He proposed instead the *Kulturbund*. He made his way to the radio station. Nothing looked the same. He met with Studtmann, who had once been the main announcer at the station including delivering the news and had performed the role of the announcer in the first *Hörspiel*, Hans Flesch's *Magic on the Air* (1924), in which Schoen was involved.[143]

They walked through the ruins to his two-room flat nearby, as he recounted his fate during the war years, when the station was run by the Nazi faithful. He was deployed to some sort of role at Siemens but after the war, found a post at RIAS (Radio in the American Sector). Eventually he found work again at the Frankfurt station. Schoen thought that men such as Studtmann moaned too much about what had happened to them. He looked forward to meeting instead with Else Mertens, who was warm-hearted compared to all these other 'larvae of those left behind in Germany.' He visited Dr Wendt, who was 'one of many pessimists of his class' and he heard sorry tales of shattered lives with only glimmers of restitution in his shattered wreck of a homeland. At a visit to Wilhelm Hollbach, Schoen was offered bitter tea and stale biscuits and saw Hollbach's ill wife and his daughter with yellow skin: both these sorry forms hang on every word of the 'great man.' Schoen was unimpressed by him, judging him as 'a sardonic, bitter liberal-individualistic fanatic, disgusted like all of them about the false denazification' – his denazification plan would have involved denunciation of the Nazi believers by their secretaries. Schoen interviewed him for the BBC about the state of the press and publishing, but dismissed the contents as 'trivial.'

Schoen took a tram to the district where he used to live, but alighted into an unfamiliar terrain. The first thing he noticed was a little poster from the German Communist Party: 'Secure the Unity of Germany. Create a unified German workers movement. Working Group of the KPD [*Kommunistische Partei Deutschlands*], locality Ginnheim.' It made him feel proud, but the sentiment soon dissipated and he groaned with the pain of homelessness, *Heimatlosigkeit*. He could not quite work out where he was. And then he saw the whole street where his home had been, from numbers 1 to 30, was a heap of rubble. The site where his home 20 Fuchshohl had likely stood was marked only by a 'ghostly' scrap of wall jutting out from the rubble. A woman told him that some people had tried to rebuild here. He tracked the corner of the wall and gazed out towards the river, where a light periodically flashed, as if it were a lighthouse in the sea. What sort of warning sign was that? In any case, the sea-like body of water was distant. He found a closer source – the mains supply for his former home was accessible. He turned it off, a gesture performed primarily to see if he could still remember how. Muscle memories persisted, even when everything else had fallen apart. In the darkening light, he boarded a tram from a 'well known but long forgotten stop' to go back to the city centre. The darkness compounded his sense of dislocation. What did he still know of this beaten up and fallen down city? Along the bus route, he caught glimpses of much rubble and destruction. In the city, he visited Studtmann again and ate, praising his wife for her culinary skills and her adeptness at sewing – for her husband wore a shirt made out of red sheets, while her own costume was made from recycled fabrics. Schoen suspected their life was good – he worked at the radio, as did she, presenting jazz programmes. He learnt through this encounter that there was little hope for him of a return to radio production in Germany. The homeland was shattered. It would be rebuilt, its networks remade, without him.

In 1951, during the night of 27 July, an image of Studtmann returned to Schoen in a dream. In the dream, he lived in an apartment one floor above Fred Zimmering, who had been prominent in anti-fascist agitation in exile in Britain. Dolf Sternberger was visiting, which was strange as he was decidedly of a different political stripe. Sternberger was wearing the then fashionable dress of young people from the continent, including a colourful round cap, which Studtmann had worn in Frankfurt in 1947 when he and Schoen walked together through town. Sternberger told Schoen in the dream that he wanted to write about Zimmering, to which the ironic reply came: 'You will write that he is an Angelus who may hide among devils, but is, after all, in God's hand'. He ascended to his apartment and the other men followed. It was full of silver. The floorboards were old, bent with a black wash on them. There was a grand piano and a bed – but everywhere was unwashed up crockery. Schoen began to dust and to wash up. Sternberger helped him. This dream seemed to be about tidying up and putting back together a battered and broken land. There were strange political bedfellows and treasures yet to be rescued.[144]

The day after seeing the crater where his home once was and after seeing Studtmann existing on stale crumbs and patched clothing, he returned to the *Innenstadt* (city centre) to get paperwork that he needed for further travel. Barbed wire stretched through the city. It protected the compound where the US Army had its headquarters, the former IG Farben administrative building. Schoen recalled walking along the street fronting the compound for the last time before emigration in 1933. The IG building loomed menacingly then. Mertens – who he had visited in the city the night before – used to live opposite and he remembered he owned a photograph of her on the balcony with the building in the background. The city had been something else then, its buildings promised chemical and technological modernity and he had been a part of this once.

Schoen had walked through ruins. His former home at 20 Fuchshohl in Frankfurt, previously an example of simple elegant Modernism, was shattered by bombing. Radio in this fractured environment was pragmatically deployed, a distraction system, a muffling or humming to try to put up a barrier against the return of fascism.

Which report on the state of defeated Germany and the needs of the future was more effective and to what ends? One recounted gaps and losses and ruins in a personal idiom, a journey into pasts amid ruins. One observed the multiple failings of the British occupying forces and made policy recommendations. Did Schoen have any authority to make these suggestions? His report appeared quite different to one by F. L. Neumann, also an employee of the German Service, filed in June 1947. This one had been forwarded to Patrick Gordon Walker, MP for Smethwick and close ally of Clement Atlee, who had reported for the BBC during the war and was present at the liberation of Bergen-Belsen concentration camp. He, in turn, forwarded it to the cabinet member, Frank Pakenham, Chancellor of the Duchy of Lancaster, with an observation written on House of Commons note paper that it contained material of value.[145]

Neumann's report painted a bleak picture of depression, hunger, exhaustion, giddiness and strange yellow skin tones. There were no clothes in the shops and a mysterious black market in potatoes. People clung to the roofs of overcrowded trains. Cash was scarce and the black market operated through barter. But Neumann's contacts while in Germany were different to Schoen's. Neumann had translated talks with 'high Russian officers' for a British colonel as they discussed the bi-zone and tri-zone situation. He then had breakfast with the colonel, before visiting another colonel and attempting to enter the Lord Chancellor's Conference, which he found out was strictly not allowed and so he visited another colonel, who made him welcome. Neumann reflected on how the British officers in Germany should be informed about the BBC's work so that they might allow them to cover the conferences. Barred from the conference, he visited 'Major General Inglis DSO etc', the chief judge in the British Zone and President of the highest British court in Germany and they spoke for a long time about legal issues and Neumann promised to let him know of legal talks on the BBC. Neumann then went to Hamburg and visited the radio station and the information centre called *Die Brücke* (The Bridge). At the latter, he was alarmed to see nothing from the BBC among all the extensive materials there. In Hamburg, he spoke to an old friend, 'the Director of a very old and big German shipping firm'. The friend told him the British were seen to be robbing the country of food and industrial goods. In Hannover he met with General Macready, the Regional Commissioner of Lower Saxony, after chatting with his aide de camp Major Murray about political difficulties in the land. The discussion was amiable, but Macready's sense of things was hopeless – there would be no upswing in German living conditions any time soon and no hope on the horizon. Neumann went on to a bunker where German refugees from the East were being 'herded together' – but he could not handle more than three hours in their proximity: 'Frankly because of the rather horrible stench there'. He also abhorred their loss of morality. Returning to Berlin, he used his friends' ration cards to see what life was like and found the lack of fats intolerable. The report was received gratefully by Pakenham: 'Very interesting though very depressing as any honest report was bound to be. If only we can put more food into the country we can effect a transformation. But the prospect of that happening is slightly better for the year ahead.'[146] Such a report could only be written by an insider, someone who was close to the occupying power, spoke its language.

Schoen had used the BBC trip to Germany to try to piece together parts of his old life and had recommended ways of bringing radio back into existence as a democratic medium of communication. Neumann had visited the British ruling class in occupation, the military, administrators and had drawn the conclusion that what was important was getting the words of the BBC to officers' ears, in order to elevate the status of the German Service. Schoen thought about the lack of paper and what lessons should be provided to ensure a democratic future. Part of Schoen's report about the state of things in his homeland might have found its way into the review of the German Service's work in the 1948 *BBC Year-Book*. The report, titled 'The German-Austrian Service', noted that there were only a few radio sets in Germany and reference to illegal trading was phrased more coyly as a lack of sets or spare parts available on the open market. The report mentioned the frequent power cuts and rationing of electricity.[147] The emphasis in the report was on the plays broadcast by the service over the year: T. S. Eliot's *Murder in the Cathedral* (1935), Sean O'Casey's *The Plough and the Stars* (1926) and, most notably for the compiler of the report, Georg Kaiser's posthumous play *Der englische Sender* (1948) (The English Broadcasting Station). There were reports on what was most popular – programmes about daily life in the UK and the Commonwealth and *Any Questions* and *Readers' Letters*. The most outstanding programme was Thomas Mann's address to the German people, captured as he passed through London to Switzerland.

In 1947, Schoen wrote a radio show for the German Service's *Youth Hour*, dated 2 February. The talk began lamentingly – fewer and fewer people were aware of Chaplin, the silent film clown, for his early films were rarely shown.[148] Schoen's thoughts turned towards the folk figure of the clown and its social role in managing fear of nature or freeing the self from the constrictions of modern civilisation. Schoen spoke of Freud, sublimation and the serious role of the joke. Chaplin was an Everyman and brought his universal audience, the watchers of silent films, as close to tears as laughter. In his dreams, Chaplin was omnipotent; in waking life powerless. The coming of sound film, noted Schoen, signalled the end of the clown. But so too, he wrote, did the current phase of bourgeois rule. The forces of industrial modernity over which it held sway had carried out the actual extermination of people as a supposedly rational solution to conflict. This eradicated the symbolic realm and purged imagination. There was no imaginative realm left in which ideas of freedom could be trialled. Reality had broken into the world of speculation. A second talk, 'The Social Tasks of Music', was broadcast on the German Service on 29 April 1948. An article about Thornton Wilder by Schoen appeared in *Die Zeit* that year too – some of Schoen's words were landing back in Germany.

Did the programmes really meet the needs of the audience? In the 1948 year-book Tangye Lean reported in 'The Listeners in Europe' that the German audience was 'too stunned by cold and hunger' to appreciate BBC radio offerings:

One woman simply scrawled across a questionnaire in June, 1947, 'Give us food instead of music and meaningless news', and another commented:

'As long as one is freezing and hungry one is scarcely interested in feature programmes of the kind dealt with in part 2 of your questionnaire or in broadcasts in the 'Countries' series, however good they may be. I have a high opinion of Mr. Lindley Fraser as a clever man. But would Mr. Fraser not also lose his zest for his work if he was hungry and freezing?'

Unfortunately a semi-conscious demand that broadcasting should act as a substitute for food and warmth does not make for good criticism or for good listening. We can expect the picture of the European audience to get clearer as well as more encouraging in the next few years if economic recovery continues.[149]

Return to the Tower

In the archive in Koblenz there is a photograph of the Eiffel Tower taken in September 1949. Ernst Schoen perches on a wall, the camera slightly tilted, his body merging with the Eiffel Tower's frame. In a previous image with the tower from 1928 he posed with illustrious friends in a fake aeroplane, all performing the role of tourists and anticipating a modern world of technology and new culture through which they soar. The later image is melancholic. The Eiffel Tower remained an erect structure, if slanting, a still proud remnant of modernity, but Schoen sits alone, his body stooped. His experience of the war, as for many, was one of disinheritance: he lost his job, he lost his friends, he was imprisoned, he lost his network, he lost his public life, his house, the objects around him. The dream of internationalism, of radio across boundaries, from towers like that built by Eiffel, ever more perilous in their height, that might, as Swiss architect and director to come of the Bauhaus Hannes Meyer wrote in 1926, 'release us from national isolation into the world community', so that our homes might unmoor, to become sleeping cars, house boats, vast liners; this too was lost.[150]

Instead of hurtling into an aesthetics of the future there was more reckoning with the past and its weight. In 1949, Suhrkamp published a short

Figure 4.2 Ernst Schoen in front of the Eiffel Tower, from 13 September 1949.

Photographer unknown. From Schoen's Archive in Koblenz: BArch N 1403 Bild-109-004.
Copyright: Sabine Schiller-Lerg.

volume by George Bernard Shaw, translated by Schoen, entitled *Musik in London*. Elsewhere were signs of a reinvented Germany – but Schoen played only a marginal role.

A letter in Schoen's archive written from Darmstadt on 24 August 1950 was signed by sixteen people who were engaged in forging the Bundesrepublik's post-war musical identity. The signatories included Adorno, Edgard Varèse, the pianists Aloys and Alfons Kontarsky and composer Brigitte Schiffer. It was written during the 'Darmstädter Ferienkurse für Neue Musik' (Darmstadt Summer Courses for New Music)[151] Along with the signed names were lines giving new current addresses or short phrases, such as 'First greeting after so many years'. The point of the Darmstadt Summer School was to reconnect Germany with music previously suppressed. It intended to re-establish, re-gauge, re-tune. The letter might have reminded Schoen of his absence, or served to absolve the group of guilt about those excluded.

* * *

Sleep Interruption: Sonic Dreams

As Schoen fell in and out of a public musical life, his dream life became a repository of sound, dotted with musical citation and notation. Sound was constructed out of the unconscious. The musical canon wove through it.

The work and anxiety of making music formed a large part of the dreams. On the morning of 1 February 1949, Schoen recalled how in his dream he was conducting *The Blue Danube*. On 1 October that year, while in Le Lavandou on the Côte d'Azur, he dreamt of a large gathering where a short melodious violin solo could be heard. Perhaps the slow second movement from a Mozart Violin Concerto. Schoen thought it might be Braun conducting, with Brinitzer playing piano, or harpsichord. Braun said: 'So, it seems as if we have cleared the matter up, gentlemen'. Schoen thought 'Aha, a rehearsal'. And now an even larger orchestra had assembled. They began to play. Schoen transcribed the music from the dream:

In an internal dialogue, he doubted himself: 'It is not Mozart but Tchaikovsky'. A steward and a secretary appeared. The conductor was a small Hoffmann-like Mephisto type. Someone said: 'Ach, Cohn is conducting. Quite good too'. The conductor led the orchestra from the side, without a baton, holding up a mirror as he did it, into which he grimaced. Each time he heard something off, he said, as if relieved: 'You see, I have proven that it won't work', and then simply continued.[152]

Music wormed its way into dreams about work. On the morning of 21 April 1950, Schoen recorded a dream set in an office at the BBC, where two secretaries, Retzer and Willott, sat opposite each other at typewriters. Behind them at the window on the right, Mr Stein. The secretaries typed. He saw Stein conducting in 4/4 time and then clocking in on the machine. He broke into two bursts of laughter, ignored by all three until he described the sight. Then he said to Stein: 'Why don't you try 7/4?'

On the night of 11 July 1958, Schoen explained to a young man who was playing a Haydn violin minuet with Puma on the piano, that it was somewhat faster than the Trio. He remarked that it was like a Ländler folk dance and transcribed the tune:

Another dream with notation was dreamt on the night of 4 August 1950. Schoen was himself as a young baritone, singing with someone called Micaela the Carmen duet. They were 'cheek to cheek'. He noted down the melody. He hoped they might sing the whole opera together but it wasn't allowed. The tune is noted down:

On the night of 12 March 1951, Schoen played a piano sonata by Beethoven in his dream. He remarked afterwards that it was strange to find one that he did not yet know. As he woke, he realised that it must indeed have been a new discovery, as he knew all the sonatas that did exist. He was able to name the sonata in the dream transcription: Op.22, in B-flat Major.

In another example, from 13 May 1959, he accompanied a 'small and hideous violinist', who had a crooked nose with a red tip, which, upon closer inspection, was made from another material. The melody seemed to be Fritz Kreisler's *Liebesfreud*, part of his Viennese Dances. Again, Schoen noted it down.

He practised it on the piano, but the father of the hideous player seemed dissatisfied with it and so he played an 'umtata, umtata' tune instead.

In a dream from 12 April 1960, Schoen was at a concert by the English Philharmonic Orchestra. A Mendelssohn symphony was coming to an end. Edward Clark looked up from the first violins to Schoen in the balcony, smiling with his round, blurry, wine-sodden face. Schoen thought, now the moment of great emotion. The conductor went to the back of the orchestra and Schoen clapped again. Clark was now sitting next to Schoen so he asked him: 'Don't they applaud in this place?' 'Never' he answered. When he woke, he thought: not with singers either? The payment or the honour must be great then.

* * *

Newspaper Clippings

By day Schoen collated reports and wrote verse dense with political attitude in something of the same fashion as Brecht's *War Primer*.[153] One poem responded to reports in the West German press about a bookshop that was selling books by the kilo. Written on 22 August 1951, it began with several stanzas evoking the book burnings in Berlin and elsewhere by the Nazis. It eulogised the Russian soldiers who had run across the dramatist Gerhardt Hauptmann and requested his autograph. The Soviet Union wanted everlasting peace; the Western powers only wanted a pause in the war. A line had been drawn through Germany and, in the East, books were printed furiously so that the East Germans could read. In the West, publishing consisted of Nazi memoirs, pornography and love poems, sold as wrapping paper. Speculation in books is replaced by speculation in armaments and the books are eventually sold by the pound. But the people did not choose books over coal or potatoes.[154] He also wrote a poem in honour of Lilli Waechter, imprisoned by the US military court in Stuttgart for reporting on what horrors she had seen in Korea.

In May 1952, he wrote a long poem on lies, the 'many thousand lying gobs', who lie for fear to get their wages, out of vanity, stupidity or ignorance.

They followed Hitler who taught them the 'lying catechism'; that the stupidest lie will be believed if repeated often enough. The final stanza reads:

> The lying wretch resembles deceived foxes
> He reveals the truth only as sour grapes
> It is said, he who lies once is never believed
> Why then believe an army of lies.[155]

The poem tabulated the many lies that circulated in the war of propaganda. In the mouth of murderers, words were turned inside out. One verse is as follows:

> In Hungary eighty chaps are killed,
> The lying radio bawls out. That he has lied
> He does not happily admit and reckons well
> That the poison is first efficiently absorbed.[156]

The verse relates to a report by Leon Griffiths he had preserved from the *Daily Worker*:

An air of mystery hangs over this mining town in Hungary's north-west – 42,000 people are wondering how eighty of their number could disappear without their knowing something about it. Last night and this morning, miners read in their newspapers the B.B.C.'s claim that 80 miners had been shot in this town for staging a go-slow movement. Men going on the last shift before the three-day Christmas holiday smiled as they told me that far from anything resembling a go-slow policy they set up on Friday an all-time output record in honour of Stalin's birthday.[157]

In another example, from 24 June 1952, Schoen wrote a poem dedicated to the memory of Georgi Dimitrov, the first communist leader of Bulgaria from 1946 to 1949 and leader of the Communist International from 1935 to 1943. He wrote it in English, but translated it afterwards into German. It opens:

> Sometimes the knell of Wallstreet's gunmen on the kill
> Seems to engulf me like the seven seas of sorry;
> I sink in nothingness, a stone bereft of will,
> Coking, with bursting veins – no hope and no tomorrow.[158]

At this point, Schoen's political persuasions faced East, but his ideas did not easily find a home there. On 24 November 1950, he had received a letter from Hans Albert Förster at Volk und Buch Verlag in Leipzig. His contact expressed regret that he was unable to offer a contract for Schoen's manuscript on the history of broadcasting: 'Were we living under normal circumstances, the decision would not ever have been in question. I would have written to you long ago with the message that we were issuing the book.'[159] But the press was impoverished and lacking in paper, so their list had to be very carefully considered, stated the missive. Förster noted that should the situation change, he would be happy to reconsider.

Schoen filed amongst his clippings a report on the staging of Barnard Rubin's *The Candy Store* at the Unity Theatre in 1951. It was a play that had run in New York for almost a year and dealt with chain store monopolisation of the market and consequent union struggles and complicity. Schoen drew a box around one paragraph in the report in the *Daily Worker*:

While the play was running in New York an appeal had to be made every night to the audience for protection for the cast on their way to the subway station. This appeal was always answered, and the cast, surrounded by their audience, used to march in a body to the station.[160]

What struck Schoen here? Perhaps the violent brutality and anti-labour politics that could be found in the USA, such that a play's themes could physically endanger its actors, matched by the gesture night after night of solidarity, of a protective armour formed around a cast.

In October 1951, Schoen sent Brecht some of his published and unpublished poems.[161] He congratulated Brecht on winning the East German National Prize and remarked on his letter to West German writers, printed in the East German daily newspaper and distributed as flyers. Brecht's letter warned of a coming war, as West Germany was beginning to remilitarise. Its final lines were much cited in political discourse: 'The great city of Carthage started three wars. After the first, it was still strong. After the second, it was still habitable. After the third, it was impossible to locate it.' Brecht lamented that, because of the denial of entry visas, an intervention by the conservative Prime Minister of Italy, De Gasperi, the Berliner Ensemble was unable to take up the invitation to the Venice Biennale. He also bemoaned the reaction that 'this latest stupidity has unleashed amongst progressive people.'[162]

In August 1952, Brecht attempted to put Schoen in touch with Maximilian Scheer (also known as Walter Schlieper), a prominent figure in East German culture, who led a radio department dealing with cultural questions. On 10 October 1952, Brecht wrote to the Communist author Alfred Kantorowicz in Berlin, recommending this 'thoroughly decent man' to him and asking if he might be able to advise him further, should he return to Germany.[163] He wrote something similar to the socialist author Arnold Zweig.

Schoen acted as a bridge between certain strands of English or British communism and socialism with comparable currents on the continent. This is evidenced is his long essay 'Christopher Caudwell and the Concept of Freedom',[164] the first work on Caudwell to appear in German. The essay opened with two quotations, one from Engels: 'Freedom is recognition of necessity',[165] and one from Lenin, arguing that those who are convinced that they have made scientific progress would not demand freedom for the new views alongside the old, 'but the substitution of the new views for the old.'[166] Schoen's essay offered a tour through Caudwell's life and work. Born Christopher Saint John Sprigg in 1907 in Putney near London, he worked as a newspaper reporter, wrote ten works of detective fiction, plus five books on flight technology, poetry and the natural sciences. Towards the end of 1934, he became acquainted with Marxism, joined the Communist Party and travelled to France to study the Popular Front movement. In December 1936 he joined the International Brigade and died on 12 February 1937 shortly after his twenty-ninth birthday, killed in the Battle of Jarama.

After these biographical notes, Schoen worked through some of his writings, commencing with *Illusion and Reality* (which was only published in German in 1966 by a German Democratic Republic [GDR] press), which argues that poetry cannot be tackled in the 'abstract, rather only as part of a sociological investigation.' Poetry reflected social upheaval and was a 'function of the economy', a kind of 'primitive communion' between people that became individualised in the bourgeois age. It represented a higher reality and it existed within a spirit of waiting, or anticipation. Schoen focused on the concept of freedom, that 'freedom is not a state, but an unspoken struggle with nature.' Caudwell tracked poetic development onto the stages of economic development. Under bourgeois modernity, poetry functioned to remove the self from the social sphere, into a world of private fantasy. In reflection on *Studies in a Dying Culture* (1938), Schoen, via Caudwell, sketched a theory of the hero, defined as someone who controls and transforms his environment: 'The hero often calls for a return to the past and, while he is doing it, opens up the future'.[167] D. H. Lawrence was the epitome of the bourgeois hero, but Lenin 'ushers in the period of the new, socialist hero', hitching the cause of freedom to the recognition of necessity, which is to say attaining revolutionary liberation through a conscious appropriation of the objective laws of nature and its transformation.

Spies

At the start of the 1950s, Schoen was under observation by the Secret Services in Britain.[168] MI5 decided that a grouping it had named the MacDonald Discussion Group, after its initiator Duncan MacDonald, harboured enemies of the state close to the Communist Party of Great Britain. The Security Services described MacDonald as a 'know-all' with a penchant for exaggeration, who, along with his wife Patricia Burke and a circle of Communist friends, appeared to be a 'typical under-cover Intellectual Communist', or, as a later report described MacDonald, 'a sinister and fanatical crypto-Communist, with a curious background and interesting connections', and a 'half-Russian background'.[169]

MacDonald and Burke, together with some of the people named as members of the discussion group, lived at a cooperative community called Saint Julian's in Sevenoaks, Kent. The Georgian house had been bought collectively in 1951. One of the instigators was Elizabeth Tylden, a London-based psychiatrist who specialised in mental trauma occasioned by battle and the Blitz. It was progressive – for example, childcare was provided in a nursery in the house to enable professional couples to work unhindered.

Various members in the so-called MacDonald Group already had MI5 'office records'. Schoen had been under observation for a while, unsurprisingly, as the BBC was subject to government vetting for any appointments it made. Also on the list, and sometimes spelt incorrectly, were Freddy (Ferdy) Mayne, Walter Bor (an architect for the London County Council), Ben Frankel, Lili Demel, Ken Annakin ('film director'), Frank Godwin ('one of Sir J. Arthur Rank's top accountants'), Arpad Rosener, R. D. Smith and Herbert Lom. The names Solly Zuckerman, George Thomson and Claude Cockburn appeared as figures invited to deliver lectures, as did the names of proposed lecturers Gordon Childe, Hyman Levy, Gordon Schaffer, J. D. Bernal, Jack Lindsay, James Aldridge, Eric Capon and Emile Burns, all of whom already had files. Others in the group's orbit were actor Mai Zetterling, Sam Wanamaker (described as 'an American who is reported to have lost his job in the States because of his Communism'), teacher Mary Miles and Bernard Berdchinger, 'a Swiss business man in the City of London', who is said 'to have played an important part during the war in the labour movement in Hatfield'.

From the first meeting on 29 November 1951, an informant seems to have been present. The source reported on conversations. 'ZUCKERMANN is one hundred percent all right,' the source recorded, adding the words of one of the Group to underline the members' common cause, 'from our point of view'. This was followed up by: 'Source has been given to understand that all lecturers are pro-Communists'. The Secret Service source reported on each contact's proximity or otherwise to the centre of the circle, or to Communist ideas.[170] The security services observed a discrepancy between the vetting of people invited into the group and the claim of the group that it was non-sectarian and educational. The security services also observed 'that there is a noticeable alien element in the Group', with speakers of various languages including Russians, Hungarians, Czechs, Austrians, a Swede. As the papers noted: 'The members and potential members consist so far mainly in professional and artistic people from the Theatrical, Film and Architectural professions'. One report noted that: 'all the forty M.D.G. [MacDonald Group] belong to the professional classes, falling into three main groups: film, theatre, architecture. It is obvious that the professional careers of such people stand to be prejudiced if their Communist sympathies and activities become too widely known'.[171]

The first meeting was at actor Ferdy Mayne's home, 61 Brompton Road, Knightsbridge, together with Duncan MacDonald, Walter Bor, Ian Gibson-Smith, Mai Zetterling and Mary Habberfield, 'who is employed in the film studios at Ealing'. The aims of the group were, according to the source, to:

(i) Afford the opportunity for Communist discussion and Communist education to Communists or Communist sympathisers whose open adherence to the Communist Party might jeopardise their employment,

(ii) Provide the opportunity for giving pro-Communist propaganda under suitable disguise of 'Progressive Discussion' to persons of left-wing sympathies, who are not Communist Party members.[172]

Discretion was the watchword. Those present were at threat of losing their employment should any affiliation be discovered. Only 'trusted persons' would know of the group's existence. At the first meeting, further names for invitation were discussed and the source conveyed to the Security Services that 'they were discussed in such a way as to leave anyone but a political ignoramus in no doubt as to the fact that the Group was left-wing'.[173]

The group met again on 27 December at Brompton Road and present were Mayne, Bor, MacDonald, Habberfield, Lom, Berdchinger, Gibson-Smith, a man called Faithful, a lecturer from Liverpool University, who had taught at Odenwald, a progressive German boarding school, and Ernst Schoen. Berdchinger addressed the meeting with the story of his life through various economic changes, or 'how slumps affect people'. The source summarised the meeting as such: 'the experience of slumps makes people desire to go to the London School of Economics to study economics, to investigate the problems of capitalism and then to turn their minds to theories of Socialism'.

On 17 January 1952, the group met again at Mayne's home. Alexander Schoen attended and those present listened to a lecture by Josef Winternitz on the present economic situation, pointing to the rise of German and American competition to British exports. The source listened out for references to the Soviet Union, drawing attention to the fact that Winternitz was a member of the Economic Committee of the British Communist Party and it was believed that he received confidential communications from the German Communist Party. The notes also observed: 'Sacha Schoen is still working for an American Chemical firm near Hampton Court'. Other names, a psychoanalyst named Morgan and his wife, are stated to be members of the Group, as is Czech translator Stephen Jolly and Sinclair Rhode, a location scout for film companies, one of a number of '"Progressive" young men', who 'all speak languages and have good contacts'.[174]

The Group met at Mayne's again on 31 January 1952 to discuss 'modern architecture in the West and in the USSR': 'The discussion was wound up by Bor, who made some excuses for the primitive state of Soviet architecture even at this date'. This time twenty-one people were present, including Alexander Schoen. John Arnold, aka Polak, was a new contact: 'He appears to be quite well off and is a technician in the Film Industry'. Helen Spalding was present too. She had just written a book, with Hyman Levy, another person of interest, on 'Literature for an Age of Science'.

A table of persons of interest was put together by the Secret Services in December 1952, along with a commentary that presented the large proportion of members who already had files on account of Communist Party membership or Communist sympathies.[175] No evidence could be found of the discussion group being in any way 'directly controlled or sponsored by the Party'. The extent to which each member's connection to communism was known was indicated in phrases such as 'crypto communist', CP member, 'sympathiser'. In one box on the chart, a note remarked on the extent to which evidence existed: 'Case is well documented' appears in several examples, including Ernst Schoen's and Alexander Schoen's. Alexander Schoen was described as a Member of the CP since 1952, at Birkbeck College: 'V active Communist'. Ernst Schoen is described as 'Announcer translator on German Service of BBC, German Nat. British 1946. Independent evidence indicates that he is a Communist sympathiser. Now living in East sector of Berlin.'

The Group appears to have petered out quite quickly and, absurdly, efforts to revive it were made by the Secret Service informer. The British state wanted a forum to keep an eye on 'extreme Left-wing and Communist intellectuals and professional persons who do not wish their political creed to affect their livelihood or advancement' and who, it observed, were 'highly intelligent' and with access to 'many different social circles'. Despite efforts, whether by the state security services or the dissidents themselves, it did not revive.

* * *

Interruption: Sleep History of the BBC

Over the period of his association with the BBC, Schoen mapped out the shape of its offices and studios in his dreams, locating in them the corporation's employees and his feelings toward them. Witnessing the dream diary, one wonders if his recurrent obsession with the BBC reflected a daily waking concern, or rather a nightly cathexis?

Schoen dreamed on 20 July 1948, though he acknowledges it was poorly remembered. Schoen was trying to deal with an impossible manuscript, sent from Germany. He saw a small, dark, skinny old lesbian, whose eye had a kind of camera shutter, or was like the extra lid of a chameleon. When it opened, small flames, like on a gas ring, darted around it. Schoen went to look for someone called Ruhm, or 'Roome', to ask what should be substituted for this manuscript tomorrow. He was in the corridor among a circle of colleagues, playfully occupied with a kind of tubular brass curtain rod, which he handed over, in lieu of an answer. Avrach was there too, a frequenter of his dreams, standing a little higher. He interfered, but Schoen told him not to, given it was none of his business, and tossed him the curtain rod. He went back downstairs, thinking that, at least, he can sign another letter himself. He saw his signature (from Frankfurt days) in front of him. He left through the wrong door to the rear of the building so had to find his way to the front, but realised it was already 10 minutes past the hour. Damn it, now, he thought, I'm already halfway home.[176]

On 3 June 1949, in a dream Schoen labelled an anxiety dream, he wondered if he had just been with Avrach. Hansi and Avrach accompanied him to the BBC and Avrach let out that Schoen had been let go from the BBC with only two weeks' notice. He avoided colleagues, whose sardonic opinions he feared. Hansi checked if they were there. Avrach forced him to come in and Avrach and Eva Sachs made him aware that they had seen an exchange of letters. He left via an old, spacious and carpeted lift to the first floor and then down some stairs to the street. He went home alone with a heavy heart and cried to himself: 'What should I do? What should I do?'

A dream from 28 April 1950: Schoen's shift was at the station. He had some soft food, like ground meat, to take home wrapped in paper. He went back because he had forgotten his folder, which was lying on a big black table. When coming back, he saw someone from behind. First it seemed to be Alexander, then someone else. He wanted to leave without talking to the person. The person turned around: it was Avrach. They exchanged a few words. Schoen thought to himself, I can put the package in the folder, otherwise the contents will spill out of me. Then, in the street, two chubby secretaries came out from the back. They got onto the back of a bus, in the Parisian way. He regretted them leaving. They held a letter. They alighted. On a wide street, they performed a rhythmic grotesque dance like two figures in a Russian toy. They stopped in a final pose as if spellbound. Schoen played along from a distance, directing imaginary traffic. A red London bus came from behind towards the secretaries. He wanted to scream, but the words got stuck in his throat. The women lunged to the side, screaming at the last moment: the bus swerved. Nothing happened to them.

In another dream dreamt in the BBC's Brooklyn Hall, from the night of 3 September 1945, a suicidal woman, Mary Tereth, appeared. In half-sleep, Schoen thought, 'Aha, the name is an anagram for "Martyr" (*Märtyrer*)'. But she was known by three names and she had locked herself in a large dark green cylinder that contained a poisonous gas to commit suicide. It had the inscription: Do come on in. The gas is quite harmless. She was French.

The dreams processed the past, lost relationships, a sense of missing out. Another, from early in the morning on 28 January 1951, detailed the process of losing self-identity in relation to others, perhaps colleagues. He dreamt he was in a magical land which was a matriarchy. The men had died – but 'that was not a problem'. He walked through the darkness along a path in a forest and to allay his fears he sang, professionally, operatically. As the light broke, he saw a girl singing too and they walked hand in hand – she nestled her fingers inside his glove. She wished she were pretty, but she was a serving girl and her mistress was much prettier. Would he come and visit this lady this evening? Schoen noted that he received this request as a third person – 'with whom I feel identical'. This dream, he observed, was unusual in that, unlike all the others, it was completely unrealistic. 'He', this third person, said he was not available – no, it could be any evening. In dreams the difficult dealings with others came out, the worry about identity, the desire to be with others only to find it impeded. The dreams, for the most part, contain fragments of reality.

On the night of 9 February 1951, just before Schoen's dismissal – the endpoint of a petering out of engagements – he was on night duty at Surrey Street, just down from the BBC buildings at Bush House, where according to a 1956 *Handbook,* 'bars, lounges, and reading-rooms are available' to members of the BBC Club.[177] But early in the morning, around 2.30 a.m., he was in the sleep room. He dreamt that he went home late. Hansi was asleep in the corner of a large dark room. He tried the light switch to find his way to bed, but it did not work, so he lay in bed in the dark. Just at that moment Hansi appeared suddenly in a white nightgown. He was so shocked that he screamed himself awake, at just the instant when the attendant shone a torch in his eye and said, just as the cleaner said in the dream from 14–15 July 1945 (this time an hour earlier): 'Three o'clock, Sir'. The cleaners and attendants at the BBC operated as his alarm clock.

In March 1951, Schoen dreamt that his watch was tangled in itself and then he found out that he had lost his job. He got a new one, with his office opposite the boss, even if his wages were to be paid in small instalments. He felt that he should call Dora Benjamin – was this a memory or reawakening of desire or guilt at losing contact with someone who had once been his intimate? He looked for accommodation in a house, number 70, on a long street. There was so much homelessness that children were sleeping in rows of beds on the street. He woke up with music in his head: a lullaby by Brahms, the 'Sandmännchenlied'. In the fairy tale that the song was based on, sand was thrown in the child's eyes to make it sleep. This explained the grit found in the inner corners of the eyes in the morning.

On the morning of 11 March 1951, he dreamt of being back at the old radio station in Frankfurt: Carl Stueber struck through the second half of a *Hörspiel* Schoen had written. Feverishly Schoen attempted to write a new second part, in order to get it broadcast, but he kept being disturbed. He tried to persuade the administrative director Wilhelm Schüller to put it out anyway. Schüller sat with his bright red head in his hands, clearly angry and embarrassed. Schoen left and was then called in again, with Hans Flesch now also present. The two men claimed to have written the *Hörspiel*. Who is the author? Who gets to decide what is broadcast? At the BBC it was not Schoen.

Another dream was from Surrey Street, within the confines of the building, on 23 March 1951, at 3.00 a.m. He was in a train carriage. There was an interaction with the train conductor. A family was travelling on the wrong tickets. The ticket collector pushed his big nose towards the little girl and asked her a question. To Schoen's surprise, she was able to answer.

The dreams were full of anxiety. He dreamed of the inability to perform tasks, that his role in a theatre might be cancelled, about missing rehearsals, about the fear of losing his wages.

On 11 April 1951, Schoen dreamt of crimes, of an England where he had only criticisms and discomfort. He was at an English music festival. At the close, it was possible to express criticisms and complaints at a desk. He stood in the queue and consulted the notes he had made during the performances: about the conductors, the presentation of the Mozart concert. Later in the dream he watched as people skied towards him. The Labour MP Aneurin Bevan approached him carefully and stopped close by. His face was repellent – yellowy green and puffed up. Then Herbert Morrison arrived. His face was red and gleaming with fat and his eye was black. He wanted a handkerchief to wipe his nose. Schoen stared straight ahead and pretended he could not hear them. The man he was with said that he could not give them his handkerchief as his daughter had a cold. Schoen commented: 'These guys not only look like criminals, they are really criminals'.

Criminals cropped up elsewhere. On 24 April 1958. Schoen went with perhaps Schmidt, a BBC colleague, through a long corridor to Mannheim. He said that the (Russian-Hollywood actor) Sokolov was setting up his own theatre there. Schoen asked: 'Probably with a virtuosic emphasis in the repertoire and staging?' They travelled to the United States for the second time. He had one suitcase in another, with padlocks on it. He heard two newspaper sellers. The one, from the *Manchester Guardian*, a grotesquely ugly one-legged person, came in. He said: 'It looks like a crime scene here'. The dream ends.

On the morning of 3 May 1951, he dreamt of writing two reports – perhaps with photos – for the Director General of the BBC, at the time Sir William Haley. Schoen saw the BBC letterhead in front of him. A colleague asked if he would earn money from this. He explains that it was something he was duty-bound to write, but he would receive a fixed amount for the photos. Upon waking, he invented a neologism: *Um-entschlossenheit*. Instead of *Un-entschlossenheit*, 'indecisiveness', this meant re-decisiveness. Was he moving towards a decision, or re-evaluating those already taken?

On 16 July 1951, Schoen dreamed that he left the BBC by the wrong exit. He went down a flight of stairs, heard a piano, urinated in a corner. An 'errand boy' passed by. He went down to the basement, but the exit there was too narrow. He found a key, but it was of no use. He went back up to the ground floor, had an argument with the doorman, but finally found an open door and went outside. The area had changed. There were market stalls. A bus came out of a wide street. He strolled around, saw children in fancy dress. A young man commented on the style of his suit. He buttoned up his shirt collar and tried in vain to wear a velvet beret as a cravat, but it did not work as the velvet band was ragged.

On the following day, he dreamt of Rosenberg and another colleague (he notes that it's perhaps Alexander, but someone friendlier), who talked about emigration. Rosenberg said: 'You won't just go there (here and there), will you?' A dispute ensued between them. Finally, Schoen interjected: 'Home is where you have interesting and useful work.' The other said: 'I will read the book up to the point where the "stillings" [which should have been "sparrows"] appear.' Rosenberg referred to a zoological name, in which the word 'Trochaeus' occurred. Schoen asked if that wasn't a rhinoceros? He thought it meant 'horn', but it meant running. The words tangled up.

A dream from 24 July 1951, around 7 a.m., brought to his troubled mind a Mr Scott Ritchie – probably Douglas Ritchie, a BBC German News Editor and clandestine organiser, as Colonel Britton, of the V for Victory radio propaganda campaign in the war years, which encouraged sabotage, assassination and industrial action in enemy territories. Ritchie insisted to Schoen that there should be frequent use, in any context, of three words: revenants, relevants and redevants. But why these words? Schoen perhaps felt like a revenant, someone who had returned from the dead, a ghost, a spectral presence existing vaguely for the airwaves, listening in, a messenger but not the maker of the message. There but not fully present. How relevant was he to what was happening, he who had once been at the centre of things, now existing in the loneliness of the night shift, on the edges. And *redevant*, the French past participle of 'to owe again'. Was he owed, or did he owe something? In whose debt was he?

In August 1951, Schoen dreamt of being at the radio station with Herbert Lom. An argument meant that they got separated. Then they were in a room in which BBC 'career women' were employing new office staff – they came in and out announcing the names of new hires. The new workers thronged around a desk. One of them was very small. Lom said: 'Wasn't this the drawing room before?' There was a sofa and chairs. Lom had thrust himself forward, curious about the new engagements that were being given out. Schoen was alone again.

On 1 September 1951, he dreamt he had two translations of Villa-Lobos' poems in an American journal. He asked Bouterweck from the BBC German department where he might publish them further and he suggested putting them in some volumes sold in music shops. But they would need music with them, said Schoen. Here he interpolated waking life into the dream. A friend of Sasha's, upon being told two days later that Schoen was writing a sort of cantata for the World Youth Congress, to be held in Berlin in 1951, asked after the music. Schoen had replied that he was writing a verse cantata. Someone else would have to do the music. Returning to his dream detailing, Schoen talked of the poems being taken to the USA and mentioned another poem, a translation of Louis Aragon. As the woman read his poems in the dream, he lay on the floor and slept. He woke up in the dream to find a Maréchal Niel rose on his cover. He thought to himself: 'That is somewhat tasteless. As if I were dead'.[178]

In December, the dream setting was transferred to the BBC, where Schoen was packing luggage, with someoe he calls 'BBC Flesch', into a 'post horn' for a young man. Hand baggage went inside a rucksack inside the horn, all shoved in with some energy. This was just one of many dreams about travel, about flights of stairs leading to the wrong place.

A dream from 19 May 1952 noted his dismissal from the BBC and his engagement instead at a police station. He attempted to flatter the master of the watch, who bore a resemblance to Krenek. He was frightened and pretended to know what to do. He wanted to visit the BBC in his lunch hour, to pick up his missing wages for the month of May. He realised he did not have the right forms with him, though.

Dreams of anxiety about getting lost at the BBC persisted. As late as 26 May 1958, he dreamed that he went to the BBC, thinking that, although fired, he would be allowed to continue to work in silence. He stood in the wide foyer, waiting with others for an elevator. One opened on another side. He ran over and jumped into it. It did not ascend, but went horizontally into another BBC building. He went through a market, stooping under tarpaulin. He still had in mind to lead someone through a series of offices and broadcasting rooms to 'our' office. He had left six years before.

On 25 September 1958, he dreamt that he was directing a TV or radio programme for the corporation. He exchanged a few words with a young man: 'We know each other from before' – 'from the old days at the BBC, in

1937! It was important to start on time. He sat around a large round table and orchestral music started up. It was supposed to be Schoen's, but he had only written a few pages of the piano version, the rest was by Seiber. He felt ashamed. He asked someone for a few cigarettes. A few days later, on the 30 September, another BBC dream happened. Schoen had to translate three articles, but could not find them. There was enough time before the broadcast but Fraser was asking for them (perhaps Ian Fraser, who features throughout the year-books as a Governor of the BBC – but likely Lindley Fraser who ran the German Section for a number of years[179]). He took some papers from a pocket, hoping that they were there, but they weren't.

* * *

Impossible Radio

On 23 March 1951, Schoen wrote a response to a letter from Adorno. Schoen wanted to know more of Adorno's recent work – he had only seen some of Adorno's writing about the state of music and an essay on Walter Benjamin in the *Neue Rundschau*.[180] He had not seen *Dialectic of Enlightenment* (1947) nor *Minima Moralia* (1951), but had acquired Benjamin's 'book of memoirs' (likely his *Berlin Childhood around 1900,* which had been published by Suhrkamp in 1950) and he awaited the selected writings. He asked if an edition of Benjamin's *Passagen-torso* was planned, in reference to the book on the Parisian arcades that Benjamin worked on between 1927 and his death: 'For sure, one cannot let [Benjamin's] most important achievement be lost.'[181]

Schoen also relayed how he felt it impossible for him to get a role in radio in Germany after all this time. Radio was an arm of the politics of the occupying forces and any employee would need to be sent out from England, a position he did not wish to adopt. He doubted he would get such a role, even if he wanted it. Schoen updated Adorno on personnel at the radio station. Adorno was back in Frankfurt – he would be able to develop a relationship with local radio.

Eberhard Beckmann, now in charge of the Frankfurt radio station, had been a sports reporter for the *Frankfurter Volksstimme* 'in his day', noted Schoen in the letter, working with 'the notorious' Paul Laven, who he had heard was back at the Frankfurt station. He recalled how he met him in October 1947 and found him to be a 'spick and span' management diplomat. He revealed to Adorno what Beckmann had told him: He, along with Hollbach, had been compelled by the Americans to take over the station. He also told him that, during the Nazi time, he had driven somebody who had shot a Lieutenant Colonel in the SS or some such as an act of self-defence, to safety in Switzerland. Schoen mocked Beckmann – why did he say the shooter acted in self-defence? Was that evidence of Beckmann-like equivocation? Schoen had previously sounded him out about whether he could attain a position in the radio station's literary department, as one had just become available, 'at which he shied away, politely, but with all the signs of vivid consternation'.[182]

Schoen reported to Adorno that he had two lines of pursuit for the future, one in Berlin, one in Munich, but these would likely not come into being. He asked Adorno to put a good word around. Adorno had mentioned what was on at the Frankfurt Music Festival, which led Schoen to recall his first arrival in Frankfurt in 1924 and his visit to a festival at which the main event was Hindemith's *Minimax: Repertorium für Militärmusik*, written in 1923 as a party piece for friends. The piece had remained unpublished requested that it never be played after his death. For Schoen, this emblematised his discomfort at music festivals and art festivals nowadays. He admitted he sounded like a grumbling old man, but he found that he felt infantilised and insulted by encountering amongst the contemporary arts 'what is at best the after-stutterings of the artistic revolts of 30 years ago or much longer'.[183] The avant-garde was a ghost of itself.

Past relations, asymmetries of existence found articulation in Schoen's sleeping life. There were anxieties about work and capability. On 21 April 1951 Schoen dreamed of taking on the role of waiter in a play. Then he found himself in a library and was searching and searching for the text of the play – one of the classics. He kept finding only the wrong thing, a book in the same series, the wrong pages of the book. Then he began to wonder about the lighting and the organisation of crockery on a tray. He panicked that he would not be able to learn the role in time, or that the role would be scrapped. Then he found himself with an old colleague queuing for a tram or bus in order to reach the theatre troupe. He resolved to walk and then realised that his colleague had in the meantime caught the bus. He then decided to take the next bus, but worried he would be late. Then he worried about not being able to learn his script in time. The whole time he is oppressed by a fear of losing the role.[184]

One evening in March in 1952, after a row with Hansi, he dreamt that she punished him by giving him untranslatable sentences to render into German.[185] That same night brought dreams of lacking food because of insufficient money – and police and soldiers and shop windows full of mountains of the finest chocolate, which led him to reflect on how often he had been alone in foreign lands. He reported that he cried bitter tears. A woman came to comfort him – she was like someone he had known before, whose name only now, in the dream, returned to him after many years: Mrs Mesniankin. Dormant in the unconscious were clues from one's own life, finding a refuge on scraps of scribbled down dreams that gather up the fragments of a damaged life.

Schoen was made redundant by the BBC. This happened at some point in 1952, but the precise date is not recorded. In a letter from the 1950s laying out his case for compensation, Schoen noted that he had been given translation work at the BBC from 1940 until 1945, which provided a yearly income of £700–800. After this date, he and his wife, he testified, were entirely without means.[186] He went back to Germany, becoming a *remigrant* – returning not to the situation as it was when he left, but to a place broken and shattered by war, his place in it uncertain.

5

Remigrant: Berlin

Early 1950s

Settling Back

1952 was the year that Ernst Schoen went to Berlin to find work and to pursue his case for compensation. We know it wasn't on the 20 August, as that day is marked, in blue biro 'Leave?', underlined and then crossed out. Days later in the year start to become populated with appointments in Germany. At the end of the year, he received a one-off compensation payment of 15,000 Deutsche Marks from Hessen Radio.[1] He put energies into attempting to get publishers in East or West Germany to commission translations and broker performances of left-wing plays in theatres and on the radio. His hopes that the radio history he had written might be published were continually dashed. A letter from the publishers Volk und Buch in September 1952 noted that the focus of the press had changed and now concentrated on regional and *Heimat* titles. Schoen's 'lovely radio book' could no longer be considered. It was not possible to recommend another publisher, as it had not yet been decided which one would cover popular science.[2]

In May 1952, the border between East and West Germany or the Federal Republic and the Democratic Republic was closed. Movement between zones was possible in the four-part divided city of Berlin, a quarter of which was the capital city of the new East German state, but tensions in East–West German relations remained and developed to such a degree that they infiltrated all aspects of life.

After the war, Berlin lay largely in ruins. The city was ripe for more or less utopian grand architectural schemes, prompted partly by a spirit of competition between East and West.[3] In the early 1950s, West Berlin's

Kurfürstendamm was rebuilt and turned into its leading shopping street, *the* showroom for consumer culture. In the late 1950s, the International Building Exhibition developed new concepts for a housing project (1957–1961) in Hansaviertel near the Tiergarten. The moderately-high buildings in modernist style, designed by an array of architects, formed a loose ensemble of blocks at angles to each other and dispersed, in order to exemplify in architectural terms the 'Western liberal principles of liberal freedom, individuality', and 'the non-authoritarianism of the order of democracy and the marketplace in the West.'[4] In the Eastern sector of the city, rebuilding resulted in the showcase architecture of Stalinallee (1951–1960), characterised by ornate monumentality, axial orientation and centralised order.[5] GDR architects had envisioned a housing project that defined itself against the formalism and cosmopolitanism of the interwar period, returning to local and national styles. Stalin mingled with Schinkel.[6] Here were apartments for party loyal GDR workers, restaurants, shops and cultural institutions.

The aesthetic expressions of the two regimes prior to the building of the Wall reflected their respective ideologies: late Western international Modernism and heroic, national, ornate, neoclassical architecture. They confronted each other along a state divide. One reached to a cosmopolitan context in order to break with both the *völkisch* and classicist monumental Nazi architectural past, whereas the other advocated an architectural style that signaled state weightiness and legitimacy. Critics of the time spoke of Communist kitsch.[7]

On 21 May 1953, Brecht, in the East of the city, wrote a recommendation for Schoen directly to West German publisher Peter Suhrkamp. 'We have already spoken about Ernst Schoen, who is in West Berlin, since returning from emigration to London and is keen to do translations from English and French.'[8] Brecht encouraged the publisher to offer him a trial translation. This garnered some income. He also was a reader for Rütten & Loening in Potsdam. He worked in the East and the West. But the relationship between the two states was changing. On 7 June, Schoen let one East German publishing house know that, owing to the state's blocking of financial transactions for those resident in West Berlin, he could no longer take on commissions from this company. It was difficult living across two states, two different political – and financial – systems.

On 21 June 1953, Schoen sent a letter to Hansi in England, in the aftermath of the Workers' Uprising in East Berlin. He wrote, as he often did, in English. He spoke of the horrors of the world: the execution of the Rosenbergs in the USA, the Korean War. He reflected on how personal happiness and security were connected to what other people do and what was done to them. Nothing came easily: it had to be fought with teeth and nails. He addressed the uprising, stating that it was not easy to give a true picture of what was happening:

A long campaign of sabotage and provocation, which is not from today or yesterday but organised and working very carefully for a long time, at least since the separation, plays certainly an important part. Of the 7 dead in Berlin all but one came from the West, and all but one were young workless hooligans. But it [is] also true that the policy and the treatment of the people over there, has been criminally wrong, and there again our own experiences may quite well be an example of the general wrongness, I almost see the demand which was made to me in '45, to come over unconditionally, in a new light now, quite apart from the idiocy of the treatment meted out to us then and still now. I read a cruel word the other day in a Westgerman paper, which Stalin is supposed to have said to Micolajchek even in '44: 'Communism fits the Germans as well as a saddle would a cow'! Well, Liebchen, it just goes to show that the right things can get very mouldy when they are handled by the wrong people in the wrong way, that is without humanity, love and understanding.[9]

His stance was ambivalent. He accepted the East German government's line that the rebellion had been stoked by outside agitation. It was true that the US-backed radio station RIAS and other organs of West-friendly Cold War propaganda had played a role in reporting on events, which could be seen as a form of encouragement. Yet he felt uneasy with what had occurred and, in any case, for him the broader question of what type of socialism existed in East Germany, or in the Eastern Bloc overall, was moot. The political deliberations in his letter to Hansi turned to reports on how lately he had fled from the brutality of humans into the fantasy worlds of films, attending film festivals in the West of the city. He also noted that he had tuned into the BBC German service on the short waveband: 'One of those features with several people, against our people, you know what I mean, and our beloved Ferdi one of the speakers!'[10] There was Ferdy Mayne again – he had worked for the Secret Services in the Second World

War and had been active in the MacDonald Group, possibly as the under-cover agent. His voice could be heard on the airwaves.

On 13 July 1953, Schoen wrote to Hansi that he had been offered a contract for the organisation of an archive and the building up of a museum of the history of theatre in one of the old Schinkel-designed buildings in the old centre in the East of the city.[11] A letter to Hansi from Charlottenburg on 14 August 1953 discussed arrangements for bringing over the family and finding somewhere for them all to live. Ernst was worried about financial affairs. They discussed purchasing one-way or return tickets for the children. Should they take on an empty flat and have their furniture shipped over or start afresh? He pondered the question of staying in one place and working in another – was that East and West Germany or Germany and England – and noted his answer to that. '1. It is my aim not to stay. 2. I might very likely be called. 3. The exchange problem. You see?!'[12] Presumably this related to the question of paying taxes on foreign income.

He reported on a letter from Friedrich Podszus, who sent him two books, a volume of Alain-Fournier about which he wanted some advice as to what would make a good German extract and a novel by Monique Saint-Hélier, of which Schoen was to do a sample translation. Should it be good enough, the full translation would appear in Suhrkamp's list. Schoen was hopeful that his old friends could provide work for him. 'And I think I wrote already in my letter to Sas that I've also got from my other publishers (sounds good, doesn't it?) the wonderful Indian short stories which I wanted so much to translate!'[13]

There was some hope that he could find enough work to keep alive and to rent a home and bring the family together again.

Dramatic Concerns

A letter to Sasha in March 1954 gives an insight into the situation of the family at the time. Schoen was translating Alain-Fournier's letters. Sasha was experiencing some difficulties at college, having 'stumbled' on one course, 'botany, or some such silliness'. Schoen comforted his son by noting that Alain-Fournier, swallowed up by the First World War, never passed a single exam. Sasha was poised to continue his studies at 'good old Birkbeck', an evening college in London. This accorded with his working during the day at Bayer's, where he had been promoted. Discussion turned to the prospect of holidays:

We are rocking once more on the waves of a situation where, financially, everything will be okeydoky, if only this, that or the other happens in time, or better still, all three of them, while on the other hand the capital still in hand is just so much that one would like to knock it down in one splendid go, and then see what happens.[14]

Life was precarious. They were bobbing along in a situation that might improve if luck arose or skills were deployed in the right places, but then again, life might be better if one were to blow everything one had in a venture and take what came of it.

East German theatre provided some opportunities for work and money. Schoen took on the role of archivist for the Deutsches Theater, pulling together the scraps of the past to build the archive anew, In this role he also edited a celebratory encyclopaedic volume, with a cover designed by John Heartfield, on its ten year post-war existence.[15] In this period, Schoen interviewed East German theatre-makers and wrote articles on progressive writers, including a piece on playwright Sean O'Casey, titled 'Das Problem O'Casey'. Heartfield remained in contact and even appeared in a photograph with Hansi, Sasha and someone unknown, posing in a line on a street in Paris.[16]

One of Schoen's articles published in *Theater der Zeit*, from March 1954, showcased the achievements of British popular theatre, by which he meant left-wing theatre. Schoen began with an observation on imperialism and how it kept people apart. This was a tragedy because all peoples have the same human dignity and the same goals. As a result of imperialist separations 'we know little of the drama of other parts of the world'. The GDR had started to introduce Soviet drama, but there were two thousand years of Asian culture about which little was known more widely in the world. There was so much still to be learned. His contribution was to discuss the work of progressive theatre makers in England. He began with a presentation of the Unity Players, the group of lay actors who set out in 1936 to create a revolutionary propaganda theatre. In January 1954, he received a report and photographs of performances for the article. He noted the strong influence communists had in culture, quite beyond their actual numbers, but could discern less influence of communists on British economics. The Unity Players developed a theatre, in a working-class area of London, Somers Town, after an appeal for help in building, which was answered by workers, artists and artisans. Now they were able to do not only agitprop on the street or other locations, but also to stage plays in their building. He described the membership structure and the ability to bring a guest – and the fact that the police kept a close eye on what was happening. In addition, there was the work of Ewan MacColl at Theatre Workshop, different in emphasis to the Unity Theatre, where all plays were revolutionary in character. Theatre Workshop was also interested in presenting classic dramas from around the world. He also mentioned the Edinburgh Festival as a showcase of popular Scottish culture.[17]

In October 1954, he mused, through a review of the work of Roger Vailland, on what a Marxist theatre aesthetic should be. Vailland was critical of Brecht. Schoen was critical of much more and insisted that theatre in the Marxist world was currently too pragmatic and too conformist.[18] The promise of a Socialist theatre worthy of the name was not being fulfilled. An article in December considered theatre in England prior to Shakespeare and emphasised the three strands that fed into the theatrical tradition: Catholic liturgy, minstrelsy and classical Humanism after the Renaissance.[19] Schoen attempted to communicate across borders, to bring about a common understanding of international human culture and to place it materially.

Radio still figured. Among Schoen's papers is a contract from November 1954 for the adaptation of Carson McCullars' *The Heart is a Lonely Hunter* as a *Hörspiel* for East German state radio. In that same year he was also contracted to adapt Elsa Triolet's *Le Cheval Roux* for radio.[20] There are letters also to the Unity Theatre, discussing upcoming performances. He sought to establish links between socialists in cultural work in the East and West, hoping to drum up work in the process. He was in contact with the theatre's director George Leeson, finding out what was happening in left-wing theatre, looking for new plays to translate and recommend in East German theatres. Leeson replied to some enquiries on 7 February 1956 concerning a possible performance of Tom Cobley's play *The Russian for Yes* on Berlin radio – it had been performed at the Unity Theatre in London in 1955.[21] The letter considered the possibility of Schoen's translation and his adaptation and overseeing of the performance. Leeson also mentioned Sartre's *Nekrassov* (1955), the talk of London, then playing at the Unity. He recommended Schoen translate it into German. The following year, Schoen wrote a lengthy summary of its themes, with proposals for how it might be adapted to radio. This was presumably to be sent to publishers and culture commissioners.

Over this time, Schoen worked on both sides of the German-German border, where he could, but tilted more to the east. One thing he signed was a contract with the newly established publisher East Berlin Henschel Verlag. His role was to scout out foreign-language plays. He wrote about theatre and he translated plays and criticism from Eduardo de Filippo, Guilherme Figueiredo, George Bernard Shaw and Frederick Antal. He also translated Charles Fenn's *Fire Eaters*, a Theatre Workshop play from 1954.[22] A long letter to Bernard Kops, on 27 October 1957, explained his sense of German-German theatre. Kops would receive royalties in good time into his bank account if a West German theatre took his play *The Hamlet of Stepney Green*. By contrast, any money paid by an East German source would be trapped in an East German bank account. The theatres in West Germany were superior and the play might then travel to Vienna or Zurich. And yet, Schoen thought that he had secured Kops a good deal in the East and was not certain such an arrangement would be forthcoming in the West. Schoen added that to date it had been impossible to have a play produced in the East transfer to the West – but it was his constant endeavour to make this happen. He blamed it on the inferior quality of work performed in East Germany. But problems persisted. On 23 November 1957, Kops telegrammed Schoen, to his Berlin Zehlendorf address, to say that the money had not arrived and that he was worried. Schoen scribbled out a telegraphic reply:

INNOCENT BUT POWERLESS STOP IT WILL
EVENTUALLY COME DESPITE CIRCUMSTANCES
PLUS HENSCHELS BUNGLING STOP
USELESS BUT EXPLANATORY LETTER FOLLOWS STOP
ALLTHEBEST = ERNST AND HANSI[23]

He continued working for Henschel, he added, despite all the difficulties because he found the publishers in the West 'uninterested, hard-headed, and always dictatorial and miserly'.[24] Schoen later spent time negotiating for a performance of his German translation of Kops' *The Hamlet of Stepney Green*, subtitled 'A sad comedy with some songs'. It was rejected by the East German Deutsches Theater as 'too private, too much reduced to a mere family conflict', he noted in a letter to Kops' agent Dina Lom.[25]

In the mid-1950s, he wrote long synopses of novels and plays by James Aldridge, Marcel Allemann, Jacques-Stephen Alexis, Georges Arnaud, Marie Louise Barron, Ugo Batti, François Boyer, William Branch, Dino Buzzati, Pierre Courtade, E. Cuffaro Montuoro, Howard Fast, Henry Fielding, Wolf Mankowitz – a hundred more or less well-known names, the re-forgotten, flashing up for a moment in Schoen's world, as he hoped someone would commission from him these works as adapted for radio, or the stage. He tried to conjure up work in the other direction too – composing in English a summary of an East German historical text by Politburo member Albert Norden, *Warnings of German History: Influence of German Capitalism and the German Junkers*.[26] This was presumably to be sent to left-wing English publishers. Schoen was a medium, a receiver and transmitter of ideas, of words, from one language into another, one context into another.

In the 1950s, Adorno began the project of collating Walter Benjamin's writings. He wrote to Schoen to request help. Schoen replied on 28 April 1955 that he was glad that Benjamin's work was being brought together, if somewhat late:

All the more I regret that I cannot contribute to your planned biographical comments. If I were among the memoir writers then I might have something to say, about our 'dramatic reading circle' of the early school years, about our sixth form 'rag magazine', which occasioned a libel suit and was the beginning of 'Der Anfang', about our re-encounter, the 'Free Student Movement', the strangely intertwined youth relationships, which surrounded us, and about the countless hours in the Delbrückstraße, at Lutter and Wegners, in Frankfurt and finally, then, in Paris, in which we spoke together, always interrupted by him reading out his works. But these memories also include several other people and events and have nothing specifically biographical about them. Most of all though I am separated from them by an abyss, out of which we try to climb today only with endless efforts, a struggle which will, I suppose, hang over us for the rest of our lives, only then to be continued by others. These considerations rather than the daily overwork make it impossible for me to provide the desired help with the work for this edition.[27]

Schoen spoke of a collective history, a shared fate that he did not wish to assume was a property of Benjamin's alone. Schoen also spoke of his pain at remembering these days, an agony at piecing together a life before the abyss of fascism. But, despite reading these personal words of pain, Adorno was convinced that Schoen had refused to assist for political reasons. He wrote to Scholem on 9 May 1955 that Benjamin's former wife Dora had agreed to assist them, but:

Ernst Schoen in contrast has refused to help, presumably out of anger that the edition is appearing in the West Zone and not with the wild peoples to whom he has given himself over.[28]

Prospects for Socialism

In August 1955, the Schoens took a trip to Yugoslavia in an attempt to find out what possibilities existed for other modes of life outside the strict frame of the Stalinist states. Schoen's report on the trip, 'Short Journey into Co-Existence', began with the journey itself, an extended journey by train through Europe.[29] At the railway station in Berlin, an opera singer, now unemployed, tried to sell a bottle of eau de cologne to Hansi. Schoen noted down conversations about politics and money with fellow passengers and train personnel, one a former Nazi, now 'sick of politics'. He was sharp in his criticism of those who lived an unreflected life. He mentioned two English travellers, both were for 'peace', but never read a newspaper. The only expression they could muster for the lakes and mountains that they passed on the train was 'lovely'. Schoen was struck by how nearly all of the tourists, and those who served them on this long journey across a continent, acted as if they had not experienced both a hot war and a cold one, 'as if everything was just as it has always been and will remain so'. History, politics, disasters had happened, it felt, to Schoen alone. The only anomaly was that in Baden the fields were flooded for miles and the train passed through them as if through lakes or a sea. Some of the farmers had sought refuge on what had become islands. This was an image of crisis, historical and ecological and of pockets of salvation – like climbing to the top of a mast on a crumbling shipwreck and making a signal.

In Italy, young workers flooded the train, women who were in service, cheap labour, returning home for a short holiday. Eventually the last part of the journey took place by bus. They reached the Yugoslavian border, but no-one in the party knew if a Yugoslavian bus would arrive to take them into the 'new land'. They sat on their suitcases and waited until a bus with a succession of friendly drivers arrived to take them across a terrain of new names to a house in Slovenia. Schoen described the people, their histories, the emigration of their children, their worldviews. He wrote of nationalisation and the prices of basic provisions and of import items, which were pegged at a much higher cost (including flour and fats). But he was also keen to relate the impact of German occupation. The sister-in-law of a village tailor, a former partisan, spent three and a half years in a German labour camp, like so many of her compatriots. Domiciled now in a new land, her husband had to give up his business as a trader and become a stock controller in a warehouse. But life was good enough, as it was, too, for her poorer sister, a seamstress, and they did not wish to emigrate to Italy, like the 'better people'. They thought they were seeking the promised land and ended up instead in refugee camps. Schoen commented: 'Now what does that remind me of?'

'Coexistence': How urgently do people need that, those people for whom life is so filled with trying to secure an existence, as necessary as the daily bread: I felt this perhaps most strongly when I stood for a few minutes here, with my grandson, in front of 'our' little house. The red moon was just climbing behind us above a mountain, in the sky there were more stars than at home, beneath us the Adriatic could only be discerned by a few reflected lights, every minute far away the light beacons of Trieste flared, and then a star plunged into the sea. Coexistence – friendly togetherness.[30]

By 1956, the real-existing socialism of the Eastern Bloc was increasingly under attack, even from within its own centres of power. On 25 February that year, Khrushchev delivered a speech behind closed doors at the Twentieth Party Congress of the Communist Party of the Soviet Union, entitled 'On the Cult of Personality and Its Consequences'. It was a denunciation of Stalin and the acknowledgement of the many thousands who had died in the gulags. Rumours about the speech surfaced in the West and a copy was acquired and reproduced at the Israeli Embassy in Warsaw. Mossad passed it on to the CIA. As well as appearing in the *New York Times*, it was broadcast by radio stations directed from the West into the Eastern zones. Radio was an effective weapon in the Cold War.

Roads Back, Roads Around

What did it mean to return to somewhere – if that place is both too much like what was left behind, but also nothing like it?

All that was hopeful and new seemed tarnished, broken and uncertain. Others returned to Germany and found a place. Adorno not only found a place, he founded a school of thought that, eventually, took on the name of the place. He was apparently proud to hear the term Frankfurt School associated with the philosophical project of Critical Theory, the school of thought which he steered in the post-war period, being its most visible representative, or survivor.[31] Adorno had a research institute in a newly opened building that was modernist in style and set itself against the neo-baroque architecture of the main university building, where philosophy proper was situated until 1958. Frankfurt was pulverised in order to repair the ruins and open up new opportunities, new styles, new tempos. Adorno's office was across the road from the new building – and between the two structures was a fast road that was a type of city motorway. He campaigned for traffic lights.[32] A small blockage on the fast flow of modernity, in order to allow human life a chance. Was the fast road new and modern? Was the new Germany modern? Were old networks being reinvented, reinvigorated, repackaged?

Konrad Adenauer, first chancellor of the Federal Republic of Germany, had not come from nowhere. According to the architect Albert Speer, Hitler was inspired by Adenauer's road-building project. From 1929 to 1932, a twelve-mile strip of motorway was built between Cologne and Bonn under Adenauer's command as Mayor of Cologne and chairman of the regional committee for roads. He also initiated the construction of a ring road around his city. Inspired by this work – this move into modernity – in the early days of the Third Reich, an ambitious road-building programme was begun, drawing in hundreds of thousands of workers to construction and supply chains of steel, concrete, maintenance equipment and signage. The motorways became a legacy of the Nazi regime – a pioneering high-speed road network. They gained the name 'Autobahn', in the plans for the Hamburg-Frankfurt-Basel network (HaFraBa) in the 1920s. The Nazis made a great deal out of the 'Reichsautobahn' from Frankfurt to Darmstadt, opened in 1935, which Nazi propaganda heralded as the first 'Autobahn'. The intellectual idea for the motorway was attributed to

Hitler by his General Inspector of German Roads, builder Fritz Todt, in 1937, who insisted – probably fancifully – that while in Landsberg Prison in 1923, Hitler had dreamt up the idea for a German network of motorways.[33] They became thoroughly Nazified, associated with the technological efficiency and expediency of the regime when it came to the control and movement of large groups of people. But the post-war state could not abolish them as a gesture of denazification. They were too useful and powered the economy of a beaten but economically robust post-war Germany. Indeed, Adenauer's regime presided over the turn away from denazification policies in order to pursue a new *Vergangenheitspolitik* or 'Politics of the Past', with amnesties for Nazi officials, reinstatements of civil servants dismissed in 1945 and the release of war criminals. Adenauer advocated reintegration at all costs and the motorways could be seen as a synecdoche of this: the network of the nation venerated as its binding ties, in a context in which the ties became a gag on speaking about the past, until the student-driven events of the late 1960s threw out its challenges to the Hitler Generation and their enduring traces.

This motorway network was the pre-condition for an accelerating supermodernity in which qualities such as mobility, connectivity, disembedding, circulation become questions of quantity It was a matter of how fast an abstract space without unique markers – village names, local landmarks – could be traversed, an experience that was regularly quantified and measured and ordered, by the signs that edged the way. Such circulation was mirrored in the installations of nowhere places, such as the electrical substations that came to occupy the landscape. The substation worked away quietly humming, as part of a network generating, transmitting and distributing electricity, moderating the grid. It powered the new Germany. The motorways were expanded. The state, or part state, was bound together again through its routes and circuits. Another nation-binding network, radio, had to be reinstated. Radio transmitters were erected or re-erected along the channels of these motorways, eventually delivering radio to the moving lumps of metal, through Blaupunkt's in-car radios. Music transformed, as did the style of presentation. The transmission cut out, you had to re-tune. But Schoen could find no place within it. It could be heard in cars as they travelled down the roads; interference heard in the car. Infrastructure had been rebuilt without his contribution. He fell back on more familiar modes: translation of books and plays, writing poetry.

Whereas Schoen hustled for work, Adorno not only had his institute: it also had a publisher, the Europäische Verlagsanstalt. Adorno published with Suhrkamp too and had outlets for his essays, in *Der Monat* and the *Neue Rundschau*. He, as well as colleague Max Horkheimer, were frequently invited to speak on the radio, just as they had done when Schoen was in charge in the years before the Nazi period. Adorno appeared on an almost weekly basis, to speak about education after Auschwitz and forgetting or repressing.[34] Through these means, the Frankfurt School was able to influence what Jürgen Habermas, Adorno's assistant from 1956–1959, would come to call the 'public sphere' of Germany, a public sphere whose mere existence was to be a guarantee against the resurgence of fascism. Perhaps Adorno felt a survivor's guilt. Or a thriver's guilt. He wrote in those terms and knew others were less able to take a place in the new Federal Republic of Germany. He also knew that to be back in place, back in Frankfurt, did not mean that nothing had changed, but sometimes he felt that way. In 1956, a radio lecture he gave on Alban Berg observed:

The period since 1935 was not one of continuity and steady growth in experience; it was disrupted by catastrophes. People forced to emigrate cannot escape the feeling that long years have been torn out of their lives and it is easy for them to succumb to the delusion that their present existence is just a continuation of what was destroyed then.[35]

It was likely hard for Schoen to succumb to such a delusion. With a position outside the institution, Schoen held tight onto the torn shreds of radical politics.

Roll Call (Dream and Reality)

On 21 August 1956, Schoen wrote a poem for Brecht, taken too young from life one week earlier.

Epitaph
Here lies Bert Brecht
Fallen nineteen hundred and fifty-six
In his fifty-ninth year of life
A victim of circumstances
Manslaughter

In life a friend of reason
And master of the word
Through which he, with exceptional power,
Held open the door to the world for his people.
Pursued by false friends
But never reached
He was always on a flight into the future
In which he was to live
Amongst people of a clarified sense
In whom he believed.[36]

Brecht could manipulate language to broadcast ideas and those were ideas of communist reason. 'In life a friend of reason and master of the word' – the idea of Brecht holding open the door for others to peer through into the world, his people, those he would coach in thinking and knowing, was an image that conveyed something radiophonic. Reason and the word – the promise of radio as a modern, rational medium, delivered through language and voice. A door held open for a people – to extend them beyond their own limits, their own borders, to enter into the world, not the small corner of the street, not the nation, but something greater, universal. And he was not of the past, but acting to bring something new into being, an angel of imminence. On a flight into the future – this promised much and it was for and of those who were a progressive community. Perhaps radio too was persecuted by false friends – by those who took its form and made it something distorted and distorting, or simply underwhelming. The people of the present fell short. Did the promise of a future community die with Brecht, with his exit, after neglect by the world? Brecht was to be added to the balance of losses that Schoen experienced, when his life was accounted for.

In 1951, Adorno published his book of vignettes and aperçus, *Minima Moralia; Reflections from Damaged Life.* He wrote about the damage done to the émigré, under the heading 'To them shall no thoughts be turned':

The past life of emigrés is, as we know, annulled. Earlier it was the warrant of arrest, today it is intellectual experience, that is declared non-transferable and unnaturalizable. Anything that is not reified, cannot be counted and measured, ceases to exist. Not satisfied with this, however, reification spreads to its own opposite, the life that cannot be directly actualized; anything that lives on merely as thought and recollection. For this a special rubric has been invented. It is called 'background' and appears on the questionnaire as an appendix, after sex, age and profession. To complete its violation, life is dragged along on the triumphal automobile of the united statisticians, and even the past is no longer safe from the present, whose remembrance of it consigns it a second time to oblivion.[37]

Had Schoen's past life been annulled through his experience of migration and exile? Was the proof of that the inability to find an adequate foothold upon returning to his broken and fractious homeland – settling in neither East nor West? Into what gaps did his knowledge and commitment fall? Adorno responded to the quantification of life in the United States, dominated by human relations and psychological profiles and forms for filling out that immigrants know more than anyone else. And as a remigrant, Schoen would know them too as he navigated the bureaucracy of compensation and complaint in post-war Germany. The past becomes reduced to a set of capacities for tick boxes. Did Schoen feel that, both abroad and at home? In any case, annulled or not, his past gathered in spectral forms with an uncommon intensity.

Schoen remembered people, people remembered Schoen. Like Adorno and Scholem, he was searching for manuscripts too, trying to piece together old work, his own – as well as his friend Walter Benjamin's. A letter in October 1956 from 'the 3 three Radts' – Grete, Fritz and Jula, old friends of Benjamin from almost five decades prior – noted that the manuscripts he had requested had all been lost in a fire in Mannheim.[38]

If, like the things, the people were all scattered or lost, from the very beginnings of the century to its latter part, they gathered periodically – even often – in dreams. The dreams were an assembly of friends, acquaintances, enemies and moments of a past or pasts lived across Europe, in accredited institutions and in none. These were the realm of a montaging of space – spaces coagulated or segued together, across time and memory and dreams.

In his dreams, the chips and fragments of the world assembled in jumbled order and a muddle of space. In one dream, transcribed from 3 November 1957, Schoen dreamt of uniforms, of school, of a broken piano, of people laughing at him. He ate on Charlotte Street in Fitzrovia, but it might also have been Paris. He bought bread rolls, but the street was destroyed. He heard that Jorge Greco was dead and woke up crying, not sure if this was because of the dream or the reality. Sometimes the dream was as bad as reality, or reality was worse than the dream. The dream became a place in which friends could be resurrected from death, or returned from afar, where reality could be inverted or crushed or denied. What roll calls occurred in sleep and waking life?

Walter Benjamin appeared in Schoen's dreams a number of times after his death in 1940. Once Schoen dreamed that he was walking down the street.[39] In front of him was an elderly nanny with a little boy. Schoen heard the boy say: 'Me and little Benjamin are the best in school'. Aha, he thought, a much younger brother of Walter. Perhaps Georg, who had, at this point, already died.[40]

Alfred Cohn was in Barcelona, where he died in 1954. His daughter Marianne, a childcare worker for a French Zionist youth organisation, the sole income earner in the home and a part of an organisation smuggling Jewish children threatened with deportation to Switzerland, was arrested, aged 21, by the Gestapo and shot dead in the summer of 1944.[41] Cohn appeared in Schoen's dreams with Georg Knepler, who was also in the GDR.[42] They were both in a cesspit. Cohn had become a pharmacist. They drove off in a car together and Schoen ran after them. Alfred was wearing a stiff black hat. They tried and failed to pick their clothes from the cloakroom.

Knepler also appeared in other dreams. In one, Schoen saw him at a Hyde Park meeting about the hunger marches and against the 'means test'. His wife said to him: 'Well, what do you gentlemen want among us poor plebs?' Shortly afterwards he dreamed he was at a procession of the King of England and his mother. All of a sudden Knepler was next to him and said: 'Well, what do you want here?' To this Schoen replied with a shameful feeling: 'Don't you know that my name is actually the Prince of Wahlheim?' (Name of a town, but literally 'elective home'.)

Schoen's one-time acquaintance dinner companion Anthony Asquith was busy making films, one a year until 1964, thrillers, romantic dramas, films about ballet and opera and adaptations of George Bernard Shaw and Oscar Wilde.[43] In Schoen's dream he appeared in a train carriage just before Surbiton. Schoen was unfolding the *New Statesman* and then began to stuff a load of things around him into a briefcase: silver tableware, an iron ashtray and a clay one and then, finally, a stash of manuscripts with the title 'Asquith's Surveys'.

Dora Sophie Kellner was in London, where she married Harry Morser (previously Heinrich Moerzer), a figure from her youth in Vienna, but divorced him in 1945. She was a hotelier with her partner Frank Shaw.[44] She also appeared in Schoen's dreams. On 20 July 1958, he walked along a street with her. A bourgeois type appeared and sang Puccini or Verdi at full volume. Schoen said to him: 'This is the only country where the people are most uninhibited. The most is Paris, but only in the popular quarters.'

Dolf Sternberger was in Heidelberg.[45] In a dream from 22–23 December 1946 he was on Regent Street where he approached Schoen. Schoen greeted him, though there is confusion over the encounter, but they have nothing to say to each other. Chinese policemen patrol everywhere in twos, always one in uniform and one in civilian clothes.

Alexander Schoen was in London. He appeared throughout the dream diary. In one he talked about the impact of the military on his feet. His father took him comfortingly by the shoulder and said that he had become nice and wide anyway. On the morning of 21 June 1959, Schoen dreamt the family were living with a young English married couple. He argued with the man and decided to have a swig of brandy from a bottle in his suitcase. The man's wife went to bed. The husband tied his shoelaces and said, in English, `Bad that Sasha is leaving again. It's as hard again, as if it were the first time.' Me: `Yes, that's what life is made of.' Him: Yes, material parting. But spiritual parting is another thing. As the priest said ...'. The man then began to deliver a litany in an artificial voice.

Hanns Eisler was in East Berlin and had composed the National Anthem for the new German Democratic Republic.[46] In a dream, he offered Schoen a volume with production designs from operas. Somehow, he would be able to make money from these. Eisler quizzed him on what operas were depicted – but the answer was on the page. In the same night, a man said how young he looked, but another said that he had the neck of a ninety-year-old.

Busoni died back in 1924,[47] but still appeared in Schoen's dreams. Once he returned to see him with the feeling that he was unwelcome. Schoen heard an orchestra in rehearsal and thought to himself: 'Oh dear, again no music of my own, and so insignificant.' He appeared again as a phantasm. Schoen went to his house. A maid answered and said no one is home. Schoen entered anyway. He found several grand pianos and harpsichord-like instruments. On top of one was a manuscript of music. He thought to himself, aha, Busoni is composing here. He opened the door to the next room. In the centre sat Busoni in his velvet smock, writing, his back turned. Schoen thought that he was home after all, but just didn't want to be disturbed, so quietly closed the door again.

Edgard Varèse was in New York, working on electronically organised sound for interpolating into *Déserts*. It premiered in December 1954 in Paris, under conductor Hermann Scherchen.[48] Varèse appeared in dreams at a dinner party. Schoen arrived unannounced. Varèse reacted warmly, but in reality, perhaps unpleasantly surprised and arrogant.

Hans Flesch slipped from all records in April 1945, somewhere and sometime in the war. He was declared dead on 31 December of that year.[49] He appeared in a dream at a communist meeting. Hansi and Ernst had sneaked in. Attendance was low. Afterwards they sat at a table, angry that loud speeches were taking place just in front of them. When Schoen pulled out a matchbox to light a cigarette, a man snatched it from under his nose.

Paul Hindemith had just been awarded the Goethe Plaque of the City of Frankfurt.[50] He doesn't feature in Schoen's dream diary.

Edward Clark had just been succeeded by Benjamin Frankel as chairman of the International Society for Contemporary Music amid claims of fraud.[51] In a dream he was offered a job in the colonies, for some position at UNESCO, with a salary of only £650 per year.

Willi Baumeister died in 1955.[52] He doesn't appear in Schoen's dreams.

Helene Weigel was in Berlin. Her husband, Bertolt Brecht,[53] appeared in Schoen's dream with Sternberger and Adorno. A man was covered in a green glaze, like in an aquarium. Someone wore a glass bowl, half filled with water, like a diving helmet. He updated Schoen on what Brecht is writing, a kind of history of literature, not yet finished.

Charlotte Wolff was in London,[54] but, as far as we know, Schoen never met with her. She did not crop up in his recorded dreams.

Late 1950s

German Dealing: Realities and Dreams

In April 1957, a letter arrived from Verlag der Nation, the ruling Socialist Unity Party of Germany's own press, established with the Republic in 1948 to issue biographies, literary writings and reissued classics. The press commissioned Schoen to put together 250 lines from his own work for a publication for the international PEN congress in Tokyo, in order to showcase German-German thinking. Schoen responded: 'Since the return from emigration I have been active almost solely, in promotional and translational terms, as an interpreter of poems from other countries.'[55]

He proposed, though, one of the long poems from his *London Elegies*, published by a Weimar-based East German press, G. Kiepenheuer, in 1950. He also drew attention to his introduction to his selection of letters by Alain-Fournier, which appeared with Suhrkamp and his contribution on 'The Problem of Sean O'Casey' in the publisher Henschel's ten-year almanac of the *Deutsches Theater* (the German Theatre).[56] These were his proposals, his high points. The publication came out under the title 'That the times are a changing!'.[57] It included 'Seestück' from *London Elegies* as part of a selection of poetry, alongside more poems from the party faithful, such as Johannes Becher and Erich Arendt.

In his dreams all the tensions of the world took on enigmatic form. One from 5 December 1957 reported on being with someone else, Hansi probably, in the Soviet Union. They were in Leningrad but wanted to go to Moscow and were short of time and money. The mood was sombre, Kafkaesque, because, he noted, they were unable to make themselves understood. A man with fluent German arrived, but said he was from Paris. All those cities, languages, communicating across borders, being stuck, moving on, being confused: it all seeped out in dreams.[58]

On the same night, he dreamed of being in the Deutsches Theater. Here he should have felt at home. In May 1957, he had contributed several essays, on stagecraft and directing and the profession of acting to the almanack of ten years of the East German playhouse that showcased the best of culture for GDR workers. He had written an essay for the programme of *Inner Voices*, a comedic play by Neapolitan Eduardo de Flippo. In this, he noted that no other dramatic form allowed the dialectic of reality to be perceived more clearly than comedy. Perhaps his dreams were comedic forms. In any case, they expressed in absurd terms the anxieties about where to belong. The theatre's manager, former actor Wolfgang Langhoff, gave a recitation, when he spied Schoen and stumbled over his words. Later he asked Schoen why he was there, when he was banned from the theatre. Schoen was unaware of this and sat down at a table. In English, he thought 'What the hell', and left.[59]

That year he recorded dreams of bombed streets and prices for food that he could not pay. One page noted a series of dream remnants from recent times. Uniformed men told him he had to face something unpleasant, an examination of some kind. He was back in the schoolroom. At another moment, he opened the lid of his new piano, but it had only one octave and its pedals were paralysed. People were about to laugh at him, but he managed to find another row of keys, differently formed and coloured. He played. He told a dream of a fat, hunchbacked old woman who wished to lie in his bed with him; he screamed repeatedly, but noticed that he was unsure if he screamed in the dream or in reality. In any case, when he woke after the event, he could hear movement in the flat below, as if he had disturbed someone.

On Christmas night 1957, his dream appeared to express concerns about his presence and purpose, not in and between the new German states, the world of culture and all that, but rather within his own home. He imagined himself desperate to get up to his own flat, but only managed to make the lift work by pulling on a rope. Others arrived in other lifts, but he was unseen. Left outside the flat, Hansi having closed the door, he saw Sasha passed out on the floor. He knelt down next to him and Sas said, weakly, while crying: 'If I don't have you, I don't know what to do'. Schoen read from a sheet of paper all the things he promised to do with him.

The start of 1958 brought news of rejection. The press declined to take on Schoen's suggestion of a translation of Emmanuel Roblès' *Les Hauteurs de la Ville* (1948). It was not a literary decision, the publisher claimed, but simply one of theme, for they already had three books on similar issues on their list.[60] Such notes and setbacks were all part of a constant hustle, to get work and, also, to bring the world's culture to the new German republic. The case for compensation dragged on. A letter on 15 April 1958 requested some final paperwork from accountant Richard Wray in England: a British Income Tax Authorities certificate, establishing the veracity of Schoen's claims about his BBC earnings.[61]

In a dream from 7 April 1958, he detailed how he was called to an unpleasant young man with the name 'Stefan Zweig' to discuss a literary work. On the way he makes a comment about the meaningless flexibility of Goethe's concept of universality. But 'Zweig' was not accessible to him, caught on the telephone, giving the 'message'. Who was to give the message in this new world? Not Schoen, who was trapped in corridors, in lifts, on the way to discussions that never happened.[62]

On 12 April, he labelled his latest dream explicitly an anxiety dream. Life and dream merged again. He had been arguing with the telegraph messenger for Ninchen's birthday telegram, early in the morning. Falling back asleep, he reported being in a train station with Puma and Nina. He stopped for a moment to search for his ticket. To catch up with them again, he found himself going first down one flight of stairs, then up another, only to arrive at the wrong platform. To get back to his family and the train, he climbed recklessly through a window. He emerged into a ticket hall and asked a reddish-haired porter – who looked like the telegraph messenger, but older – where the train to West Berlin's main station, the Zoo, was leaving from. He replied that he did not understand Italian. 'Berlin' said Schoen and was then pointed on his way. Reaching some kind of platform, he saw women hurriedly dress up in carnival costumes. Then it became clear that there were no train tracks – and so he screamed out in anger and fear: 'Apparently I was really screaming because Puma woke me up.'[63]

Carousel of Jobs (Revisited)

Some of Schoen's efforts made for a sorry tale, at least according to the fragments of letters back and forth that are held in the Schoen archive. In December 1957, Schoen wrote to Ewan MacColl:

I have read *So long at the fair* with great pleasure and admiration. I think, the theme, that every human being is entitled to act only, if he knows the reason why, and accepts it as right – a theme which carries such an important lesson just for a German audience –, comes out excellently in the drama of the five soldiers, who are as different as they are representative. It is enhanced by the fruity dialogue (of which I am not afraid, if it should come to my translating the play, quite on the contrary, which will stimulate me); and the scenic effect is, so it appears to me, beautifully coloured by the fairground, its characters, and the songs. I shall recommend the play warmly, and hope very much that my recommendation will meet with the desired success.[64]

In March 1958, Schoen wrote again with news that he had translated a scene from the play – a love scene between Turk and Moll – and had written a synopsis. This is 'for the attention of the leading theatres of the GDR'. The work had met with enthusiasm and German rights were sought. Schoen wanted to clarify issues concerning payment and confirm that the contract should go to MacColl and Joan Littlewood.[65] By the end of the year, he reported to Gerald Raffles and Hannes Fischer of the Dresden State Theatre that he had translated about half of the play. Raffles replied immediately from the Theatre Royal that work on *So long at the fair* had been abandoned and he had no copy to convey. Schoen by return of post sounded exasperated. 'For God's sake!' He had the play and discussions about its production in Dresden in the coming season were advancing. 'So, please don't tell me, the authors won't let us have it now: I for one can't see what's unfinished about it; I think, it is the goods!'[66] Raffles replied that all is then well and good, if MacColl has given him the script.[67]

The play, now called *Der Rummelplatz*, was scheduled for performance at the Maxim-Gorki Theater Berlin. On 11 March 1960 a letter arrived from Theatre Workshop, signed by Gerald Raffles. It speaks of distress at finding that *So long at the fair* was to be produced in Berlin without any authorisation from the company. It insisted that on no account may Joan Littlewood's name be associated with it. Raffles wrote:

As far as we are concerned the play is unfinished, and we do not wish it to be presented as an example of our work. You may regard this as formal permission to make whatever arrangements you may like with Ewan MacColl about presenting the play, but the authorship of the play must rest with him alone.[68]

Schoen replied that the protest was misdirected. The agreement concerning performance of the play would be a concern for Henschel, the play's publishers, and it was to them that the protest should be directed. Schoen had been caught in some aesthetic, political and personal crossfire. The play went ahead, as *Der Rummelplatz*, only under MacColl's name, at the Maxim-Gorki Theater in October 1961, a long run and the only staging of it. Schoen is not mentioned in the play's description.[69] It was broadcast on GDR TV in 1964.

There were other sorry tales. At the end of 1957, an excited letter from Maria Sommer at Kiepenheuer Bühnenvertrieb discussed plans for a theatrical production of a play by Luigi Squarzina in Düsseldorf. Schoen had put them onto it, along with English and American works. He had translated Squarzina's *La sua parte di storia* (1952–1955) into German and it was staged at the Düsseldorfer Schauspielhaus. This was followed by Schoen's co-direction with Squarzina of the production at the Volkstheater in Vienna in November 1958. In June 1958, discussions began for a contract from Kiepenheuer Bühnenbetrieb in Berlin-Dahlem, for the adaptation of Squarzina's *Il Pantograf* (1958) as a radio play for Hamburg radio. There was word of a contract also for Squarzina's *Romagnola* (1951–1957).[70] In July 1958 Schoen wrote to Sommer, requesting timely notification of when his translated plays would be performed in Germany: 'I am always interested in the career of my "godchildren"'.[71] He bemoaned that he had not received proofs and asked if the publisher occasionally sold *Hörspiele* to

East German radio. If it were the case, the Squarzina play appeared to be a good candidate. He requested he be proposed as director, as he was known for such work there. But perhaps, he mused, it was not possible to repeat plays from the West on the radio stations of East Germany, or vice versa. He also requested the return of various manuscripts that were 'spoiling' in the office.

As January 1959 drew to a close, Schoen was compelled to write a difficult letter to his contact at Henschel, Fritz R. Schulz, on account of an unpleasant business that had blown up at the publishers.[72] He reminded Schulz that, for years, it had been hard to bring to the stage the most progressive socialist works and that Henschel had, in resignation, decided not to translate the best of them, because of the official state drama policy. Schoen had asked Schulz whether there were any West German theatre publishers interested in similar works – socialist in tendency, of course, because he would translate nothing else. Schulz put him onto Maria Sommer, with whom Schoen had already been in touch, given she had once worked for Henschel. She had taken the second drama by Squarzina, which he had offered previously to Henschel, and also a play by a young Englishman, Frederic Raphael, a polemic against atomic bases in England, and then a third play by Squarzina, which had been adapted for radio. He reported that he was happy to translate the play, because he agreed with its political message and he cited its main theme as expressed by the protagonist:

I was aware of doing something that had to be done, in spite of all the difficulties, even in secret, even against the law, because, of course, it is not right to make oneself comfortable with the laws, as long as not one of them says what a man, who dies after an exhausting life, should have done, in order to be sure that the children he brought into the world were left with a few pennies.[73]

Schoen had suggested to Maria Sommer that she offer the radio play to 'democratic radio', and that he would gladly direct. She wanted to try it with Radio Bremen, a station that had already broadcast his translation of Squarzina's second play before its staging in Düsseldorf and Vienna – a situation to which he could not raise any objections given the contract already signed. To put the next play on the radio, in a co-production by Radio Bremen, Südwestrundfunk and RIAS, seemed to him in some regards a kind of smuggling of socialist politics into West German radio. But it was RIAS that was the problem. Upon hearing the plans, he had not, he said, taken in that RIAS were involved. It had dawned on him only in conversation with Schulz. RIAS stood for Radio in the American Sector. It was explicitly the enemy of the Russian Sector, self-named 'a free voice in the free world', and, after the Berlin Blockade, it became a news service particularly favoured by East Berliners who wanted to hear something different to what was state-sanctioned. The East German state blamed the events of the Workers' Uprising in 1953 on RIAS. Schoen expressed, in a letter to Schulz, the sentiment of a party-liner: 'Of course I know from reports the dark role that RIAS plays in German internal politics. But the mention of my honourable name in its programme hit me like a virgin having a child.'[74] Schoen requested Schulz explain something of this to Henschel. He feared being crossed off the books.[75]

On 2 February 1959, he wrote to George Raffles at the Unity Theatre, noting that he had left Henschel 'to freelance again'. It was all the more important, therefore, to get good material. He inquired after Shelagh Delaney's *A Taste of Honey* (1958).[76] Efforts, again and again.

In March 1959, there was more bad news for Schoen. Maria Sommer had looked over his translation of Squarzina more thoroughly than her first perusal. She had compared it to the original and had also examined another of his translations – *Il Pantograf* (1958). She reported that they were full of errors that distorted the meaning.[77] Squarzina had spoken out against Schoen's translations in the autumn, and, as a result of her investigation of the quality, she would not step in to change his mind. The previous translation and adaptation contracts were to be cancelled, so that new translators could be contracted. Sommer stated bluntly, in case he should find it unfair, he must remember that 'such huge costs and unpleasantness have arisen for the publishers as a result of your work.'[78] The play would not be performed again in the version that had appeared in Germany and Austria and accruing to Schoen would be only a percentage from any previous ticket receipts and for any repeats of the radio play. Some money arrived in his account from the radio broadcast of *Il Pantograf* in his translation as *Der Unfall* (The Accident) in the next months, and, in the following years, Hansi received the royalties as they accrued, minus a foreign earnings tax.

The debacle with Squarzina may have made Schoen nervous about future translation work. In any case, on 12 August 1959, he sent a note to a Mr Branco, noting that he had translated a play by Jorge Amado, *O Amor do Soldado* (1947) for Henschel. He had, he revealed, only a pocket dictionary at his disposal and was stumped by half a dozen constructions. He wanted to meet with Branco at the press club, presumably a Portuguese native speaker, to go over those parts.[79]

On 8 July 1959, Schoen presented Charles Prost's *Adieu Jerusalem* (1962) to Kiepenheuer & Witsch, in Cologne, a company distinct from the ones in Berlin and Weimar with a similar name. He sent it to his contact there, Jörg Wehmeier, with some recommendations of young Argentinian writers and writing from Guatemala. He received an acknowledgement signed on behalf of Wehmeier. In September he was informed that Wehmeier had left the press in August and that the manuscript could not be found. Another copy was requested. Then he was assured, on 13 October, that it had been found to be in the possession of a reader, but the reader was away travelling. By November, it transpired that it was in fact lost and the publisher acknowledged the 'fiasco'. The publisher offered something in compensation, for Schoen had already informed them that it was a transcript available only in a magazine, *Theatre Populaire*, which formed part of his collection. Eventually, by February 1960, plays from Prost were with a reader and further materials, such as reviews and production photographs, were requested from Schoen for consideration. On 22 February, having returned from a trip, Schoen sent theatre programmes and other materials, lent to him by the playwright Myriam Lempereur whose *La Moisson de Pilar*, first performed in Belgium in 1919, was with a reader.[80] He asked that they be quickly returned and pressed for a speedy decision, as well as a decision on *I Giacobini* (1955) by Zardi which was 'one of the greatest successes of the Piccolo Teatro di Milano'. Late in March 1960, he received a letter from Rudolf Jürgen Bartsch, assuring him that he and his texts had not been forgotten, but the publisher understood his impatience. However, Bartsch was able to say that the publishers did not want to take on Prost's work.[81] Other proposals were still being deliberated. So many farces. So much effort for so little gain.

Poems Backwards and Forwards

From Berlin's Zehlendorf, on 25 June 1958, Schoen wrote a little poem in English, 'A Sailor to a Siren'. It was staccato and sonic, playful and modernist, a warning from beyond or atop a mast, at sea or by a radio station, as the thin vertical line on the page evokes:

Crickets
Play Cricket
On your rocky
Isle
Rockets
Croquet
With a croco-
Dile
I've
Got my ticket
And
Stand
Hand
In Pocket
In a picket
Line
Your beacon
Beckons
Sailor be
Mine
I chase
A march-hare
Here and there
Your beacon
Beckons
Sailor be-
ware.[82]

Britain appeared to him in his memory as a craggy island of crickets and croquet players, strikers and sailors. It beckoned him, he got his ticket, but its calling, like a siren, lured him only into a dangerous or unappealing situation. Beyond all that, the language is playful, confusing, punning and slippery. The English language's curious, historically tinged irregularities revolve expertly in the words of the person who adopted the language.

On 1 January 1959, Schoen received an elegant card from the East German publisher, Verlag der Nation. The card stated on its front: 'At the change of the year'. And then inside, in cursive print, a ponderous salutation: 'All best wishes for firm solidarity as regards the solution of the weighty tasks ahead for one's own successes and personal well being'. The recto displayed an extract from 'Poetic Journey', a sixty-two-page poem by Georg Maurer, which the press published that year:

> I heard through the sleeping of the hemisphere
> Like a deluge a flood of waves
> Each peered to see where a cliff stood its ground
> Not yet vaulted by this sea's flood
> Then I saw columns grow, here and there in the furthest East
> The ruins of a world amid crashing waves
> Threatened thunderously by this cliff outpost
> Deafened I suffered every night the same noise.
> But in each breaking morning there rose
> The young columns of our republic[83]

This was a New Year's Greeting, East-German style.

A few days later a letter from the same publisher thanked Schoen for his letter and a manuscript intended for the PEN Almanack.[84] This belonged to the small tally of moments of success.

Correspondence Continued and Interrupted

Scholem and Adorno planned an edition of Walter Benjamin's letters. They knew Schoen was a good source for the early correspondence. Adorno tried to contact Schoen, but his letter was returned. Bloch told Adorno that Schoen was now living in the Eastern Zone and now Adorno wondered how he would find his address.[85] It was all the more unpleasant because he was sure Schoen was the only person able to contact Alfred Cohn – Adorno was presumably unaware that Cohn was dead, nor did he know whether to spell his name with a K or a C.[86] Scholem took up negotiations, because, as Adorno put it in a letter from 7 November 1960: 'He seems to have *gravamina* against me, which are connected to my anti-Soviet position'.[87] Scholem replied to Adorno on 28 November, noting that he had already been in contact with Schoen, who had written a friendly letter and informed him he had letters from Benjamin from 1913 to 1920 and was prepared to lend a dozen of them, if they passed into 'loyal hands'. Schoen thought they were of theoretical interest, but Scholem wanted to tell him that they were keen on personal materials too. Scholem reported also that Schoen stated bluntly that they might only be touched by him and no other person.[88] Scholem indicated to Adorno he would agree to the condition, but that he would have copies made straight away. Schoen also informed Scholem that he and Hansi were to leave Germany in March or April 1961 to move to Upper Italy. On 2 December Adorno replied to Scholem, stating that he had no idea why Schoen was so opposed to him and he found it ridiculous to transfer political differences to personal relations.[89] He asked Scholem to find out what was the cause – but only once they had got their hands on the booty. In the following letter, from 6 December 1960, Scholem repeated to Adorno that Schoen had insisted that no one other than Scholem should be able to see the original letters.[90] The no one other than Scholem was Adorno. Scholem promised to find out why such a feeling existed on Schoen's part. It was too late for this. Schoen died in Berlin, in the Martin Luther Hospital in Berlin-Schmargendorf on 10 December 1960 at 5:30 in the morning.

1960: Death Notice

Schoen's death was recorded by Hansi in one of the little diaries as 'Ati sleeps'. The cause of death was noted at the bottom of the diary's page: cardiovascular failure. A telephone call with a doctor at 1 p.m. that day was roughly scribbled out in the diary.[91] The family's official death notice followed in the *Frankfurter Allgemeine Zeitung*. It found a more permanent home inside a book of scraps and cuttings relating to his death compiled by Hansi.[92] Inside a black box, the date span of his life was supplemented by a line that summarised the contribution of that life, in its most public, most successful aspect: 'from 1924 until 1933 pioneer of German radio in Frankfurt am Main'. And then, after a small gap, like a moment's delay to maximise the effect, 'he died as a victim of National Socialism'. It was issued on behalf of the family by 'Hansi Schoen, née Liman', the address given as Berlin-Wilmersdorf, 3 Ravensberger Straße.

Communications of condolences were pasted into the commemorative scrapbook. Letter-headed and black-banded stationery from across the world, fading signals from far-flung networks, voices from childhood, professional contacts, echoes from a dozen exploded address books. The first cutting was a letter written on 16 December from Eberhard Beckmann, the director of Hessen's radio network, Hessischer Rundfunk, successor to the radio station where Schoen had worked. The words were grandiloquent. He assured Hansi that Ernst Schoen had not been and would not be forgotten in Frankfurt: 'His name will forever have a prominent place on the memorial stone dedicated to those men who gave a face to radio in its earliest days'. Beckmann stressed how different radio had become in organisational terms after the Second World War, but those involved did not forget how much the foundations had been laid prior to 1933. The conceptual and artistic principles from those days continued to be relevant. The final paragraph was a strong articulation of Schoen's reputation:

Ernst Schoen, the successor to Hans Flesch, will forever be valued as one of the most significant pioneers of German radio. His artistic activities and his championing of a matter that was most deeply despised by the National Socialists, brought upon him a martyrdom, which commits us to more than I can express in words.[93]

The next letter pasted in the scrapbook is from Edgard Varèse in New York who expressed sadness at the loss of Schoen, whom he names as 'his young pupil', and mentioned how some weeks ago he had been talking about him with the filmmaker and theorist, Hans Richter, and the chief conductor of the Frankfurt Radio Orchestra, Hans Rosbaud. Family members also wrote: grandson Mike's condolences are swiftly followed by his own news of working in Liberia, after visiting Lisbon, where he heard Fado for the first time. Old neighbours from Kingfisher Court wrote, as did various publishers in Berlin. Letters arrived from the director of Berliner Ensemble Joachim Tenschert and Martin Lawrence, the communist publisher, who had last met Schoen at a Theatre Workshop event. Others, including Dr S. Fink of Sydney, sent their condolences while also reporting the death of their own loved ones: 'my Lotte' in Fink's case. Another, C. E. Hardinge, reports the death from thrombosis of a 'Mr. Mann', map drawer for *The Times*, and the demolition of several houses on the road in Belsize Park where the Schoens used to live. The widow of Hans Flesch recalled the pioneering days at the Frankfurt radio station. Bernard Kops wrote of how happy he had been to be translated into another language for the first time, of how he could not understand the words, but was struck by the sounds that came from them and how he felt a personal loss in Schoen's passing.[94]

There was also a letter from childhood friend Friedrich Podszus, who bemoaned the multiplication of black rimmed letters as the years progressed, like those that litter Schoen's archive boxes. The tragic news evoked a flood of memories in him: long walks in Heidelberg in 1919, a Berlin room in the Lietzenburger Street with his grandmother and mother, Walter Benjamin and 'his aura', meeting Schoen from the Wolff Telegraphenbüro after work, a visit to Frankfurt in 1930 and a meeting, after all the evil they had both endured in the Nazi years, at a publishers.[95] A childhood friend was sent into reverie and into his own wrestling with death and the human condition. Others stayed on the plane of efficiency. Telegrams have a particular curtness: 'WE MOURN WITH YOU = HERRERA', one reads.[96] Another: SHAKEN BY THE DEATH OF THIS TRULY NOBLE MAN = HANSS EISLER'[97].

Adorno and Scholem worried about the Benjamin letters that Schoen had promised them. Adorno wrote to Scholem on 14 December 1960. He had read of Schoen's death in the *Frankfurter Zeitung*. It could not be the death notice of another man of the same name, for Hansi Schoen had placed 'extremely ostentatious formulation'. He wrote:

What is especially strange is that Hansi writes that he died as a victim of National Socialism. He emigrated, after all, just like me. We saw each other a lot in England, and, aside from the material difficulties posed for us by the first years of immigration, he got through this time fairly well. The only explanation might be that he really did suffer from hunger during those years and that this damaged his health, or that some Nazis did something nasty to him now, although I can hardly imagine that. In all likelihood, Hansi, who is a thoroughly irresponsible character, wanted to appear important and to elevate Ernst, without thinking at all about the gravity of her formulation[98]

Adorno wondered if, given the 'strange way that both the Schoens acted' towards him in the recent years he should send condolences. He did not wish to appear to curry favour, or be tactless, but he also did not wish to betray an old friendship. He asked for advice.

Scholem replied to Adorno from Jerusalem on 20 December 1960. He had received the death notice from Berlin. He presumed it came from Schoen's wife:

All it says is 'A poet and a friend of mankind is mourned by all.' I will write to her today and can only hope that she will send the letters promised to me by her husband. My letter to him left here on the 28th of November, so it should have reached him just a week or so before he died. I don't know what he died of; I suspect a heart attack. He was 66 years old.

He recommended to Adorno that he send condolences, despite the tension between them. They wanted to still get hold of the letters. They had a legacy to curate. Adorno wrote a remarkable letter on 4 January 1961, lavish in praise of someone who was a combination of 'endless sensitivity and gentleness with a fearlessness' and 'a unique being' who 'stood just as aslant to the business of the culture industry as to official cultural ideology and its products.'[99] He also attributed to Schoen the few humanly decent years in material terms that Walter Benjamin experienced between around 1928 to 1933. He mentioned that Schoen and Hansi had refused to meet him the last time they were in Frankfurt and he wondered why that was. He asked if it was due to divergences in their political development, but wished that something could have exceeded that, on account of their having shared such intense experiences. He then raised the issue that hit him most forcefully: the end of the notice. He asked if Schoen had been literally killed by the Nazis. Had perhaps some lingering Nazi fanatic (of which there were many) burst into the hospital where he lay and snuffed out his life in 1960? Had he not known something concrete of Schoen's fate dealt out by the fascists in the time during or after his escape? He asked Hansi to reply and signed off as Teddie.

The issue arose again in his letters to Scholem. On 22 June 1961, Adorno mentioned to Scholem that he had heard nothing from 'Frau Schoen':

It is also entirely unclear to me what is meant in the obituary by the claim that Schoen died as a victim of National Socialism. I believe that the memory of the victims is far too serious a matter to be abused for such an effect. But Mrs. Schoen is apparently lacking the necessary sensitivity for such matters.[100]

Even though it was not literally true, Schoen's death was a result of the consequences of the Nazi horror that had broken Schoen's vital energies. The Nazis had killed so many possibilities, of life, culture and politics. Schoen was shattered by these losses and suffered, so his loved ones felt his was a premature death, a demise brought about by the particular way in which the horrors and injustices of the century had impacted on him. There was a concrete link between the loss of his work and context and the decline in his health. In his statement requesting compensation on 22 October 1952, he had noted: 'Finally, the terrible events of that time and the years that followed had as a consequence a severe worsening of a nervous speech impediment, and furthermore, a heart complaint, as a result of which I am under the permanent watch of Frau Dr H. Kaltenhäuser, Charlottenburg, Kaiserdamm.'[101] The radio producer's voice was fractured, his heart broken.

Schoen's cremation took place on 15 December 1960 and the journalist and human rights campaigner Joachim G. Leithäuser, a cousin of Schoen, delivered the eulogy. Leithäuser spoke of Schoen as a presence so large, so lively that it was as if he had just left the room, closing the door behind him. He was a 'Gentleman', a cavalier, of the type rarely seen today. He was modest and this obscured the many talents he possessed, especially in music and literature. He remained friends with the Busoni family. He studied in Berlin, Marburg, Heidelberg and Bern. He had skills as a poet and as a translator. He employed those skills in many ways. He spoke many languages and he translated between them. 'Life unfortunately did not allow him to develop those talents, as would have befitted him'. War interrupted his progress and he was compelled to do things that were not in his nature. There was a period of uncertainty following the war, but finally he found a role in radio and tasks that matched his capacities until 1933. These included overseeing the first international broadcast from Paris to Frankfurt, the first opera transmission from a radio station, and the promotion of modern music, Stravinsky and Hindemith, as a result of which these composers became known. These are historic events, but, noted Leithäuser, they are not catalogued anywhere – except in a book that he has only partly written and now cannot finish.

Leithäuser recounted how Schoen was imprisoned twice and managed to escape with the family that he loved very much. He came to

England but found no support from any significant political institution. He set up his Opera Group, with three of the day's most significant singers and worked for the German Service of the BBC, with bombs falling around him. After the war, life was 'unjust' once more. He found no place abroad or at home to contribute to culture, despite the pre-war service he had given to German culture. He was a true humanist. Leithäuser added: 'If one considers his life as a whole, one word stands over it – a small word perhaps, but one that has a lot of meaning here: integrity. Whoever thinks about how seldom it is encountered in our contemporary world will know what we have lost.'[102]

Coda: 1960–

6

Afterlife Echoes

After a death, time goes on, but with different flows. Hansi continued to keep a record of the schedule of appointments, the duties associated with family life. One diary from 1961, extra thin, held a card, upon it written: 'AHOY! MERRY CHRISTMAS Frau Ati!', dated from 1948. On the inside she wrote her new name and address, one she now used in England: 'Countess Johanna Rogendorf. 52 Hamilton Terrace, NW8'. A purple threepenny stamp also lurks between the pages. She wrote down the weather, those she met, reminders, appointments, holiday plans, ailments. The name of Charles Fenn, one of Ati's contacts, appears, as do many others.[1] From the end of the decade, 1969, a diary, red with metallic lines, had on its inside cover the words: 'The bridge of love is the only link between the land of the living and the land of the dead'.[2] There were references to saving bonds, tax firms. She visited Leatherhead, then marked coming home. Chessington Zoo. A note to self to ask someone about Heinrich Böll, a reminder to fetch photos. She met Miss Bridgewater for tea from time to time. On 24 January she wrote: 'At Paul's who is better', likely her grandson.[3]

As work on Benjamin's collected letters progressed, Scholem and Adorno tried to elicit materials from Hansi. On 21 October 1963, Adorno copied what he perceived to be an extraordinary letter from Hansi, received 6 days earlier, and sent it to Scholem in Jerusalem. In it, she stated how finally, after three years, she had enough strength to emit a sign of life.[4] She had wandered for a while, including a year in Australia with her daughter Nina, who had emigrated there, but now she had a nice small flat in London and she wanted to clarify the position of Ernst vis-à-vis Adorno and other old friends. She informed Adorno that she read the *Frankfurter Allgemeine* every day and was aware of both his successes, large and small. She mentioned Scholem, and the edition of Benjamin's letters, as well as seeing the theologian of their circle, Paul Tillich, on TV. He once appeared at a fancy dress party as Napoleon, she recalled. Do greet your wife, whom she nicknames *Schwanenhals*, swan-neck, in her closing line. She also offered to explain, when they next met, why she had adopted her aristocratic title.

Hansi sent Schoen's book on broadcasting to Adorno, as she wished to find a publisher for the manuscript. On 10 March 1964, he wrote a response, informing her that his wife Gretel had read it and recommended, instead, a journal for parts of it. He also reported that *The Cold Heart* (a play co-written by Schoen and Benjamin and first broadcast on 16 May 1932) had turned up amongst Benjamin materials and that she need not seek it out.[5] Benjamin's archive was coming together, he reported, and so would his posthumous publications. Schoen's – Hansi might have thought – would not.[6]

Hansi wrote to Gretel Adorno on 2 May 1965. She thanked her for sending through galley proofs, though noted that the surname 'Schoen' is not spelt with an umlaut. Then she doubted herself, wondering if that was a spelling only adopted in England. Names circle and reform again and again.[7] Indeed, documents show that Schoen's father, decades ago, had spelt it with an umlaut. Had Schoen changed the spelling as a modernising gesture or in homage to Schoenberg? Hansi related in her letter that Benjamin and Schoen, even long ago when they sat together on school benches, spoke the formal 'Sie' to each other, rather than the informal 'Du'. She attributed it to intellectual snobbism. The Du form was for the plebs, the *other* school children. The anecdote was followed by some news on the campaign that would grip her for the rest of her life – compensation. She was about to travel to Berlin to meet with politicians and other figures to press and plead their case. A nota bene mentioned that Schoen was able to get over the loss of everything left behind in Germany but one thing: 'the poems, handwritten, by Heinle, lost forever and mourned by him.'[8] She wondered too what had happened to Ati's poem cycle, *Circle of Love*, which she thought she had left with Adorno in Frankfurt.[9]

Two years later, on 16 March 1967, Hansi wrote to Adorno. She was still desperate for justice for all they had suffered. She began by noting how she heard frequently of his good fortune. Then she emphasised the duration of their friendship. The true matter of the letter is that the compensation claim was before the courts in Wiesbaden. She reminded 'Teddy' that, after imprisonment in Frankfurt and Hamburg, Schoen was 'a broken man' who 'could no longer withstand leaving his country, the loss of his beloved pioneering radio work'. Having fled, with a wife and two children of 4 and 6 years old, he was in no position, financially or temperamentally, to plead that remaining friends take care of possessions and money left behind in Germany. She hoped Adorno and his wife had not forgotten entirely that they had often been guests at 20 Fuchshohl in Frankfurt. She had proof: photographs of them in the garden together. When Schoen fled, in May 1933, he lost his part in this world.

Hansi then made a request: a document, written under oath by Adorno, to testify that when Schoen fled he took nothing with him. She asked Adorno to provide details about his visit to their home in London, as he made his way into exile in the USA. She prompted him to recall how modest the home was where they found themselves. There were simply a few second-hand pieces of furniture donated by the Quakers. Schoen had testified to this in a statement of 22 October 1952 in his compensation file: 'After our flight to London we lived for seven years, from 1933 to 1940, almost completely through support'. He also listed there his loss of wages and the loss of the entire home's contents, including a library worth over 20,000 marks, none of which he ever saw again.[10] Hansi included a list of things that were at the Frankfurt home, in an attempt to jog Adorno's memory, so that he might affirm the scale of the loss. Other people, she felt, had been compensated, but Ernst had never bothered to see it through. She was compelled to undertake this mission, because the radio station had treated her so poorly in financial terms. The letter ended with a request for her daughter, Nina, to receive an edition of Walter Benjamin's letters, which drew on some that she had donated to Adorno.[11]

Presumably hard times led to the sale of one valuable possession that had made its way into exile. On 3 May 1961, the painting, gifted to the Schoens by Willi Baumeister in 1930, *Still Life with Head* was auctioned through the Stuttgarter Kunstkabinett in the 36th Auction of Modern Art. The listing states a guide price of 14,000 Deutsche Marks.[12] Roman Norbert Ketterer had set up the gallery and auction house in 1947, after discovering Expressionism, which he had not known or seen during the Nazi years. It was his mission to bring this art back into public view, to give it its due and to reinstate the art that had been condemned as degenerate. *Still Life with Head* was sold for 11,000 marks. The catalogue entry noted that it was signed and dated 1930 on the back of the canvas. It had been reproduced in Will Grohmann's book on Baumeister for Gallimard in 1931. The painting, the entry noted, derived from a private collection in Frankfurt.[13] *Still Life with Head* came into the possession of Morton D. May, who had built himself a house in Saint Louis in 1941 on the family fortune that accrued from owning May Department Stores Company, one of the largest retail chains in the US. May began to build a collection of modern art, including Picasso, Rouault and Stuart Davis. In 1946, he too discovered German Expressionism, having been attracted to Max Beckmann's work during a merchandising trip to New York. One of his purchases was Beckmann's *Birds' Hell* (1938). It is garish and chaotic. In the upper right corner are loudspeakers, barking Nazi propaganda into the scene. The eagles and vultures rip apart a man. A many-breasted figure, in quasi-Greek form, proffers a Hitler-Salute, as the sacrificial man looks up helplessly. May was a breezy and busy figure in Saint Louis, serving also on the boards of the Boy Scouts of America, the Saint Louis Symphony and the Saint Louis Arts and Education Council. Quoted in the *New York Times*, in 1970, he said happily: 'I've got a jillion things to do.'[14] *Still Life with Head* now hangs in Saint Louis Art Museum as a bequest of May in a room entitled 'European Art: The Modern Still Life' in new company – next to a Giorgio Morandi and opposite a Georges Braque.[15]

When we were at Sasha and Leda's house one day, they fetched a large folder of documents that all related to the restitution of the Willi Baumeister painting. Inside the file was correspondence with the Saint Louis Art Museum, plus reams of papers to and from lawyers specialising in art restitution. One image jumped out: a photograph that includes a cat, perched upon a table in front of a small vase of chrysanthemum-like daisies. The cat has ruffled the tablecloth, on which lies a newspaper. The image is slightly overexposed, almost layered. It is seemingly suburban. In the background: a painting, framed, *Still Life with Head*. It looks like Kingfisher Court. This photograph is used to prove the possession of the painting.

How to survive when your worldly possessions have scattered, when your means of survival – your circles, your abilities – are no longer present?

What questions of justice arise, moves to undo the work of fascists who originated the scattering, to retrieve something of the shattered rings, lost vessels? Sasha always spoke of the wish to go to Saint Louis. What would it mean for him to stand in front of the painting, the one of *his* mother, her head within a network of radio, so valuable, and just stand there, look at it and leave?

The selected correspondence of Walter Benjamin appeared in a two-volume hardcover edition with Suhrkamp in 1966. As is customary in such collections, only Benjamin's letters were included. To read the letters – with various ellipses – is like listening in on something interrupted, subject to interference, full of drop outs. The various letters to Schoen from across the years indicate a lively exchange of ideas, but Schoen's part of the dialogue is lost. The introduction to the volume provides a roll call of those who had aided them, now scattered, some widowed or left behind. There Scholem wrote:

Finally, I would like to extend our most heartfelt gratitude to everybody who has assisted in making this book a reality by contributing letters, above all to Mr. Herbert Belmore (Rome), Mrs. Hansi Schoen (Countess Johanna Rogendorf, London), Mrs. Jula Radt-Cohn (Naarden), Mrs. Grete Cohn-Radt (Paris), Dr. Werner Kraft (Jerusalem), Dr. Kitty Steinschneider (Jerusalem), Prof. Fritz Lieb (Basel), and Mrs. Susanne Thieme (Lorrach), as well as the heirs and executors of the estates of Brecht, Hofmannsthal, and Rang. [...] Thus this collection, which is meant to be a living monument to our deceased friend, now appears twenty-five years after his death.[16]

Letters continued to be sent. On 22 March 1966, Friedrich Podszus wrote a long reflective letter to Hansi on sky blue paper. He wanted to clarify his relation to Schoen. They were not at school together. Podszus was born five years later and grew up in Königsberg. In 1919, he had gone to Heidelberg where he met Jula Cohn and it was through her that he had become friends with Schoen. Once he moved to Berlin in 1922, he saw Schoen often. He described himself as the youngest and most stupid in the circle around Benjamin. He knew, as he had already said in his condolence letter, Ernst's rather disturbed mother and his wonderful grandmother. When Ernst moved to Frankfurt, he visited him once in 1930. It was after a concert that Hans Rosbaud conducted, where he also met Hansi and Adorno. Podszus heard from Dr Claasen and Hans Flesch that Ernst had made it to London.

In 1935, he tried unsuccessfully to find him in London. When he returned to Germany, both were eager to meet again. Podszus and Schoen did meet up again: Podszus wrote in his characteristic neat, almost childlike hand, a dedication in a gifted copy of his book of poems, *Wassermusik* (1952): 'Ernst Schoen, for our reunion in Frankfurt, 1953.'

Podszus worked as chief reader for Suhrkamp, then an up-and-coming press, though he left in 1956 to make his own way.[17] He mentioned the appearance of Walter Benjamin's letters in the summer, noting that Scholem was right to be ruthless, for sloppiness would be disgraceful, especially in the case of Benjamin. Podszus reported that he lost everything in 1943, after an attack on Berlin, including all his Benjamin relics, except for a couple of pages, which turned up again later and needed to be kept very safe. 'What else remains for us?'

The papers around Schoen pile up through the decades that follow, collected by Hansi: theatre programmes, exhibition guides, newspaper clippings, obituaries and death notices and correspondence. In the 1980s, some interest in Schoen as a radio pioneer began to flicker. August Soppe contacted Hansi as he was writing a PhD on radio in Frankfurt. He was seeking material and wished to interview her. It eventually happened in London, with Hansi and Nina, and resulted in radio programmes, a chronology of Schoen's life and an assessment of extant materials. For a while he brokered negotiations with Hessen Radio, with an eye to buying the archive. Soppe mentioned the publication of a significant book on Benjamin and radio by Dr Sabine Schiller-Lerg,[18] which had references to Schoen. He brought in his friend Gary Smith, a Benjamin scholar, who wanted to know more of Schoen's relationship to Benjamin and who attempted to find buyers for numerous photographs by Sasha Stone in Hansi's possession. Attempts to sell the material were protracted and difficult. Hansi wanted Schoen to re-gain the reputation proper to him. She also wanted to realise the legacy in cash. Eventually, in 1991, the extant materials were acquired by the Bundesarchiv in Koblenz. They were sorted through by archivist Ulf Rathje as best he could, for there were gaps left through private sales and the damage wrought by historical process. The catalogue was published in 1993.

There is a letter from Nina regarding the legacy, which found its way to the Bundesarchiv after Hansi's death. She wrote apropos the Alfred Cohn ring – yes, I have it but it is changed I fear. Many years ago whilst wearing it (on my little finger) I was sweeping out a fireplace and it slipped off into the still hot embers! When I was able to get it out again I saw that the stone itself was badly cracked and the head rather distorted. I have had it re-mounted but it is not the same and probably not suitable to photograph any more. But I often wear it anyway.[19]

This ring – likely the one bought at the antiques shop at the start of the First World War, worn also in the photograph in Heidelberg in 1921, a gift from Alfred Cohn to Schoen – ended up in Australia, its form altered by the heat of a fire. Objects travel and transform, as do people, who exchange objects in various circles and circuits, under conditions not necessarily of their own making, themselves shattered and scattered. As much as legacies buckle and hopes are dashed, they remain for us, in transfigured forms, vectors of new connections, emblems of experimental positions, in the fight against everyday and extraordinary fascisms and for a liberated future.

Notes

Introduction

1 Phoebe Blatton, *Art Monthly*, no. 441, November 2020, 42–44.
2 Theodor W. Adorno, *Essays on Music*, trans. Susan H. Gillespie and ed. Richard Leppert (University of California Press, 2002), 251.
3 Theodor W. Adorno, *Current of Music: Elements of a Radio Theory*, ed. Robert Hullot Kentor (Polity, 2008), 116.
4 Scattered among articles in a radio journal from 1930 are warnings about radio interference from other devices and how to avoid it. Readers are advised not to use anything with electrical motors – vacuum cleaners, hair dryers – during the main hours of broadcast from 4pm to 11pm. To interfere with radio transmission, a little graphic proclaims, is a sin against one's fellow humans who seek consolation and joy in radio. See *Rundfunk Jahrbuch* (Reichs-Rundfunk-Gesellschaft, 1930), 142.
5 Walter Benjamin, 'The Crisis of the Novel' (1930), *Selected Writings*, vol. 2, trans. Rodney Livingstone (Cambridge, MA: Harvard University Press, 1999), 299.
6 From Ernst Schoen's compensation file at the Entschädigungsamt Berlin: 602.385. From the Landesamt für Bürger- und Ordnungsangelegenheiten (LABO).
7 Sabine Schiller-Lerg, 'Ernst Schoen 1894–1960. Ein Freund überlebt. Erste biographische Einblicke in seinen Nachlaß', in *Global Benjamin*, ed. Klaus Garber and Ludger Rehm (Wilhelm Fink Verlag, 1999), 994.
8 Ibid., 1001.
9 According to records at the Landesarchiv Berlin, the birth certificate has the name Ernst Fritz Erich Schön (14 April 1894, document number: 1084/1894). His father was the architect in private practice Otto Carl Schön and his mother Jeanette Schön, née Grodnick Grodsinsky. The father signed the certificate with the umlaut as 'Schön'.

Assembling and Composing: Youth

1 Walter Benjamin, 'Berlin Chronicle' (1932), *Selected Writings*, vol. 2, trans. Edmund Jephcott (Cambridge, MA: Harvard University Press, 1999), 595–637.
2 For a history of this school life see Momme Brodersen, *Klassenbild mit Walter Benjamin* (München: Siedler Verlag, 2012).
3 Benjamin refers to Alois Riegl's work in 'Berlin Chronicle', 615. Benjamin's reading led to the 'The Rigorous Study of Art' (1932/3) trans. Thomas Y. Levin, *Selected Writings*, vol. 2, 666–670.
4 Benjamin, 'Berlin Chronicle', 615.
5 Ibid., 616.
6 Sabine Schiller-Lerg and August Soppe, 'Ernst Schoen (1894–1960). Eine biographische Skizze und die Geschichte seines Nachlasses', in *Mitteilungen Studienkreis Rundfunk und Geschichte*, vol. 20, no 2/3 (1994): 79–80; Sabine Hock, 'Schoen, Ernst', in *Frankfurter Personenlexikon* (Online edition), https://frankfurter-personenlexikon.de/node/1119 [version: 6 January 2018]; Solveig Ottmann, *Im Anfang war das Experiment: das Weimarer Radio bei Hans Flesch und Ernst Schoen* (Berlin: Kulturverlag Kadmos, 2013), 90–94.

7 Fernand Ouellette, *Edgard Varèse: A Musical Biography*, trans. Derek Coltman (London: Calder & Boyars, 1973), 34. Translation amended. This paragraph is based on a letter to Ouellette dated 30 May 1960 and reprinted in Erinn Knyt, *Ferruccio Busoni and His Legacy* (Bloomington: Indiana University Press, 2017), 117. Busoni's thesis *Ästhetik der Tonkunst*, literally *Aesthetic of Sound Art*, was written in 1907 and expanded in 1916. It developed ideas on the specific capacities of technologically mediated music and sound in general.

8 Knyt, *Ferruccio Busoni and His Legacy*, 2. Knyt's study also details many of the ways that Busoni's teaching techniques were unconventional.

9 Schiller-Lerg, 'Ernst Schoen 1894–1960. Ein Freund überlebt', 990.

10 Knyt, *Ferruccio Busoni and His Legacy*, 117.

11 Ludwig Thuille (1861–1907) co-authored a harmony textbook together with Rudolf Louis Harmonielehre (1907). See Ouellette, *Edgard Varèse*, 34. This paragraph is based on a letter to Ouellette dated 30 May 1960 and reprinted in and translated by Knyt in *Ferruccio Busoni and His Legacy*, 117.

12 Ottmann, *Im Anfang war das Experiment*, 94.

13 Benjamin, 'Berlin Chronicle', 614.

14 Ibid., 596.

15 See the appendix of Walter Benjamin's *Sonnets*, ed. and trans. Carl Skoggard (Albany: Fence Books, 2017), 358, for a copy of the facsimile of this letter, which is held at the Deutsches Literaturarchiv in Marbach.

16 See Sabine Schiller-Lerg, 'Ernst Schoen vertont sechs Gedichte von Christoph Friedrich Heinle', in *Klang und Musik bei Walter Benjamin* (Leiden: Brill, 2013), 129–141.

17 See Johannes Steizinger, *Christoph Friedrich Heinle: Lyrik und Prosa* (Berlin: Kulturverlag Kadmos Berlin, 2016).

18 According to Erwin Loewenson, those around Heinle 'adopted the same gesture, the same smile (of being over and above everything) and the same physical movements as he'. See William Collins Donahue and Martha Helfer (eds), 'Nexus 1', in *Essays in German Jewish Studies* (Columbia: Camden House, 2011): 155. The original quotation is from Erwin Loewenson, 'Über Wolf und Fritz Heinle' (from c. August 1914), 1, from Loewenson's archive that is at the Deutsches Literaturarchiv Marbach.

19 Howard Eiland and Michael Jennings, *Walter Benjamin: A Critical Life* (Cambridge, MA: Harvard University Press), 91.

20 Ernst Schoen Archive (Koblenz): *Tagebuch*, BArch N 1403/1. With thanks to Daniela Aharon for help in deciphering this handwriting and its significance.

21 'Chronology' in Walter Benjamin, *Selected Writings*, ed. by Marcus Bullock and Michael W. Jennings, vol. 1 (Cambridge MA: Harvard University Press, 1996), 493.

22 See Theodor W. Adorno Archiv, Frankfurt am Main, Br 1346/6.

23 Ernst Schoen Archive (Koblenz): *Tagebuch*, BArch N 1403/1.

24 In Franz Hessel's journal *Vers und Prosa* from 1924, there are a number of translations of Baudelaire poems published by Benjamin, Wolff and Hessel. Benjamin translated: 'An Den Leser', 'Frohsinn des Toten', 'Einer Madonna: Ex-voto im spanischen Sinne'. Wolff translated: 'Der Balkon', 'Spleen', 'Die Seele des Weins'. Hessel translated: 'An die Viel zu Frohe'. For more on this circle's translation practice, see Alex Wild Jespersen, ' "The Seventies Meet the Twenties": Charlotte Wolff as writer, public figure and "period piece" ' (PhD thesis, University of Auckland, 2013), chapter 2.

25 See Ernst Schoen Archive (Koblenz): BArch N 1403 Bild-110-091.

26 Private conversations with Alexander Schoen.

27 Walter Benjamin held onto a copy of this verse in his collection of Heinle poems.

28 With thanks to Daniela Aharon for this material and context, whose work on Jula Cohn is forthcoming in her PhD thesis 'Andere Gefühle. Authentizität und jüdische Differenz in der Jugendkulturbewegung zu Beginn des 20. Jahrhunderts' (Technische Universität Berlin), along with further work on the letters between Ernst Schoen and Jula Cohn.

29 In German: 'Wesen Kreatur und Zahlen / Traum und Leben überm Grund / Dichter werden Stunden malen / Über dem geliebten Mund'. Translated by Esther Leslie.

30 Images of this bust are held in the collection at the Museum der Dinge in Berlin.

31 Ernst Schoen Archive (Koblenz): *Tagebuch*, BArch N 1403/1.

32 With thanks to Samuel Draper for playing these lines through with us and offering his thoughts on them. This notebook can be found among Schoen's papers at the Bundesarchiv in Koblenz.

33 Walter Benjamin Archive, University of Giessen: Letter from Locarno, 2 March 1918. Translated by Esther Leslie.

34 Eva Weissweiler, *Das Echo deiner Frage. Dora und Walter Benjamin* (Hamburg: Hoffmann und Campe Verlag, 2020), 145. Gershom Scholem recounts some details of the event in his *Walter Benjamin: The Story of a Friendship*, trans. Harry Zohn (New York Review of Books, 2001), 111–112.

35 Review in *Die weißen Blätter*, Zürich, July-September 1918, 59. Another part of the review is cited in Weissweiler, *Das Echo deiner Frage*, 145. Translated by Esther Leslie.

36 In his 1907 *Aesthetic of Sound Art*, Busoni wrote of how renunciation and restraint and 'the all-controlling intelligence' in composition allows 'feeling' to arise, rather than the sentimental and pathetic. See first English translation, as *Sketch of a New Esthetic of Music* (New York: G. Schirmer, 1911), 38.

37 Ferruccio Busoni, *Das Wandbild. Eine Szene und eine Pantomime*, in *Die weißen Blätter*, Zürich, July-September 1918, 29–36.

38 Knyt, *Ferruccio Busoni and His Legacy*, 239.

39 See Benjamin, 'The Work of Art in the Age of its Technological Reproducibility' and Other Writings on Media, ed. Michael W. Jennings, Bridget Doherty and Thomas Levin, trans. Michael W. Jennings (Cambridge, MA: Harvard University Press, 2008), 40. He also relates it in the 1934 version of his *Berlin Childhood around 1900*, in *Selected Writings*, vol. 3, trans. Howard Eiland (Cambridge, MA.: Harvard University Press, 2002), 393.

40 Letter from 7 September 1912, in Paul Scheerbart, *70 Trillionen Weltgrüsse. Eine Biographie in Briefen 1889-1915*, ed. Mechthild Rausch (Berlin: Argon Verlag, 1991), 442–443.

41 Walter Benjamin and Dora Sophie Kellner (then Pollak) married on 17 April 1917 in Berlin. According to Michael Jennings and Howard Eiland: 'As the only nonrelative in attendance at the ceremony, Scholem presented his friends with a copy of Paul Scheerbart's utopian "asteroid novel" *Lesabéndio* (1913)', in *Walter Benjamin: A Critical Life*, 91.

42 Benjamin, 'Berlin Chronicle' (1932), *Selected Writings*, vol. 2, 616.

43 Ibid., 616.

Radio and Experiment: Weimer

1 Ernst Schoen Archive (Koblenz), from the manuscript: *Broadcasting: How It Came About*, BArch N 1403/63.

2 Ibid.

3 As related in private communication with his son Alexander Schoen and Leda Schoen.

4 Schiller-Lerg and Soppe, 'Ernst Schoen (1894–1960). Eine biographische Skizze und die Geschichte seines Nachlasses', 80.

5 As reported by Schoen in files held by the Stasi, ref: MfS AP 12155/65.

6 Peter Reuter, 'Walter Benjamin in Gießen: Die Benjamin-Sammlung in der Universitätsbibliothek', in *Aus mageren und aus ertragreichen Jahren*, ed. Irmgard Hort and Peter Reuter (Gießen: Universitätsbibliothek Gießen, 2007), 229.

7 See Christopher Williams, 'The Concrete "Sound Object" and the Emergence of Acoustical Film and Radiophonic Art in the Modernist Avant-Garde', *Transcultural Studies*, vol. 13, no. 2 (2017): 242.

8 Enzo Ferrieri published 'La radia, forza creativa' ('Radio as a Creative Force') in 1931, preceding Marinetti by two years. See Williams, 'The Concrete "Sound Object"': 239–263.

9 László Moholy-Nagy, 'Dynamic of the Metropolis', in *Painting, Photography, Film* (London: Lund Humphreys, 1969), 128. It was originally published in the Bauhaus book series: László Moholy-Nagy, *bauhausbuch 08, malerei photographie, film*, 1925. The sketch, according to Moholy-Nagy, was first conceived in 1921–1922.

10 Sibyl Moholy-Nagy, *Moholy-Nagy: Experiment in Totality* (Cambridge: MIT Press, 1950), 72.

11 Sigfried Giedion, *Building in France, Building in Iron, Building in Ferro-Concrete* (The Getty Center for the History of Art and the Humanities, 1995), 91. Cited in Walter Benjamin, *The Arcades Project*, trans. Howard Eiland and Kevin McLaughlin (Cambridge, MA, & London: Belknap Press, 1999), 459, [N1a,1].

12 Benjamin, *The Arcades Project*, 459, [N1a,1].

13 'Materials for the Exposé of 1935' in Benjamin, *The Arcades Project*, 901.

14 See Benjamin, *The Arcades Project*, 160–161, [F4a,2].

15 Walter Benjamin, *Radio Benjamin*, ed. Lecia Rosenthal and trans. Jonathan Lutes with Lisa Harries Schumann and Diana Reese (London: Verso, 2014), 170–175.

16 Benjamin, *Radio Benjamin*, 175.

17 Cited in Benjamin, *The Arcades Project*, 160–161, [F4a,2]. Translation slightly altered.

18 Karl Marx, *Grundrisse*, trans. Ben Fowkes (London: Penguin, 1973), 699–743.

19 'Glass before its time, premature iron', in Benjamin, *The Arcades Project*, 150, [F1,2].

20 'Materials for the Exposé of 1935' in Benjamin, *The Arcades Project*, 901.

21 Germaine Krull, *Germaine Krull, Fotografien, 1922–1966* (Cologne: Rheinland-Verlag, 1977), 123.

22 For background see David Travis, 'In and of the Eiffel Tower', *Art Institute of Chicago Museum Studies*, vol. 13, no. 1 (1987): 5–23, 6.

23 Weissweiler, *Das Echo deiner Frage*, 183.

24 For a thorough exploration of the relations between Walter, Dora, Jula and Ernst, drawing on correspondence between the participants, as well as letters from Dora to Gershom Scholem, see Weissweiler, *Das Echo deiner Frage*: this section draws especially on 187–197. Weissweiler's material, including the citing of correspondence, which also

draws on the Masters dissertation by Daniela Aharon, 'Jugendliche Erotik: Widerständige Liebeskonzeptionen in der Jugendzeitschrift Der Anfang und im Kreis um Walter Benjamin' (Masters dissertation, Technische Universität Berlin, 2014). Her PhD thesis 'Andere Gefühle. Authentizität und jüdische Differenz in der Jugendkulturbewegung zu Beginn des 20. Jahrhunderts' (forthcoming, Technische Universität Berlin) develops this work.

25 Letter cited in Weissweiler, *Das Echo deiner Frage*, 187.

26 Letter from Dora to Scholem cited in Weissweiler, *Das Echo deiner Frage*, 191.

27 Rolf Tiedemann, Christoph Gödde, Henri Lonitz, *Walter Benjamin, 1892–1940: eine Ausstellung des Theodor W. Adorno Archivs in Verbindung mit dem Deutschen Literaturarchiv* (Marbach: Literaturarchiv, 1990), 148.

28 Weissweiler, *Das Echo deiner Frage*, 192.

29 Ibid., 194–195.

30 Charlotte Wolff, *Hindsight: An Autobiography* (London: Quartet Books, 1980), 75–77.

31 Florence Tamagne, *History of Homosexuality in Europe: Berlin, London, Paris 1919–1939 Volume I* (New York: Algora Publishing, 2004), 55. For a wider history see Robert M. Beachy, *Gay Berlin: Birthplace of a Modern Identity* (London: Penguin, 2014).

32 Weissweiler, *Das Echo deiner Frage*, 196. One can read Benjamin's essay 'Goethe's Elective Affinities' (1921) as a reflection on these entanglements: *Selected Writings*, vol. 1, trans. Stanley Corngold, 97–356.

33 Wolff, *Hindsight*, 69.

34 Ibid.

35 Details surrounding these events can be found in Weissweiler, *Das Echo deiner Frage*, 194–198.

36 Ouellette, *Edgard Varèse*, 66. For a detailed account of the ICG, see R. Allen Lott, '"New Music for New Ears": The International Composers' Guild', *Journal of the American Musicological Society*, vol. 36, no. 2 (1983): 266–286. Lott, however, does not mention Schoen.

37 Ouellette, *Edgard Varèse*, 66.

38 Quoted in Lott, ' "New Music for New Ears" ', 267.

39 Ibid., 276.

40 Reproduced in Ouellette, *Edgard Varèse*, 66.

41 See Igor Stravinsky, *Die Hochzeit/Les Noces: russische Tanzszenen mit Gesang und Musik*, trans. Ernst Schoen (Mainz: Schott's Söhne, 1922).

42 Ouellette, *Edgard Varèse*, 67.

43 Ouellette, *Edgard Varèse*, 68. See also Knyt, *Ferruccio Busoni and his Legacy*, 121.

44 Ouellette, *Edgard Varèse*, 67. See also Knyt, *Ferruccio Busoni and his Legacy*, 121.

45 Ibid.

46 Quoted from Lott, ' "New Music for New Ears" ', 266.

47 'Moving Music by Moderns–But the Audience Moves Out', *New York Sun*, 5 March 1923, quoted in Lott, ' "New Music for New Ears" ', 266.

48 W. J. Henderson, 'Concert Ends in Uproar', *New York Herald*, 5 March 1923, quoted in Lott, ' "New Music for New Ears" ', 266.

49 See in Lott, " 'New Music for New Ears" ', 266.

50 This account of the early days of radio in Germany is drawn from the *Rundfunk Jahrbuch* (Reichs-Rundfunk-Gesellschaft, 1930), 27–41.

51 See Karl Christian Führer, 'A Medium of Modernity? Broadcasting in Weimar Germany, 1923-1932', *The Journal of Modern History*, vol. 69, no. 4 (December 1997): 722-753.

52 An authoritative account of early German radio history is provided in Winfried B. Lerg, *Die Entstehung des Rundfunks in Deutschland: Herkunft und Entwicklung eines publizistischen Mittels* (Frankfurt: J. Knecht, 1965).

53 Christoph Borbach, 'Experimentelle Praktiken: Apparative Radioexperimente in der Weimarer Republik', *Navigationen: Zeitschrift für Medien- und Kulturwissenschaften*, vol. 17, no. 1, 2017: 120.

54 *Berliner Börsen-Zeitung*, 28 October 1923. These three reviews were sourced and translated by Samuel Draper.

55 *Berliner Börsen-Zeitung*, 1 April 1924.

56 Klaus Mann, 'Erinnerungen an Anita Berber', *Die Bühne*, vol. 7 (1930), 43-44.

57 In 1930 Flesch declared 'Im Anfang war das Experiment' (In the beginning was the experiment) in 'Das Studio der Berliner Funkstunde' in *Rundfunk Jahrbuch* (1930), 117-120. See Ottmann, *Im Anfang war das Experiment*, 9.

58 *Moderne am Main 1919-1933*, ed. Klaus Kemp, Annika Sellmann, Matthias Wagner K and Grit Weber (Frankfurt: Avedition, 2019), 66.

59 Ottmann, *Im Anfang war das Experiment*, 108.

60 See Paul Hindemith, *Selected Letters of Paul Hindemith*, ed. and trans. Geoffrey Skelton (New Haven and London: Yale University Press, 1995), 34.

61 *Südwestdeutsche Rundfunkzeitung*, 1 April 1926.

62 Letter from 19 February 1925, in Benjamin, *Gesammelte Briefe*, vol. 3, (Berlin: Suhrkamp, 1997), 15.

63 For a detailed discussion of this history see Schiller-Lerg, 'Ernst Schoen 1894-1960. Ein Freund überlebt', 993. In 'Ernst Schoen (1894-1960): Eine Biographische Skizze und die Geschichte seines Nachlasses', Sabine Schiller-Lerg and August Soppe cite this source: 'The witnesses to the civil marriage were Reinhold Merten, leader of the Frankfurter Rundfunk band, and Eugen Lewin' (BA Kblz NL 403). Johanna Liman's father, Paul Liman, as a free-conservative journalist and friend of Bismarck, had developed the *Leipziger Neueste Nachrichten* into a right-wing newspaper with a large circulation (in *Studienkreises Rundfunk und Geschichte*, vol. 20, no. 2/3, April/July 1994, note 25, 87, trans. Esther Leslie).

64 Birgit Hammers, ' "Sasha Stone sieht noch mehr": Ein Fotograf zwischen Kunst und Kommerz' (PhD thesis, Philosophischen Fakultät der Rheinisch-Westfälischen Technischen Hochschule Aachen, 2013), 23-24.

65 Schiller-Lerg, 'Ernst Schoen 1894-1960. Ein Freund überlebt', 994.

66 Ernst Schoen Archive (Koblenz): BArch N 1403 Bild-110-014.

67 Hans Richter, *Köpfe und Hinterköpfe* (Zurich, 1967), 69, in Hanne Bergius, *'Dada triumphs!': Berlin Dada 1917-1923: artistry of polarities: montages, metamechanics, manifestations* (Farmington Hills: G.K. Hall & Co, 2003), 70.

68 See Eiland and Jennings, *Walter Benjamin: A Critical Life*, 172.

69 Ernst Schoen, 'Die Theatermuse', *G: Zeitschrift für elementare Gestaltung*, ed. Hans Richter, vol. 3, 1924, 64-65. Translated by Esther Leslie.

70 This point is made in Lecia Rosenthal, 'Introduction', in 'Magic on the Air: Attempt at a Radio Grotesque', Hans Flesch, trans. Lisa Harries Schumann *Cultural Critique*, vol. 91 (2015): 14-31.

71 Ibid.

72 Ibid.

73 Ibid.

74 Noah Eisenberg (ed.), *Billy Wilder on Assignment: Dispatches from Weimar Berlin and Interwar Vienna*, trans. Shelley Frisch (Princeton University Press, 2021), 172.

75 Ernst Schoen Archive (Koblenz): *Broadcasting: How It Came About*, BArch N 1403/63.

76 Ibid.

77 Ibid.

78 Ibid.

79 See Ottmann, *Im Anfang war das Experiment*, 163.

80 Ibid., 110, 155.

81 See *Rundfunk Jahrbuch* (Reichs-Rundfunk-Gesellschaft, 1930).

82 Walter Benjamin/Dora Kellner, *Vossische Zeitung*, 29 June 1925, published in Walter Benjamin *Gesammelte Schriften*, vol. 4, no. 1, 462. Translation here by Flossie Draper. This work went into Kellner's writing of *Gas gegen Gas*, a novel serialised in the *Südwestdeutsche Rundfunkzeitung* in 1930–1931, when Schoen was working at Frankfurt Radio.

83 *Südwestdeutsche Rundfunkzeitung*, 25 April 1926.

84 *Südwestdeutsche Rundfunkzeitung*, 1 April 1926.

85 Hans-Erhard Haverkampf, *Benjamin in Frankfurt: Die zentralen Jahre 1923-1932* (Frankfurt: Societäts-Verlag, 2016), 174.

86 *Südwestdeutsche Rundfunkzeitung*, 27 December 1925.

87 Ibid.

88 Ibid.

89 Ibid.

90 *Südwestdeutsche Rundfunkzeitung*, 26 August 1928.

91 *Südwestdeutsche Rundfunkzeitung*, 6 December 1925.

92 *Südwestdeutsche Rundfunkzeitung*, 3 March 1926.

93 *Südwestdeutsche Rundfunkzeitung*, 7 March 1926.

94 *Südwestdeutsche Rundfunkzeitung*, a four-leaf clover from 10–17 May 1931, a house from an issue in 1925, a star from 1926, a rabbit from 1931 and a ship from 1932.

95 See introduction to *Rundfunk Jahrbuch* (Reichs-Rundfunk-Gesellschaft, 1929), n.p.

96 Siegfried Kracauer, *The Salaried Masses: Duty and Distraction in Weimar Germany*, trans. Quintin Hoare (London, Verso, 1998), 88.

97 See *Rundfunk Jahrbuch* (Reichs-Rundfunk-Gesellschaft, 1929).

98 Ibid.

99 Jonathan Wipplinger, *The Jazz Republic: Music, Race, and American Culture in Weimar Germany* (University of Michigan Press, 2017). On the complex structure of radio, public, jazz, classical and popular music at SÜWRAG, see Michael Stapper, 'Unterhaltungsmusik im Rundfunk der Weimarer Republik' (Dissertation, University of Würzburg, 1999/2000).

100 See Carlo Bohländer, 'The Evolution of Jazz Culture in Frankfurt: A Memoir', in *Jazz and the Germans: Essays on the Influence of 'Hot' American Idioms on 20th-Century German Music*, ed. Michael Budds (Hillsdale: Pendragon Press, 2002): 167–78.

101 See Florian Scheding, *Musical Journeys: Performing Migration in Twentieth-Century Music* (Martlesham, Suffolk: Boydell Press, 2019), 57.

102 Ibid., 58.

103 Ernst Schoen, 'Jazz und Kunstmusik', in *Melos*, 1927: 512–519. Translated by Esther Leslie.

104 Ibid.

105 Eiland and Jennings, *Walter Benjamin: A Critical Life*, 263.

106 Peter Reuter, 'Walter Benjamin in Gießen: Die Benjamin-Sammlung in der Universitätsbibliothek', in *Aus mageren und aus ertragreichen Jahren*, ed. Irmgard Hort and Peter Reuter (Gießen: Universitätsbibliothek Gießen, 2007), 227.

107 Ernst Schoen Archive (Koblenz): *Scrapbook*, BArch N 1403/114.

108 Ernst Schoen Archive (Koblenz): BArch N 1403 Bild-109-037.

109 Hammers, ' "Sasha Stone sieht noch mehr" ', 20.

110 See *Sasha Stone: Fotografien 1925–39*, ed. Eckhardt Köhn (Berlin: Verlag Dirk Nishan, 1990), 102.

111 *Südwestdeutsche Rundfunkzeitung*, 11 September 1927.

112 This includes 'Alte und neue Graphologie' which marked a lecture on the same topic by Walter Benjamin scheduled for Sunday 23 November 1930.

113 *G: An Avant-garde Journal of Art, Architecture, Design, and Film, 1923–1926*, ed. Detlef Mertins and Michael W. Jennings (Los Angeles: Getty Research Institute, 2010), 176.

114 See *Sasha Stone: Fotografien 1925–39*, ed. Eckhardt Köhn (Berlin: Verlag Dirk Nishan, 1990), inside cover.

115 See Hanns Eisler, *Composing for the Films* (New York: Oxford University Press, 1947), 4–6.

116 Ernst Schoen Archive (Koblenz): BArch N 1403 Bild-110-036.

117 Ouellette, *Edgard Varèse: A Musical Biography*, 65–73. For a detailed account of the ICG, see Lott, " 'New Music for New Ears'": 266–286.

118 Paul Morand, 'Foire à la Floride' (1924), in *Poèmes* (Paris: Gallimard, 1973), 36. See also Clément Chéroux, *Since 1839: Eleven Essays on Photography*, trans. Shane B. Lillis (Cambridge, MA: The MIT Press, 2021).

119 Jean-Gérard Fleury, 'À la fête du Trône: Royaume des forains', *L'ami du peuple*, 3 April 1929, evening edition, 4. Translated by Shane B. Lillis.

120 *Südwestdeutsche Rundfunkzeitung*, 20 November 1927.

121 Mark E. Cory, 'Soundplay: The Polyphonous Tradition of German Art Radio', in *The Wireless Imagination: Sound, Radio, and the Avant-Garde*, ed. Douglas Kahn and Gregory Whitehead (Cambridge: MIT Press, 1992), 339.

122 Ibid., 336.

123 *Rundfunk Jahrbuch* (Reichs-Rundfunk-Gesellschaft, 1930), 116.

124 See Lott, " 'New Music for New Ears' ", 266.

125 See Alan Clayson, *Edgard Varèse* (London: Sanctuary, 2002), 107.

126 See *New Worlds of Edgard Varèse: Papers and Discussion from a Varèse Symposium at the City University of New York*, ed. Sherman Van Solkema (New York, Institute for Studies in American Music, 1979), 27–29.

127 Chou Wen-Chung, 'Varèse: A Sketch of the Man and His Music', *The Musical Quarterly*, vol. 52, no. 2 (1966): 151–170.

128 Compare the language of waves and technology with Caroline Adler's review of 'Walter Benjamin's antifascist education: from riddles to radio' (2021): 'Benjamin's youthful writing: the language of swelling, of waves crashing, or of the spilling of truth that carry

the weight of Benjamin's early metaphysical writings, which he himself abandons in his later work in favour of a more radicalised notion of education mediated through technology.' In *Contemporary Political Theory*, vol. 21, no. 4 (2021): 154–158, 155.

129 Walter Benjamin, *Rundfunkarbeiten: Werke und Nachlaß. Kritische Gesamtausgabe*, ed. Thomas Küpper and Anja Nowak (Frankfurt: Suhrkamp, 2017), 568.

130 Benjamin, *Radio Benjamin*, 289.

131 Ibid., 290–91.

132 Ibid., 284.

133 *Rundfunk Jahrbuch* (Reichs-Rundfunk-Gesellschaft, 1930), 101.

134 Bertolt Brecht, 'Radio as a Means of Communication: A Talk on the Function of Radio', in *Brecht on Theatre*, ed. and trans. John Willett (London: Eyre Methuen, 1964), 51–52. Translation slightly altered.

135 Ernst Schoen Archive (Koblenz): *Broadcasting: How It Came About*, BArch N 1403/63.

136 *Südwestdeutsche Rundfunkzeitung*, 1 April 1926.

137 *Südwestdeutsche Rundfunkzeitung*, 27 March 1927.

138 *Südwestdeutsche Rundfunkzeitung*, c.11 December 1927.

139 *Südwestdeutsche Rundfunkzeitung*, 28 October 1928.

140 *Südwestdeutsche Rundfunkzeitung*, 'Alles hört Rundfunk!', 1 January 1928.

141 *Südwestdeutsche Rundfunkzeitung*, 29 December 1929.

142 Hock, 'Schoen, Ernst', in *Frankfurter Personenlexikon (Onlineausgabe)* (accessed online: https://frankfurter-personenlexikon.de/node/1119) [version: 6 January 2018].

143 Ibid.

144 Ernst Schoen Archive (Koblenz): BArch N 1403 Bild-109-023.

145 Ernst Schoen Archive (Koblenz): BArch N 1403 Bild-110-022.

146 Ernst Schoen Archive (Koblenz): *Eigene Träume. Niederschriften* [1938–1960], BArch N 1403/14.

147 Ibid.

148 *Rundfunk Jahrbuch* (Reichs-Rundfunk-Gesellschaft, 1930), 319–326.

149 *Südwestdeutsche Rundfunkzeitung*, 15 May 1932.

150 *Südwestdeutsche Rundfunkzeitung*, 21 February 1932 (after a competition held on 19 January 1932).

151 *The Pedagogy of Images: Depicting Communism for Children*, ed. by Marina Balina and Serguei Alex. Oushakine (University of Toronto Press, 2021), 50.

152 *Südwestdeutsche Rundfunkzeitung*, listing for 3 January 1932.

153 Esther Leslie, *Walter Benjamin: Critical Lives* (London: Reaktion, 2008), 126.

154 Ernst Schoen Archive (Koblenz) [sound]: BArch N 1403 TON-24.

155 Ibid.

156 *Südwestdeutsche Rundfunkzeitung*, 17 January 1926.

157 Ibid.

158 *Südwestdeutsche Rundfunkzeitung*, 7 March 1926.

159 *Südwestdeutsche Rundfunkzeitung*, 14 February 1926.

160 *Südwestdeutsche Rundfunkzeitung*, 28 November 1926.

161 *Südwestdeutsche Rundfunkzeitung*, 1 May 1927.

162 'The Cold Heart: A Radio Play adapted from Wilhelm Hauff's Fairy Tale' in Benjamin, *Radio Benjamin*, 221–248.

163 *Rundfunk Jahrbuch* (Reichs-Rundfunk-Gesellschaft, 1931), 277.

164 *Südwestdeutsche Rundfunkzeitung*, 6 April 1930.

165 *The BBC Year-Book* (London: BBC, 1932), 39.

166 *The Pedagogy of Images: Depicting Communism for Children*, ed. Marina Balina and Serguei Alex. Oushakine (University of Toronto Press, 2021), 302, 314.

167 Benjamin, *Radio Benjamin*, 201–220.

168 Kasper appears throughout the pages of the *Südwestdeutsche Rundfunkzeitung*. There are a number of adverts for a visit from the Kasperle-Theater to the Funkhaus for 12 February 1933. A spread shows documentation from the performance of *Kasperl*. It is captioned 'For the radio play for children by Dr. Benjamin on 10 March'. There are images of performers and a large audience. Puppet theatre was also part of radio culture. On a front cover from 3 November 1929 there is an image of two people operating hand puppets. The caption reads 'Hansi plays theatre'.

169 Benjamin, *Radio Benjamin*, 220.

170 Ernst Schoen Archive (Koblenz): *Kompositionen ('Ati's Compositions')*, BArch N 1403/55.

171 See *Konzertführer Berlin-Brandenburg 1920–2012, Führer durch die Konzertsäle Berlins*, held at the Universität der Künste Berlin.

172 'Programm des elften Abends der Novembergruppe, 30. Januar 1925', held by the Berlinische Galerie, no. BG-HHC D 549/79.

173 Erwin Loewenson, 'Über Wolf und Fritz Heinle' (from c. August 1914), from Loewenson's archive that is at the Deutsches Literaturarchiv Marbach.

174 Vera Ibold, 'Alice Jacob-Loewenson', *Hochschule für Musik und Theater Hamburg* (2015) (accessed online: www.ezjm.hmtm-hannover.de/en/library/biographical-sketches/alice-jacob-loewenson) [accessed: 19 April 2022].

175 Ibid.

176 See Barbara von der Lühe, *Die Emigration deutschsprachiger Musikschaffender in das britische Mandatsgebiet Palästina* (Frankfurt: Peter Lang, 1999).

177 Thanks to Samuel Draper for sourcing this cutting.

178 See 'Music in the Foreign Press', *The Musical Times*, vol. 74, no. 1080 (1933), 137.

179 Ibid.

180 Ernst Schoen Archive (Koblenz): *Kompositionen ('Ati's Compositions')*, BArch N 1403/55.

181 Alice Jacob-Loewenson, רקב' לפסנתר ארץ-ישראלי-בית אלף: רקב in *Boker, Boker: A Palestinian A-B-C Book for the Pianoforte* (accessed online: www.nli.org.il/he/scores/NNL_MUSIC_AL997010359107105171/NLI) [accessed: 3 May 2023]. With thanks to Liran Lev Fisher for help with translation here.

182 Jascha Nemtsov, 'Alice Jacob-Loewenson', *Lexikon verfolgter Musiker und Musikerinnen der NS-Zeit*, ed. Claudia Maurer Zenck and Peter Petersen (Hamburg: Universität Hamburg, 2006).

183 See Walter Benjamin's review of Tom Seidemann-Freud's primers 'Verdant Elements', in *The Storyteller: Tales out of Loneliness*, ed. Sam Dolbear, Esther Leslie and Sebastian Truskolaski (London: Verso, 2016), 199–204.

184 See Walter Benjamin, 'To the Planetarium', *One Way Street* (1928), in *Selected Writings*, vol. 1, trans. Edmund Jephcott (Cambridge, MA: Harvard University Press, 1996), 487.

185 Ernst Schoen Archive (Koblenz): Kompositionen (*'Ati's Compositions'*), BArch N 1403/55. Translated by Samuel Draper.

186 Ibid.

187 These two examples come from conversation with Samuel Draper.

188 *Südwestdeutsche Rundfunkzeitung*, 15 May 1927.

189 *Südwestdeutsche Rundfunkzeitung*, 28 November 1926.

190 See Walter Benjamin's 'Colonial Pedagogy', in *The Storyteller: Tales out of Loneliness*, ed. Sam Dolbear, Esther Leslie and Sebastian Truskolaski (London: Verso, 2016), 195–196.

191 See the score of Paul Hindemith's *Wir bauen eine Stadt* (1930).

192 Hock, 'Schoen, Ernst'.

193 For context on Hanna Mandello (who renamed herself Jeanne Mandello upon emigration to Paris), see Andrea Nelson, with contributions by Elizabeth Cronin, Mia Fineman, Mila Ganeva, Kristen Gresh, Elizabeth Otto and Kim Sichel, *The New Woman Behind the Camera* (New York: Distributed Art Publishers, 2020).

194 *Südwestdeutsche Rundfunkzeitung*, 4 November 1928.

195 'Siedlung Höhenblick', on *ernst-may-gesellschaft e.v.* (accessed online: https://ernst-may-gesellschaft.de/wohnsiedlungen/siedlung-hoehenblick.html) [13 October 2022].

196 Ernst Schoen Archive (Koblenz): BArch N 1403 Bild-110-010.

197 Walter Benjamin, 'Thought Figures' (1933), *Selected Writings*, vol. 2, trans. Rodney Livingstone (Cambridge, MA: Harvard University Press, 1999), 724–725.

198 *Südwestdeutsche Rundfunkzeitung*, 5 April 1932.

199 *Südwestdeutsche Rundfunkzeitung*, 1 May 1932.

200 Walter Benjamin, 'A Family Drama in the Epic Theatre' (1932), *Understanding Brecht*, trans. Anna Bostock (Verso: London, 1996), 33.

201 Ibid.

202 Ibid., 34.

203 Ibid., 35. Translation slightly altered.

204 Quoted from *Kompositionen ('Ati's Compositions')*, BArch N 1403/55. Translation by Esther Leslie.

205 Nemtsov, 'Alice Jacob-Loewenson'.

206 Mitchell L. Margolis, 'Brahms' lullaby revisited. Did the composer have obstructive sleep apnea?', *Chest*, July 2000, vol. 118, no. 1: 210–213.

207 Brecht, 'Radio as a Means of Communication', 52.

208 See Benjamin, *'The Work of Art in the Age of its Technological Reproducibility'*, 398.

209 *Südwestdeutsche Rundfunkzeitung*, 9 November 1930.

210 Ernst Schoen, 'Über Strawinskys Einfluss', *Melos*, no. 8, 1929: 162–166.

211 Ibid., 166.

212 Ibid.

213 Ibid.

214 *Südwestdeutsche Rundfunkzeitung*, listing for 13 June 1930.

215 Letter deposited in the Ernst Schoen Archive (Koblenz): *Korrespondenzen*, BArch N 1403/21. From the Walter-Benjamin-Archiv, marked with number 16.

216 Haverkampf, *Benjamin in Frankfurt*, 186.

217 Ibid., 198.

218 Ibid., 188.

219 *Rundfunk Jahrbuch* (Reichs-Rundfunk-Gesellschaft, 1929), 227. Translated by Esther Leslie.

220 *Rundfunk Jahrbuch* (Reichs-Rundfunk-Gesellschaft, 1930), 1–10.

221 Ibid., n.p.

222 Ibid., 6.

223 Ibid., 8.

224 *Rundfunk Jahrbuch* (Reichs-Rundfunk-Gesellschaft, 1930), 10.

225 *Südwestdeutsche Rundfunkzeitung*, 8 January 1928.

226 *Rundfunk Jahrbuch* (Reichs-Rundfunk-Gesellschaft, 1931), 25–30.

227 *Rundfunk Jahrbuch* (Reichs-Rundfunk-Gesellschaft, 1929), 63.

228 Ibid., 71.

229 Benjamin, 'The Work of Art in the Age of its Technological Reproducibility', 398.

230 Ibid., 398.

231 Benjamin, *Radio Benjamin*, 292–303.

232 Benjamin, 'The Work of Art in the Age of its Technological Reproducibility', 398.

233 Ibid., 398.

234 Ottmann, *Im Anfang war das Experiment*, 150.

235 See Peter Dahl, *Sozialgeschichte des Rundfunks für Sender und Empfänger* (Hamburg: Rowohlt, 1983), 93.

236 Sabine Hock, 'Laven, Paul', on *Frankfurter Personenlexikon* (online edition), https://frankfurter-personalenlexikon.de/node/3037 [version: 24 January 2022].

237 *Südwestdeutsche Rundfunkzeitung*, 27 September 1929.

238 *Südwestdeutsche Rundfunkzeitung*, c.8 January 1930.

239 *Rundfunk Jahrbuch* (Reichs-Rundfunk-Gesellschaft, 1930), 456–460.

240 *Rundfunk Jahrbuch* (Reichs-Rundfunk-Gesellschaft, 1931), 46. For reflection on Flesch's contribution to *Hörspiel* in this period, see Katy Vaughan, 'From prop to producer: the appropriation of radio technology in opera during the Weimar Republic' (PhD thesis, Bournemouth University, 2020), 92–95. See also Cory, 'Soundplay', 341.

241 *Rundfunk Jahrbuch* (Reichs-Rundfunk-Gesellschaft, 1929), 48.

242 Ibid., 148.

243 Ibid., 149.

244 Ibid., 151.

245 Ibid., 153.

246 Ibid., 163.

247 *Südwestdeutsche Rundfunkzeitung*, 18 February 1934.

248 Benjamin, 'The Work of Art in the Age of its Technological Reproducibility', 397.

249 *The Correspondence of Walter Benjamin: 1910–1940*, ed. Gershom Scholem and Theodor W. Adorno (Chicago & London: University of Chicago Press, 1994), 85.

250 Letter from 31 July 1918. Ibid., 132.

251 See *Portsmouth Evening News*, 14 July 1930, 12.

252 *Rundfunk Jahrbuch* (Reichs-Rundfunk-Gesellschaft, 1931), 101.

253 The character of Frankfurt Radio in this period is discussed by Wolfgang Schivelbusch, *Intellektuellendämmerung. Zur Lage der Frankfurt Intelligenz in den zwanziger Jahren* (Frankfurt: Suhrkamp, 1985), 62–76.

254 Haverkampf, *Benjamin in Frankfurt*, 201.

255 *Südwestdeutsche Rundfunkzeitung*, 7 September 1930.

256 Ibid.

257 Ibid.

258 All citations from the letter exchange between Schoen and Hausmann are taken from the Berlinische Galleriee's extensive online Raoul Hausmann Archive (accessed online: https://uclab.fh-potsdam.de/hausmann/attributebased.html#211832) [accessed: 17 September 2022].

259 *Rundfunk Jahrbuch* (Reichs-Rundfunk-Gesellschaft, 1930), 117.

260 Ibid., 120.

261 *Der Klang der zwanziger Jahre: Reden, Rezitationen, Reportagen* (Stimmen des 20. Jahrhunderts, DHM 2004).

262 As discussed in Schiller-Lerg, 'Ernst Schoen 1894–1960. Ein Freund überlebt', 982–1013.

263 This thinking draws on Miri Davidson's work: 'The reification of speech: I learned recently that I began to stutter not because of an inherited neurological abnormality, but because of a malfunction in my Fisher-Price sing-along cassette recorder. At two or three years old, I was speaking into it when the playback tripped and my voice came back at me in unrecognizable form. From that moment, the story goes, I stuttered. The tape recorder and I had entered into an irreversible unity, inside of which speech did not coincide with the will to speak. Speech was reconfigured as a machine, an object, an apparatus to be wielded with great difficulty and to wield the machine wrongly meant to invite the wrath of the social world. Speech was reified for me, from then on, as a thing of the tongue.' See Miri Davidson, 'Speech Work', *Social Text Online*, 28 October 2019.

264 See Ernst Schoen's compensation file at the Entschädigungsamt Berlin: 602.385.

265 This epigraph is taken from Bertolt Brecht, 'Second Poem on the Unknown Soldier beneath the Triumphal Arch', from *Das Berliner Requiem* (1928).

266 From Wolfgang Marx, 'Who telleth a tale of unspeaking death?', *Dublin Death Studies*, vol. 2, ed. Wolfgang Marx (Dublin: Carysfort Press, 2017).

267 See Peter Jelavich, *Berlin Alexanderplatz: Radio, Film, and the Death of Weimar Culture* (University of California Press, 2009), 119.

268 John Willett, *Art and Politics in the Weimar Period: The New Sobriety, 1917–1933* (Pantheon Books, 1978), 186.

269 *Südwestdeutsche Rundfunkzeitung*, 2 July 1933.

270 *Rundfunk Jahrbuch* (Reichs-Rundfunk-Gesellschaft, 1931), 53.

271 Kurt Tucholsky, *Gesammelte Werke*, vol. 8 (Hamburg: Rowohlt, 1975), 346. Originally in *Die Weltbühne*, 30 December 1930.

272 *Moderne am Main 1919–1933*, ed. Klaus Kemp, Annika Sellmann, Matthias Wagner K and Grit Weber (Frankfurt: Avedition, 2019), 66.

273 Alfred Braun, 'Rundfunk-Bühne-Tonfilm: Erfahrungen an der 'Rundfunkversuchstelle': Ein Brief an den Funk', in *Funk* 7, no. 13 (1930): 72.

274 Included in *Brecht on Theatre*, trans. and ed. Jon Willett (New York: Hill and Wang, 1964). Originally 'Der Rundfunk als Kommunikationsapparat', in *Blätter des Hessischen Landestheaters*, Darmstadt, no. 16, July 1932.

275 See Erdmut Wizisla, *Walter Benjamin and Bertolt Brecht: The Story of a Friendship*, trans. Christine Shuttleworth (London: Lebris, 2009), 115.

276 Walter Benjamin, 'Theatre and Radio', in *Selected Writings*, trans. and ed. Rodney Livingstone, vol. 2 (Cambridge, MA: Harvard University Press, 2005), 585.

277 Ernst Schoen, 'Broadcast Opera in Germany', *The BBC Year-Book* (London: British Broadcasting Company, 1934), 71.

278 Ibid., 71.

279 Ibid., 67.

280 Ottmann, *Im Anfang war das Experiment*, 330–331.

281 Schoen quoted in Ibid., 341–342.

282 Schiller-Lerg, 'Ernst Schoen vertont sechs Gedichte von Christoph Friedrich Heinle', 135.

283 *Moderne am Main 1919–1933*, ed. Klaus Kemp, Annika Sellmann, Matthias Wagner K and Grit Weber (Frankfurt: Avedition, 2019), 62.

284 Willett's translation omits this section in Bertolt Brecht, 'The Radio as an Apparatus of Communication', in *Brecht on Theatre*, ed. and trans. John Willett (London: Eyre Methuen, 1964). It is included in the translation in Niel Strauss (ed.), *Radiotext[e]* (New York: Semiotext[e],1993), 15–17.

285 Borbach, 'Experimentelle Praktiken', 126–127.

286 Kurt Weill, 'Möglichkeiten absoluter Radiokunst', in *Weill, Musik und Theater: Gesammelte Schriften* (Berlin, 1990), 191–196.

287 Klaus-Dieter Krabiel, *Brechts Lehrstücke: Entstehung und Entwicklung eines Spieltyps* (Stuttgart: Metzler, 1993), 36.

288 Schiller-Lerg, 'Ernst Schoen vertont sechs Gedichte von Christoph Friedrich Heinle', 135.

289 See Ralph Kogelheide, *Jenseits einer Reihe 'tönender Punkte': Kompositorische Auseinandersetzung mit Schallaufzeichnung, 1900–1930* (PhD thesis, University of Hamburg, 2017).

290 Ernst Schoen Archive (Koblenz) [sound]: N1403 TON-23.

291 Translated by Richard Wigmore and found on the online *Oxford Lieder*.

292 *Rundfunk Jahrbuch* (Reichs-Rundfunk-Gesellschaft, 1931), n.p.

293 Ibid., 40.

294 Bertolt Brecht, 'Radio as an Apparatus of Communication', in *Brecht on Theatre*, ed. and trans. John Willett (London: Eyre Methuen, 1964), 52.

295 Ibid.

296 *Moderne am Main 1919–1933*, ed. Klaus Kemp, Annika Sellmann, Matthias Wagner K and Grit Weber (Frankfurt: Avedition, 2019), 66.

297 *Südwestdeutsche Rundfunkzeitung*, 4 December 1926.

298 *Südwestdeutsche Rundfunkzeitung*, 16 March 1930.

299 *Südwestdeutsche Rundfunkzeitung*, 2 December 1928.

300 *Südwestdeutsche Rundfunkzeitung*, 4 January 1932.

301 *Südwestdeutsche Rundfunkzeitung*, 8 February 1931.

302 *Rundfunk Jahrbuch* (Reichs-Rundfunk-Gesellschaft, 1931), 310.

303 Ibid., 312.

304 Ibid., 312.

305 Ibid., 318.

306 Ibid., 318.

307 Ibid., 13.

308 Ibid., 16.

309 Ibid., 17.

310 *The BBC Year-Book* (London: BBC, 1932), 12.

311 *Südwestdeutsche Rundfunkzeitung*, 11 December 1932.

312 *The BBC Year-Book* (London: BBC, 1932), 74.

313 Ibid., 51.

314 Ibid., 20.

315 Ibid., 50.

316 Ibid., 295.

317 See Maja Adena, Ruben Enikolopov, Maria Petrova, Veronica Santarosa and Ekaterina Zhuravskaya, 'Radio and the Rise of the Nazis in Prewar Germany', in *The Quarterly Journal of Economics*, vol. 130, no. 4 (November 2015): 1885–1940.

318 See Corey Ross, 'Mass Politics And The Techniques Of Leadership: The Promise And Perils Of Propaganda In Weimar Germany', in *German History*, vol. 24, no.6, 2006: 206.

319 See 'Die Schriftleitung: Wer nennt das literarische Gleichberechtigung?', in *Deutsche Zeitung*, 16 June 1932.

320 Walter Benjamin and Theodor W. Adorno, *The Complete Correspondence 1928–1940*, ed. Henri Lonitz and trans. Nicholas Walker (Cambridge: Polity Press, 1999), 16.

321 Walter Benjamin, *Briefe 1931–1934*, ed. Christophe Gödde and Henri Lonitz (Frankfurt: Suhrkamp, 1998), 130.

322 A thorough exploration of this material is in Schiller-Lerg, 'Ernst Schoen vertont sechs Gedichte von Christoph Friedrich Heinle', 129–141. Schoen's music is deposited in the archive under *Kompositionen ('Ati's Compositions')*, BArch N 1403/55.

323 These poems were taken from *Christoph Friedrich Heinle: Lyrik und Prosa*, ed. Johannes Steizinger (Berlin: Kulturverlag Kadmos Berlin, 2016). These sonnets are here translated by Alexander Schoen.

324 See Benjamin, *Sonnets*, ed. and trans. Carl Skoggard (Albany: Fence Books, 2017).

325 Ibid., 'Sonnet 34', 154.

326 Wolff, *Hindsight*, 69.

327 See Benjamin, *Radio Benjamin*, 366.

328 The drawing and notes on the election results appear on the manuscript of Benjamin's Lichtenberg script, held as part of the Sammlung Walter Benjamin in the University Library at Gießen. Thanks to Erik Granly Jensen for drawing attention to this in his work presented at a colloquium 'Faire nôtre Expérience et pauvreté de Walter Benjamin?', organised by Christophe David in Rennes, October 2021.

329 Theodor W. Adorno and Walter Benjamin, *The Complete Correspondence 1928–1940*, ed. Henri Lonitz and trans. Nicholas Walker (Cambridge: Polity, 2018), 26.

330 See *Die Sendung*, vol. 9 (1932): 1659.

331 *Südwestdeutsche Rundfunkzeitung*, 18 February 1934.

332 *Südwestdeutsche Rundfunkzeitung*, 2 July 1933.

333 A page was devoted to this in *Südwestdeutsche Rundfunkzeitung*, 27 August 1933.

334 Horst J. P. Bergmeier and Rainer E. Lotz, *Hitler's Airwaves: Jazz, Swing, and Nazi Radio Propaganda* (Yale University Press, 1997), 6.

335 *Südwestdeutsche Rundfunkzeitung*, 25 October 1933.

336 Ansgar Diller, *Rundfunkpolitik im Dritten Reich (Rundfunk in Deutschland)*, vol. 2 (Munich: Deutscher Taschenbuch Verlag, 1980), 115.

337 *Südwestdeutsche Rundfunkzeitung*, 18 June 1933.

338 Diller, *Rundfunkpolitik im Dritten Reich*, vol. 2, 131.

339 Ibid., 111.

340 Ibid., 132.

341 *Südwestdeutsche Rundfunkzeitung*, 3 September 1933.

342 Letter from Benjamin to Scholem dated 17 April 1931, in Benjamin, *Gesammelte Briefe*, vol. 2, 532. See also Susan Buck-Morss, *The Dialectics of Seeing: Walter Benjamin and the Arcades Project* (London: MIT, 1989), 37. Buck-Morss connects this remark with Benjamin's radio lecture 'The Mississippi Flood 1927', broadcast on Radio Berlin on 23 March 1932, translated in Benjamin, *Radio Benjamin*, 176–181.

Wires Cut and Crossed: 1933

1 Ernst Schoen Archive (Koblenz): *Diarien (Taschenkalender)*, BArch N 1403/18.

2 Ibid.

3 Edward Said, *Reflections on Exile and Other Literary and Cultural Essays* (Harvard University Press: Harvard, 2002), 186.

4 Ernst Schoen Archive (Koblenz): *Diarien (Taschenkalender)*, Barch N 1403/18.

5 See Ernst Schoen's compensation file at the Entschädigungsamt Berlin: 602.385.

6 Hock, 'Schoen, Ernst'.

7 Ernst Schoen Archive (Koblenz): *'Scrap-book' von Ernst Schoen. – Zeitungsausschnittsammlung*, Barch N 1403/114. Translated by Esther Leslie.

8 Kurt Magnus is described in an article 'Radio in Germany' in *Popular Wireless*, from 14 May 1932, as the 'Sir John' of Germany, equivalent of Reith at the BBC.

9 Ernst Schoen Archive (Koblenz): *Diarien (Taschenkalender)*, Barch N 1403/18.

10 See also Schiller-Lerg and Soppe, 'Ernst Schoen (1894–1960). Eine biographische Skizze und die Geschichte seines Nachlasses', 87.

11 Schiller-Lerg, 'Ernst Schoen 1894–1960. Ein Freund überlebt', 998.

12 A letter sent from Schoen to his lawyer in relation to questions of compensation after the Second World War, Dr Fraustädter, 2 August 1958. Ernst Schoen Archive (Koblenz): Barch N 1403/17.

13 See Schoen's compensation file at the Entschädigungsamt Berlin: 602.385.

14 Ibid.

15 See Brodersen, *Klassenbild mit Walter Benjamin*, 91, 137, 188–189.

16 See Ernst Schoen's compensation file at the Entschädigungsamt Berlin: 602.385.

17 Ibid.

18 Ibid.

19 Ibid.

20 Ibid.

21 Alexander Schoen, *Mutti's Story* (unpublished manuscript). No speech seems to be scheduled in the *SWZ* around the dates in question, though it is also possible that it might not have been listed prior to its broadcast.

22 Alexander Schoen, *Mutti's Story* (unpublished manuscript).

23 Ibid.

24 Ernst Schoen Archive (Koblenz): *Diarien (Taschenkalender)*, Barch N 1403/18.

25 Heiko Morisse, *Ausgrenzung und Verfolgung der Hamburger jüdischen Juristen im Nationalsozialismus* (Göttingen: Wallstein Verlag, 2013), 111. With thanks to Holger Tilicki and Holger Schultze from the Willi Bredel Gesellschaft Geschichtswerkstatt e.V. for this source.

26 Christa Fladhammer/Silke Wenzel, 'Betty Francken', *Stolpersteine Hamburg* (accessed online: www.stolpersteine-hamburg.de/index.php?MAIN_ID=7&BIO_ID=2592) [accessed: 2 February 2022].

27 Ernst Schoen Archive (Koblenz): *Filmmanuskripte. – Typoskripte*, Barch N 1403/70.

28 Morisse, *Ausgrenzung und Verfolgung der Hamburger jüdischen Juristen im Nationalsozialismus*, 111–112.

29 See Schoen's *Lebenlauf* in his compensation file at the Entschädigungsamt Berlin: 602.385.

30 Alexander Schoen, *Mutti's Story* (unpublished manuscript).

31 Hans Werdmann [Ernst Schoen], *Londoner Elegien* (Weimar: Kiepenheuer, 1950), 14–18. Translated by Esther Leslie.

32 Alexander Schoen, *Mutti's Story* (unpublished manuscript).

33 Ibid.

34 See Schiller-Lerg and Soppe, 'Ernst Schoen (1894–1960). Eine biographische Skizze und die Geschichte seines Nachlasses' 1994: 81.

35 Alexander Schoen, *Mutti's Story* (unpublished manuscript).

36 Ibid.

37 Ernst Schoen Archive (Koblenz): *Diarien (Taschenkalender)*, Barch N 1403/18.

38 See 'Gustav Krukenberg' on the webpage of the *Beamte nationalsozialistischer Reichsministerien* (accessed online: https://ns-reichsministerien.de/2019/08/09/gustav-krukenberg) [accessed: 1 June 2022].

39 Schiller-Lerg, 'Ernst Schoen 1894–1960. Ein Freund überlebt', 998.

40 'Schoen, Ernst* Fritz Erich', in *Hessische Biografie* (accessed online: www.lagis-hessen. de/pnd/12229386X) [version: 15 April 2021].

41 Schiller-Lerg and Soppe, 'Ernst Schoen (1894–1960). Eine biographische Skizze und die Geschichte seines Nachlasses', 81.

42 Alexander Schoen, *Mutti's Story* (unpublished manuscript).

43 See Ernst Schoen's compensation file at the Entschädigungsamt Berlin: 602.385.

44 Ibid.

45 Haverkampf, *Benjamin in Frankfurt* (Frankfurt: Societäts-Verlag, 2016), 188.

46 Ibid., 199.

47 See Ansgar Diller, ' "Führer der Sender". Rundfunkintendanten im "Dritten Reich"', in *Geschäft mit Wort und Meinung: Medienunternehmer seit dem 18. Jahrhundert. Büdinger Forschungen zur Sozialgeschichte 1996 und 1997*, ed. Günther Schulz (Berlin: Walter de Gruyter, 1999): 245.

48 Ernst Schoen Archive (Koblenz): *Diarien (Taschenkalender)*, Barch N 1403/18.

49 Ibid.

50 Ernst Schoen Archive (Koblenz): *Aufsätze*, Barch N 1403/43.

51 Ernst Schoen Archive (Koblenz): Barch N 1403 Bild-110-077 and -069.

52 Kitty Hauser, *Bloody Old Britain: O. G. S. Crawford And The Archaeology Of Modern Life* (London: Granta, 2009), 115.

53 In 1934, Violet Bonham Carter published a pamphlet *Child Victims of the New Germany: A Protest* (London: McCorquodale, 1934). There is also correspondence in Schoen's archive discussed later in this work: *Korrespondenzen*, Barch N 1403/20.

54 John Reith, *The Reith Diaries*, ed. Charles Stuart (London: Harper Collins, 1975), 128–129.

55 Ibid., 57.

56 Ibid., 56.

57 Ernst Ritter, *Das Deutsche Ausland-Institut in Stuttgart 1917–1945* (Wiesbaden: Franz Steiner Verlag, 1976), 55.

58 Reith, *The Reith Diaries*, 56.

59 Ibid., 209.

60 Gordon Bathgate, *Radio Broadcasting: A History of the Airwave* (Barnsley: Pen and Sword History, 2020), 81.

61 Richard Lambert, *Ariel and All His Quality: An Impression of the BBC from Within* (London: Victor Gollancz, London 1940), 31.

62 Alexander Schoen, *Mutti's Story* (unpublished manuscript).

63 Ernst Schoen Archive (Koblenz): *Diarien (Taschenkalender)*, Barch N 1403/18.

64 Ibid.

65 Ibid.

66 Ibid.

67 See Mel Gordon, *The Seven Addictions and Five Professions of Anita Berber* (London: Feral House, 2006).

68 For more on Ball's life see Hugo Ball, *Flight Out of Time: A Dada Diary*, trans. Ann Raimes (New York: Viking Press, 1974).

69 Benjamin, *Gesammelte Briefe*, vol. 4, 111–122.

70 Thanks to Angela Miller for investigating this for us.

71 See Peter Zudeick, *Der Hintern des Teufels* (Zürich: Elster Verlag, 1987) and *Bloch. Eine Bildmonographie*, ed. Ernst Bloch Zentrum Ludwigshafen (Frankfurt: Suhrkamp, 2007).

72 See Wizisla, *Walter Benjamin and Bertolt Brecht: The Story of a Friendship*, xiv.

73 See discussions in *Italian Jewish Musicians and Composers Under Fascism: Let Our Music Be Played*, ed. Alessandro Carrieri and Annalisa Capristo (Berlin: Springer International Publishing, 2021).

74 See the death record for Zion Church of the City of Baltimore. Châtin-Hofmann is mentioned in Kate Elswit, *Watching Weimar Dance* (Oxford: Oxford University Press, 2014), 2; and Gordon, *The Seven Addictions and Five Professions of Anita Berber*, 145–147.

75 Letter from 9 July 1933 in Benjamin, *Gesammelte Briefe*, vol. 4, 266.

76 Ruth Federspiel, 'Marianne Cohn', *Stolpersteine Berlin* (accessed online: www.stolpersteine-berlin.de/en/biografie/1269) [accessed: 19 April 2021].

77 Ottmann, *Im Anfang war das Experiment*, 63–79.

78 Morisse, *Ausgrenzung und Verfolgung der Hamburger jüdischen Juristen im Nationalsozialismus*, 111–112.

79 See National Archive record: HO 334/233/3960.

80 Susan Manning, 'Review of Valeska Gert: Tänzerin, Schauspielerin, Kabarettistin; Anita Berber: Tanz Zwischen Rausch und tod, 1918–1928 in Berlin', in *Dance Research Journal*, vol.18, no. 2, 1986: 70–73.

81 See Sabine T. Kriegel, *Revolutionary Beauty: The Radical Photomontages of John Heartfield* (Berkeley: University of California Press, 2014).

82 See Raoul Hausmann, *Hyle: Ein Traumsein in Spanien*, ed. Adelheid Koch-Didier (München: Belleville, 2006).

83 See Hindemith, *Selected Letters of Paul Hindemith* ed. and trans. by Geoffrey Skelton (New Haven and London: Yale University Press, 1995), 34.

84 Ibold, 'Alice Jacob-Loewenson', *Hochschule für Musik und Theater Hamburg* (2015) (accessed online: www.ezjm.hmtm-hannover.de/en/library/biographical-sketches/ alice-jacob-loewenson) [accessed: 19 April 2021].

85 See Claudia Maurer Zenck, 'Challenges and Opportunities of Acculturation: Schoenberg, Krenek, and Stravinsky in Exile' in *Driven Into Paradise: The Musical Migration From Nazi Germany to the United States*, ed. Reinhold Brinkmann and Christoph Wolff (Berkeley: University of California Press, 1999).

86 Stefan Müller-Doohm, *Adorno*, trans. Rodney Livingstone (London: Polity, 2005), 186.

87 See Kim Sichel, *Germaine Krull: Photographer of Modernity* (Cambridge: MIT Press, 1999).

88 See Eva Weissweiler, *Villa Verde oder Das Hotel In Sanremo – das italienische Exil der Familie Benjamin* (München: btb Verlag, 2022).

89 Hock, 'Laven, Paul', on *Frankfurter Personenlexikon* (online edition), https://frankfur ter-personalenlexikon.de/node/3037 [version: 24 January 2022].

90 Klaus Mann chronicles much of his life post-1933 in his autobiography *The Turning Point: Autobiography of Klaus Mann* (Princeton NJ: Markus Wiener, 1995). Their relationship, and their work in the cabaret, is detailed in Andrea Weiss, *In the Shadow of the Magic Mountain: the Erika and Klaus Mann Story* (Chicago: University of Chicago Press, 2008).

91 Muriel de Bastier, 'Jeanne Mandello de Bauer, ou la mémoire disparue d'une photographe / Jeanne Mandello de Bauer – oder das verlorene Vermächtnis einer Fotografin', in Anne Grynberg, Johanna Linsler (eds.), *Irreparabel. Lebenswege jüdischer Künstlerinnen, Künstler und Kunstkenner auf der Flucht aus dem «Dritten Reich» in Frankreich* (Veröffentlichung der Koordinierungsstelle Magdeburg), vol. 9, 2013: 332–341.

92 Chronicled in Moholy-Nagy, *Moholy-Nagy: Experiment in Totality.*

93 Ludwig Marcuse, *Mein zwanzigstes Jahrhundert: auf dem Weg zu einer Autobiographie* (Zurich: Diogenes, 1975).

94 Peter Donhauser, *Elektrische Klangmaschinen: die Pionierzeit in Deutschland und Österreich* (Weimar: Böhlau, 2007), 220.

95 Madlen Lorei, Richard Kirn, *Frankfurt und die goldenen zwanziger Jahre* (Verlag Frankfurter Bücher, 1966), 220.

96 See Carolyn Birdsall, 'Radio Documents: Broadcasting, Sound Archiving, and the Rise of Radio Studies in Interwar Germany', *Technology and Culture*, vol. 60, no. 2 (2019): 96–128.

97 Hanna Eckhardt, 'Simon, Liesel', in *Frankfurter Personenlexikon* (Accessed online: https://frankfurter-personenlexikon.de/node/6434) [version: 31 January 2021].

98 See David Biale, *Gershom Scholem: Master of the Kabbalah* (New Haven: Yale University Press, 2018).

99 See *Sasha Stone: Fotografien 1925–39*, ed. Eckhardt Köhn (Berlin: Verlag Dirk Nishan, 1990).

100 Scheding, *Musical Journeys*, 61.

101 See Gwendolen Webster, *Kurt Merz Schwitters: A Biographical Study* (University of Wales Press, 1997).

102 Anonymous, 'Introduction to Simone Weil', *New Left Review*, no. 111, May–June, 2018. https://newleftreview.org/issues/ii111/articles/simone-weil-meditations-on-a-corpse

103 Michael Steinberg, Larry Rothe, *For The Love of Music: Invitations to Listening* (Oxford: Oxford University Press, 2009), 114.

104 Ouellette, *Edgard Varèse: A Musical Biography*, 112–125.

105 See Susan Manning, *Ecstasy and the Demon: Feminism and Nationalism in the Dances of Mary Wigman* (University of California Press, 1993).

106 Wolff, *Hindsight*, 107.

Exile Life

1 'Ernst Schoen, Reich Playwright, Joins British Broadcasting Corporation', *Jewish Telegraphic Agency*, 19 November 1933 (accessed online: www.jta.org/archive/ernst-schoen-reich-playwright-joins-british-broadcasting-corporation) [accessed: 2 April 2022].

2 Ernst Schoen Archive (Koblenz): *Diarien (Taschenkalender)*, BArch N 1403/18.

3 Walter Benjamin and Theodor W. Adorno, *The Complete Correspondence 1928-1940*, ed. Henri Lonitz and trans. Nicholas Walker (Cambridge: Polity Press, 1999), 50.

4 Ernst Schoen Archive (Koblenz): *Diarien (Taschenkalender)*, BArch N 1403/18.

5 Ibid.

6 Ernst Schoen Archive (Koblenz): *Korrespondenzen*, BArch N 1403/29.

7 Ernst Schoen Archive (Koblenz): *Diarien (Taschenkalender)*, BArch N 1403/18.

8 See Schiller-Lerg and Soppe, 'Ernst Schoen (1894–1960). Eine biographische Skizze und die Geschichte seines Nachlasses', 81. Albrecht von Bernstorff was later executed by the SS after daily torture at Lehrterstraße Prison in Berlin on 24 April 1945, after imprisonment in concentration camps for his role in the opposition. See also Knut Hansen, *Albrecht Graf von Bernstorff: Diplomat und Bankier zwischen Kaiserreich und Nationalsozialismus* (Frankfurt: Peter Lang, 1996).

9 Ernst Schoen Archive (Koblenz): *Diarien (Taschenkalender)*, BArch N 1403/18.

10 Raymond Price, 'The Bright Young Men of the B.B.C.', *The Strand Magazine*, vol. 35, January-June 1933: 26–35, 30.

11 Ernst Schoen Archive (Koblenz): *Korrespondenzen*, BArch N 1403/20.

12 John Reith, *Broadcast over Britain* (London: Hodder and Stoughton Ltd, 1924), 217.

13 Ibid., 181.

14 Ibid., 34.

15 'What the Children Like', *BBC Year-Book* (London: British Broadcasting Company, 1934), 108.

16 Ernst Schoen Archive (Koblenz): *'Scrap-book' von Ernst Schoen. – Zeitungsausschnittsammlung*, BArch N 1403/114.

17 That same year, his friend Walter Benjamin wrote an essay on technological culture and the shifting role of the artist. See Walter Benjamin, 'The Author as Producer', *Selected Writings*, vol. 2, trans. Edmund Jephcott (Harvard University Press, 1999), 768–782.

18 Schoen, 'Broadcast Opera in Germany', 69.

19 Ibid.

20 John Gloag, 'Learning to Broadcast', *BBC Year-Book* (London: British Broadcasting Company, 1934), 77.

21 Ernst Schoen, 'Music from Austria', *Radio Times*, 24 November 1933, issue 530 (southern edition).

22 Ibid.

23 Ernst Schoen, 'Hindemith and Applied Music', *Radio Times*, 12 January 1934, issue 537 (national edition).

24 Ernst Schoen, 'Bartok and Musical Folklore', *Radio Times*, 9 February 1934, issue 541, (national edition).

25 Audax, 'Wireless Notes', *The Musical Times*, vol. 75, no. 1094 (April, 1934): 335.

26 Ibid.

27 Ernst Schoen Archive (Koblenz): *Diarien (Taschenkalender)*, BArch N 1403/18.

28 Bertolt Brecht, *Briefe in 2 Bände*, ed. Günter Glaeser (Frankfurt: Suhrkamp, 1981), 411, letter 538.

29 Benjamin, *Briefe 1931-1934*, 371.

30 Ernst Schoen Archive (Koblenz): *Diarien (Taschenkalender)*, BArch N 1403/18.

31 Ibid.

32 See Theodor W. Adorno and Ernst Krenek, *Briefwechsel* (Frankfurt: Suhrkamp, 1974), 236.

33 Laurel Leff, 'A Tragic "Fight in the Family": *The New York Times*, Reform Judaism and the Holocaust', in *American Jewish History*, vol. 88 (March, 2000): 3-51, 19.

34 In Schiller-Lerg and Soppe, 'Ernst Schoen (1894-1960). Eine biographische Skizze und die Geschichte seines Nachlasses', 87.

35 See Walter Benjamin, 'Rastelli's Story' (1935) in *Selected Writings*, vol. 3, trans. Howard Eiland and Michael Jennings, based on an original translation by Carol Jacobs (Harvard University Press, 2006), 96-98.

36 See Theodor W. Adorno and Ernst Krenek, *Briefwechsel* (Frankfurt: Suhrkamp, 1974), 169.

37 Ernst Schoen, 'Music for Broadcasting: Should It Be Specially Arranged', *BBC Annual* (London: British Broadcasting Company, 1935), 174.

38 Ibid.

39 Ibid., 171.

40 Schoen, 'Music for Broadcasting: Should It Be Specially Arranged', 174.

41 Ibid.

42 For more on the colonialist and anti-colonialist mobilisations of radio, see Franz Fanon, 'This is the Voice of Algeria', *A Dying Colonialism*, trans. Haakon Chevalier (New York: Grove Press, 1965), 69-98.

43 See *Daily Worker*, 'Wireless Notes' from 27 January 1934, 29 January 1934 and 3 March 1934, as pointed out by Ben Harker in ' "The Trumpet of the Night": Interwar Communists on BBC Radio', *History Workshop Journal*, Spring 2013, vol. 75: 81-100.

44 See Harker, ' "The Trumpet of the Night" ', 81-100.

45 *BBC Year-Book* (London: British Broadcasting Company, 1934), 294.

46 Ibid., 297.

47 Ibid., 295-298.

48 See Nick Chadwick, 'Mátyás Seiber's collaboration in Adorno's jazz project, 1936', *The British Library Journal*, vol. 21, no. 2, (Autumn, 1995): 259-288.

49 See Heinz Steinert, *Die Entdeckung der Kulturindustrie: oder: Warum Professor Adorno Jazz-Musik nicht ausstehen konnte?* (Vienna: Verlag für Gesellschaftskritik, 1992), 93-95.

50 All letters plus excerpts from Schoen's in Theodor W. Adorno and Max Horkheimer, *Briefwechsel*, vol. 1, 1927-1937 (Frankfurt: Suhrkamp, 2003).

51 Theodor W. Adorno and Max Horkheimer, *Briefwechsel*, vol. 1, 1927-1937 (Frankfurt: Suhrkamp, 2003), 173-174.

52 Ibid., 174.

53 Ibid., 174.

54 Ibid., 172.

55 Ibid., 200–202

56 Theodor W. Adorno and Max Horkheimer, *Briefwechsel*, vol. 1, 1927–1937 (Frankfurt: Suhrkamp, 2003), 200–201. Carl Dreyfuss, first husband of Sibyl Moholy-Nagy, was a Frankfurt associate of Adorno's and he undertook studies of white-collar worker professions and attendant ideologies: see *Beruf und Ideologie der Angestellten* (Duncker & Humblot, 1933); this work was later translated by Ernst E. Warburg, Eva Abramovitch and William Dittmar as *Occupation and Ideology of the Salaried Employee* in 1938.

57 Theodor W. Adorno and Max Horkheimer, *Briefwechsel*, vol. 3, 1945–1949 (Frankfurt: Suhrkamp, 2005), 202.

58 Ibid., 220.

59 Ibid., 220.

60 Ibid., 221.

61 Ibid., 247.

62 Ibid., 293.

63 Theodor W. Adorno and Max Horkheimer, *Briefwechsel*, vol. 3, 1945–1949 (Frankfurt: Suhrkamp, 2005), 328.

64 Ernst Schoen Archive (Koblenz): *Zeitungsausschnitte, Fotos, Prospekte*, BArch N 1403/112.

65 Adorno's letter to Seiber from 28 May 1936, cited in Chadwick, 'Mátyás Seiber's collaboration in Adorno's jazz project, 1936': 259–288, 267. Translated by Esther Leslie.

66 Ibid.

67 *The Daily News*, London, 10 March 1937, 8.

68 Schoen, 'Music for Broadcasting: Should It Be Specially Arranged', 174.

69 Quoted in Ottmann, *Im Anfang war das Experiment*, 139. Ottmann lists the reference from the Koblenz archive: *Zeitungsausschnitte, Fotos, Prospekte*, BArch N 1403/112.

70 *Kurt Weill: The Threepenny Opera*, ed. Stephen Hinton (Cambridge University Press, 1990), 73.

71 See Hans Severus Ziegler, *Entartete Musik* (Düsseldorf: Völkischer Verlag Deutsches Reich, 1939).

72 See Dina Gusejnova, 'Jazz Anxiety and the European Fear of Cultural Change: Towards a Transnational History of a Political Emotion', *Cultural History*, vol. 5, issue 1: 26–50.

73 Ernst Schoen Archive (Koblenz): *'Scrap-book' von Ernst Schoen. – Zeitungsausschnittsammlung*, BArch N 1403/114.

74 *Deutscher Reichsanzeiger und Preußischer Staatsanzeiger*, no. 138, 19 June 1939, 2.

75 See the broader context of the organisation in Alban Webb, *London Calling: Britain, the BBC World Service and the Cold War* (London: Bloomsbury, 2014).

76 *BBC Year-Book* (London: British Broadcasting Company, 1948), 43.

77 Antonia White, *BBC at War* (London: British Broadcasting Corporation, 1942), 40

78 See Vike Martina Plock, 'Erika Mann, the BBC German Service and Foreign-Language Broadcasting during WWII', *Modernism/modernity*, vol. 27, no. 1, January 2020, 103–123.

79 Diller, *Rundfunk in Deutschland*, vol. 2, 179.

80 Ibid., 183.

81 See *Merkblatt zur Bedienung des Wehrmacht-Rundfunkempfänger*, 4 October 1941, WR1/P, Bundesarchiv, BArch RHD 8/1665.

82 *The Brecht-Eisler Songbook*, ed. Eric Bentley (New York: Oak Publications, 1967). Translation modified.

83 Details taken from 'German Broadcasting Corporation: Propaganda Broadcasts: Names of Participants: British; National Archives', Kew, GFM 33/449.

84 National Archives Kew Reference: KV 2/1290.

85 National Archives Kew: Divorce and Matrimonial Cause Files, J 77/2725.

86 Stephen Michael Cullen, 'Strange Journey: The life of Dorothy Eckersley, *The Historian*, Autumn 2013, no. 119, 18–23.

87 National Archives Kew Reference: CRIM 1/1736.

88 Ibid.

89 Ibid.

90 Ibid.

91 Ernst Schoen Archive (Koblenz): *Bühnenstücke, Filmmanuskripte und Rundfunksendungen*, BArch N 1403/69.

92 Ernst Schoen Archive (Koblenz): *Diarien (Taschenkalender)*, BArch N 1403/18.

93 Nikolaus Pevsner and Ian Nairn, *Surrey*, editions by Bridget Cherry (Yale University Press, 2002), 206.

94 See Ottmann, *Im Anfang war das Experiment*, 136.

95 Ibid.

96 Ernst Schoen Archive (Koblenz): *Korrespondenzen*, BArch N 1403/37.

97 Werdmann [Ernst Schoen], *Londoner Elegien*, 7. Translated by Esther Leslie.

98 Ibid., 11.

99 Ernst Schoen Archive (Koblenz): *Kompositionen ('Ati's Compositions')*, BArch N 1403/55. Translated by Esther Leslie.

100 Ibid.

101 Werdmann [Ernst Schoen], *Londoner Elegien*, 41. Translated by Esther Leslie.

102 Diller, *Rundfunk in Deutschland*, vol. 2, 435–436.

103 *BBC Year-Book* (London: British Broadcasting Company, 1944), 74.

104 Ernst Schoen Archive (Koblenz): *Eigene Träume. Niederschriften* [1938–1960], BArch N 1403/14.

105 Ernst Schoen Archive (Koblenz): *Eigene Träume. Niederschriften* [1938–1960], BArch N 1403/14.

106 *BBC Year-Book* (London: British Broadcasting Company, 1934), 47.

107 *BBC Year-Book* (London: British Broadcasting Company, 1943), 5.

108 *BBC Year-Book* (London: British Broadcasting Company, 1934), 48.

109 *Wireless World*, 9 November 1934, 374.

110 *BBC Handbook* (London: British Broadcasting Company, 1942), 79.

111 *BBC HandBook* (London: British Broadcasting Company, 1928), 42.

112 Ibid., 365.

113 *BBC Year-Book* (London: British Broadcasting Company, 1932), 171.

114 *BBC Handbook* (London: British Broadcasting Company, 1938), 24.

115 *BBC Year-Book* (London: British Broadcasting Company, 1948), 40.

116 *BBC Handbook* (London: British Broadcasting Company, 1939), 45.

117 Ernst Schoen Archive (Koblenz): *Eigene Träume. Niederschriften* [1938–1960], BArch N 1403/14.

118 Ibid.

119 Ernst Schoen Archive (Koblenz): *Gedichte und Kompositionen*, BArch N 1403/49. Translation by Esther Leslie.

120 See Brecht's poems on Walter Benjamin, in Erdmut Wizisla, *Walter Benjamin and Bertolt Brecht: The Story of a Friendship*, 181–184.

121 Ernst Schoen Archive (Koblenz): *Gedichte und Kompositionen*, BArch N 1403/49. Translation by Esther Leslie.

122 Ibid.

123 Ibid.

124 Ernst Schoen Archive (Koblenz): *Korrespondenzen*, BArch N 1403/30.

125 Hannah Arendt and Gershom Scholem, *The Correspondence of Hannah Arendt and Gershom Scholem*, ed. Marie Luise Knott and trans. Anthony David (Chicago: University of Chicago, 2017), 38.

126 Ibid., 65.

127 Ibid., 66.

128 Ibid., 67.

129 Ernst Schoen Archive: 'Gedanken zur Schaffung und Durchführung eines Rundfunkprogramms in der britischen Besatzungszone Deutschlands', in *Aufsätze*, BArch N 1403/43.

130 Ernst Schoen Archive (Koblenz): *Korrespondenzen*, BArch N 1403/37.

131 Ibid.

132 Ibid.

133 Ibid.

134 Ibid.

135 *London Gazette*, 20 September 1946, 4759.

136 See Benjamin, *Berlin Childhood around 1900*, 344–413.

137 See Gusejnova, *Jazz Anxiety and the European Fear of Cultural Change*: 26–50.

138 Ernst Schoen Archive (Koblenz): *Aufsätze (Essays); z. T. als Rundfunkmanuskripte verfasst*, BArch N 1403/45.

139 Ernst Schoen, 'Germany Report', dated 11.47, from the BBC Written Archives.

140 Ibid.

141 See *Magnetic Recording: The First 100 Years*, ed. Mark H. Clark, Eric D. Daniel, C. Denis Mee (New York: IEEE Press, 1999), especially chapter 5.

142 Ernst Schoen Archive (Koblenz): *Persönliches*, BArch N 1403/13.

143 See Hans Flesch 'Magic on the Air: Attempt at a Radio Grotesque', trans. Lisa Harries Schumann, *Cultural Critique*, vol. 91 (2015): 14–31.

144 Ernst Schoen Archive (Koblenz): *Eigene Träume. Niederschriften* [1938–1960], BArch N 1403/14.

145 FO 938/108: P. C. Gordon-Walker: report on visit to Germany by BBC official; National Archives, Kew. There is a chance that this F. L. Neumann could be the Neumann of the Frankfurt School, involved in Office of Strategic Services activities and part of the team collecting testimonies for the Nuremberg Trials.

146 FO 938/108: P. C. Gordon-Walker: report on visit to Germany by BBC official; National Archives, Kew.

147 *BBC Year-Book* (London: British Broadcasting Company, 1948), 118.

148 'Charlie Chaplin and the Social Function of the Clown', Ernst Schoen Archive (Koblenz): *Aufsätze*, BArch N 1403/42.

149 *BBC Year-Book* (London: British Broadcasting Company, 1948), 36.

150 Quoted in Helmut Lethen, *Cool Conduct: The Culture of Distance in Weimar Germany*, trans. Don Reneau (University of California Press, 2002), 14.

151 Ernst Schoen Archive (Koblenz): *Korrespondenzen*, BArch N 1403/30.

152 Ernst Schoen Archive (Koblenz): *Eigene Träume. Niederschriften* [1938–1960], BArch N 1403/14. With thanks to Lucy Strauss for the transcriptions.

153 See Bertolt Brecht, *War Primer*, ed. John Willett (London: Verso, 2017).

154 Ernst Schoen Archive (Koblenz): *Zeitungsausschnitte. Gedichtzyklus*, BArch N 1403/53.

155 Ibid. Translated by Esther Leslie.

156 Ibid.

157 Ibid.

158 Ibid. Originally in English.

159 Ernst Schoen Archive (Koblenz): *Korrespondenzen*, BArch N 1403/32.

160 Ernst Schoen Archive (Koblenz): *Zeitungsausschnitte. Gedichtzyklus*, BArch N 1403/53.

161 Brecht, *Briefe in 2 Bände*, 521. See note.

162 David Barnett, *A History of the Berliner Ensemble* (Cambridge: Cambridge University Press, 2015), 134–135.

163 Brecht, *Briefe in 2 Bände*, 143.

164 Ernst Schoen Archive (Koblenz): *Aufsätze*, BArch N 1403/43.

165 From Friedrich Engels' *Anti-Dühring* (1877). Translation taken from David Margolies (ed.), *Culture as Politics: Selected Writings of Christopher Caudwell* (London: Pluto Press, 2018), xvi.

166 From Lenin, *What Is to Be Done? Burning Questions of Our Movement* (1902), in *Selected Works*, vol. 1 (Moscow: Foreign Languages Publishing House, 1952): 210.

167 Ernst Schoen Archive (Koblenz): *Aufsätze*, BArch N 1403/43.

168 Details in this section are drawn from the National Archives file: KV5/80.

169 National Archives File: KV 5/80, serial 11a, B.1.F/GHL note on the MacDonald Discussion Group, 2 December 1952.

170 James Smith makes the case for the source being the host of the meetings, Ferdy Mayne, in the essay 'The MacDonald discussion group: A communist conspiracy in Britain's Cold War film and theatre industry – or MI5's honey-pot?', *Historical Journal of Film, Radio and Television*, vol. 35, no. 3 (2015): 454–472. It is certainly the case that Mayne does not appear in the Top Secret 'List of Persons Attending the MacDonald Discussion Group'. There is also discussion of this file in Harker, ' "The Trumpet of the Night" ', 81–100.

171 National Archives File: PRO KV 5/80, serial 11a, B.1.F/GHL note on the MacDonald Discussion Group, 2 December 1952.

172 National Archives File: PRO KV 5/80, serial 1a, B.1.K/WAY source report, report number 999, 10 December 1951.

173 Ibid.

174 Ibid.

175 Ibid.

176 All dreams from Ernst Schoen Archive (Koblenz): *Eigene Träume. Niederschriften* [1938–1960], BArch N 1403/14.

177 *BBC Handbook* (London: British Broadcasting Company, 1956), 229.

178 Ernst Schoen Archive (Koblenz): *Zeitungsausschnitte, Fotos, Prospekte*, BArch N 1403/112.

179 The 1947 *BBC Year-Book* relays the history in an article 'The German-Austrian Service': 'During the year there have been some important changes in staff. In particular, Hugh Carleton Greene, who took an important part in building up the German Service, has been seconded to the Control Commission, Germany, to be Controller of Radio in the British Zone of Germany and has been replaced by Lindley Fraser who, almost from the beginning, has been the principal commentator in the German Service.' *BBC Year-Book* (London: British Broadcasting Company, 1947), 108.

180 Theodor W. Adorno, 'Charakteristik WBs', *Neue Rundschau*, no. 61 (Frankfurt am Main: S. Fischer, 1950).

181 Theodor W. Adorno Archiv, Frankfurt am Main, Br 1346/4.

182 Ibid.

183 Ibid.

184 Ernst Schoen Archive (Koblenz): *Eigene Träume. Niederschriften* [1938–1960], BArch N 1403/14.

185 Ibid.

186 See Ernst Schoen's compensation file at the Entschädigungsamt Berlin: 602.385.

Remigrant: Berlin

1 See Ernst Schoen's compensation file at the Entschädigungsamt Berlin: 602.385.

2 Ernst Schoen Archive (Koblenz): *Korrespondenzen*, BArch N 1403/32.

3 See Emily Pugh, *Architecture, Politics, and Identity in Divided Berlin* (University of Pittsburgh, 2014), 11.

4 Brian Ladd, *The Ghosts of Berlin: Confronting German History in the Urban Landscape* (University of Chicago Press, 1997), 188.

5 Ibid., 181–183.

6 Ibid., 183.

7 As Brian Ladd argues, while Stalinallee's false pomp was heavily criticised in the West as totalitarian kitsch, after the fall of the Wall it was re-discovered by postmodern architects who had distanced themselves from the formal purity of modernism and playfully returned to the importance of ornament in architectural design, in *The Ghosts of Berlin: Confronting German History in the Urban Landscape* (University of Chicago Press, 1997), 187.

8 Brecht, *Briefe in 2 Bände*, 173.

9 Ernst Schoen Archive (Koblenz): *Persönliche Briefe von Ernst und Johanna Schoen an den Sohn Alexander ('Sascha')*, BArch N 1403/35. Original in English.

10 Ibid.

11 Ibid.

12 Ibid.

13 Ibid.

14 Ibid.

15 *Deutsches Theater. Bericht über 10 Jahre,* ed. Ernst Schoen (Berlin: Henschelverlag, 1957).

16 This photograph is held by the Museum der Dinge in the Sondersammlung Walter Benjamin.

17 Ernst Schoen Archive (Koblenz): *Aufsätze,* BArch N 1403/43.

18 Ibid.

19 Ibid.

20 Ernst Schoen Archive (Koblenz): *Korrespondenzen,* BArch N 1403/31.

21 Ibid.

22 Ernst Schoen Archive (Koblenz): *Übersetzungen und Vorarbeiten,* BArch N 1403/76.

23 Ernst Schoen Archive (Koblenz): *Korrespondenzen,* BArch N 1403/26.

24 Ibid.

25 Ibid.

26 Ernst Schoen Archive (Koblenz): *Übersetzungen und Vorarbeite*n, BArch N 1403/108.

27 Theodor W. Adorno Archiv, Frankfurt am Main, Br 1346/6.

28 Theodor W. Adorno and Gershom Scholem, *«Der liebe Gott wohnt im Detail» Briefe und Briefwechsel 1939-1969. Band 8: Theodor W. Adorno/Gershom Scholem,* ed. Asaf Angermann (Frankfurt, Suhrkamp: 2015), 126-127. This was translated into English by Sebastian Truskolaski and Paula Schwebel as Theodor W. Adorno and Gershom Scholem, *Correspondence 1939-1969* (Cambridge: Polity, 2021), 92.

29 Ernst Schoen Archive (Koblenz): *Kleine Reise in die Koexistenz. - Reise nach Jugoslawien, Aug. 1955,* BArch N 1403/5.

30 Ibid.

31 Detlev Claussen, *Theodor W. Adorno: One Last Genius,* trans. Rodney Livingstone (Belknap Press of Harvard University Press, 2008), 337.

32 Ibid., 264.

33 See Richard Vahrenkamp, *The German Autobahn 1920-1945: HaFraBa Visions and Mega Projects* (Lohmar: Josef Eul Verlag, 2010).

34 See Sonja Boos, *Speaking the Unspeakable in Postwar Germany: Toward a Public Discourse on the Holocaust* (Ithaca: Cornell University Press, 2014), 195-210.

35 Theodor W. Adorno, *Sound Figures,* trans. Rodney Livingstone (Stanford University Press, 1999), 69. Quoted in Claussen, *Theodor W. Adorno: One Last Genius,* 245.

36 Ernst Schoen Archive (Koblenz): *Gedichte und Kompositionen,* BArch N 1403/49. Translated by Esther Leslie.

37 Theodor W. Adorno, *Minima Moralia: Reflections from Damaged Life,* trans. Edmund Jephcott (London: Verso, 2020), 46-47.

38 Ernst Schoen Archive (Koblenz): *Korrespondenzen,* BArch N 1403/28.

39 All dreams from Ernst Schoen Archive (Koblenz): *Eigene Träume. Niederschriften* [1938-1960], BArch N 1403/14.

40 See Uwe-Karsten Heye, *Die Benjamins. Eine deutsche Familie* (Berlin: Aufbau, 2014) and Hilde Benjamin, *Georg Benjamin. Eine Biographie* (Leipzig: Hirzel, 1987).

41 Some of Marianne Cohn's biography is set out on a page relating to her Stolpersteine, placed at Wulfila Ufer 52, in Tempelhof-Schöneberg, Berlin, written by Dr Ruth Federspiel based on research by Hannelore Emmerich and translated by Charlotte Kreutzmüller: www.stolpersteine-berlin.de/en/biografie/1269 [accessed: 9 November 2022].

42 See Gerhard Oberkofler and Manfred Mugrauer, *Georg Knepler: Musikwissenschaftler und marxistischer Denker aus Wien* (Vienna: Studien Verlag, 2014), 195-217.

43 Tom Ryall, 'Asquith, Anthony (1902-1968)', in *Reference Guide to British and Irish Film Directors*, accessed on the BFI website: www.screenonline.org.uk/people/id/447391/index.html [accessed: 9 November 2022].

44 See Weissweiler, *Das Echo deiner Frage. Dora und Walter Benjamin*.

45 See Detlev Schöttker, 'Dolf Sternberger und Walter Benjamin. Ein Photographie-Aufsatz und seine Folgen', in *Sinn und Form*, vol. 4 (2010): 437–444.

46 See Albrecht Betz, *Hanns Eisler: Musik einer Zeit, die sich eben bildet* (München: text+kritik, 1976) and Friederike Wißmann, *Hanns Eisler: Komponist, Weltbürger, Revolutionär* (München: Edition Elke Heidenreich bei Bertelsmann, 2012).

47 See Knyt, *Ferruccio Busoni and His Legacy*.

48 See Ouellette, *Edgard Varèse: A Musical Biography*, 179–194.

49 See Ottmann, *Im Anfang war das Experiment*.

50 See Hindemith, *Selected Letters of Paul Hindemith*, and Simon Desbruslais, *The Music and Music Theory of Paul Hindemith* (Woodbridge: Boydell Press, 2019).

51 David Huckvale, *Hammer Film Scores and the Musical Avant-Garde* (London/Jefferson NC: McFarland, 2008), 54.

52 See Will Grohmann, *Willi Baumeister: Leben und Werk* (Cologne: DuMont, 1963).

53 See Erdmut Wizisla, *Walter Benjamin and Bertolt Brecht: The Story of a Friendship* (New Haven: Yale, 2014).

54 See Charlotte Wolff, *Hindsight* (London: Quartet Books, 1980).

55 Ernst Schoen Archive (Koblenz): *Korrespondenzen*, BArch N 1403/32.

56 Ernst Schoen, 'Das Problem O'Casey', in *Deutsches Theater: Bericht über 10 Jahre* (Berlin: Henschelverlag, 1957), 220–223.

57 *daß die Zeit sich wende! Ein Almanach*, PEN-Zentrum Ost und West (Berlin: Verlag der Nation, 1957).

58 Ernst Schoen Archive (Koblenz): *Eigene Träume. Niederschriften* [1938–1960], BArch N 1403/14.

59 Ibid.

60 Ernst Schoen Archive (Koblenz): *Korrespondenzen*, BArch N 1403/32.

61 Ernst Schoen Archive (Koblenz): *Korrespondenzen*, BArch N 1403/30.

62 Ernst Schoen Archive (Koblenz): *Eigene Träume. Niederschriften* [1938–1960], BArch N 1403/14.

63 Ibid.

64 Ernst Schoen Archive (Koblenz): *Korrespondenzen*, BArch N 1403/31.

65 Ibid.

66 Ibid.

67 Ibid.

68 Ernst Schoen Archive (Koblenz): *Korrespondenzen*, BArch N 1403/31.

69 Ernst Schoen Archive (Koblenz): *Übersetzungen und Vorarbeiten*, BArch N 1403/103.

70 Ibid.

71 Ibid.

72 Ernst Schoen Archive (Koblenz): *Korrespondenzen*, BArch N 1403/32.

73 Ibid.

74 Ibid.

75 Ibid.

76 Ibid.

77 The Bundesarchiv (Koblenz) holds a letter from Squarzina to Schoen giving seven pages of extensive notes and critical observations regarding Schoen's initial translation of *La sua parte di storia* (*Die Teilnahme*). There is also a response from Schoen complaining of the 'indecent haste' demanded by Sommer and his fears that he will receive no more translation work, as a result of these necessary revisions. See *Korrespondenzen*, BArch N 1403/29.

78 Ernst Schoen Archive (Koblenz): *Korrespondenzen*, BArch N 1403/32.

79 Ibid.

80 *World Premieres* (France: International Theatre Institute, 1959), 41, 43.

81 Ernst Schoen Archive (Koblenz): *Korrespondenzen*, BArch N 1403/32.

82 Ernst Schoen Archive (Koblenz): *Gedichte und Kompositionen*, BArch N 1403/49.

83 Ernst Schoen Archive (Koblenz): *Korrespondenzen*, BArch N 1403/32.

84 Ibid.

85 Adorno and Scholem, «*Der liebe Gott wohnt im Detail*» *Briefe und Briefwechsel 1939-1969*, 199. Translated by Sebastian Truskolaski and Paula Schwebel in Theodor W. Adorno and Gershom Scholem, *Correspondence 1939-1969* (Cambridge: Polity, 2021), 147.

86 Adorno and Scholem, *Correspondence 1939-1969*, 146-147.

87 Ibid., 169.

88 Ibid., 170.

89 Ibid., 171-172.

90 Ibid., 174.

91 Ernst Schoen Archive (Koblenz): *Diarien (Taschenkalender)*, BArch N 1403/18.

92 Ernst Schoen Archive (Koblenz): *Trauerpost zum Tode von Ernst Schoen (10.12.1960)*, BArch N 1403/39.

93 Ibid.

94 Ibid.

95 Ibid.

96 Ibid.

97 Ibid.

98 Adorno and Scholem, «*Der liebe Gott wohnt im Detail*» *Briefe und Briefwechsel 1939-1969*, 235; Adorno and Scholem, *Correspondence 1939-1969*, 175.

99 Ernst Schoen Archive (Koblenz): *'Scrap-book' von Ernst Schoen. Zeitungsausschnittsammlung*, Barch N 1403/114. Translated by Esther Leslie.

100 Adorno and Scholem, «*Der liebe Gott wohnt im Detail*» *Briefe und Briefwechsel 1939-1969*, 250; Adorno and Scholem, *Correspondence 1939-1969*, 186.

101 See Ernst Schoen's compensation file at the Entschädigungsamt Berlin: 602.385.

102 Part of the 'Ernst Schoen Collection', from the Leo Baeck Institute Archives (accessed online: https://archive.org/details/ernstschoenf001/page/n11/mode/1up?view=theater) [accessed: 22 February 2022].

Afterlife Echoes

1 Ernst Schoen Archive (Koblenz): *Diarien (Taschenkalender)*, BArch N 1403/18.
2 Ibid.
3 Ibid.
4 Adorno and Scholem, «*Der liebe Gott wohnt im Detail*» *Briefe und Briefwechsel 1939-1969*, 294–295; Adorno and Scholem, *Correspondence 1939-1969*, 219–220.
5 See 'The Cold Heart: A Radio Play adapted from Wilhelm Hauff's Fairy Tale', in Benjamin, *Radio Benjamin*, 221–248.
6 Ernst Schoen Archive (Koblenz): *Korrespondenzen*, BArch N 1403/20.
7 Ibid.
8 Ibid.
9 Ibid.
10 See Ernst Schoen's compensation file at the Entschädigungsamt Berlin: 602.385.
11 Ernst Schoen Archive (Koblenz): *Korrespondenzen*, BArch N 1403/20.
12 *Stuttgarter Kunstkabinett Roman Norbert Ketterer Auktionskatalog 36*, vol. 1, ed. Werner and Nachbauer, 10.
13 See Grohmann, *Willi Baumeister*.
14 Grace Glueck, 'Morton D. May Shows His German Art', *New York Times*, 17 January 1970: 27.
15 With thanks to Angela Miller for helping to locate this painting in its current context.
16 Scholem and Adorno (eds), *The Correspondence of Walter Benjamin, 1910-1940*, (Frankfurt: Suhrkamp, 1966), xv.
17 Ernst Schoen Archive (Koblenz): *Korrespondenzen*, BArch N 1403/27.
18 Schiller-Lerg went on to contribute the most extensive research on Schoen to date, including in her essay Schiller-Lerg, 'Ernst Schoen 1894-1960. Ein Freund überlebt'. Here Sabine Schiller-Lerg makes a powerful analogy for Schoen's exile and remigration: 'Neither as emigrant nor as remigrant has Ernst Schoen been considered by research, even though precisely his fate can serve as a typical example of exile as an amputation, in which the severed nerves remind painfully of what has been lost and the return to Germany can only enable more attempts at protheses' (983). Translated by Esther Leslie.
19 Ernst Schoen Archive (Koblenz): *Korrespondenzen*, BArch N 1403/Supplementary papers.

Index

Acknowledgements

Our greatest thanks go to Alexander ('Sasha') Schoen and Leda Drucaroff, for their friendship, courage and hospitality. This project, from the start, was motivated by meeting them and hearing the stories of their lives. We also owe a great deal to their daughter Nadine Schoen, whom we also met early on in this process, a fierce activist and educator. We would also like to thank Mickie, Flossie and Samuel Draper for being part of this project in so many ways and for sharing so much of Walter Benjamin and Dora Sophie Kellner's lives with us. Thanks are also owed to Mona Benjamin for allowing us to include reference to some letters between Schoen and her grandmother Dora Sophie Kellner. Also, to John Knepler for meeting and discussing his father's life with us. This project produced a number of collaborations along the way.

Thanks are due to Tom Allen for including a number of Alexander Schoen's translations of Fritz Heinle's verse in a collection *We Do Not Believe in The Good Faith of The Victors* (2019). Also, for having us read at the launch of the publication in London in August 2019. To Lotte Betts-Dean and Joseph Havlat for taking on the Heinle songs with such sensitivity and power. Also, to those who took part in our first event at the Bishopsgate in December 2019: Flossie Draper for reading, Florence Warner for playing the flute and everyone at The New Factory of the Eccentric Actor, especially Anthony Best, Hilary Derrett, Penelope Dimond and Gary Merry for their performance of the radio play. Also, to Henri Vaxby and Rachel Prosser for being so supportive and generous with the organisation.

Huge thanks also go to everyone involved with *Tanz 23/24*: to Samuel Draper for preparing and performing the music (also being so open to conversations about Schoen's music throughout this process and for sourcing various reviews), to Alka Nauman and Lucie Palazot for the performance and Alicia Gladston for the costumes. Also, to Joanna Klass and everyone at Curie City for everything they did in hosting the performance and making it happen in a small window of possibility during the first stages of the COVID-19 pandemic. It was incredibly thrilling to see a leaflet discovered in an archive find its life again on stage.

We would also like to thank various archives and libraries, without which this research would not have been possible. To the librarians at the ICI Berlin (Saori Kanemaki and Corinna Haas and especially Christine Niehoff who was so helpful in the final stages of preparing the manuscript), the Staatsbibliothek in Berlin, the London School of Economics Library, the German Historical Institute in London and the National Archives in Kew. A number of archives also helped provide documents along the way: Rita Wolters at the Museum der Dinge; Anna Krutsch and Florian Preiß at the Deutsches Museum; Berit Walter and Jasmin Brötz from the images section of the Bundesarchiv in Koblenz; Jason Gray at the Saint Louis Art Museum; Susanne Knoblich at the Landesarchiv Berlin; the Deutsche Literaturarchiv Marbach; Stephan Bachtejeff-Mentzel and Antonia Kausch of the Stasi-Unterlagen-Archiv in Berlin; Oliver Kleppel of the Universitätsarchiv Frankfurt; the Akademie der Künste Berlin; Dr Peter Reuter and Olaf Schneider of Universitätsbibliothek der Justus-Liebig-Universität Giessen; the Landesamt für Bürger- und Ordnungsangelegenheiten, the compensation authority for victims of National Socialism; the BBC Written Archives Centre at Caversham. We would also like to thank everyone at the Bundesarchiv in Koblenz for their support and hospitality on our two visits there in 2019 and 2021. Thanks go also to Erdmut Wizisla and Ursula Marx of the Benjamin-Archiv and Michael Schwarz of the Adorno-Archiv, both based at the Akademie der Künste, Berlin, who have been so generous and supportive over a number of years.

Thanks also to: Daniela Aharon for sharing some of her research with us; Monica Bohm-Duchen of the Insiders/Outsiders festival for her support; Knud Breyer who kindly helped us navigate some materials relating to Hanns Eisler; Derek Burgess, Peter Sanders, John Wakely, Richard Stow who so kindly showed us around the British Vintage Wireless and Television Museum; Anthony Charlesworth for his kind hospitality and generosity at Kingfisher Court; Tony Drake and Keith Dolbear for helping decipher some electronic circuits; Ben Harker for orientation as regards to the MI5 file at Kew; Erinn E. Knyt for help navigating the Busoni archive; Angela Miller for searching down the Willi Baumeister painting in Saint Louis for us; everyone at MayDay Radio and MayDay Rooms; Jan Gerber and Rosemary Grennan for help with photography; Lucy Strauss for transcribing Schoen's dream musical notations; Holger Tilicki and Holger

Schultze at the Willi Bredel Gesellschaft Geschichtswerkstatt in Hamburg, for their hospitality and generosity and for their commitment to examining the legacies of fascism in that city. And, finally, to the copyright holder of Schoen's archive, Dr Sabine Schiller-Lerg, for granting us permission to look at the archive and quote from it in this work. We also want to acknowledge the work of Solveig Ottmann and the late August Soppe, for their work on Schoen. Our endnotes can be also read as a list of acknowledgements of previous work done by innumerous others.

We have also been so generously supported by a number of institutions. The Lipman-Miliband Trust generously supported this project in its early and late stages. A pot of funding allowed us to travel, make new discoveries for ourselves and put on a number of events. The Research Centre for German and Austrian Exile Studies at the School of Advanced Study, University of London, supported Sam with a postdoctoral fellowship in 2018–2019. Sam also owes a huge thanks to the Institute of Cultural Inquiry Berlin for the support and environment it has provided for over two years: to my cohort of fellows, as much as to staff, especially Christoph F. E. Holzhey, Manuele Gragnolati, Claudia Peppel, Jakob Schillinger, Arnd Wedemeyer, Chris Wunsch, Christoph Breuer, Silke Schwarz and Walid Abdelnour, among others. As the final touches of the manuscript were underway, Sam was supported from a post-doctoral grant from the Leverhulme Trust. Also, a hurrah to the School of Arts at Birkbeck, especially Anthony Shepherd, for being hospitable when we needed space to plan and work.

And finally, thank you to everyone at Goldsmiths Press for supporting this project: Atau Tanaka, Susan Kelly and Ellen Parnavelas.